088703

BCFTCS

ENVIRONMENTAL

BUSINESS
MANAGEMENT

D1135875

ENVIRONMENTAL BUSINESS MANAGEMENT

Sustainable Development in the New Millennium

Andrew Hutchinson and
Frances Hutchinson

B.C.F.T.C.S.
088703

The McGraw-Hill Companies

London · New York · St Louis · San Francisco · Auckland · Bogotá · Caracas · Lisbon
Madrid · Mexico · Milan · Montreal · New Delhi · Panama · Paris · San Juan · São Paulo
Singapore · Sydney · Tokyo · Toronto

Published by
McGraw-Hill Publishing Company
Shoppenhangers Road, Maidenhead, Berkshire, SL6 2QL, England
Telephone 01628 502500
Facsimile 01628 770224

British Library Cataloguing in Publication Data

Hutchinson, Andrew,
    Environmental business management: sustainable development in the new millenium
    1. Industries – Environmental aspects 2. Sustainable development 3. Environmental
engineering
    I. Title II. Hutchinson, Frances
    658.4′08
    ISBN 0077091957

Library of Congress Cataloging-in-Publication Data

Hutchinson, Andrew,
    Environmental business management: sustainable development in the new millenium /
Andrew and Frances Hutchinson.
        p.   cm.
    Includes bibliographical references.
    ISBN 0–07–709195–7 (pbk.)
    1. Industrial management – Environmental aspects. 2. Green movement. 3. Sustainable
development. I. Hutchinson, Frances, II. Title.
    HD30.255.H869   1996
    658.4′08–dc20

96–41879
CIP

McGraw-Hill
A Division of The **McGraw·Hill** Companies

Copyright © 1997 McGraw-Hill International (UK) Limited. All rights reserved. No part of
this publication may be reproduced, stored in a retrieval system, or transmitted, in any form
or by any means, electronic, mechanical, photocopying, recording, or otherwise, without the
prior permission of McGraw-Hill International (UK) Limited.

 234 CUP 998

Typeset by Computape (Pickering) Ltd, Pickering, North Yorkshire

Printed and bound in Great Britain at the University Press, Cambridge

Printed on permanent paper in compliance with ISO Standard 9706

'Commit your Works to the Lord and your thoughts will be established'
(Proverbs 16.3, *King James Version of the Bible*)

The text is dedicated to Keith Hutchinson, whose devoted support and encouragement have proved invaluable.

CONTENTS

PART 2 ■ THE INTERNAL ENVIRONMENT AND ECO-MANAGEMENT

CHAPTER 5 Environmental Strategic Management

LIST OF FIGURES AND TABLES

FIGURES

TABLES

PREFACE

Environmental Business Management: Sustainable Development in the New Millennium is an introductory text which tempts the reader to delve further into the complexities of sustainable development and corporate environmentalism. Traditionally the environment has appeared as a strategic threat to industry to be tackled alongside other economic, political and social pressures. *Environmental Business Management* challenges this view. It involves the student in an ongoing learning process as industry continues to adjust to a new scenario.

The decade 1986–95 has demonstrated that environmental excellence is synonymous with both competitive and co-operative advantage in the market-place. The environment is no longer a threat to industry, but an opportunity. Where perhaps environmentalists have been too demanding on industry, industry has often been far too demanding on the environment. It is as much in the interests of industry as the environment to have secure, well-balanced and sustainable economic and social systems. Realistic co-operation is a vital essential. Recycling a few drinks containers and a pile of in-tray paper is not the type of co-operation which will produce an ecologically sustainable society.

Consideration of environmental impacts is not merely an extension of total quality management and ethical business practice. It offers a unique challenge of its own. In the last analysis, business cannot survive cocooned from the environment. Without an environment there will be no market-place in which to thrive and do business. It is, therefore, of primary importance that today's business leaders and decision-makers recognize the pivotal nature of the environmental question and attempt to address the problem of how to live and act in an ecologically sustainable manner. For this reason, this book has been written to aid the understanding of sustainable development from a management perspective.

Environmental Business Management is designed to be used in conjunction with traditional management textbooks. It is not a radical re-think of traditional management theory. Environmentalists may hold the opinion that the only truly green business is no business at all. This book, however, draws upon material written in the real world and provides some solutions to the ongoing challenge of environmental management.

The underlying philosophy of this book is that the profit-driven shareholders are not the only stakeholders to be affected by corporate decisions which have environmental impacts. Stakeholders also include the local communities affected by poor environmental practice. *Environmental Business Management* is written from a holistic perspective, appreciating the complex interrelationships involved in environmental management.

It is possible, and more satisfactory, to have a 'win-win' scenario, where all parties are satisfied. The solution is for the twenty-first-century business and environmental activists to both think and act globally and locally, in co-operating for the common goal of sustainable development. This textbook introduces the reader to this debate and demonstrates that this co-operation is well underway. It draws upon a whole range of academic disciplines in order to present this holistic view.

Words that are italicized at first appearance are given in the glossary on p. 379. Most of the acronyms used in the text are also in the glossary.

ACKNOWLEDGEMENTS

We thank all who gave such generous support in the preparation of material for this text. In particular, we are grateful to Dr John Huddleston, Clive Smallman, Guy Dauncey, Dorothy Sharpe, Tony Edwards, Colin Hunter, Pauline Ford, Grace Evans, Karen Spencer, Isabelle Guillot and all at JB Priestley Library and Inter-Library Loans, Bradford Management Centre and Plymouth University Library staff, David Turner, Lowana Veal, Danyal Sattar, Ed Mayo, Pat Conaty and all at the New Economics Foundation and UK Social Investment Forum, Peter Hopkinson, Penny Shepard, Reenha Chudha, Keith Pitcher, Jayne Breach, James Shackleton, Mary Harrowsmith, Andrea Ballard, Ted Trainer, John Kaler, Kevin Leather, Simon Payne, Chris Seldon, Lisa Page, Peter Hopkinson, Don King and Terry and Eileen Waters for Proverbs 16.3. We thank all those we may have forgotten to name, and take full responsibility for any mistakes or omissions.

PART 1

Foundational Concepts

Environmental management and sustainable development are perhaps the most eclectic academic disciplines of all. They include aspects of philosophy, economics, management strategy, operations management, biology, physics, metaphysics and law to name but a few. Part 1 of this book places some of the key ideas behind the subjects into their historical perspective and introduces the reader to the foundational concepts that underpin environmental management and sustainable development. The themes and ideas that are introduced in Part 1 reoccur throughout the book. They provide the reader with the contextual setting of the subject area, the extent of the task of achieving sustainable development and the opportunities that can prevail from a strategy that manages for sustainability.

OVERVIEW

The predator and the preyed upon exist not alone, but as part of a vast web of life, all of which needs to be taken into account.

(Carson 1962: 239)

Now is the time for a paradigm shift to carry us forward into the next century. International competition has changed dramatically over the last few decades. Senior managers who grew up at a time when environmental regulation was synonymous with litigation will see increasing evidence that environmental improvement is good business. Successful environmentalists, regulatory agencies, and companies will reject old trade-offs and build on the underlying economic logic that links the environment, resource production, innovation and competitiveness.

(Porter and Van der Linde 1995)

By the start of the Christian era it is estimated that the planet's total human population was in the region of 250 million. It took roughly 1600 years to double. By 1850 it was around 1 billion (1000 million) and by 1950 it was 2.5 billion. By the turn of the century it will be 7 billion, set to rise to 10 billion. The effect that this rise will have on the environment and the quality of life for the human species is uncertain; what is certain is that the current estimated extinction rate of 50–100 plant and animal species per day will continue to rise dramatically. A typical 4 mile square patch of Amazonian rainforest contains up to 1500 different plant species, 400 species of bird and 250 different species of mammal. Currently it is estimated that in any single year rainforests covering an area the size of the state of Washington (176 617 km^2, compared to the UK which is 244 750 km^2), are being destroyed.

Every year in the UK alone 2.5 billion tonnes of waste is produced by industry, agriculture and households, much of which could be recycled and some of which need not be created in the first place. The prevailing industrial philosophy is one of 'out of sight out of mind'. The environment is viewed as a free resource to be used at will with no immediate or apparent cost to the user.

The year 1996 was the hundredth anniversary of the car manufacturing industry. The occasion has led to recognition of the fact that in the mid-1990s there are over 21 million cars on the roads of a small country like the UK producing 14 per cent of all UK emissions of carbon dioxide. Since 1926, when the first statistics were kept, almost 430 000 people have been killed in road accidents in the UK alone. Over 3500 people still die annually and it is calculated that another 11 000 die prematurely due to air pollution associated with exhaust fumes. There are now about 480 million cars world-wide, 1.4 million of which were scrapped in 1992. Every year the British dispose of between 25 million and 30 million tyres and spend 16 per cent of their annual household income on transport. On average car drivers spend 5.4 days per year in traffic jams and the government response to this has been to spend 114 per cent more on road networks in the UK than on rail (Friends of the Earth (*FoE*) 1995).

One-fifth of the world's population now uses four-fifths of the world's resource output and is living on a *gross national product* (*GNP*) per capita that is 45 times greater than that of the poorest half, while 50 000 die every day from deprivation (Orr 1994). Our solution is to produce more and more unnecessary goods, to trade more and more resource-depleting luxuries and to argue that the increase in this economic 'growth' will not only raise the standard of living of the already rich north but also improve global standards through increased investments. In reality the rich get richer, the poor get poorer and the earth becomes less and less capable of sustaining the human race. The effects are becoming apparent within our bodies. Human sperm counts have fallen by 50 per cent (Orr 1994) (Maynard 1995) on a global scale since 1938, for reasons which remain inexplicable. Human breast milk often contains more toxins than would be permitted in milk sold by dairies, and at death human bodies are often so heavily contaminated with toxins and *heavy metals* as to be classifiable as hazardous waste (Orr 1994).

THE CONSERVER SOCIETY

All industrial activity has an effect on natural resources, energy sources, water supplies and on the land. Where the continued supply of resource materials were the primary initial environmental concern of the 1970s, since the mid 1980s there has been a shift. Although resource supply is still a significant environmental question, what is perhaps more significant is the awareness that the globe has a finite capacity to absorb industrial waste and pollutants. This realization has led to the development of what is known as *sustainable development*, 'development that meets the needs of present generations without compromising the ability of future generations to meet theirs' (World Commission on Environment and Development 1987: 89).

Within this definition (taken from the Brundtland Report) there is an implicit acceptance of the interrelationship between society, economics, the environment and futurity. There is a recognition that industry is not isolated in time or indeed from society and that it has a critical role to play in the equity of the new millennium. Industrialists can no longer hold that the disposal of waste and energy use is a private matter. International commitment to sustainable development has ensured the requirement for international public industrial accountability.

It is also no longer acceptable to argue that the more goods and services we produce, the higher the quality of life will be. It is not so much the amount of goods and services *per se* that produce quality of life but the right type and amount of goods and services. The challenge for the new millennium is to develop an industrial system that has minimal socio-ecological impacts without compromising quality of life.

Where many *environmentalists* blame technological developments and science for the current environmental crisis, this book places all dimensions of research into context and concludes that we have, in fact, not been scientific enough in our approach to the environment. Where chemicals have been used on the land without due research and testing as to the long-term implications for the health of the land and of humans, we have not been scientific enough; where machines have been employed that are energy-inefficient wasting valuable resource capacity, we have not been scientific enough; where trade has encouraged thousands of miles of transportation, we have not been scientific enough; where the human industrial legacy has led to holes in the *ozone* layer, *global warming* and forestry depletion, we have not been scientific enough. Science aspires to be objective and rational. The human–environment interface, however, has neither been managed rationally nor scientifically. Decisions have been made from positions of ignorance and based upon short-term greed. It is time to become more scientific, more rational and more logical about the environment. What is required is a rethink of how we trade and why we trade, taking into account all of the interests of all of the stakeholders. This book draws from a whole host of sources and from a number of selected disciplines to prove that there are alternatives to the current ecological abyss. What is required is a paradigm shift from a consumer society to a conserver society before the minority remove the majority's security altogether.

> The aim of the conserver society is to develop an economic system that has a high quality of life with the lowest possible resource use, placing more worth on leisure time. It is aiming towards developing small regionally autonomous and decentralised, participatory efficient economies.

> **(Trainer 1995)**

There are now over 73 definitions of sustainability and many argue that it is important to distinguish between them. Although we do distinguish between ecological sustainability and financial sustainability, the text uses terms such as ecological sustainability, sustainability and sustainable development interchangeably. Despite the existence of differing applications and understandings, the general meaning of sustainability is encapsulated in the Brundtland Report definition (see Chapter 3). Therefore, as with 'ecological' and 'environmental' management, we have sidestepped the maze of semantics. For a detailed discussion of the main areas of sustainable development see Kirkby *et al.* (1995). This collection of readings will give the inquiring observer an excellent initial overview in the field of sustainable development.

THE MANAGEMENT PERSPECTIVE

> The time has come to recognise the lead taken by industry in finding solutions to the world's environmental problems adding that there is now no conflict between industry and nature and this harmonic relationship can be achieved through eco-efficiency and leadership from the business sector.
>
> (Stigson 1995)

Stoner *et al.* (1995) put the environment top of the list of issues that frame the workplace for the twenty-first-century manager. This is ahead of ethics, social awareness, globalization, entrepreneurship, culture, diversity, multiculturalism and quality. Not only is there a priority case for environmental concerns to be holistically incorporated into all decision-making structures of the firm, but also many organizations are now accepting this fact and looking to move towards sustainable development. The proactive company is no longer dragging its heels but is seeking to be co-operative and engage in partnership with environmentalists to determine the optimum solution to their mutual concerns.

With the World Bank organizing conferences on *Financing Sustainable Development* and the establishment of the international organization, the Business Council for Sustainable Development (*BCSD*, now the *WBCSD*), who published *Changing Course: A Global Business Perspective on Development and the Environment* (Schmidheiny 1992), the international business community is clearly taking the challenge of sustainable development seriously with more than words. The BCSD opening statement declares:

> Business will play a vital role in the future health of this planet. As business leaders we are committed to sustainable development, to meeting the needs of the present without compromising the welfare of future generations. ... This concept recognises that economic growth and environmental protection are inextricably linked, and that the quality of present and future life rests on meeting basic human needs without destroying the environment on which all life depends. ... New forms of co-operation between government, business, and society are required to meet this goal.
>
> (Schmidheiny 1992: xi)

In its report to the June 1992 *Earth Summit* (United Nations Conference on Environment and Development: *UNCED*) in Rio de Janeiro, and in subsequent workshops, the BCSD promoted the concept of *eco-efficiency*. It defined eco-efficiency in terms of the delivery of competitively priced goods and services designed to satisfy human need and enhance quality of life while 'progressively reducing environmental impacts and resource intensity throughout the entire life cycle'. A life-cycle and system approach is regarded as necessary to bring human economic activity in line with the earth's estimated carrying capacity. The BCSD advocated progress towards eco-efficiency through seven key routes:

- Minimization of the material intensity of goods and services.

- Minimization of the energy intensity of goods and services.

- Elimination of toxic dispersion.

- Enhancement of material recyclability.

- Maximization of sustainable use of renewable resources.

- Extension of product durability.

- Increase the service intensity of goods and services.

(Fussier 1994: 10)

The endorsement of the principle of eco-efficiency and the construction of guidelines for progress towards its attainment by international business interests is a development which could not have been predicted in 1962 on the publication of Rachel Carson's *Silent Spring*. Lord Shackleton, in his introduction to *Silent Spring*, the first comprehensive text on the effects of the use of toxic chemicals upon the countryside, observed that 'however artificial his dwelling, [man] cannot with impunity allow the natural environment of living things from which he has so recently emerged to be destroyed' (Shackleton 1964). In this book we explore the historical background to the acceptance by the global business community of the requirements to reduce mass and energy utilization and enviro-toxic dispersion, and the associated quest for improvements in recycling, use of renewable resources and innovation in service life and extensions of functionality. We examine the extent of change in the light of the pressures to adapt to growing awareness of the limits to the earth's carrying capacity and the unrealistic demands of traditional forms of economic activity upon that capacity.

Getting to where we want to be must necessarily entail starting from where we are, however unsatisfactory that may seem to be. It is therefore essential to understand the guidelines and systems being developed, in order that change may be effected, both within industry and within the political and legislative framework of society as a whole.

Speed and extent of change

'Reduce, Reuse, Repair, Recycle.' 'Buy food locally and try to go organic.' 'Invest in low energy lightbulbs.' These quotes, with their ring of some 1970s/1980s 'beard and sandals' environmental pressure group pamphlets, appeared in a National Westminster Bank advertising brochure in 1995. They are characteristic of the extension of concern within a growing group of proactive companies in the mid-1990s, well beyond the early exclusive focus on recycling as a means to reduce environmental degradation. The wording in the National Westminster Bank brochure is indicative of the shift in attitudes to the environment which have occurred with increasing speed as the 1990s move towards the millennium. This shift requires investigation in an attempt to evaluate the pressures towards change in the socio-economic and environmental setting within which managers are required to operate.

The inclusion of 'reduce' as the first of the four Rs signifies a fundamental move away from the increasingly discredited business axioms that more is beautiful and growth is vital for survival regardless of the form it may take. The realization is growing that a higher quality of life can be sustained only by learning to consume *less* through the generation of less waste. Inevitably, after two hundred years of industrialization founded upon the apparent inevitability of technological progress towards the satisfaction of unlimited material wants, such realization produces initial reactions of denial (there is no problem). Subsequent reactions include displacement of blame (someone else is causing the problem) and refusal (I /we do not have the resources to change course of action). All three forms of reaction can be detected within the business community. Nevertheless, many organizations and companies have moved and are moving rapidly towards the final stage of constructive co-operative dialogue. Proactive environmentalism has already superseded purely reactive initiatives. It is now being replaced by a recognition that long-term sustainability can be achieved only by firms ceasing to act as predators upon their social and ecological environments.

Pressures for change include an increasing public awareness of the scale of hazards resulting from environmental degradation coupled with an increasing propensity to claim legal redress for environmental damage. Environmental risks bring new demands from insurance companies, forcing all types of enterprise into holistic assessments of their environmental impacts, signalling a general paradigm shift in the relationship between commercial activity, society and the natural environment. Ignorance of environmental issues and their implications for business can no longer be regarded as a tolerable option for organizations seeking to face the future with confidence and with a determination to succeed.

ALTERNATIVE APPROACHES

Environmental scientists have produced increasing documentation of the degree and extent of environmental degradation, from the discharge of toxic waste into land, water and air to global warming, ozone depletion and loss of species diversification. Solutions vary. At one extreme solutions are offered on a 'one-off' short-termist, reactive basis. For example, lead particles in the atmosphere have been found to be harmful to human health in general, and to child development in particular. The remedy, proposed by a university annual report referring to research undertaken in 1994–5, is to hang net curtains at the windows, so as to trap lead particles and prevent them from entering the house (Annual Report, University of Bradford, 1995: 28). No less inauspicious was Sydney City Council's attempt to reduce the volume of rubbish being produced—by providing fewer litter bins! Reactive, short-termist and piece-meal solutions like these are typical of the now very dated business-as-usual, technofix approach which is in fact a 'no-tech-fix' approach in many cases. Solutions to our current communal problem lie in removing the disease rather than tinkering with the symptoms. In this book we explore the relationship between business and the natural environment from a diametrically opposite angle, by examining the complex relationships between society, *ecology* and commercial activity,

The linear model

Over the past two hundred years western society has been conducting a massive experiment. The development of industry and commerce has been premised upon the assumption that it is possible to draw indefinitely upon the material resources of the natural environment and the institutions of society in order to create 'wealth'. In a linear process, raw materials and labour are drawn into the economy, consumed as wealth and disposed of as waste (Figure 1.1). Wealth is shared among the creators of wealth and their dependants, including such taxation and charitable donations as they can sustain. Meanwhile nature is expected to

MATERIALS
ENERGY
HUMAN
RESOURCES
→ PRODUCTION → CONSUMPTION → WASTE

FIGURE 1.1 *Linear model*

continue to provide raw materials and to absorb the waste. Defending his company's clean-up operations in Alaska in 1989, Charles Sitter, senior vice-president of Exxon, explained:

> I want to point out that water in the [Prince William] Sound replaces itself every 20 days. The Sound flushes itself out every 20 days. Mother Nature cleans up and does quite a cleaning job.
>
> **(quoted in Seager 1993: 221)**

The belief that 'Mother Nature' will clean up the mess is giving way to a more mature and responsible attitude towards human stewardship of the planet. In the old linear scenario, profitability could be left to dominate at all levels of decision-making, and social justice and environmental sustainability were regarded as peripheral to technical elegance and economic success. Linear-style management based upon this short-termist model now belongs to an experiment which has run its course. As a part of this process, linear-style management is being replaced by a diversity of models based upon security and sustainability.

Limitations of the linear model

The linear global market model is becoming increasingly inappropriate as a mechanism to regulate the relationship between human society and the planet as a whole. In this model the predatory firm draws on natural and human resources, using purely financial accounting systems. Natural resources include soil, air, water, *fossil fuels*, minerals, plant and animal life, which are taken in, consumed and deposited as wastes. The human resources in the linear model are 'mushroom people' who appear 'ready-made' on the firm's doorstep. They have no childhood, no social responsibilities and no respect. After being used by the system to benefit the system, they are deposited as any other industrial input as unwanted waste, laid off or pensioned off. Humans are valued in this model only when they are given an exchange or economic value in terms of a cash price.

Within the linear model a firm can be profitable even though it may degrade its natural and human resources and deposit toxic and non-biodegradable wastes into the land, air and water of the natural environment. Over the past two hundred years in the countries of the 'developed' north, this type of enterprise has grown and been highly successful in increasing the amount of materials consumed. While human life can be comfortably sustained on a yearly intake of 6 tonnes of air and food per person, in the 'developed' world each person requires an additional 83 tonnes of material for shelter, mobility and to clean up the mess created. A very small fraction of this extra consumption adds to the permanent infrastructure supporting human life and activity. The vast bulk of it results in environmental degradation and unsustainable discharges to water, land and atmosphere. In nature the predatory species which destroys its source of supply dies. On the same principle, human enterprise, however sophisticated its technological trimmings, remains viable only so long as it is supported by its natural environment. The evidence, explored more fully in later chapters of this book, suggests that the human species has come a long way towards the irreversible fouling of its nest.

Humankind shares the planet with a host of other species which together form the complex chain of support systems necessary for human survival. As solar energy is converted into net *biomass* production, however, around 40 per cent of annual net growth of vegetation is consumed and destroyed by humans. At the same time they are extracting, and destroying through combustion, the fossilized biomass laid down through millions of years of prehistoric time. The resultant emissions of carbons, sulphur and other particulates is impacting upon the atmosphere, causing instability through rapid unprecedented climate changes.

Not all humans are responsible for, or benefit from, this vast depletion of resources. About 20 per cent of the earth's population consumes 80 per cent of the mineral and energy resources and is responsible for 80 per cent of global trade. Meanwhile, the needs of the poorest 20 per cent go unmet as they struggle in poverty and malnourishment. Hence the linear model draws in an unprecedented amount of resources, deposits an unviable volume of waste, and results in the type of poverty and social unrest which precipitates famine, uncontrollable plagues and sickness (Fussier 1994). As mounting evidence reinforces these conclusions, pressure grows to bring the human enterprise into line with the limits which will enable it to exist within its natural environment.

The holistic model

In nature, all waste products are reused to regenerate the living system. By contrast, a linear system based on a calculus of single inputs and single outputs fails to account both diversity of output and costs of degradation. Human technology, however sophisticated, requires to be assessed in the light of its ability both to draw upon and to stimulate the regeneration of diversity in the natural and social environments. A holistic approach is required if total degradation of the environment is to be avoided over the long term.

Although all human activity impacts upon the natural environment, these impacts can be controlled. In most non-western socio-economic systems, prior to colonization, human activity is monitored so that the end result is sustainable growth. Due regard is given to the natural environment in which the human economy operates. Historically, in the industrialized western socio-economic system, the natural environment has been degraded as nonrenewable resources are taken from it and non-degradable and toxic wastes are discharged into it. Ultimately, such degradation renders land unproductive and incapable of sustaining life. In the absence of a spare planet parked alongside, concerned citizens in the 'north' and in the 'developed' world generally are placing the environmental challenge closer to the top of their list of concerns in national and international politics.

As the *Sustainable Germany* study indicated: 'Nature permits to each individual a form of independent activity, but links in a co-operative manner the activity patterns of all species. Co-operation and competition are intermeshed and are held in a dynamic balance—for individual companies and the overall economy, too, this provides a sensible orientation' (Wuppertal Institute: 1995: 20). The study was undertaken on behalf of Bund für Umwelt und Naturschutz Deutschland (*BUND*), an environmental pressure group with 220 000 members and 2500 local groups, and Miseror, one of the largest development *non-governmental organizations* (*NGOs*) in Germany. Noting that 'The economic sub-system is threatening to destroy the two others—society and ecology', the study called for holistic approaches and 'new forms of economy and management. This cannot happen in opposition to industry and economic institutions, but only with them. They must be an active part of the fundamental systemic transformation processes' (Wuppertal Institute: 1995: 20). Furthermore, the study notes the links between environmental degradation and social disintegration and advocates increased flexibility on the part of the state. The study provides a quantitative assessment of reduction goals for a sustainable Germany, offering guidance for policy actors in the different sectors of German industry and government. It carries recommendations for the reduction of external resource dependence as a means to increase peace and security and to reduce international conflict such as, for example, the Gulf War.

The successful firm of the future will recognize the significance of the global ecological social market economy emerging in the *Organization for Economic Co-operation and Development* (*OECD*) countries and the UN sustainable development project which followed on from the Rio Earth Summit. Alongside the concern of citizens, scientists, politicians and planners is a growing realization that business and commerce, being at the heart of the problem, are central to the solutions. Equally, however, it is clear that commerce as a whole and individual firms in particular cannot 'clean up their act' single-handedly in a vacuum. Each concerned individual, each firm, whatever its size, operates within a social, environmental, economic, technological and political context. Within this evolving scenario, the successful firm will require the capacity to react from an informed standpoint to Political, Economic, Social and Technological (*PEST*) pressures as the added 'E' for Environment (which makes Social, Technological, Economic, Environmental and Political, giving rise to the acronym *STEEP*) colours all the other pressures.

Sustainable development cannot be viewed as a simple matter of cutting back on the use of natural resources independently of other considerations. A simplistic reaction of this type would lead to decline in industry and commerce, leaving contamination and degradation of resources to the anarchic forces of chance. Humans have so far changed their environment that they cannot now opt out of responsibility for its management. In this respect, management must involve working with and through natural resources and processes to achieve sustainability. It must also involve working in co-operation with the full range of human institutions in order to construct social mechanisms capable of pre-empting pressures from the marginalized (or the greedy) to precipitate further environmental degradation. The firm of the future will operate within the non-linear, holistic model of co-operative advantage (Figure 1.2), in which resources are used with a view to securing the three vital securities:

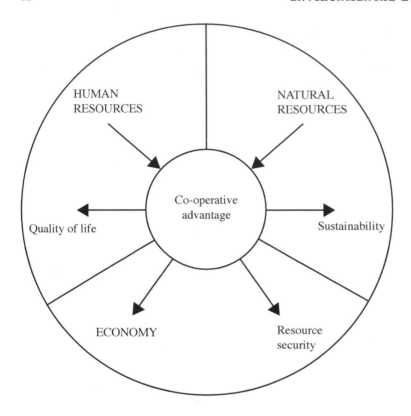

FIGURE 1.2   *Holistic model of co-operative advantage*

- **Ecological security** Based on the need to maintain the planet's capacity to support healthy life systems.

- **Social equity** Based on the need to provide food, security, education and appropriate technologies for all to avoid the necessity for environmental destruction.

- **Economic sustainability** Requires an economic system based on the need to live from the planet's dividends while leaving its *natural capital* intact.

Environmental management is premised upon an understanding of the fundamental inter-connections between economic, social and environmental sustainability. This requires acceptance of the need to conserve, rather than degrade, the vital elements of a sustainable economy. These are:

- **Human resources** Work provided and products supplied will enhance the quality of life.

- **Natural resources** The very best available technology will ensure *cradle-to-grave* mini-mization of long-term adverse impact on the environment and maximization of beneficial impacts in terms of ecological sustainability.

- **Economic resources** Financial success will be increasingly dependent upon successful management of the other two forms of resources, as legislative pressures, risk minimization and consumer pressures discriminate against the environmentally unsustainable enterprise.

The chapters which comprise the four parts of this book introduce the pressures for change from within business itself and from the wider society in which it must operate. They also review the stages traversed by organizations across the globe in the transition from unsustainable industrial practices and towards a new vision of a sustainable, equitable, socio-economic system.

SUMMARY

Disasters like Bhopal, Chernobyl and the *Exxon Valdez* (see Chapter 2) added weight to the more general pressures for business to adopt environmental policies and strategies arising out of the findings of scientific studies and reports from agriculturalists and climatologists. On a global scale, businesses have accepted that environmental issues will not go quietly away, but are here to stay. Nevertheless, one strategy is to seek to use 'respectable' journals to discredit the evidence of scientists as presented by the media as a whole. For example, Richard North (1995), dismisses the human misery caused by the Chernobyl disaster in a single phrase, before proceeding to describe several 'useful outcomes' of the accident. These included:

■ The provision of a 'textbook example of how not to run a nuclear power station'.

■ The prejudicial effects of media reporting on the debate about risk.

■ The opportunity to test the effects of radiation on the human population, particularly relating to thyroid cancers.

By the mid-1990s the 'balanced' approach to environmental issues, in which facts cited by environmentalists and scientists are systematically countered by refutation or claims of 'lack of sufficient evidence', effectively confused the issues. The first task of this textbook is to explore whether business should be expected to adopt an ethical viewpoint, or whether the dominant ethic in business is to continue with 'business as usual' in order to stay in business.

Part 1 therefore starts with an examination of the ethical theories which underlie business practices in general, and with respect to the environment in particular. The necessity to operate in an ethical fashion within business cannot be taken for granted. In a world where profitability is endorsed as the primary motivation to action, the requirement to consider the needs of others, be they citizens, customers, neighbours or future generations can appear to be an irrelevant side issue. Chapter 2 explores the fields covered by *ethics*, business ethics and environmental ethics. This is followed by a chapter on the historical build-up of environmental concerns within society as a whole on a global scale. Chapter 3 reviews the key texts and developments which have led to the altered perceptions of consumers and legislators in the light of mounting evidence of the need for a proactive approach to environmental degradation. Chapter 4 covers the evolution of management structures and the growth of business interest in the environment in the context of the development of international trading patterns in the last decades of the twentieth century.

In Part 2 the reactions of management to the pressures described in Part 1 are examined in more detail. Part 2 analyses the internal business environment, covering the internal decision-making process. It also offers new insight into the development and application of management theory, proposing various newly developed models of eco-management. Chapter 5 explains the strategic approach to environmental and ecological management as progressive firms have sought to review their environmental impacts and assess alternative approaches. Chapter 6 deals with operational management and techniques used to minimize external environmental impacts. In Part 2, as in Parts 3 and 4, case study material provides illustration of good practice. It also includes substantial material on the greening of the Small and Medium Sized Enterprise (*SME*) sector with new material from the European Union (*EU*) Small Company Environmental and Energy Management Assistance Scheme (*SCEEMAS*).

Part 3 is concerned with the external business environment, those issues that influence decision-making from outside the four walls. It also looks at the growing pressures upon organizations to prioritize environmental issues. Chapter 7 looks at legislation and regulation arising out of political pressures for environmental protection, with particular reference to the UK within the EU. Alternative or 'green' approaches to economics are explored in Chapter 8, which contains discussion of environmental taxation, pollution permits and the case for other economic incentives to reduce environmental degradation. Chapter 9 introduces the emerging concepts of social responsibility for investment which is steadily moulding a new social investment paradigm. Chapter 10 covers the changes in technology and design which offer scope for environmental management to pursue viable alternatives to polluting industrial processes. Part 3 provides the broad picture within which the firm of the new millennium will operate.

Part 4 places management in the broader social and environmental framework within which it must operate on a global scale. Throughout this section examples are drawn from best practice in the SME sector wherever possible. Chapter 11 reviews emerging good practice in co-operative strategies and networking, based primarily upon localities, in the search for solutions to environmental problems. Chapter 12 is concerned with the spatial dimension, focusing on local economic development, alternative forms of inward investment, *bioregionalism* and *permacultural* design concepts. The final chapter explores the potential for ecological and economic regeneration through sustainable cities developing in a symbiotic relationship with their hinterlands. Throughout the text it is recognized that industry draws upon natural resources to meet economic demands, and that industrial activity results in the production of wastes and the degradation of natural resources.

No single text can provide a definitive introduction to so diverse a range of subject areas. Hence the student is directed to key specialist texts. References to these texts may be made both within the body of the text and at the ends of the chapters.

CONCLUSION

Companies have adopted environmental policies for a number of reasons. According to Frances Cairncross (1995: 179), these include:

■ Management morale: it can be advantageous, and improve general management morale, to have an environmental policy in which pride can be taken.

■ Staff morale: pressure to adopt environmental policies has often come from a firm's staff.

■ Consumer pressure: often consumers wish to know more about the origins of the goods they buy.

■ Desire for good publicity, and a good image generally.

■ Desire to reduce unpredictable risks deriving from the costs of environmental damage, particularly in view of legislative change.

■ Desire for cost reductions, through savings in material and energy use and waste disposal costs.

Cairncross concludes that despite the mid-1990's green battle fatigue and anti-environmentalist backlash, the environment is an issue which is here to stay, now and for the rising generation. The implications of this for management into the new millennium are explored in the following pages.

Guy Dauncey (1988) has developed a model for the holistic business that places business firmly within the social context it operates in (Figure 1.3). Rather than viewing management theory as detached from the real world the business seeking to follow this model will be engaged in the culture of the new millennium. The stakeholders are the beneficiaries in this win-win scenario where both business and the environment coexist. The model shows how values inform and stimulate action which in turn benefits all of the stakeholders involved. The theme forms a central tenet of this book, which covers a number of diverse subject areas. The model draws together interrelated themes and highlights the derived benefits of sustainable and holistic development strategies. Not only can businesses derive benefit from caring for the environment but also customers, investors and the local community within which the business operates can benefit from a healthy environment. The book develops this idea by suggesting that environmental management and sustainable development is more than recycling schemes in offices, and the *greenwashing* of corporate logos. The challenge is to understand how our vibrant and dynamic globe functions and how to develop socio-economic systems that will have a minimum long-term impact on the environment.

The issue of cultural values affecting the commercial decision-making process is often neglected within the management field, yet it is a central element of the sustainability debate. Without a vision positive change will never come. We often forget that managers and decision-makers are individuals themselves who are open to family and ethical pressure just as much as the interested independent individual is. Although it is true that there is a level of corporate compromise in most decision-making that can nullify any individual ethical values,

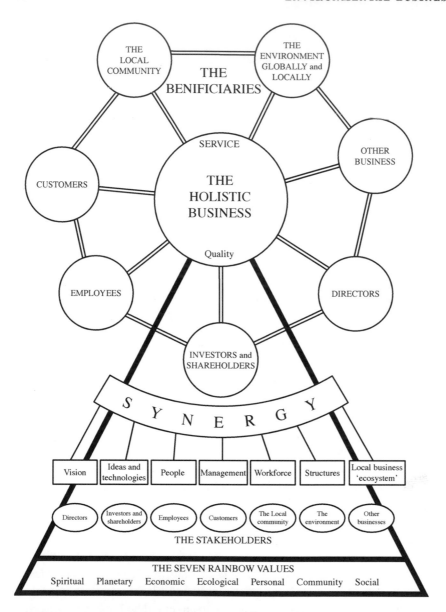

FIGURE 1.3 *Holistic business (Source: Dauncey 1988: 143)*

a healthy environment is not only in the interest of the environment but also in the interest of industry. An ethical stance is, in this case, not only morally commendable but also commercially desirable in the long term.

It is the aim of this book to move towards this model by providing the reader with a basic understanding of the relevant subject areas within this eclectic discipline of ecological management. The book is not exclusive in coverage; it provides an introduction to all of the central elements of ecological management in the twenty-first century, post-modern society, while pointing towards the references of most use for the reader to take a line of inquiry further. The book also attempts to engage the mind of the reader by removing any false presuppositions regarding the place, purpose and philosophy of local and international business in the new millennium.

The 'out of sight out of mind' philosophy towards resource use is now, clearly, totally out of date within international business. It is ironic that within the isolationist post-modern 'self' society where 'looking after number one' is the dominant prevailing wisdom of the day, where financial profit is sold as the gateway to freedom to be grasped at all cost, even if that includes cultural and sociological disengagement, that we are being called as a human race to interact, communicate and re-engage once again to solve a problem that is communal to us all. The challenge is now to learn how to co-operate with the environment and society to develop a sustainable, healthy economy and environment.

BIBLIOGRAPHY

Useful introductory texts

Carson, R. (1962) *Silent Spring*, Hamish Hamilton, London
Rachel Carson's *Silent Spring* remains 'brilliant and controversial', and is as relevant in the 1990s across the globe as when it was first published in the USA in 1962. It was almost immediately translated into almost every language of the industrial world, and gave rise within a few years of publication to environmental legislation in those countries in which it was widely read. Following the publication of Carson's book it was no longer possible to sell pollution as a necessary evil in the march of progress.

Wackernagel, M. and Rees, W. (1996) *Our Ecological Footprint: Reducing Human Impact on the Earth*, New Society Publishers, Gabriola Island, BC, and Philadelphia, PA
The concept of an *'ecological footprint'*, an accounting tool facilitating the estimation of resource consumption and waste assimilation, has been developed on an international basis. The potential of this new tool is explored by Mathia Wackernagel and William Rees in *Our Ecological Footprint*. The authors demonstrate that traditional economics is capable of evaluating trade and money flows, but is less capable of reflecting ecological flows and their environmental consequences. The work provides an impressive resource for policy-makers across the globe. It includes illustrations and explanations on carrying capacity, resource use, waste disposal and sustainability.

Cairncross, F. (1995) *Green Inc.: A Guide to Business and the Environment*, Earthscan, London
Traditionally, economists and environmentalists have adopted antagonistic roles. Economists favour economic growth, while environmentalists have blamed the economy for ecological malaise. In *Green Inc.* Cairncross, environment editor for *The Economist* from 1989 to 1994, argues the case for co-operation between the two. The book was originally conceived of as a résumé of her journalistic writings over the five years, which covered

the emergence of global warming as a serious worry, the successful completion of several environmental treaties, rows about trade and the environment, the discovery of the severity of pollution in the Soviet empire, the greening of the World Bank and the emergence of a widespread view that industry could make money by pursuing responsible environmental policies.

(Cairncross 1995: vii)

As a completed text, the work offers a valuable account of the main environmental issues of the period.

The text highlights the productive antagonism between the concerns of the environmentalists and the interests of the business community. Cairncross has little sense of affinity with environmentalists. She dismisses their 'web of nature' arguments in favour of the more pragmatic approach to saving the least endangered species on grounds of costs, and 'making nature pay' through green tourism. Although the text introduces major issues and developments from the early 1990s, at times it requires the reader to adopt a critical perspective in order to assess the wider implications of developments in understanding and practice.

Cairncross is confident that environmental problems can and will be solved through advances in technology and improved business practice. In her checklist of 10 points for governments she makes it clear that 'a cleaner environment will not come about entirely as a result of unfettered market forces'. Governments and industry will need to continue to work in partnership towards a sustainable future.

Shell *Interactive* Magazine, Shell Better Britain Campaign, Victoria Works, 21a Graham Street, Birmingham, B1 3JR, UK

In 1995 the Shell Better Britain Campaign celebrated its twenty-fifth anniversary year by launching its annual *Interactive* magazine. This information service seeks to provide access to local grants for environmentally sustainable development and to stimulate local involvement in environmental issues. It provides:

- An A–Z of information on everything from computers to permaculture, indicators to recycling, stakeholders to Local Agenda 21, city farms to windfarms.

- A list of contacts of community and conservation organizations, with descriptions.

- A list of publications, including footpaths, *Food Miles* and Who's Who in the Environment.

The magazine, updated each year, provides articles covering good practice in action in a range of schemes and projects involving active participation of the general public in conjunction with Shell. Compendia like these are being produced in more and more countries as a result of co-operation between multinational companies and leading environmentalists.

References and further reading

Cairncross, F. (1995) *Green Inc.: A Guide to Business and the Environment*, Earthscan, London.

Carson, R. (1962) *Silent Spring*, Hamish Hamilton, London.

Dauncey, G. (1988) *After the Crash*, Green Print, London.

Friends of the Earth (FoE) (1995) *Cars Cost the Earth*, FoE Publications Despatch, 56–8 Alma Street, Luton, LU1 2PH, UK.

Fussier, C.R. (1994) 'The Sustainability Revolution and the Eco-Efficiency Imperative', Paper to Greening of Industry Conference, Copenhagen, 13–14 November, pp. 10.

Kirkby, J., O'Keefe, P. and Timberlake, L. (1995) *The Earthscan Reader in Sustainable Development*, Earthscan, London.

Maynard, R. (1995) 'Sperm Alert', *Living Earth*, No. 188, October, pp. 8–9.

North, R. (1995) *Life on a Modern Planet: A Manifesto for Progress*, Manchester University Press, Manchester and New York.

Orr, D. (1994) *Earth in Mind: On Education, the Environment and the Human Prospect*, Island Press, Washington, DC.

Porter, M.E. and Van der Linde, C. (1995) 'Green and Competitive: Ending the Stalemate', *Harvard Business Review* Sept.–Oct. 5: 120–34.

Schmidheiny, S. and The Business Council for Sustainable Development (BCSD) (1992) *Changing Course: A Global Business Perspective on Development and the Environment*, BCSD and MIT Press, Cambridge, MA, and London, May.

Seager, (1993) *Earth Follies*, Earthscan, London

Shackleton, Lord (1964) Introduction, in R. Carson, *Silent Spring*, Hamish Hamilton, London, (Reader's Union Edition).

Stigson, Björn (1995) Speech by executive director of WBCSD, UNED–UK Conference, 'Sustaining Developments since the Rio Summit,' 27 November 1995, London, UK.

Stoner, J., Freeman, R. and Gilbert, D. (1995) *Management*, 6th edn, Prentice Hall, Englewood Cliffs, NJ.

Trainer, T. (1995) *The Conserver Society: Alternatives for Sustainability*, Zed, London.

University of Bradford (1995) *Annual Report*, University of Bradford, March, p. 28.

Wackernagel, M. and Rees, W. (1996) *Our Ecological Footprint: Reducing Human Impact on the Earth*, New Society Publishers, Gabriola Island, BC, and Philadelphia, PA.

Wehrmeyer, W. (1994) *Environmental References in Business*, Greenleaf Publishing, Sheffield.

World Commission on Environment and Development (1987) *Our Common Future*, Brundtland Report, Oxford University Press, Oxford.

Wuppertal Institute (1995) *Sustainable Germany: A Contribution to Sustainable Global Development* (Résumé), Wuppertal Institute for Climate Energy and the Environment, Doppersberg 19, Wuppertal, Germany, December.

CHAPTER 2

BUSINESS ETHICS AND THE ENVIRONMENT

If a man hasn't discovered something to die for, he isn't fit to live.

(Martin Luther King Jr 1963) (1929–68)

INTRODUCTION

Ethics form part of the complex web of human relationships within which decisions relating to people, organizations and competitors are taken. Profit-making is not a morally neutral activity. This chapter seeks to explain what business ethics are, why they are important and what they have to do with ecological sustainability. As business involves individual interrelationships as well as forming a social function, there are significant ethical questions to consider. This chapter delineates these ethical questions and analyses their importance to the proactive manager of the new millennium.

WHY STUDY BUSINESS ETHICS?

The term 'business ethics' could be regarded as a contradiction in terms. An organization which exists to make money appears to have little or no reason to be interested in morality. It has been argued that as long as governments regulate for the welfare of citizens, business should be content to put morality to one side. Indeed, Milton Friedman (1984) says that business has no social responsibility beyond that of increasing its profits 'so long as it stays within the rules of the game, which is to say, engages in open and free competition without deception or fraud' (Friedman 1984: 131). In other words, business has no business to consider questions of 'good' or 'evil', still less of social justice or environmental sustainability. Even in this extreme view, however, there are 'rules of the game' which 'ought' not to be broken. As Friedman recognizes, there are actions which are 'wrong' in the sense that they break the rules.

The examples in Case Study 2.1 will give the reader an understanding of why the

CASE STUDY 2.1
Environmental Disasters

Union Carbide's Bhopal catastrophe

One of the worst industrial disasters of all time occurred in Bhopal, India, on the night of 3 December 1984. Union Carbide was the third largest US chemical company, operating plants in 38 countries. The Bhopal plant was 49.1 per cent Indian owned, and was, essentially, an Indian operation. The accidental release of methyl-isocyanate in the congested, low-income district of Old Bhopal killed 3000 people and left many thousands more with chronic disabilities leading to premature deaths. Since the selection of the site 17 years earlier, the local population had tripled as people sought jobs. The tragedy raised the question of the ethics of siting a plant capable of such devastation in a highly populated urban site in a country where labour costs and government-prescribed safety standards were low.

Chernobyl nuclear plant, USSR

On 26 April 1986 the Chernobyl nuclear plant came close to a core melt-down. As a result, large quantities of radioactive material were discharged into the environment, killing 10 000 people in the former USSR. The radioactive cloud which drifted across most of western Europe is considered likely to be responsible for many more thousands of premature deaths through cancer. The tragedy confirmed doubts about the nuclear industry's assurances of the impossibility of acute systems failure. Despite the accident and its implications of nuclear risks now attached to conventional warfare, nuclear power stations continue to be commissioned.

Exxon Valdez Alaskan oil spill

The most catastrophic maritime oil spill in US history occurred on the night of 24 March 1989 in Prince William Sound, Alaska. The oil tanker *Exxon Valdez* spilled 10.1 million gallons, creating an oil slick which eventually covered 1000 square miles, damaging some of Alaska's most pristine waters, extinguishing wildlife and decimating the tourist and fishing industries. The Exxon Corporation, the USA's second-largest corporation and the world's third largest oil company, with sales of over $86 billion that year, was reluctant to accept responsibility to fund the $2.5 billion clean-up operation.

All three accidents raise the question of the ethics of the production of highly contaminating materials which may be released into the environment. Whether through carelessness, negligence, bad judgements, terrorism or acts of God, accidents are likely to occur whenever hazardous substances are manufactured and transported. Indeed, the cumulative effect of minor leakages and careless waste disposal procedures may cause greater long-term environmental damage than the more noticeable disasters.

Source: News items and Hartley (1993)

considerations of business ethics are so important and what the implications are of ignoring their existence.

Hoffman and Moore (1990: 1) explore the complexity of business ethics underpinning corporate morality by setting business within the wider social context within which all transactions take place. Although corporate relationships are essentially economic, business can operate only within the context of the wider society in which it is located. It is towards the rules and the approaches to ethical theory which inform the decision-making processes in business and the community that we now turn.

ETHICS AND PROFITS

All businesses have to consider moral questions. It is an important strategic variable. If a business focuses solely on the bottom line without considering the implications of its relationship with the community as a whole, its short-termist position could undermine the bottom line. For example a company choosing to ignore the environment because it is too 'costly' to review its processes could face expensive litigation following a disaster of the type described in Case Study 2.1. Negative publicity surrounding litigation may have adverse effects on marketing. Profit maximization on a long-term basis is incompatible with a short-termist strategy.

A company may choose to implement environmental reform for reasons of profit maximiza-tion and long-termist strategic planning. This raises the question of whether there is a distinction to be drawn between ethical action and good business sense. Green marketing may be viewed as a strategy for the future or for profitability. Problems may occur, however, when there is a conflict of interest between the motivating factors. If there are two central motivating factors, where financial profit and futurity appear incompatible, it may be difficult to determine precedence in a conflict of interest. A strategy may undermine the financial motive but satisfy the futurity motive. In this event, the soundest approach may not be to resort to the archaic of the short-term profitability yardstick.

Decision-making in business has become increasingly complex as environmental questions have been raised about all aspects of corporate activity. Since business is in the community, and works within a physical and ethical framework, it has to consider the environment as an ethical issue and needs to respond to the challenge of ecological sustainability.

A QUESTION OF ETHICS

So, what is ethical? And who says that it is so? One person's morality could be, and very often is, another person's immorality. Are there any absolutes and are there any codes of practice for businesses to use as measures of morality? Some ethical theorists have argued that it is so difficult to differentiate between the action and the motivation that only the consequences of the action are relevant in establishing the ethical nature of the action (consequentialist theories). If the action has overall good for the majority it is deemed to be ethical (*utilitarianism*). The problem then becomes a semantic one, what after all is 'good'?

Within the post-structuralist, post-modern world, words have begun to mean less and less. As a host of interest groups call for a more 'sustainable' society, their different motivations encompass totally different ideas of what they are demanding. One individual may accept the need to move towards a 'sustainable' society by taking 'sustainable' development to mean 'sustainable economic growth'. Another may regard 'sustainability' as merely 'sustained economic growth' placing the focus on the conservation of market leadership rather than on the conservation of resources. Given that there are around 73 definitions of sustainability in the English language, the ethics which underlie the quest for it must remain tentative.

As Moore said in his seminal work *Principia Ethica*: 'It appears to me that in Ethics, as in all other philosophical studies, the difficulties and disagreements, of which its history is full, are mainly due to a very simple cause: namely to the attempt to answer questions, without first discovering precisely what question it is which you desire to answer' (Moore 1903: *vii*). It is for this reason writers have begun to prefix environmental or ecological before sustainability to clarify the focus of the word.

The problems of semantics and definitions are central to the understanding and prescription of environmental sustainability. Take for example the statement: 'Environmental sustainability is an ethical concept'. First, one has to decide and agree what environmental sustainability is, and second, what an ethical concept is; then and only then is one in a position to decide if environmental sustainability is an ethical concept. Undefined terms lead to undefined problems and undefined solutions.

Chryssides and Kaler (1993: 8) have argued that many of the more contemporary works on business ethics, particularly from the USA, have tended to reject consideration of questions of personal and social morality, concentrating solely on linguistics and semantics. Although consistent with the post-modern society where words have increasingly lost their meaning, there is a need for detailed definitional construction. Words must still be used to give social morality contemporary relevance.

There are three general terms used that require initial explanation: 'ethics', 'business ethics' and 'environmental ethics'. Ethics will be considered in detail, but first, definitions of business and environmental ethics are briefly considered. Business ethics has been described as 'the systematic study of moral (ethical) matters pertaining to business, industry or related activities, institutions, or practices—or beliefs' (Donaldson 1992). Environmental ethics has been defined as 'the attempt to apply moral theory to the human treatment of natural objects' (Sorell and Hendry 1994: 185). This is not a new ethical paradigm that excludes humans and is created specifically for plants and animals but rather an ethic that recognizes the inter-relationships and ethical imperatives that exist in a co-habitational moral world.

ETHICS DEFINED

In the conduct of business, questions of what is good or bad, moral or immoral, right or wrong have given rise to considerable discussion. The question arises as to whether there are any guidelines, rules or codes of conduct that classify what is or is not moral. What is 'right' and what is 'wrong' may be no more than a matter of personal judgement. On first reading, many statements appear reasonable enough. We may agree that 'Ethics is about moral choices. It is about the values that lie behind them, the reasons people give for them, and the language they use to describe them' (Thompson 1994: 5). We may also agree that 'It is about the moral value of human conduct and of the rules and principles that ought to govern it' (Sorell and Hendry 1994). Defining the values, and the principles that 'ought' to govern human conduct, however is not so straightforward.

The word *ethic* comes from two main Greek words. *Ethos* means moral—habit, culture, distinctive character, attitudes, principles of conduct, all of which are actions. The second derivation is from *ethikos*, which means custom. Apart from attitudes, the rest of the variables are concerned with the ensuing actions of morality. The distinction between the action itself, including the consequences of the action, and the motivation behind the action we will come on to in a little while.

Settling on a definitive statement of what ethics are is problematic. Indeed it has been the source of philosophical debate since the early Greek civilizations. Ethics or ethical theory is a central element within the academic discipline of philosophy. Philosophy, which is derived from the Greek word *philosophos* meaning 'lover of wisdom', attempts to explain what wisdom is. Philosophy is concerned with what is wise and who says that it is so. It is the academic discipline concerned with making explicit the nature and significance of ordinary or scientific beliefs, investigating the intelligibility of concepts by means of rational argument concerning their presuppositions, implications and interrelationships. Philosophy *per se* is split into four main areas:

- The rational explanation of the nature and structure of reality (metaphysics).
- The resources and limits of knowledge (epistemology).
- The principles and import of moral judgement (ethics).
- The relationship between language and reality (semantics).

In this context, ethics is a central component of the discipline of philosophy. 'The goal of ethical theory is to identify and defend some fundamental principle that can serve as the foundation for all morality' (Desjardins quoted in Chryssides and Kaler 1984: 136). This is what all ethical *meta-theories* attempt to construct. There are a number of theories and approaches to ethics in the literature that have evolved through time. However, due to the limitations of space within this text we are able to cover only the mainstream theories. For a more comprehensive analysis of ethical meta-theories and their application to business ethics, see Sellars and Hospers (1952), Chryssides and Kaler (1993) and Sorell and Hendry (1994).

The ethical meta-theories underlying the decision-making process are of interest in order to ascertain what actions are right and what are wrong. They assist in the clarification and explanation of the motivations behind actions taken and future possible strategies. Ethical meta-theories try to explain what is right and wrong and to offer reasons for such classification. But are there any objective criteria by which we can say that certain actions are right, and other actions are wrong? For example, is it right or wrong to be concerned about the future of society and its ability to farm the earth's resources? If yes, who says that this is so? What is 'wrong' with asserting that future generations have done nothing for the people of the present, and therefore do not deserve consideration by decision-makers of the present? 'What have future generations done for me?' appears an entirely rational argument. Indeed, it has been argued that conserving the earth's resources and moving towards sustainability cannot be justified at the expense of industrial expansion and providing jobs for the stability of society in the present day. If there are any conflicts of interest the question is whose interests should be compromised?

To judge the relative importance of these kinds of questions, the roots of morality need to be understood. This next section briefly covers the work of the early Greek philosophers. It reviews the general framework that has arisen from that period in history, providing a clearer understanding of the ethics involved in the corporate decision-making process (both conscious and subconscious). It also allows us to place business into perspective in assessing the importance of the environment and the ethical criteria behind being interested in green issues.

Moral philosophy—more than words

Moral philosophy has two dominant paradigms of thought, encapsulated in two periods of history. The first relates to the classical Greek period, the second to the modern period (since the 1920s). The two periods are distinct in focus, although the former has had a strong influence over the development of the latter. Early Greek philosophy was interested in defining good and bad, right and wrong, not just for the sake of defining the terms but to enable the citizen to become good and to act with justice. The motivation was associated with practicality rather than with the theory. Contemporary philosophers, however, due to the dilution of the meanings of contemporary language, have often been more concerned with the semantics (the meaning of words) than the application of the theory in any practical sense.

For the purpose of this book, due to the practical requirement for action to achieve ecological sustainability, we are interested primarily in the practical implications of ethical theory. We must, however, have an understanding of the importance of anachronistical development and some sympathy for the problems of transliteration and semantics. A word coined in the Greek like *ethikos*, for example, when transliterated into English, and still used over 2000 years later, could well have a different meaning today from that which applied when it was first coined.

Both Plato and Aristotle regarded ethics as part of the science of politics, whose function it was to provide the conditions under which the individual members of the community could achieve happiness (Rowe 1976). Their view of moral philosophy was interactive and dynamic, providing society with its moral foundation and codes of conduct. The main motivation of the Hellenistic philosophers, however (post-Aristotle and including the Stoics) was a desire for security, through embracing the doctrine of universal brotherhood of man as a means to freedom from violent feelings and emotions. Violent competition was seen as dysfunctional in terms of social cohesion.

The central elements, therefore, of early Greek moral philosophy were the application of theory to questions of security and freedom in the operation of society within the framework of the state. These same elements are central to the movement towards an ecologically sustainable society today. It can be argued that a secure, ecologically sustainable society can provide freedom from the constant threat of extinction and the economic and social disruption which may be predicted to arise from the early stages of ecological disintegration.

Many of the problems the Greek philosophers wrestled with stay unresolved by philosophy today, namely:

- The problem of the justification of moral beliefs.
- The problem of moral knowledge.

Plato and Socrates were in general agreement that moral conflict came from a lack of knowledge. They concluded that it is possible to know what is right and to do what is right only on the basis of information. The problem is, as Socrates himself said, 'the more I know, the more I realize I do not know anything'. If it is impossible to gain enough information, for example on environmental issues, in order to understand the whole picture, it may appear impractical to act in accordance with the ultimate ethical code. Where there are contradictions of motives between finance and ethics, it may appear more pragmatic to allow financial considerations to predominate other considerations. Certainly the area of moral decision-making can be a complex web of inexhaustible choices. For example, undertaking environmental measures that necessitate employment redundancies due to efficiency gains could be viewed as ethical from one angle, or unethical from another. Individual views may differ as to the correctness or otherwise of an action. Hence we have a system of laws backed by physical sanctions to settle those differences.

Although the law is seen by most to be the final arbiter of rights and wrongs, even the law has discernible origins. In the UK, for example, human law has in the main been derived from the Ten Commandments of the Bible. Western businesspeople can go about their daily business in relative security on the basis of a set of ethical rules which are Divine in origin. According to those rules, it is wrong to steal, and to bear false witness, and those who break the rules can be apprehended and punished. Ethics did not begin in ancient Greece, although the word was coined there. To understand how ethics has developed as a discipline over the years we are now going to take a brief look at the general ethical meta-theories that have evolved.

ETHICAL META-THEORIES

Cognitivism and non-cognitivism

Two major strands of ethical theory, cognitivism and non-cognitivism, can be identified. Cognitivism claims that it is possible to know moral right from wrong. Non-cognitivism, on the other hand, claims that you can not know what is morally right or wrong and that morality can be culturally differentiated. The implications are evident. Unless one can say what is right and what is wrong and agree on it then all decisions are to be made up on an individual level. In this event, corporate desire to unite in common purpose (for example towards a more sustainable future) can be compromised for the sake of short-term gains and cultural values.

Non-cognitivism stems from the reasoning that there are no 'absolute truths' but there are general cultural preferences and social ideals. This is known as moral *relativism*. A cognitivist perspective of morality, however, holds that truth (rights and wrongs) exists, regardless of what people believe. Societal preferences do not make morality.

This is one of the central questions of ethical theories. What is morally right and who says? It is central because one needs to be able to judge what is right to do what is right. An obvious source of moral determinants is God. If God is omniscient then God should be able to understand the whole picture and be the 'infallible authority on matters of ethics' (MacIntyre 1966: 84). The problem is then one of belief, understanding, interpretation and communication. For example we can know what the Bible says about ethical morality but not necessarily agree what it means or with the source of its authority.

The non-cognitivist theories argue against any transcendent influence and against any external controlling deity. Ethical *relativism*, for example, argues that there is no single universal objective set of standards by which to judge an action's morality. Different cultures have different rules, and even within a culture different subgroups may vary in their standards. Indeed, where acts are viewed as either moral or immoral, ethical relativism would not see them as either. Non-cognitivist theories do not say why an action is right or wrong, just what is viewed as right or wrong from a descriptive perspective. The majority of ethical theories derive from the cognitivist camp within which there is a further significant dichotomous divide which we must consider. This divide is between consequentialist and non-consequentialist theories.

Consequentialism and non-consequentialism

Consequentialist and non-consequentialist theories are those which assess the consequences of the action and those that do not. 'With consequentialist theories we look at the results of the action to determine the truth or falsity of moral judgements about them' (MacIntyre 1966: 88). Ethics here are not so much concerned with the motivation or the action in itself, but with the consequence of the action. 'Right or wrong is a question of good or bad; and good or bad a question of benefit or harm' (MacIntyre 1966: 88). A statement like 'what is the good of that?' would be typical. There can be agreement of action between consequentialists and non-consequentialists but for totally different reasons. Take an action like the avoidable generation of waste in industry. The action can be defined as wrong from both a consequentialist and a non-consequentialist perspective, albeit for different reasons. For the consequentialist it is wrong because of the waste of money and the detrimental social effects of the action. For the non-consequentialist the exploitation of the earth's resources over and above what is required to produce the good in the most efficient manner may be viewed as intrinsically wrong.

The non-consequentialist has one option available, that is to adhere to the determining set of codes of conduct. For the Christian, for example, this would be the Ten Commandments. This is known as the Divine Command theory. The consequentialist, however, has a number of options open and judges what will achieve the best result. The consequentialist assumes that the individual has full knowledge and total ability to judge all of the implications of an action. The non-consequentialist would argue that this is unlikely and there is a need, therefore to look elsewhere for guidance. 'Adherence to principle is the basis of the non-consequentialist approach, pragmatic flexibility that of the consequentialist' (MacIntyre 1966: 90).

Consequentialism

Utilitarianism

It can be argued that the 'greatest happiness of the greatest number' provides the most reliable guide for morality. Happiness is viewed as 'good'. In cost-benefit analysis the detrimental effects of a project are totalled and weighed against the estimated benefits to indicate the most beneficial course of action. Similarly, utilitarians argue that an act's moral quality is revealed by subtracting its painful consequences from its pleasurable ones. This approach raises the question of distribution of pleasure. It could be that total pleasure is increased if a few very rich people experience very high standards of enjoyment. The physical misery and moral depravation of the many may not outweigh the pleasure of the few. It all depends who is measuring what, and on what subjective basis. Motives are incidental: they matter only in how they affect the performance of the action and maximizing utility. Utilitarianism is a calculation of consequences. If a common preference is shared by the majority it then becomes the accepted good, even if the premise of the action is evil (Sorell and Hendry 1994: 41).

But, if the common good is in the interests of the majority, who is to say that the majority are right? History has proved time and time again that this is not always the case. Infanticide in China is one example of a practice which appears inherently evil, but arises from the perceived necessity to secure the common good of controlling population growth. It is also true to say that events can make individuals happy although the means are potentially unethical. For example, increased profit is the desire of most commercial enterprises, is in the interests of the shareholders and rarely makes a businessperson sad! However, if these increased profits are at the expense of good ethical business practices the businessperson could be happier, yet acting in an unethical manner. What makes us happy is not necessarily what is good and morally right.

Ethical egoism

Ethical egoism (debated primarily in the USA) holds that to act contrary to one's own self-interest is immoral. Each person has a duty to promote the greatest possible balance of good over evil for themselves. According to this theory, even altruism is ultimately a means to personal satisfaction. Other people have value only to the extent that they promote your own self-interest. Hence Friedman (1984: 131) can argue that 'good business is good ethics', and *not* vice versa. Social welfare, for example good working conditions, may be promoted only *in order* to increase productivity, efficiency, turnover and profits. Welfare measures are unethical if introduced for any other reasons.

Non-consequentialism

Kantianism

Immanuel Kant (1724–1804) argued that there are binding moral commands. Unlike other forms of animal life, humans are not governed by instinct and self-interest, but are capable of making moral choices. Indeed, humans have a duty to make these moral choices, and to refrain from using other humans as means to their own ends. One thing only is good in itself and for Kant that is good will.

> An action is morally right only if the person performing it is motivated by a good will; morally wrong if it is not. The possession of such a will alone makes the action right; its absence alone makes it wrong. Nothing else matters.
>
> **(Kant, from Chryssides and Kaler 1964: 97)**

What does Kant mean by good will? Essentially he means the action is done for reasons of principle, from a sense of duty and nothing else. The consequences of the action are not a motivating factor, the only thing that matters is doing your duty. We can tell if the action has been done for the right motives (i.e. out of a sense of duty) if the action is done in accordance with what Kant calls his categorical imperatives, two of which are detailed here:

- **Categorical imperative 1** Treat others as you would want them to treat you. 'I ought never to act except in such a way that I can also will that my maxim should become a universal law' (Kant, from Chryssides and Kaler 1964: 98–9). Maxim means 'the principle upon which I act'; this could actually be good or bad. Effectively, Kantianism is not engaging in practices that you could not recommend to others.

- **Categorical imperative 2** That people are an ends rather than a means and they have intrinsic worth.

> To act morally we must respect the personhood of people and never treat them simply as a means to an end but always, and primarily, as an end in themselves.
>
> **(Chryssides and Kaler 1993: 99)**

Kant refuses to accept as morally good any action that is not in keeping with purist motivation, that is any action done from fear, for appearance, or for any personal gain like financial profit. Kant associated moral worth only with actions undertaken because they are intrinsically right and not done for any consequentialist reasoning. The consequences of the action could not be the motivation for the action. The motivation for the action would be the satisfaction of the moral codes. Kant held that by reflecting on the ordinary concept of duty, people would recognize that the demands of morality were actually in their own interest in the long term and also in the interests of the people making their satisfaction desirable. The problem is the lure of short-term financial profit and humankind's insatiable consumptive appetite.

While there may be nothing ethically wrong with the pursuit of profit *per se*, it is the place of the pursuit of profit within the decision-making priority list of the corporate decision-maker that is important within the constraints of Kantianism. However, Kantianism fails to address the fundamental problem of the determination of 'right' and 'wrong'. Kant assumes a categorical imperative to perform certain actions because they are intrinsically 'right'. But duty is hard to define, and contradictions not easily reconciled.

For example, a firm seeking to do 'right' could face the following ethical dilemma. It produces hazardous substances which provide the basis for the production of a substance used in traditional industrial production methods. The ethical imperative to steward the earth's resources and not to pollute the waterways of the environment are clear. There are no substitutes to the production process and the idea of making the product more durable would mean the need for a smaller workforce.

The company faces several choices.

■ It may close down.

■ It may introduce less wasteful production processes and reduce the outflow of hazardous wastes into the water supply. The introduction of new and cleaner technology may lead to the loss of 100 jobs, increasing poverty, reliance on the welfare state and taxation.

■ It may seek to avoid detection and keep the jobs intact.

The categorical imperative to recognize one's duty may take the form of one of these choices. No option emerges as intrinsically 'right', due to the opportunity cost of failing to undertake the other duties. Without a hierarchy of moral duties the solution would seem to be compromise or achieving the optimum balance between duties which would only partially satisfy the optimum ethical morality.

Natural law

Natural law concentrates on human rights. The focus shifts from the theocentric view of Divine Command theory to a more (but not exclusively) anthropocentric view. This approach discerns an objective moral order of natural law which underpins human laws. By this line of reasoning, if human law contradicts the natural law, natural law takes precedence. Rights are bestowed on us by virtue of being human. These rights, which may include life, liberty, justice and the ownership of property, cannot legitimately be taken away by government or the state. Since John Locke (1632–1704), the list of human rights has gradually extended to include aspects of freedom of expression, belief, rights to education, welfare, fair wages and holiday pay in employment (Chryssides and Kaler 1993: 102). Where human rights clash it is accepted that the most important right will prevail. Clearly there will be matters of dispute about what are the higher order rights but generally life and liberty are seen as the most important. Parallels have been made with Kantianism in so far as human rights should be respected and adhered to as a duty. The link is between the Kantian duty to treat others as you would want them to treat you and other people's right to be treated well.

Ethics have been formally acknowledged within the business context in Europe from at least as far back as medieval times when the Catholic Church were involved with issues of usury, fair wages and employment rights. Although the subject was for a time the almost exclusive preserve of academics, there has recently been an upsurge of academic interest in business ethics, most notably within the USA (Chryssides and Kaler 1993). Having considered the main ethical meta-theories we now turn to their application to business. In order to understand the place of ethics within the industrial context it is necessary to see how industry has evolved, with particular emphasis on the ethics of employment.

ETHICS OF EMPLOYMENT

In the UK, the cradle of the industrial revolution, early industrialists faced a problem in converting rural peasants into an urban workforce. Rural subsistence farmers directed their own daily work in home, field and woodland, following the seasons and adapting local customs and practices as they saw fit. The early entrepreneurs had to be hard taskmasters to create a disciplined workforce. Singing or opening windows were regulated by fines and dismissals, and workers were often beaten or starved. In many towns and villages, workers were summoned from their beds at 5 a.m. by 'knockers up' to start their 12-hour working day. Workers, particularly young children, had a tendency to doze, and were often caught up in machinery. The resultant injuries or deaths were of particular inconvenience to the employers, since machines had to be stopped to free the child or adult workers. This resulted in significant periods of time when capital investments were idle.

The work of enlightened paternalistic employers such as Robert Owen and Titus Salt, coupled with public pressure marshalled by trade unions, an early form of *non-governmental organization* (NGO), led to legislation compelling employers to accept responsibility for terms and conditions of employment. From the time of the first Factory Acts in 1833 and 1847, the state fostered good practice not only with regard to employment but also in the provision of education, health, housing and the transport and services infrastructure. As production increased so did the paperwork. Research and development, administration and banking, advertising and promotion, all required an educated and healthy workforce. The sound ethical practices of the employers of the day were, with the support of trade unions and politicians, embedded in legislation applicable to all employers. Throughout the nineteenth and twentieth centuries the ethics of employment developed as a learning curve for employers and employees alike.

Employers could not, however, guarantee an income for the entire urban population from the cradle to the grave. Without a social security safety net, old, infirm, sick and unemployed people faced starvation in the gutters or degradation in the workhouses. In the course of the twentieth century, ethical employment practices were supplemented by various social security measures, which were designed as a co-operative venture by employers, trade unions, politicians and pressure groups.

The conversion of rural populations into urban workforces occurred throughout Europe (east and west), North America, Australia and New Zealand. Despite local variations—the early degradation of workforces was most severe in the UK and USA—by the late nineteenth century industrialists had a readily available, wage-dependent workforce, able and willing to accept directions from the employer to maximize profits. The self-motivation of pre-industrial craft workers was a thing of the past. Even so, the day-to-day administration of the workforce remained in the hands of foremen and skilled workers. The organization and supervision of work, basic operational and personnel management decision-making was undertaken by the shop-floor.

Scientific management

In the early twentieth century the US engineer Frederick Winslow Taylor (1856–1915) introduced the concept of scientific management into the workplace to further maximize profits. Taylor advocated:

- **The increased division of labour** Tasks should be broken down into their smallest component parts. Each worker should have a single, simple task. The reasoning was that increased specialization would lead to greater efficiency. It was also accepted that the de-skilling of the labour force offered opportunity to employ cheaper, unskilled labour. Specialization among managers was also encouraged.

- **Management control co-ordination** For the first time managers could control and co-ordinate the entire production process.

- **Information diffusion through cost accounting** Cost accounting based on time and motion study could provide managers with the information they needed in order to control the workplace.

Taylor believed that workers were motivated predominantly by financial gain. The most effective way to secure their full co-operation was therefore through a scientific system of payment by results. In this way individual workers would share in the profits arising from their efforts. The removal of managerial skills and organizational autonomy from lower-level employees established management as a distinct role, neither owner nor skilled worker. The potential conversion of the workforce into little more than mindless robots, as caricatured by Charlie Chaplin, was attractive to employers in the USA prior to the First World War, and later in Europe and the Soviet Union. These general philosophies in workplace theory became known as 'Taylorism' or '*Fordism*', as scientific management, as it has been termed, has underpinned economic relations throughout the twentieth century in the developed world.

The global labour market

One legacy of the introduction of scientific management and the 'managerial revolution' which followed it (see Burnham 1942) was the entrenched belief that the purpose of industry was to create money, and that workers were 'human resources'. The conversion of workers into commodities in the labour market resulted in employers and managers recognizing the dignity of labour as and when it was financially expedient to do so. Financial gain soon became the primary motivating factor for employees, replacing the more responsible vocational motivations. By the late twentieth century managers and employers in a global market could shift production and investment on purely financial grounds. Charles Handy (1994) has examined business organizations and outlined the paradoxes of the time. With new technologies, fewer and fewer people are required to produce more and more goods. Training schemes become more elaborate, graduate unemployment rises, part-time and temporary employment replaces full-time employment and income insecurity is rife. Yet those remaining in full-time employment work longer hours and incur greater stress (Crawhurst 1995).

Meanwhile, the import of cheap goods from countries with low wage rates threatens the destruction of industries in the developed world. Crawhurst (1995) cites hourly labour costs in the mid-1990s:

Germany	$25.00
Britain	$12.00
Taiwan	$5.50
Mexico	$2.50
Czech Republic	$1.00
China	$0.50

Manufacturers are moving their production processes to areas where labour costs are low and regulation of employment conditions virtually non-existent, thus enabling cheap goods to be imported into the developed world. Therefore European manufacturers who retain home plants lose market share to the imported stock. As in the first industrial revolution, although for slightly different reasons, small farmers in developing countries are forced off the land, providing the pool of cheap labour essential for this process to take place.

BUSINESS ETHICS—THE APPLICATION

Ethics may be defined as the study of what is good or right for human beings. It asks what goals people ought to pursue and what actions they ought to perform. Business ethics is a branch of applied ethics; it studies the relationship of what is good and right to business.

(Hoffmann and Moore 1990: 1)

Having considered the theory behind the roots of ethics and a brief history of the evolution of ethics within employment, it is appropriate now to turn to the application of those theories to business and business practice today.

Milton Friedman (whose ethical position is primarily rights-based *libertarianism* and utilitarian in nature) argues that participants are motivated purely by self-interest, and that this can be seen as an ethical stance for business to take. He argues that the sole purpose of a business is to generate profit. The successful entrepreneur produces goods and services which people want, and does so with the maximum efficiency. This alone satisfies the social function of business, in that investment, employment and flows of money serve the community. Hence social responsibility can be satisfied by profit maximization. Few businesses are actually run purely on an ethical or altruistic basis, where morality and consistent action is the overriding motivator in the decision-making process. Taking a relativist perspective the morality of an action would depend on a variety of individual standpoints:

- From Milton Friedman's (1984) perspective, broad ethical considerations are secondary, since the only ethical responsibility is to maximize profits.

- From a non-consequentialist perspective, the validity of correctness of ethical judgements is dependent upon accepted moral laws.

- From a Kantian and relativist perspective, the morality of actions is dependent upon individual perception of their appropriateness for universal law status.

- From a utilitarian perspective the consequences need to be assessed to judge ethical priorities.

A business perspective

At the turn of the twentieth century, the following list of practices are commonly viewed as ethical within a business context:

- Employing good environmental practices.

- Contributing to good causes.

- Participating in community activities.

- Paying employees a fair wage.

- Providing safe and clean working conditions.

- Not fixing the books.

- Being loyal to customers.

- Keeping your word in a deal.

- Not fixing prices with competitors.

- Exaggeration in advertisement.

- Avoiding false advertising claims regarding competitors.

- Not building in product obsolescence.

- Negotiating morally with customers.

- Equal employment opportunities.

This selective list offers indications of good ethical practice. As we have seen, business ethics can be defined as 'the systematic study of moral (ethical) matters pertaining to business, industry or related activities, institutions, or practices—or beliefs' (Donaldson 1992). Since the primary commercial motive would seem to be profit (rather than adherence to overriding moral laws), tension is created at the interface between profit and other questions of moral law. This is indeed the case with sustainability. Sustainability and the environmental question in general have challenged the industrial bottom line and corporate responsibility (and will continue to).

The free rider

Recognizing the pressures to integrate environmental considerations in their production and marketing strategies, a firm may nevertheless opt for short-term rewards by adopting a '*free rider*' strategy. Free riders assume that while everyone else will be socially responsible, their own irresponsibility will be negligible in relationship with the whole, and will therefore remain unnoticed. In effect, such people act as parasites. While enjoying the common good, the free rider relies upon the contribution of others *to* the collective good. Were all to follow the same principle, a collective catastrophe would ensue.

The free rider strategy relies upon anonymity. A firm may dump plastic wastes on derelict land, rely upon illegal incineration or discharge untreated wastes into water courses during the hours of darkness. Large quantities of toxic wastes may legally be shipped overseas to be dumped at nominal prices in Third World countries, with unknown effects on the long-term health of the men, women and children living in the locality. *DDT*, an insecticide, the use of which is banned in many developed countries, may still be sold for use on cash crops in the Third World. The food-importing firm which opts to ignore the effects of DDT upon the health of the workers in the Third World, and upon consumers of foodstuffs in the First World, is no less a free rider.

Although not condoning specific free rider activities, senior management may encourage profit maximization by turning a blind eye to unethical practices. Thus deceptive advertising, adulterated products, casual waste disposal and the legal or illegal release of genetically modified organisms (*GMOs*) may be tacitly condoned. The free rider strategy remains a short-termist option in large, centralized markets. Within small local markets the failure to contribute to the collective good or the production of a collective bad is more immediately identifiable.

While such activities may benefit a firm's short-term accounts, it is becoming increasingly recognized as unsustainable practice, both for the individual firm and the environment. Growing environmental awareness on the part of consumers, investors, employees and the local community will increasingly undermine the survival prospects of the free rider firm (see Chapter 8). In the mean time, ethically sound practices introduced throughout an organization in the context of worker participation and commitment are the hallmark of a progressive management aspiring to long-term survival.

ENVIRONMENTAL ETHICS

Until the UK industrial revolution began in the middle of the eighteenth century, production, trade and commerce had little discernible impact upon the global environment. However, as manufacturers generated more and more trade, workers needed to be supplied with food, housing and fuel. Concurrently, suppliers, manufacturers, wholesalers and retailers required transport systems and infrastructures and the services of finance and communications. As service industries, retail and distributive trades sprang up around the original centres of manufacturing, a new mind-set was created in which manufacturing industry was equated with wealth generation. In the process, science, technology and industry became accepted as ends in themselves and ceased to be regarded as a means of optimizing human well-being.

Forests were cut down, soils polluted and toxic substances permeated the workplace. As individual symptoms of malaise appeared they were dealt with on a piecemeal remedial basis, with little or no pre-planning. Eventually, legal restraints on the siting of industry and the development of health and safety regulations came to accompany industrialization. For the most part, new industrial processes were introduced with little analysis in research and development (*R&D*) of environmental impacts resulting from the sourcing of material, production, use or disposal of the product. In general, science, technology and industry were slow to develop an environmental perspective. When Abraham Darby erected the world's first iron bridge in Coalbrookdale in 1779, he did not make an environmental impact assessment (*EIA*) of the project!

Perhaps it is unreasonable to have expected him to foresee that his use of coke-coal to smelt iron would lead to replacement of pack horses, wagons and tall ships by iron horses, iron ships and the internal combustion engine. Still less can the early industrialists be blamed for failing to anticipate the problems associated with the production of methods of transportation and packaging which were not, like the pre-industrial artefacts, biodegradable. The new products required fossil fuels for their production and use, new methods looked highly attractive, and a naive optimism was, perhaps, understandable.

Eighty years later, however, the environmental impact of industrialization was becoming apparent. J. S. Mill (1806–73) questioned the pursuit of wealth through industrial progress which failed to take the environment into account. He noted 'disagreeable symptoms' in the 'northern and middle states of America':

> [As a result of progress] the life of the whole of one sex is devoted to dollar-hunting, and of the other to breeding dollar-hunters. ... I know not why it should be a matter of congratulation that persons who are already richer than anyone needs to be, should have doubled their means of consuming things which give little or no pleasure except as representative of wealth. ... Nor is there much satisfaction in contemplating a world with nothing left to the spontaneous activity of nature; with every rood of land brought into cultivation, which is capable of growing food for human beings; every flowery waste or natural pasture ploughed up, all quadrupeds or birds which are not domesticated for man's use exterminated as his rivals for food, every hedgerow or superfluous tree rooted

out, and scarcely a place left where a wild shrub or flower could grow without being eradicated as a weed in the name of improved agriculture.

(Mill 1857, in Daly 1973: 12–13)

Mill recommended improvement in the 'industrial arts' as a means to reduce labour, offering scope for 'human improvement' through 'all kinds of mental culture, and moral and social progress'. However, despite early warning signs, industry continued to adopt ecologically unsound materials and techniques, with no vision beyond the abstracting of resources and the dumping of toxic and degraded materials back into the natural environment. In the USA the extraction of oil fuelled the rise of the automobile industry, petrochemicals and plastics, each of which paid little regard to the long-term environmental effects. Like the shipping of slaves across the Atlantic and the employment of child labour, 'everybody' indulged in these practices as a part of business survival.

Nevertheless, well into the twentieth century, the bulk of food supplied to urban areas was locally sourced. A walk into the countryside provided workers with evidence of the animal husbandry and horticulture which supplied their foods. Household wastes, even in inner cities, remained minimal, with sacks and rags converted into rugs, milk and beer collected in jugs, and food scraps fed to chickens, pigs and pets. Although good practice survived in many parts of the world, even in the urban situation (see Chapter 12), in practice the profit motive predominated in business, and there was little attempt to apply moral theory to the human treatment of natural objects (Sorell and Hendry 1994).

Principles of ecologically sustainable development

In the 1990s industrial and household waste has reached gigantic proportions across the developed world. Pressure groups and forward-looking firms attempt to backtrack on the environmental devastation caused by science, technology and industry by introducing schemes based upon 'old fashioned' values of thrift and common sense. Ecologically sustainable development (*ESD*) is an ethical framework providing for an holistic approach to ecological sustainability.

The speed and extent to which this approach may be adopted by management will vary from firm to firm, and over time and place. Thorsby (1993) has identified six principles of ecological sustainability:

- **Advancement of material and non-material well-being** In ESD terms the definition of 'development' extends beyond the narrow concept of economic growth. It includes GDP as a measure alongside a broader view which encompasses concern for standards of education and health, equity, cultural values and environmental security, each of which has a contribution to make to the total quality of life.

- **Inter-generational equity** ESD is concerned with the relationship between present behaviour and its impacts on future generations. Concern stems from the ethical belief that the planet we hand on to our children and grandchildren should be in no worse shape than the one we inherited from our forebears. In Margaret Thatcher's words, we have inherited the 'full-repairing lease'.

- **Intra-generational equity** Inequitable distribution of access to goods and resources within our own generation has been shown to lead to social disruption and environmental degradation. Social injustice is therefore ecologically unsustainable. Environmental policies which impact heavily upon the disadvantaged will therefore be counterproductive.

- **Protection of *biodiversity* (biological diversity) and the maintenance of ecological processes and systems** The fundamental importance of the interdependence between ecological systems is receiving increasing recognition. Environmental effects are coming to be regarded as of more significance than mere spillovers from the important activities of business.

- **Dealing cautiously with risk and uncertainty** Some technological developments and industrial processes involve risk of irreversible damage to the environment. In the face of such prospects, a 'risk-averse' stance, postponing actions with possible irreversible consequences until further information is to hand is being recommended. This is known as the *Precautionary Principle*.

- **Recognition of global dimensions** Few environmental issues are purely national in their impacts and ramifications. One country's energy policy may increase the effects of global warming for all. Land degradation and water pollution have effects which ignore national boundaries. Additionally, environmental policies are increasingly affecting trade and impacting on economies.

Ecological sustainability can be defined as desirable, and ethical in each of the senses defined above. Since the market cannot function to meet the interest of the egoist unless there are resources to fuel the supply, even the egoist has a rational interest in ecological sustainability. It can also be argued that ecological sustainability is ethical from a Kantian perspective, in the sense that it is our duty to treat others as we would like to be treated and this includes future generations. If the sustenance of the present quality of life enjoyed in the north requires amended lifestyles it is our duty to address the issue. Equally it is our ethical duty to question the interrelationship between the rich north and the poor south. According to Kant, if the rich are getting richer at the expense of the poor, it is our duty to move towards a more egalitarian society. Equally, from a utilitarian perspective, ESD is ethical because the consequences of a deleterious environment are not in the best interests of the global population as a whole. For example if holes in the ozone layer continue to expand, and temperatures in the Arctic continue to increase, the corresponding sea-level rises in areas of low-lying terrain will force more and more people into less and less space. Environmental refugees will move into already crowded areas, spreading social and environmental problems into the remaining habitable lands. There are many examples of how micro-behaviour can and will (unless checked) rebound on the economies of the north.

TOWARDS AN ECOLOGICAL BUSINESS ETHIC

It is one thing to agree that from a theoretical perspective, ecological sustainability is ethical and desirable. It is quite another to prescribe what can be done to attain or move towards it. As it has been said, there is a need for people not only to 'talk the talk' but also to 'walk the walk'. Actions are more powerful than words, and mere belief in ecological sustainability while undertaking business as usual is unlikely to result in an ecologically sustainable global society. Mobilization for ethical action may come from a number of sources and for a number of motivations. These include:

■ Moral motives.

■ Information flows.

■ Government pressure (e.g. legislation).

■ Economic pressure (e.g. market incentives).

■ Stakeholders' pressure (e.g. media, investors and customers).

■ Company policy.

Although from a non-consequentialist perspective the only truly ethical action is the one fuelled or mobilized by a moral law, other ethical theories suggest there are a number of other acceptable motivations for action that can just as equally be called ethical.

For ecological sustainability to be achieved, the motivation to aspire to ecological ideals has to be as strong an influence as financial gain. There are large areas of overlap, where financial and ecological goals can be satisfied together. However, there are also major areas of action where they do not. For example, a truly sustainable society and economic system would require a radical revision in our thinking regarding production. With 20 per cent of the world using 80 per cent of the world's energy, a rise in demand by industrializing countries for energy, coupled with the generation of more waste, can be predicted. Solutions to the anticipated problems require an ethically informed realism in which financial and environmental goals are skilfully reconciled. In practice, although businesses increasingly regard the environment as a significant social issue, firms have been slow to change their practices to the extent that an ecologically sustainable society appears assured. Production is basically motivated by profit, with the long term appearing distant and abstract. Waste management reduction and green marketing policies have been introduced from short-term profit motivations rather than long-term ethical considerations.

In practice, ecological ethics may be little more than a selective marketing strategy. Where it suits, decisions may be termed 'ethical'. Where morality is inconvenient, it can be compromised in favour of 'sound business practice'. The motivation is nearly always primarily 'self' and financial. While this may not be set to change, what is important from an ethical perspective is to realize that when people talk about ethical business practices they are often talking about little more than a good marketing strategy. 'As Aristotle recognised we can know what ought to be done, we can even desire to do it, and yet we find our selves giving in to temptation' (Brennan 1992: 4). Assuming, both from a consequentialist and non-consequentialist perspective, that ecological sustainability is desirable, how can it best be achieved?

Ecological sustainability requires a fundamental shift in the ethics employed by decision-makers from reactionary action ethics to proactive attitudinal ethical decision-making. For

ESD to be achieved, there needs to be this foundational desire to aspire to the best practice. ESD demands economies that produce fewer goods which are made to last longer, generating more money through services than manufacturing goods. As Lee (1989) has suggested we need to move towards producing more 'inner goods', like teaching, and services in general whose existence does not detract from others participating in the economy. The production of so-called 'outer goods' like cars or freezers uses up resources. Because there is only a limited amount of resources available within a finite world (substitutes apart) the production and use of these resources diminishes the ability of others to participate in this economy. Inner goods do not use unsustainable resources and can be produced *ad infinitum*. These goods add to the wealth of the nation without detracting from the resource base and anyone else's ability to consume.

SUMMARY

In the real world, the average businessperson, with limited knowledge of the total effects of any action, is likely to choose the most apparently beneficial option, from an individual short-term perspective. In this event, the ethical meta-theory most accurately describing the position of industry at the present is *ethical egoism*. The issue, however, is not so much which is the most descriptive ethical meta-theory but what may be the outcome of the employed theory in the long term. There is a significant distinction between what is and what ought to be aimed for.

In the absence of a simple rule-of-thumb definition of ethics, there is little possibility of watertight analysis within business ethics. As long as one person believes that ethics can be egocentric (as in egoism) and another argues that morality and ethics require external focus for the good of others or adherence to universal laws, there will always be disagreement on what is required of business, and what is or is not ethical. Perhaps the more pertinent issue relates to the question of whether industry can be said to be morally inclined at all. Although sustainability is clearly beneficial to industry over the long term, its attainment in itself may not be pursued for ethical reasons. Furthermore, what people believe to be moral does not on its own necessarily make the action moral.

Within the theory of ethics, and moral philosophy, ecological sustainability would seem to be one of the primary ethical considerations of the twenty-first century. This book will cover the requirement to manage waste and operate in a more ecologically sensitive way in Part 2. However, it also stresses that this approach to environmental management is not, on its own, sufficient to achieve an ecologically sustainable society. This chapter has stated why ethics are a critical dimension of ecological sustainability by reviewing the standard ethical theories and moral philosophies of yesterday and today. Although ethics have the potential to be isolated in theory, it is argued that ethics and morality have a central part to play within the corporate environmental decision-making process, particularly for the proactive twenty-first century business. With the tide of public opinion moving towards more localized environmentally accountable socio-economic structures, a holistic eco-strategy for business ethics is increasingly becoming standard corporate practice.

QUESTIONS

2.1 Does a manager have a moral responsibility to consider the ethical implications of the entire production process of the plant where hazardous substances are used? In the last analysis, when an accident occurs, does responsibility rest with the perpetrator of the final 'mistake' (e.g. in the case of the *Exxon Valdez*, her drunken captain)?

2.2 Should managers consider the ethical implications of new products? Technology enables us to supply a machine to do almost everything and advertising techniques to market it. Liquid food could be supplied on tap. Babies' nappies could be changed as well as washed by machines. The production of babies outside a human mother's body is also being researched. Using a concrete example, consider the courses of action available to a firm that discovered that products being developed may be considered unethical.

2.3 Taken cumulatively, every economic decision has significant environmental effects, with potential economic implications over the long term. To what extent are ethical considerations legitimately involved in the search for solutions to this problem?

BIBLIOGRAPHY

Key texts

Chryssides, G. and Kaler, K. (eds) (1993) *An Introduction to Business Ethics*, **Chapman & Hall, London**
An excellent résumé of the central ethical questions facing industry today. This book of readings comprises classic ethical texts interspersed by profound educational and accessible comment.

Hoffman, W. and Moore, J. (eds) (1990) *Business Ethics*, **McGraw-Hill, New York**
Another classic book of readings, this book comprises five main sections which include theoretical developments, corporate fabric analysis (two sections), the place of the corporation within the broader external environment and the future.

References and further reading
Brennan A. (1992) 'Environmental Decision-making', in R. J. Berry (ed.) *Environmental Dilemmas, Ethics and Decisions*, Chapman & Hall, London.
Burnham, J. (1942) *The Managerial Revolution*, Putnam, New York.
Carr, A. (1968) 'Is Bluffing Ethical?', *Harvard Business Review* Jan.–Feb., reprinted in G. Chryssides and K. Kaler (eds) (1993) *An Introduction to Business Ethics*, Chapman & Hall, London.
Chryssides, G. and Kaler, K. (eds) (1993) *An Introduction to Business Ethics*, Chapman & Hall, London.
Crawhurst, S. (1995) 'Is the Market Economy Sustainable?', Conference Proceedings

Abstract, The 1995 International Sustainable Development Research Conference, Manchester, 27–28 March.

Daly, H. E. (1973) *Towards a Steady State Economy*, W. H. Freeman, San Francisco.

Desjardins, J. J. (1984) *Virtues and Business Ethics Corporate Governance and Institutionalising Ethics* (ed.) M. Hoffman *et al.*, Lexington Books, Lexington, MA, reprinted in G. Chryssides and J. Kaler (eds) (1993) *An Introduction to Business Ethics*, Chapman & Hall, London.

Donaldson, J. (1992) *Business Ethics—A European Casebook*, Academic Press, London.

Friedman, M. (1984) 'The Social Responsibility of Business is to Increase its Profits' in W. Hoffman and J. Moore (eds) (1990) *Business Ethics*, McGraw-Hill, New York.

Handy, C. (1994) *The Empty Raincoat*, Hutchinson, London.

Hartley, R. F. (1993) *Business Ethics*, John Wiley, Chichester.

Hoffman, W. and Moore, J. (eds) (1990) *Business Ethics*, McGraw-Hill, New York.

Kant, I. (1964) *Groundwork of the Metaphysic of Morals*, trans. H. J. Paton, Harper & Row, London, reprinted in G. Chryssides and K. Kaler (eds) (1993) *An Introduction to Business Ethics*, Chapman & Hall, London.

Lee, K. (1989) *Social Philosophy and Ecological Scarcity*, Routledge, London.

MacIntyre, A. (ed.) (1966) *A Short History of Ethics*, Routledge & Kegan Paul, London.

Mill, J. S. (1857) *Principles of Political Economy*, vol. II, Parker & Son, London.

Moore, G. E. (1903) *Principia Ethica*, Cambridge University Press, Cambridge.

Rowe, R. (1976) *An Introduction to Greek Ethics*, Hutchinson University Library, London.

Sellars, W. and Hospers, J. (eds) (1952) *Readings in Ethical Theory*, Appleton-Century-Crofts, New York.

Sorell, T. and Hendry, J. (1994) *Business Ethics*, Butterworth Heinemann, London.

Thompson, M. (1994) *Ethics*, Cox & Wyman, Reading, UK.

Thorsby, D. (1993) 'Ecologically Sustainable Development and the Transport Sector', *UNEP Industry and Environment* 16 (1–2): 15–17.

3

GREENING OF THE POLITICAL ECONOMY

Most of today's decision-makers will be dead before the planet suffers the full consequences of acid rain, global warming, ozone depletion, widespread desertification and species loss. Most of today's young voters will be alive.

(World Commission on Environment and Development 1987)

INTRODUCTION

Managers advocating the adoption of environmentally sustainable business practices require some evidence that there is a problem. Furthermore, actions must be premised on the knowledge that the problem has been noted and solutions advocated in the light of the evidence. This chapter, therefore, has two interdependent themes. First, it explores causes for concern at the physical effects of industrial activity on the human life-support systems of the planet. Second, it reviews expressions of awareness of those causes for concern within the literature, in political movements and within legislation. Since no single text can cover the whole of this vast subject, this chapter will have served its purpose if it tempts the reader to explore further the work of individual environmentalists.

Facts, fatalism and the political economy

The naive fatalism encapsulated in the view that 'since you can't stop progress there is no need to question the destination' has come under increasing pressure throughout the world since the late 1960s. Until then, 'the economy will provide' was the dominant guiding philosophy.

Definitions of 'the economy' are hard to come by: 'economy' in the *Collins English Dictionary* is 'the careful management of resources to avoid unnecessary expenditure or waste'. However, *the* economy, as understood in terms of workaday management of trade and industry, pays very little attention to the husbanding of environmental or human resources. *The* economy is strengthened by the extraction of limestone from a hillside, its transportation across the countryside in order to extract pollutants from the gases emitted by a power station, and the use of landfill sites to receive the resultant wastes. Such activity, however, is hardly sustainable. In the short term, environmental discharge from energy production can be diverted by creating another form of pollution. But reduction in the total level of polluting activity offers a shorter route to long-term sustainability. The problem is that forms of polluting activities (including the subsequent clean-up processes) accord well the definition of an economy as a system of rules and ceremonies. Outdated rules and ceremonies are not particularly helpful when there is a serious problem at hand.

Facts alone do not influence opinions. In the face of overwhelming evidence of cumulative environmental degradation, its present effects and the predicted outcomes, motivation to change is moderated by the institutions in which people live and work and the habits of thought which flow from our education and training. A commonly rehearsed argument is to advise caution in the absence of 'conclusive' scientific evidence of adverse results flowing from environmental degradation from some identifiable cause. In this view, industry is innocent until proven guilty and the 'precautionary principle' is neutralized. There is no justification for adopting expensive measures to protect the environment. It is rather like the person in free fall past the twenty-first floor window of a skyscraper, who calls out 'everything is perfectly all right so far'.

Nevertheless, as the contributors to Calori and de Woot (1994: 55) demonstrate, a business system naturally tends to fit with the society in which it is embedded and any change in the 'business system' is linked to changes in the whole society. Business operations are governed by the institutions which form the cultural base of a society, its church and family structures. The effects of these on the firm are less easy to detect than the influence on the firm of the formal institutions of political systems, financial and labour markets. 'Here the role of the state is crucial as it defines the rules of the economic game and designs the education system and communication networks' (Calori and Woot 1994: 59–60). This chapter examines the growing pressure towards environmental management originating in these institutions.

CAUSES FOR CONCERN

Very few environmental problems can be accounted for on a simple cause-and-effect basis. Problems usually stem from a multitude of causes, with a single course of action having multiple effects. Environmental problems fall into two main categories:

- **Biological responses** A multitude of living, interdependent organisms are affected in a chain reaction by any single human activity. The cutting down of mountain forests on a large scale to provide pasture leads to soil erosion and flooding, silting up of water courses, reduction of water sources and desertification. Some damage may be irreversible, some potentially reversible. Some consequences may be remedial, some not. Cumulative responses, for example to the residues from toxic substances used in agriculture and deposits in water courses fall into this category, as do global warming and ozone depletion.

■ **Resource depletion and depletion of natural assets** We are already using 40 per cent of our basic energy resource—the sun's energy made available from green plants on the land.

The effect of depreciation of the 'free' gifts of Nature, initially ecological, is ultimately economic in its consequences. Economic effects of environmental degradation are most immediately visible in developing countries which are economically dependent upon primary production. Nevertheless, not even the most sophisticated state-of-the-art information technology (*IT*) business in the developed world will survive total destruction of the planet's life-support system. Causes for concern range over a number of issues and are discussed in this section.

Atmospheric pollution

Atmospheric pollution has long been associated with the burning of fossil fuels, the resulting sulphur dioxide being a major atmospheric pollutant. Since the early 1960s those most closely associated with the land—agriculturalists, biologists and foresters—noticed adverse effects upon crops and trees down-wind of industrial smoke as the sulphuric acid dissolved in water and fell as rain. In countries like Sweden, forest decline and reductions in fish populations were attributed to the spread of *acid rain*. Acid rain in Europe has been calculated to cause 3–5 per cent reduction in returns to European tourism and timber. It similarly results in extra costs in building restoration and domestic water treatment.

Acid rain can be reduced by forcing the effluent gases from power stations through beds of limestone or dolomite. The problem is that this process is not cheap. It necessitates the transportation of limestone from distant hillsides, the production of new machinery and the deposition of the resultant gypsum in economically and ecologically expensive *landfill* sites.

Combustion of motor fuels causes an added influx of a range of volatile organic compounds, coupled with carbon dioxide (CO_2), and NO_x, nitrous oxides. These gases interact to create the gas ozone and nitric acid which affect plants, animals and humans. At low levels the gas ozone is affected by sunlight and causes photochemical smog, as witnessed in cities throughout the world with increasing frequency (Department of Health 1993).

Deteriorating agricultural sustainability

Food production is vital to the sustainability of the human species. It is threatened in two ways. First, ecologically unsustainable food production methods are degrading soil quality and water supplies. Second, industrial production is generating waste products which, in the air, water and land systems, further degrade the agricultural resource base. Mounting evidence indicates that the profusion of products on the supermarket shelves is not as sustainable as it appears.

Agrochemical residues

Expanding urban populations require vast quantities of food. The application of the economies of scale supported by agrochemicals has enabled intensive farming to produce high yields from given acreages. The uprooting of hedgerows to facilitate the use of oil-driven machines, the sprinkling of herbicides to clear the weeds, of fertilizers to feed the soil, and of pesticides and herbicides as the crops grow, all use vast quantities of energy. *Monoculture* results in environmental damage as the residues feed into water courses and impact upon the *food chain*, affecting plants, animals and humans.

Soil erosion

The loss of ground cover caused by monoculture leaves soils bare. Without roots to bind the soils, irreplaceable nutrients and humus are washed out. Nitrogenous fertilizers inhibit the growth of plants and micro-organisms vital to the delicate balance of the soil's composition. Soils are further eroded by removal of forest cover and over-grazing of grasslands. Each year billions of tonnes of once fertile soils are being washed away into the sea or blown away with the wind. Yet this little-publicized resource is the basis of civilization.

Water pollution

The production and use of a multitude of products, from agrochemicals to cleaning agents, paints and dyes, lead to environmental damage and create wastes. Dispersal of those wastes—directly into water courses or indirectly through seepage from landfill sites—results in reduced potability. Nitrates and phosphates, largely derived from detergents, combine with organic wastes in sewage to increase the biological productivity of water courses. The resulting micro-organisms absorb oxygen, causing the death of fish and water animals. The cocktail effect of *eutrophication* is enhanced by the presence of persistent insecticides, industrial contaminants and toxic heavy metals like lead or mercury.

Marine pollution

Water draining from the land through water courses flows eventually to the seas. Since the 1970s the effects of toxic and de-oxygenating wastes have become increasingly apparent in the shallower waters of the North Sea, the Baltic and the Mediterranean. Microscopic algae, heavy metals and nuclear contamination become concentrated in the food chain, affecting fish and humans. The microscopic plants of marine vegetation vastly outnumber all terrestrial vegetation and, although at least seven-tenths of the earth is covered by seas, we are still remarkably ignorant of the workings of the oceans and the effects of contamination upon the deep seas. There appears to be a connection between human activities which reduce marine vegetation and increases in atmospheric CO_2.

Materials disposed of in the seas fall into two categories (although particular waste inputs may contain elements from both categories):

- **Non-conservative wastes** These may take the form of degradable wastes, in the form of sewage or slurry, wastes from food-processing industries, brewing and distilling, pulp and paper, and chemical industries. They may include dissipating wastes in the form of energy in the heat that cooling water discharges, acids and alkalis. They may also include agrochemical fertilizers.

- **Conservative wastes** These come in two forms. First, particulates in the form of inert plastics or mining wastes from colliery spoils. Second, heavy metals, halogenated hydro-carbons (e.g. DDT and other chlorinated hydrocarbon pesticides) and radioactive materials.

Discharges may be the result of accident or negligence, as in the case of major oil spills, e.g. the *Torrey Canyon* (1967, Cornwall) or the *Exxon Valdezy* (1989, Alaska). The major source of pollution is, however, the routine discharge of hazardous substances into the sea as a means of cheap disposal. This may include discharges from nuclear power stations and reprocessing plants, the discharge of raw or partially treated sewage, liquid effluents and cooling water from industry and the deballasting and tank-washing operations of oil tankers and other ships (Mannion and Bowlby 1992). The cumulative effect of accidental and deliberate discharges from all sources is unlikely to be supportive of the long-term sustainability of the marine ecosystem.

The greenhouse effect

Another complete unknown is the long-term effects on the global environment of the accelerated output of atmospheric CO_2, methane and other gases since the onset of the industrial revolution. It can be argued that the build up of 'greenhouse gases' is nothing new and therefore no cause for alarm. The glass in a greenhouse admits solar energy but traps the infrared energy which the soil and plants inside the greenhouse generate. Similarly, the layer of clouds surrounding the earth, including water vapour, carbon dioxide, methane, nitrous oxide, chlorofluorocarbons (*CFCs*) and ozone, admits incoming solar radiation and traps outgoing long-wave radiation. Without a layer of gases to trap the heat, the temperature on the earth's surface would be around − 18 degrees C, and there would be no life on earth.

The gases which produce a balanced temperature of 15°C are produced by natural events and augmented by human activity.

Natural events include the decay of organic materials in the oceans and the dung of herbivores which produce methane. The activities of microbacteria in soil and water also create nitrous oxides. Ozone is created in the upper atmosphere through the actions of sunlight. Carbon dioxide is absorbed by plants and released into the atmosphere by decomposition.

Human activities include rice paddy fields and cattle farming, which cause increased production of methane and nitrous oxides. The use of nitrogenous fertilizers and the combustion of fuel result in further emissions of nitrous oxides. Photochemical reactions, most notably vehicle emissions, result in the production of ozone near the earth's surface. Forests act as carbon sinks, taking in carbon dioxide and giving out oxygen. Deforestation adds to both heat radiation (from the bare soils) and increased carbon dioxide levels (Leggett 1990).

According to the UN's Intergovernmental Panel on Climatic Change (*IPCC*) 1995 Report, concentrations of greenhouse gases (*GHGs*) continue to rise. The projected concentration of carbon dioxide by the end of the twenty-first century is more than 700 parts per million (*ppm*). This compares with 355 ppm at the turn of the twentieth century and 280 ppm in 1800. In other words, since the beginning of western industrialization (around 1750) the amount of carbon dioxide in the atmosphere has risen by 25 per cent, mainly caused by the burning of fossil fuels, with the greater part of that rise (around four-fifths) taking place since

1960. The effects, extent and timing of the rise of this and other greenhouse gases remain unknown. Uncertainty surrounds the following problems:

- How much of that rise will be absorbed by the sea, mitigating the warming effect.

- The extent to which atmospheric haze from industrial pollution leads to cooling in industrial areas.

- Whether the warming process will be speeded up by the release of methane from peat bogs.

- How the melting of ice-sheets will affect ocean currents.

Possible consequences include a rise in sea levels, accelerated by melting of the ice caps and changes in climatic zones. Drier conditions in the northern land masses of America and the former USSR may be accompanied by wetter conditions in the subtropical zones. The effects upon coastal areas, agricultural production, world trade, international economy and international relations are potentially devastating.

Ozone layer depletion

The stratospheric ozone layer, which covers the 15–50 kilometres above the surface of the earth, acts as a shield. It absorbs high-energy ultraviolet radiation (*UV–B*) which is harmful to life, and it heats the outer layer of the atmosphere. Wholly human-made chemicals with an active life of over 70 years, most notably CFC 11 and CFC 12, have been identified as active ozone destroyers. The chemicals interact with sunshine and ice crystals in the atmosphere above the poles, resulting in the destruction of ozone. Since 1979, 15 per cent of the ozone above the Antarctic zone has been destroyed.

Ozone depletion may have effects upon humans, animals and climate.

- **Humans** Cataracts and cornea damage result from exposure to UV-B. A predicted loss of up to 25 per cent of ozone by the year 2000 could result in 3 million cases of blindness. Cases of non-cancerous skin disorders and the skin cancer melanoma are also predicted to rise.

- **Wildlife and domestic animals** The eyes of land mammals and cattle are being affected by acute exposure to UV-B resulting from the decrease in ozone cover. Equal cause for concern is the effect on single-cell organisms in shallow waters. Destruction of marine plankton, which plays a vital role in absorbing excess carbon dioxide, could accelerate global warming.

- **Climate** Another unquantifiable effect is the link between ozone layer and weather patterns. The stratospheric heating caused by radiation absorption of ozone may have effects close to the earth's surface.

It was for these reasons that the Montreal *Protocol UNEP* (United Nations Environment Programme 1987), an international agreement on levels of permitted CFC dispersion, was drawn up and signed by international governments. The main aim was to cut the production of the five most deleterious CFCs by 20 per cent by 1993 and by a further 30 per cent by

1998. The Montreal Protocol was followed in 1990 by the London Agreement which stated that all CFCs and other key ozone-depleting substances, should be phased out by the year 2000 (DOE 1990). There were also further developments made in 1992 through the Copenhagen Agreement (DOE 1992).

Loss of biodiversity

In the course of micro-evolution, species of plant and animal life have become extinct, to be replaced by others more adapted to changing habitats. This natural process has, however, been accelerated since 1900 from an estimated annual rate of species loss of under 6000 to an estimated annual rate of 50 000 by the turn of the 21st century (Myers 1994). Current estimates suggest a loss of 50–100 species per day from the total of between 5 million and 30 million species thought to exist. Continued habitat destruction may result in a quarter to a half of all species being lost. As with the pollution of the deep seas, the effects of species loss can only be guessed at. Myers (1994) offers one example of how destruction of a part of the web of life can have far-reaching impacts. Destruction of the roosting sites and feeding grounds near Kuala Lumpur (Malaysia) of the little-known *Eonycteris spelaea* bat was considered necessary to mine limestone and reclaim swamplands. The bat was responsible for pollinating the drurian fruit tree, the crops of which were worth c.$120 million in South East Asia. Environmental literature abounds with examples of genetic erosion due to habitat destruction.

In the mean time, food crop diversity is being replaced by a dangerous homogeneity. Professor Garrison Wilkes of the University of Massachusetts likens this to 'taking stones from the foundation to repair the roof' (quoted in Myers 1994: 156). Agrotechnology is based upon wide species diversity and *genetic diversity*, with scientists constantly referring back to nature for new gene stock when new pests and diseases threaten the limited varieties of monocultured stocks. There is increasing concern that the very foundations of agriculture are being undermined. A naive faith in gene banks or some other technofix solution looks set to persist as we pass the point of no return.

The cumulative effect

All the categories of the natural environment interact to produce a 'climate system.' This system has five component parts:

1. The Atmosphere.
2. The Oceans.
3. The *Cryosphere*—ice caps, glaciers, seasonal snow cover, permafrost.
4. The *Biosphere*—the zone in contact with the earth's surface in which all life exists.
5. The *Geosphere*—the solid portion of the earth.

(Leggett 1990: 15)

The stable equilibrium produced by the natural interaction between these five elements was disrupted by the industrial revolution. Vastly expanded emissions of greenhouse gases resulting from industrial activity have altered the balance between absorbed solar radiation and radiation emitted to space by the planet and its atmosphere. The long-term effects of industrial activity—the production and use of consumer goods and the production of food by agri-business methods—remain unquantifiable. All that can be said with any certainty is that some degree of global warming, the results of which remain uncertain, is inevitable. The uncertainty indicates the advisability of a precautionary approach both to future levels of gaseous emissions and to other environmental impacts.

Equally uncertain are the cumulative effects of the production of hazardous or potentially hazardous waste materials. In the USA over 21 000 hazardous landfill sites have been identified, of which at least 1750 require urgent remedial action. Several thousand potentially hazardous sites exist all over Europe, with considerable as yet unquantified contamination in central and eastern Europe. On a global scale, the volume of hazardous wastes continues to grow.

Added to the sheer volume of waste is the problem of the nature of waste. Many synthetic chemicals have been developed to be resistant to corruption when employed in industrial uses. Placed in the natural environment, these chemicals often cannot be easily broken down. CFCs, for example, may last for 100 years. Polychlorinated biphenyls (*PCBs*) also enter the food chain, accumulating in the fatty tissues of fish and mammals, as do heavy metals. There is increasing evidence that the cocktail effect of exposure to these substances is associated with cancers and interference with reproductive fertility in mammals and humans. Since the 1930s there has been a two-fold fall in average human sperm counts and a similar increase in testicular cancer.

In the absence of firm evidence either way, there appear to be only two options. The first is to proceed with 'business as usual' until conditions become unworkable. The second is to adopt the 'Precautionary Principle', erring on the side of caution while seeking to minimize the number of actions with unquantifiable side-effects. Either human beings use the tools of science with discretion in order to stabilize the relationship between the species and its life-supporting planet, or the earth's adaptive mechanisms could conspire to reject the offending species. There is very little evidence of a middle way which will enable the 'real world' of business and commerce to maintain its ostrich-like stance.

EXPRESSIONS OF AWARENESS

It can no longer be assumed that disposal of wastes from a particular firm, however small, in one industrial sector is a purely private matter. In this section we explore the sources of pressures for environmental change which have been impacting on industry and commerce during the growth in awareness of the need for environmental sustainability. Many of the works mentioned make fascinating reading, having informed and motivated proactive business leaders as well as activists in environmental pressure groups.

Early warnings

Concern at the impact of industrial activity on the environment is not confined to the latter decades of the twentieth century. The term 'acid rain' was invented in the nineteenth century by Britain's first Chief Alkali Inspector, as attempts were made to combat the effects of London's blanket smogs. It was not, however, until the 1950s and the introduction of the first environmental legislation in the form of the *Clean Air Acts*, that effective measures were taken to overcome the hazards caused by industrialization.

Many late twentieth century environmental scientists, philosophers and economists were inspired by the work of Henry David Thoreau (1817–62). A US field ecologist and philosopher of nature, Thoreau was a Romantic, arguing for the restoration of the place of humanity in nature and opposed to anthropocentric commercialism. In his poetic and evocative writings he depicted the folly of a species attempting to reshape the world in total disregard of the evidence of the need for a balanced *ecosystem*. He argued that scientifically and spiritually, humans are rooted in the living world. Uprooted, in the concrete desert of commercialism, they may survive for a while on a dead science and a nature-hating metaphysics, but not for long. An ardent animal-lover, Thoreau regarded the whole creature, with its body and perceived spirit set within its living environment, as of far more interest than a carcass in a laboratory. He argued that the rational dualistic laws of the scientist might explain mechanisms to human satisfaction, but fell a long way short of holistic understanding of the natural world (Worcester 1977: 86–93).

A century later in the UK, Massingham (1942) explored the implications of the separation of people from the soil. He noted the pressures to abandon balanced farming for specialization in crop production, with its destruction of hedgerows, lanes and copses as 'nuisance' features. He argued that the unlimited use of machinery with the profit-making motive as the sole stimulus to initiative in agriculture, was resulting in 'spend-thrift wastage of capital resources in soil-fertility, phosphates, timber and the like' (Massingham 1942: 131–2).

In the mean time, at least one scientist, the Swede Svante Arrhenius, calculated the physics of the greenhouse effect and documented the likely implications for the atmosphere of the heat-trapping gases as long ago as the turn of the nineteenth century. The prospect of a warmer climate to counteract the predicted return of an ice age seemed not unattractive. Similarly, species loss, soil loss and acidification, air pollution and non-renewable resource depletion were noted but thought to be of short-term relevance. Science and technology would inevitably progress to find substitutes for depleted resources and mechanisms to clean up the mess. Public appreciation of the scale and seriousness of the adverse impact on the environment of industrial and agricultural activities did not emerge on a global scale until the second half of the twentieth century.

Emerging green theory and practice in the 1960s

Rachel Carson's (1962) *Silent Spring* remains the most eloquently written scientific text on the vulnerability of nature to organic pesticides made from chlorinated hydrocarbons. Perhaps more significantly, however, her work was translated into two dozen languages and inspired environmental consciousness on a global scale of the dangers of the manufacture and use of toxic substances.

In her earlier scientific work Carson documented the impact of radioactive wastes upon the oceans, a part of the earth hitherto imagined to be vast and secure against degradation by industrial activity. *Silent Spring* was the first work by a scientist to seriously question the inevitability of progress towards the total subjection of the natural world and its eventual replacement by human technology.

Carson wrote with a 'feeling mind and thinking heart', documenting the harm to nature, naming those responsible for it, those who profited from it, and describing the techniques used to obscure the facts of the matter. She demonstrated that human overcrowding, poor sanitation and deprivation caused problems which required alleviation. Chemical pest control, however, merely worsened the conditions it was supposed to remedy. Julian Huxley ended his Preface to *Silent Spring* with the words 'We must control the pest-controllers before the process [of destruction of the human habitat] gets out of hand' (Carson, 1962). It was to be thirty years before any serious attempts at control emerged in the market-place.

In *Our Synthetic Environment*, published within a year of *Silent Spring*, Murray Bookchin (1962) also noted the pollution of the natural world and its impacts on human health and society. Public pressure arising from the writings of Carson, Bookchin and others, for example Charles Reich's (1971) *Greening of America*, gave rise to the earliest codification of environmental protection in the legislative process in the USA.

In 1969 the National Environmental Policy Act (USA) established the Environmental Protection Agency (*EPA*) to monitor environmental impact statements on any major development work involving construction of roads, dams and housing (The Environmental Protection Act 1990 applies to the UK only). This early attempt to monitor environmental impacts was not without its problems. In 1983 corruption charges were brought against officials in the so-called 'sewergate' scandal. Nevertheless, the EPA established the principle of monitoring environmental impacts.

The 1960s also saw the emergence of green politics in the form of the world's first green party, the short-lived Values Party of New Zealand. Following the example of the Values Party, concerned environmentalists outside the USA have sought to influence political processes by entering the political arena. Although difficult to quantify, the impact of green politics upon policy formation has been considerable. Most notable has been the historical impact within Europe in general and Germany in particular, of the German *Die Grünen,* and their charismatic leader Petra Kelly (1947–1992).

Whistle blowers in the 1970s

In 1970 a group of industrialists and scientists, inspired by Dr Aurelio Peccei, an Italian industrial manager and economist, worked with the Massachusetts Institute of Technology (MIT) to produce computer projections of the future ecological impacts of five fields of human activity:

- Population.

- Agricultural production.

■ Natural resource use.

■ Industrial production.

■ Pollution.

The Club of Rome Report, *The Limits to Growth* (Meadows *et al.* 1972), was the first attempt at a systematic assessment of the global impact of industrial progress and development. It predicted a world-wide scarcity of resources, leading to a collapse of world trade and the demise of the industrial system. Throughout the 1970s and 1980s, fuelled by the oil price rises of 1973–4 and 1979–80, resource issues dominated economic and political discussions. In the event, technological developments, more efficient resource use and more extensive explorations combined to eliminate resource scarcity as the major cause for concern.

Scientists, industrialists and academics have, since the early 1970s and the *Limits to Growth* study, continued to monitor the impacts of industrial activity on a global scale. The leading ecological journal the *Ecologist* (1972) published *A Blueprint for Survival*, outlining the unsustainability of an unlimited expansion of human numbers and *per capita* consumption. In the same year the United Nations Conference on Economic Development and the Environment was held in Stockholm, followed by the establishment of the UN Environment Programme (UNEP). Since 1974 Lester Brown's Worldwatch Institute has continued to issue annual *State of the World* reports, available in all the world's major languages. Such reports informed debate on the growing concern in private and public bodies at the impact of industrial activity on the earth's ecosystems. Already in 1971 IBM had established a corporate environmental policy, one of the first companies to do so.

One of the most significant influences on policy formation by governments with the European Community was the adoption by the *EC* of its first environment action programme on 22 November 1973, to run from 1973 to 1976. Further action programmes followed every four to five years, providing a basic reference charter for the Community Environment Policy. Aims included:

■ Prevention, reduction and approaches to elimination of pollution and nuisances.

■ Management of natural resources by avoidance of damage to ecological balances.

■ Improvement of working conditions and quality of life.

■ Incorporation of environmental considerations in town planning and land use.

■ Seeking solutions to environmental problems in co-operation with non-EC states and international organizations.

Public awareness of environmental issues was enhanced in the 1970s with the publication of Schumacher's (1973) *Small is Beautiful*. Eloquently argued, this controversial text presented the drawbacks of progress and development. Increased specialization and the pursuit of profit through giant corporations was the recipe not for wealth and happiness, but for gross economic inefficiency, environmental pollution and inhumane working conditions. As journalist Peter Lewis explained in a newspaper article:

> Man is pulling the earth and himself out of equilibrium by applying only one test to everything he does: money, profits and therefore giant operations. We have got to ask instead, what about the cost in human terms, in happiness, health, beauty and conserving the planet?

Schumacher's answer was to emphasize the *person* not the product, by using technology appropriate to smaller working units, set in regional workplaces and using local labour and resources.

An often neglected aspect of environmentalism is the role of business in accepting standards of ethics in employment. While Schumacher's *Small is Beautiful* will be known to the aspiring environmental manager, his exploration of the purpose of work in *Good Work* (Schumacher 1979) has tended to be overlooked. Schumacher noted that although legislation ensures that workers' bodies are protected from physical harm, no checks on the impacts of work on workers' minds exist.

> Considering the centrality of work in human life, one might have expected that every textbook on economics, sociology, politics and related subjects would present a theory of work as one of the indispensable foundation stones for all further expositions.
>
> **(Schumacher 1979: 2–3)**

Yet a job in which one finds no personal satisfaction is soul destroying, sapping initiative. Drawing on his experience in industry, Schumacher explored alternatives to work as a 'dark wood of meaningless existence'. He expressed the view that the true purpose of work is:

- To produce necessary and useful goods and services.

- To enable us to use and perfect our skills.

- To serve and collaborate with other people in order to liberate ourselves from our inborn egocentricity.

> **(Schumacher 1979: 3–4)**

An enlightened and motivated workforce is, perhaps, the first prerequisite for sustainable development.

There are those, however, within the green movement, who argue that development and sustainability cannot be reconciled. While Schumacher, like Bookchin and other '*social ecologists*' adopts a reformist approach, '*deep ecologists*' argue that the rights of the non-human world should be prioritized over human welfare. Many deep ecologists like Arne Naess (see *The Basics of Deep Ecology* in Button 1990) are influenced by James Lovelock's (1979) 'Gaian' hypothesis. Developed in the 1960s, the hypothesis suggests that the biosphere operates as if it were a single living entity. All the organisms on the planet co-operate to create conditions optimal to the sustainability of life. This living entity, named Gaia after the Greek goddess of the earth, can accommodate human beings only so long as their activities do not seriously interfere with its complex mechanisms. While humans are dependent upon their environment, Gaia may be able to survive only through reacting to human activities and by making adaptations which may not be human-friendly.

In 1978 the Blue Angel Award scheme was introduced in Germany. Based on the environment emblem of the United Nations, the quality seal awarded by the German Institute for Quality Assurance and the Federal Environment Office, motivates manufacturers to supply environment friendly products. The process of independent, neutral testing assists consumers in making their ethical purchases.

Post-1980s

The 1980s saw the publication of a number of texts of enduring relevance. For example, *The Gaia Atlas of Planet Man* (Myers 1985; updated 1994), offers 'a definitive guide to a planet in transition', and has been rated as one of the Top Ten books on the environment. *The Living Economy* (Ekins 1986), offers readings from leading analysts of the impact of industrial activity on the environment.

Although evidence of causes for concern continued to mount, by the mid-1980s attention had shifted from future supply shortages to the impact on the environment of the use of those resources. The impacts of population growth and the increased volume of industrial production were evaluated in 1980 in an authoritative document (IUCN 1980) by the International Union for Conservation of Nature and Natural Resources (*IUCN*), the UNEP and the Worldwide Fund for Nature (formerly World Wildlife Fund: *WWF*). Noting that since the industrial revolution human numbers have risen eight-fold, while industrial production has risen more than 100 times in the past 100 years, the report entitled *World Conservation Strategy* (IUCN 1980) documented the major impacts on the environment resulting from these two factors. The report was dedicated to preventing environmental catastrophe. The three powerful organizations pointed out that 'unless the vitality and productivity of the planet are safeguarded, the future for humanity is at risk'. The impact of this study (a later report on the 1980 World Conservation Strategy, IUCN 1980) was immediate and world-wide, establishing the still novel concept that sustainable development was our only rational option (IUCN, UNEP and WWF 1991).

The United Nations Brundtland Report *Our Common Future* was published in 1987. Prepared by the World Commission on Environment and Development, the study set out a broad agenda for change. It advocated the adoption of long-term environmental strategies on a holistic basis. Exploration of the complex interrelationships between people, resources, environment and development were considered essential to the development of sound strategies of co-operation and mutual trust within the world community.

The Brundtland Report was one of the first to address the major stumbling block to mutual comprehension and co-operation between environmentalists, scientists and pressure groups on the one hand and concerned industrialists on the other. The central issue here was economic growth. In the view of the former group, industrialists were at the root of environmental degradation through their insistence on the pursuit of profit through growth at all costs. The latter group, on the other hand, argued that without sound strategies based on R&D and generated by successful growth, existing environmental damage could not be cleaned up, neither could cleaner and more efficient technologies be introduced. Adapting the concept of 'sustainable development' from the 1980 IUCN *World Conservation Strategy* (IUCN 1980) the Brundtland Report defined a sustainable society as one which 'meets the needs of the present without compromising the ability of future generations to meet their own needs' (Beaumont *et al.* 1993: 19).

The momentum of studies on the complexity of the environmental problems accelerated over the following decade, culminating in the publication by IUCN, UNEP and WWF of their second report, *Caring for the Earth: A Strategy for Sustainable Living* (1991). The work claims to 'provide an agenda for immediate action' and calls for a 'new ethic . . . based on affirming the community of life and cherishing its diversity'. This ethic 'has to be reflected in our personal attitudes and the organisation of our communities as much as in wider policies' (IUCN, UNEP and WWF, in Beaumont *et al.* 1993: 19). Sustainable development cannot be imposed by governments on an unwilling public and the organizations in which they live and work. It must come, say the authors of this report, from our personal attitudes. *Caring for the Earth* is designed to be used not only by politicians but also by executives in the public and private sectors at the national and international levels as well as businesspeople and other citizens. Its authors note 'the reality that the environmental, economic and social issues are joined in a network of sobering complexity' and recommend that their text should be read as a whole. A valuable resource, which clearly sets out the scientific evidence of the multiplicity of causes for concern, the text provides evidence and arguments for a constructive dialogue between governments, international bodies, NGOs and business.

The environment first came on to the political agenda in the UK with Prime Minister Margaret Thatcher's 27 September 1988 speech to the Royal Society. The following summer, the so-called Pearce Report, *Blueprint for a Green Economy* (Pearce *et al.* 1989), was enthusiastically endorsed in the UK by the then Environment Secretary, Chris Patten. The report reviewed and summarized research and discussion on the apparent incompatibility between economic growth and environmental preservation, recommending a mixture of regulation and market forces. Growth concerned with quality of life, rather than mere increases in income was advocated through the manipulation of market forces, rather than the free play of unfettered markets. Given the government's preoccupation with market forces, this was a firm commitment on the part of the UK government to 'sustainable development' as defined in the Brundtland Report. *Blueprint 1* called specifically for environmental concerns to be:

> integrated into economic policy from the highest (macroeconomic) to the most detailed (microeconomic) level. The environment must be seen as a valuable, frequently essential input to human well-being. Sustainable development means a change in consumption patterns towards more environmentally benign products, and a change in investment patterns towards augmenting environmental capital.
>
> **(Pearce *et al.* 1989: xiv)**

On a practical level, the report viewed sustainable development as dependent upon a proper evaluation of the environment based on long-term considerations and both intra-generational and inter-generational equity. Over the following years government policy has been to follow the guidelines proposed in *Blueprint 1* by following a dual approach. Measures introduced fall into two broad categories:

- Command and control measures include regulation through the setting and enforcement of standards.

- Market-based instruments include taxation, *tradable permits*, deposit-refund systems and grants for the development of new technologies.

Future green legislation is also likely to be influenced by *Blueprint 3: Measuring Sustainable Development* (Pearce *et al.* 1993), a later sequel to *Blueprint 1*. *Blueprint 3* takes the argument much further, reviewing the UK's existing political and institutional structures and presenting new options. As its title implies, progress towards sustainability can be monitored and measured. Chapters cover the quantification of air quality, water and water quality, solid and hazardous waste, biodiversity, agriculture and the environment, forestry and transport and the environment. The central argument is that it is 'possible to have economic growth (more gross national product—GNP) *and* to use up fewer resources [by] driving the ratio of resource use to GNP downwards, and encouraging the transition to renewable resources' (Pearce *et al.* 1993: 4–5). If this is to happen, however, governments will have a vital role to play. Free markets will not lead to a gradual but inevitable sustainable equilibrium, since the resources most at risk are those without markets: 'the receiving capacities of the oceans, atmosphere and stratosphere for example, and the greater part of the world's biological diversity' (Ibid.: 4–5). Even where they exist, free markets are not environmentally benign. 'No-one can argue that they can be expected to resolve environmental problems "naturally" if they do not exist at all' (Ibid.: 4–5).

Caring for the Earth was followed by the publication, prior to the Earth Summit in Rio, of a report by Schmidheiny (1992) for the Business Council for Sustainable Development; its opening statement declares:

> Business will play a vital role in the future health of this planet. As business leaders we are committed to sustainable development, to meeting the needs of the present without compromising the welfare of future generations.
>
> **(Schmidheiny 1992: xi)**

This concept recognizes that economic growth and environmental protection are inextricably linked, and that the quality of present and future life rests on meeting basic human needs without destroying the environment on which all life depends. New forms of co-operation between government, business, and society would of course be required to meet this goal (Schmidheiny 1992).

BUSINESS AND THE ENVIRONMENT

Notable among the many publications on the subject of business and the environment are Paul Hawken's (1993) *The Ecology of Commerce* and James Goldsmith's (1994) *The Trap*. A leading thinker on sustainable business in the USA, Hawken takes the Pigovian (i.e.

derived from the economist A. C. Pigou) line that free markets are 'superb at setting prices, but incapable of recognising costs', and argues for price/cost integration. Traders with the lowest prices are usually the ones with the highest unrecognized costs, a result which flows from a system which rewards short-termism and large-scale, centralized structures. He advocates three routes to sustainability:

1. Redesign systems of production to have little or no waste on a cyclical principle (waste = food).
2. Change from an economy based on carbon to one based on hydrogen and sunshine.
3. Create systems of feedback and accountability based on local production and distribution, to reinforce restorative behaviour.

Hawken's approach is designed to increase real productivity by bringing human activity, and hence life, back to fields, forests, watersheds and even factories. 'It is ironic,' he comments, 'that we define productivity as the elimination of labour in the manufacturing process' (Hawken 1993: 38). Hawken calls for environmentalists to redirect their battle to save the planet by uniting with business people to save business from the soul-destroying ugliness of huge corporations. He likens the large corporations which dominate the US economy—400 companies employ or support one-quarter of the US population—to feudal barons. Serfs were devoted to the welfare of their lords because they believed 'that the lord who exploited them was better than the uncertainty of no lord at all' (Hawken 1993: 17). However, most global problems are merely global symptoms of local problems, and can be solved only locally. According to Hawken new businesses are the source of new ideas and diversity. It is necessary to encourage the 'restorative economy' for innovative commercial options to survive the 'monoculture of corporate capitalism'.

In *The Trap,* which was a best-seller in France before publication in the UK, Goldsmith (1994) is equally dismissive of the ability of the global market system's ability to solve global environmental problems. It is perhaps surprising to note one of the world's most successful capitalists advocating local participation in decision-making. It has, however, been remarked that 'if Sir James is reading the political climate as astutely as he used to read the markets, the European Parliament may find it has opened its doors to a take-over' (from the small circulation newsletter, *Planetary Connections* review). As a Member of the European Parliament (*MEP*), Goldsmith was well placed to advocate that Europe should close its doors and impose community preference in its trading policies, while wresting back power from the European Commission.

The European Fifth Environmental Action Programme, *Towards Sustainability* (Commission of the European Communities (*CEC*) 1993), was adopted at the end of December 1992 and designed to run 1993–2000. Following the Rio Summit (1992) and the adoption of the Single European Act (*SEA 1986*), this Action Programme was highly proactive, seeking effective means to address the root causes of environmental degradation before problems become overwhelming and damage irreversible. Recognizing that the whole internal market programme would be at risk if natural limits were breached, the Action Programme was designed to change behavioural patterns in producers, consumers, governments and citizens.

The programme addressed issues of climate change, *acidification* and air pollution, depletion of natural resources and biodiversity, depletion and pollution of water resources, deterioration of the urban environment, deterioration of coastal zones (CEC 1993).

These issues are addressed not so much as problems, but as symptoms of mismanagement and abuse. The real 'problems' which cause environmental loss and damage are the current patterns of human consumption and behaviour. With this distinction in mind, and with due respect to the principle of *subsidiarity*, priority will be given to the following fields of action with a view to achieving tangible improvements or changes during the period covered by the programme:

1. Sustainable management of natural resources: soil, water, natural areas and coastal zones.
2. Integrated pollution control and management of waste.
3. Reduction in the consumption of non-renewable energy.
4. Improved mobility management, including more efficient and rational location decisions and transport modes.
5. Coherent packages of measures to achieve improvements in environmental quality in urban areas.
6. Improvement of public health and safety, with special emphasis on industrial risk assessment and management, nuclear safety and radiation protection.

The programme followed three main approaches:

1. Statutory authorities (national and local governments) are centrally placed to enforce legislation, make planning decisions and inform and educate the public.
2. Public and private enterprise, especially large consumers of resources generating wastes, are well placed to take effective remedial actions.
3. The programme recognized that the greatest influence on future policy is the actions of the public, as producers, consumers and citizens.

The programme selected five target areas for special attention, not only because of their impacts upon the environment but also recognizing the potential benefits to be gained by the sectors themselves: industry, energy, transport, agriculture and tourism.

Industry
Industry is centrally placed to govern present decision-making and choices impacting upon the immediate future. Recognizing the limitations of prescriptive legislative measures, the programme's strategy was to work through industry (including SMEs) to promote environmentally sustainable production methods. Industry was held responsible not only for improving resource management but also for enhancing consumer information on environmental issues.

Energy
Energy was recognized as a key factor in the programme. The aim was to improve energy efficiency and to develop strategic technology programmes based on less carbon-intensive energy sources and with the emphasis on renewable energy options.

Transport

Transport demand and traffic were set to add to problems of pollution, congestion and wastage of time and value, following the completion of the internal market and the opening up of central and eastern Europe. The programme therefore set out a strategy for sustainable mobility in conjunction with the publication of the Green Paper *A Community Strategy for Sustainable Mobility* (Commission of the European Communities 1992).

Agriculture

Although EC policy had increased availability of food supplies at reasonable prices, changes in farming practices had led to considerable over-exploitation and degradation of natural resources of soils, water and air. Policies had also led to commodity overproduction and rural depopulation. It would therefore make sound agricultural, social and economic sense to pursue more environmentally sustainable policies.

Tourism

Tourism is uniquely placed to synthesize economic growth and environmental protection. A profitable tourist trade is dependent upon respect for nature, especially in coasts and mountain areas, and stands to lose most from the problems created by the solid wastes and waste waters which it generates. While the EC has some responsibility for infrastructures, effective action and the transition to more appropriate forms of tourism are best taken within member states.

PARALLEL GROWTH OF PRESSURE GROUPS AND CONSUMER AWARENESS

A Department of the Environment (1995) survey of public attitudes towards the environment (conducted in 1993) found that 85 per cent of adults in England and Wales were 'quite concerned' or 'very concerned' about the environment. The two issues of greatest concern were chemicals being discharged into rivers and seas, and the import of toxic wastes. The survey indicated increasing concern about exhaust fumes, urban smog, traffic congestion and noise. Well over half of those surveyed were also 'very concerned' about radioactive waste (60 per cent), sewage on beaches and in bathing water (56 per cent) and oil spills at sea (52 per cent).

In 1995 the UK Co-operative Wholesale Society (CWS) conducted a market research programme of their retail customers. The survey of 30 000 people confirmed that animal welfare, environment and related topics were of concern to these consumers in their purchasing decision-making. Close on 70 per cent said they had, in the past, boycotted stores and products because of opposition to retailers' policies on these issues. Almost 80 per cent regarded it as the retailer's duty to provide more information on environmental and ethical issues surrounding the production of individual products. Similar studies in Germany indicate that by 1988, 59 per cent of households were prepared to take environmental considerations into account in making their purchases (Worcester, 1994).

The growth of consumer awareness flows from the work of pressure groups. Many, like *Greenpeace*, Friends of the Earth (FoE) and the Worldwide Fund for Nature (WWF) are international organizations with national bases in many countries across the world. WWF has been involved in over 4000 projects in 140 countries since its foundation in 1961, while Greenpeace has over 4 500 000 members world-wide and offices in 30 countries. Other groups form around a single local issue in one locality, often opposing a landfill site or airborne or water pollution from a particular industrial premises. For example, residents in the 250 houses and school built over a toxic waste dump at Love Canal in New York campaigned to get the area evacuated by the US federal government in 1978, after much suffering and protest. Traditionally, the interests of pressure groups have been diametrically opposed to those of industry, with the incidence of confrontation high and the incidence of co-operation low. Hence the tendency of industry to seek to mislead, rather than lead. Public awareness on environmental issues has been countered by the threat of aggressive negative publicity by pressure groups.

The confrontational approach has obscured the valuable role of voluntary pressure groups in sponsoring scientific research into the causes of environmental degradation and highlighting those areas where more research is needed. Pressure groups concerned with environmental issues operating at national and international levels include:

■ Greenpeace.

■ Friends of the Earth.

■ Oxfam.

■ Christian Aid.

■ Council for the Protection of Rural England (*CPRE*).

■ Worldwide Fund for Nature (*WWF*).

This list is far from exhaustive and should include a growing number of church and religious-based charities, for example Justice and Peace. In order to raise awareness through their non-violent direct action campaigns, Greenpeace alone has documented information on:

■ Whales in the Southern Ocean.

■ Ancient forests in Canada.

■ Effects of dumping toxic wastes in Latin America.

■ Pollution in Britain's rivers and coastal waters.

■ Wilderness of Antarctica.

■ Effects of testing nuclear weapons in the Pacific.

■ Depletion of fish stocks through large-scale drift-netting.

■ Rise in children's asthma due to car exhaust emissions.

■ Global effects of the use of ozone-destroying chemicals.

Taken as a whole, pressure groups possess a fund of scientific, geographical, agricultural, biological and locally based knowledge of infinite potential value to the business community. The trend has therefore been towards increasing co-operation between businesses and pressure groups. Through the 1995 Group, for example, WWF works with businesses like the do-it-yourself chain B&Q to vet sources of tropical hardwoods to ensure that they originate from managed forests.

PUBLIC POLICY INITIATIVES IN THE 1990s

By the late 1980s a dramatic change in the public mood, reflected in the UK Green Party's 15 per cent share of the vote in the 1989 European elections, brought environmental issues firmly onto the political, economic and business agendas. Over the following years the twin recommendations of the Pearce Report (Pearce *et al.* 1989), for command and control mechanisms and market-based instruments, were followed through by the British government in a series of measures designed to support management initiatives towards environmental sustainability. By the mid-1990s EC-inspired environmental legislation was starting to jolt British commerce and industry into environmental action.

Despite the weak White Paper *This Common Inheritance* (DOE 1990), the Environmental Protection Act (*EPA 1990*) established a legal obligation on industry to minimize waste production on the Best Available Technology Not Entailing Excessive Cost (*BATNEEC*) principle. The same cost-effectiveness approach was reflected in the series of Department of Trade and Industry (*DTI*) publications under the title *Business and the Environment* (DTI, constant updates). The Advisory Committee on Business and the Environment (*ACBE*) was founded in 1991 by the DTI and the Department of the Environment (*DoE*) to encourage dialogue between business and government on environmental issues, and to foster examples of good practice. The need to raise awareness of environmental issues among small and medium-sized enterprises was highlighted by ACBE, and the provision of support for local green business clubs was advocated. Local initiatives such as the Newcastle Initiative Environmental Services, Blackburn Groundwork Business Environment Association, Sheffield Green Business Club, Leeds Environmental Business Forum (part of Leeds Environment City Initiative: see Chapter 11), Amber Valley Business Environment Association, Dudley Environment Business Forum, Sutton Business and Environment Initiative, West Herts and Dacorum Business Environmental Association and the Payback Environmental Business Association (Plymouth) were supported by this venture. The first UK *Environmental Business Club Directory*, issued free by Business in the Environment (*BiE*) in 1994 (DTI 1994), listed 80 separate clubs and networks set up specifically to provide information, advice and guidance on environmental matters. The dissemination of good practice through publications and joint events was considered essential, as was partnership between large and small companies and local environmental pressure groups.

The Environmental Protection Act 1990 also introduced a system of integrated pollution control. Following the *Polluter Pays Principle*, the Act requires companies to meet charges to meet the costs of the regulatory and control bodies which are being phased in. Industry faces heavy financial penalties for breaking imposed emission limits, while environmental impact assessments are required for all new industrial and commercial activities.

Rio and its aftermath

The United Nations Conference on Environment and Development (UNCED), the Earth Summit held in Rio de Janeiro in 1992, forced the issues and challenges of managing our environment on to the world-wide stage. At Rio, over 150 governments signed the *Climate Change Convention* (the Framework Convention in Climate Change), the *Biodiversity Convention* (Convention on Biological Diversity) (UNCED 1992a) and the 500-page document entitled *Agenda 21* (UNCED 1992b). Agenda 21 accepts that sustainable development will not occur by accident. The protection of fragile ecosystems through reduction in use of energy and raw materials, and reduction of pollution and waste production, require conscious planning and work at local, national and international levels. Signatory governments accepted the requirement to:

■ Develop policies to encourage processes and products with lower environmental impacts.

■ Secure ethical management of products and processes to produce a healthy and safe environment.

■ Make environmentally sustainable technologies available to developing countries at moderate prices.

■ Establish national councils for sustainable development to unite the formal business community and the informal sector, including small-scale businesses.

■ Increase research and development into environmentally sound technologies and management systems.

(Adapted from UNCED 1992b)

Agenda 21 delegates a key role to local government: hence it is often referred to as 'Local Agenda 21' (LA21). Two-thirds of the actions in Agenda 21 required the active involvement of local authorities, and Chapter 28 of the Agenda called on local authorities to adopt a partnership approach to initiate process at local level by 1996.

For the first time, governments made pledges to work with industry on a range of actions and initiatives to combat poverty and environmental degradation. Southern governments combined with NGOs to bring recognition that sustainability was as much dependent upon consumption patterns in the north as on population control and forest protection in the south. Among the inevitable greenwashing platitudes, since the time of Rio an underlying sea-change in attitudes towards the environment can be detected on the part of northern governments and industry.

The change in attitudes is typified by the introductory statement by John Gummer, Secretary of State for the Environment, in *Sustainable Development: The UK Strategy*, the UK government's post-Rio statement which accompanied reports on climate change, biodiversity and sustainable forestry in 1994 (Department of the Environment (DoE) 1994a, 1994b, 1994c, 1994d). Recognizing the need for 'a change of attitudes throughout the nation' in view of the urgency of the situation because 'time is running out', Gummer presents the report as a 'spur to action'.

> Man has grown used to living as conqueror. So sure are we of our title to the planet that we have long taken it for granted. Science, which has enabled us to discover the intricacies and the wonders of our world, has not led us to treasure it. Instead it has fed our desire to dominate all things. Disease must be eradicated, weeds destroyed, pests eliminated. Road and railways could blast their way through mountain ranges, dams hold back mighty rivers, and bulldozers turn forests into pasture. There seemed no limit to what man could do.
>
> **(Department of the Environment 1994a: 5)**

'Then science began to show the measure of our human weakness,' continues Gummer, '. . . We began to see that growth and development demanded a price, and that price was increasingly beyond our ability to pay' (ibid.).

> For hundreds of years we had accepted the growth of pollution and only when it became utterly intolerable did we take effective action against it. Now we are seeing how much it has deprived us. As the fish come back to our rivers and the wild flowers to the unsprayed margins of more and more of our fields we learn just how much we have lost. Like a former smoker recovering his sense of smell, we have begun to rediscover a richness in the world which we had all but forgotten.
>
> **(Ibid.)**

This and its three sister publications prepared the way for the appointment of the Government Panel on Sustainable Development by the UK Prime Minister in January 1994 (Tufts, 1990). The panel, which meets four times a year, is available for consultation by the government and has access to all ministries, keeping in contact with different sectors of British society and with developments in other countries. Its remit is to identify problems and monitor progress. The panel's first report (published in January 1995) made recommendations with far-reaching implications on:

- Environmental pricing and economic instruments.
- Depletion of fish stocks.
- Ozone depletion.
- Technology transfer.
- Reform of the Common Agricultural Policy (*CAP*).
- Climate change.

(Department of the Environment 1995)

The most significant section of the report focused on environmental education and training. The section opens with a quote from *Sustainable Development: The UK Strategy*.

> Education and training are crucial to the achievement of sustainable development. They can provide the population, including the workforce, with an understanding of how the environment relates to everyday issues and what action they can take personally to reduce

their own impact on the environment at home, at work or in their leisure activities. The influence of education and training thus applies across the boundaries of the voluntary, public and private sectors.

(Department of the Environment 1994a: para.32.12)

The panel goes on to recommend:

■ The government should establish a comprehensive database, with local applications, to draw attention to the many resources available, including written material, lectures and facilities on offer from official and voluntary bodies, from industry and commerce, and in local communities.

■ That universities and higher education institutions in [Britain] should subscribe to the Talloires Declaration of 1990 [which recommended interdisciplinary approaches to environmental management and co-operation with international institutions, governments, industry and the general public].

(Department of the Environment 1995)

This holistic approach recognizes the crucial role of education as an agent for change towards an environmentally sustainable future. Change can come from many different directions, including:

■ Government regulations and legislation requiring enforcement.

■ Green marketing and consumer awareness.

■ Green business strategies.

■ Changes in food acquisition patterns and adoption of green lifestyles.

■ Altered fishing and agricultural practices.

■ Environmentally conscious transport policies.

■ Local government monitoring and regulation of land use.

■ Green accounting and reporting.

(Department of the Environment 1995)

The holistic approach recognizes that change in any one of these directions cannot stand alone. It can be effective only in the context of a generic approach to change attendant upon co-operation and communication between industry and commerce on the one hand and statutory bodies and other private and voluntary agencies. For initiatives to be effective it is necessary to break down the barriers between public and private lives, between 'work' and 'leisure' and to consider the effects of decisions over the long term. Individuals are not workers *or* members of trade associations or trade unions *or* members of extended families *or* citizens with a vote *or* consumers *or* holiday-makers *or* members of community organizations: as we conduct our daily lives we fall simultaneously into all of these categories. Hence government recognition of the role of education, in all its multifaceted forms, to the project of sustainability is highly significant (Department for Education and Welsh Office, 1993).

Other UK government publications include the 1994 *Royal Commission on Environmental Pollution Eighteenth Report: Transport and the Environment* (Department of the Environment 1994e). This report came to the unpopular conclusion that the projected growth of road traffic into the twenty-first century was unsustainable and offered clear objectives and quantified targets to remedy the situation, while emphasizing the role of public transport. As the first government report recognizes, transport affects every aspect of the economy and the community. Its significance cannot be overestimated.

Additionally, governments provide a variety of incentives to new initiatives. Acting alone or in conjunction with the EC, a European national government may work in partnership with business organizations or voluntary NGOs to promote environmental sustainability. Examples of this type of co-operation include grants for R&D, e.g. the UK DTI Non-Fossil Fuel Renewable Orders for England and Wales. By 1995 these included projects utilizing hydro-electric power (28), landfill gas (46), municipal and general industrial waste (6), sewage gas (26), wind (33) and other waste (5).

The UK government-sponsored initiatives were timely in view of the comparative ignorance of UK companies of environmental developments within the EC. *Directives* concerning control of air and water pollution and waste disposal had reached triple figures by the mid-1990s and were set to rise.

BS 7750, EMAS and ISO 14001

An environmental management system (*EMS*) is a programme which enables firms to:

- Take specific measures to identify the environmental effects of the firm.

- Decide how to deal with any negative environmental impacts.

- Provide an audited account of steps taken to minimize environmental impacts.

Since 1994 a range of quality systems for environmental management have been developed to provide management with a body of non-mandatory guidance order to satisfy environmental demands from employees, shareholders, supply-chain customers and the public. The first of these, the UK *BS 7750*, was set up in 1992 as a voluntary certification scheme for the holistic assessment of a company's environmental impact. The standard was designed by the British Standards Institution (*BSI*) in conjunction with government, business and service industries, trade associations, technical committees and environmental organizations to enable individual businesses to create and monitor an environmental management system tailored to their own particular activities. Modified in 1994 in the light of experience, this pioneering work provided a model for other European and international standards. It is compatible with the EU Eco-Management and Audit Scheme (*EMAS*) agreed by 11 of the 12 EU states in December 1992, with Germany holding out on a technicality, and introduced in late 1994. These two schemes contributed to the development of the ISO 14000 series prepared by the Geneva-based International Standards Organization (*ISO*). Following pressure from the International Chamber of Commerce (*ICC*), ISO, the leading developer of standards for the private sector, negotiated for a standard which was less prescriptive and less detailed (see Chapter 5).

Case Study 3.1 describes 3M's introduction of *'eco-economies'*.

CASE STUDY 3.1
3M

The US firm 3M was one of the first companies to discover the cost-saving advantages of 'eco-economies'. Manufacturers of a range of over 60 000 different products from Post-It notes to abrasives, and operating in 52 countries, 3M launched its 'Pollution Prevention Pays' (3P) programme in 1975. Based on the principle that prevention is easier than clean-up, the programme cut the firm's pollution by half, eliminating over 453 000 tonnes of waste emissions and bringing an estimated saving of £500 million. A typical tactic was to eliminate solvents used to bind abrasive discs to the paper backing. At its South Wales plant, solvents were replaced by a system of hot melting, a process which required no major capital outlay and saved the company £150 000 per year into the bargain.

Source: Aspengreen (1994) and Hopfenbeck (1992)

SUMMARY

Solutions proposed by different factions at local, national and international levels are as diverse as the problems are complex. The issues are reoccurring throughout the book and positive solutions are developed in Parts 2, 3 and 4. Approaches include:

■ **Deep ecology** The call to reduce human numbers (especially in the Third World), to abandon growth and to adopt 'back-to-nature' lifestyles.
 Problem: This approach has been viewed as racist and elitist.

■ **Social ecology** Seeks to adopt energy-efficient lifestyles based on green technology and intrinsically satisfying work. This approach is premised upon global security through equitable distribution of the earth's scarce resources.
 Problem: This would require a radical transformation of the basic institutions of western civilization.

■ **Business as usual** Opts to continue with business as usual in the hope that the environmental problem will go away.
 Problem: It will not.

■ **Local economy** Recognizes the advantages of local control over labour and natural resources as source materials for industry and in minimization of hazardous wastes.
 Problem: The same as for social ecology.

■ **Reformist** Business is the cause of the problem, therefore the answers must flow from business. As members of churches, charitable institutions and other community groups, managers and their families are involved with environmental issues. Through social contacts with politicians and other industrialists at local, national and international levels, environmental managers are well placed to work towards minimization of environmental impacts on a co-operative basis.

Problem: Lack of training and expertise in environmental issues among older senior management.

■ **National legislation** Governments create the climate, including the educational systems, within which business operates. Governments can therefore introduce legislation and regulatory measures to control adverse environmental impacts.

Problem: Assessment and monitoring of specific causes of pollution may be expensive. It may also merely translate one problem, such as marine pollution into another, like disposal of solid wastes to landfill or incineration. National legislation can be evaded and avoided, for example by shipping toxic wastes across boundaries. It may also be considered antagonistic to the principles of international free trade. Lang and Hines (1993) refer, for instance, to the *GATT* (General Agreement on Tariffs and Trade) ruling which declared unacceptable Canada's attempt to protect its west coast fisheries by banning the export of unprocessed herring and salmon.

■ **Pressure groups and political parties** Within democracies interest groups conduct research and media campaigns on specific issues with a view to influencing legislation and business practice. Although environmental pressure groups and corporations initially tended to view each other with suspicion, co-operation between specific groups and corporations has proved mutually beneficial.

Problem: Lack of a holistic approach may merely lead to solutions which are as problematic as the original problem.

■ **Green consumers** Environmentally conscious or *green consumers* may influence production and distribution of goods and services, minimizing adverse ecological impacts through purchase choice. A firm with a green marketing strategy is therefore advantageously placed.

Problem: This approach is unlikely to lead to long-term holistic solutions.

■ **Risk management and ethical investment** Investors are increasingly seeking assurances that hazardous production and disposal strategies are being minimized.

Problem: This approach requires integration with a holistic management strategy.

QUESTIONS

3.1 Take any one chapter of *Caring for the Earth* (IUCN, UNEP and WWF 1991) and provide evidence from the rest of the book to show that the issues raised in your chosen chapter cannot be considered in isolation from other factors.

3.2 Select one of the texts mentioned in this chapter and review it in the light of its comparative importance for developing awareness of routes to environmental sustainability.

3.3 The EU Programme *Towards Sustainability* recommends a transport policy based upon 'improved land use/economic development planning at local, regional, national and trans-national levels, to reduce the need for mobility and allow for the development of alternatives to road transport.' List and analyse the implications for strategic management of this approach to mobility.

3.4 Quoting examples from actual campaigns, analyse the effectiveness of consumer boycotts in recent years.

BIBLIOGRAPHY

Key texts

Brown, L. R. (annually) *State of the World: Worldwatch Institute Report on Progress Toward a Sustainable Society*, **Worldwatch Institute, New York**
This annually updated work documents the economic and social realities which result from the unsustainable harvesting of the earth's natural resources. Essays by a range of contributors document the over-fishing of the seas, the deforestation of the rainforests and other types of resource depletion. It also documents the growing revolution in the energy industry, including new transport technologies, the shift to hydrogen and the use of more energy-efficient materials and architecture. This major publication of the Worldwatch Institute is translated into 27 languages and is used by national governments, UN agencies and the international development community. It provides an invaluable resource for students.

Meadows, D. H., Meadows, D. L., Jørgen, R. and Behrens, W.W. (1972) *The Limits to Growth: A Report for the Club of Rome's Project on the Predicament of Mankind*, **Pan, London**
This report arose from a meeting of 30 individuals from 10 countries in Rome in 1968. Participants included scientists, educators, economists, humanists, industrialists and national and international civil servants. In the early meetings the members noted the complex number of problems faced by nations across the world. These included: 'poverty in the midst of plenty; degradation of the environment; loss of faith in institutions; uncontrolled urban spread; insecurity of employment; alienation of youth; rejection of traditional values; and inflation and other monetary and economic disruptions' (Meadows *et al.* 1972). They noted that while all can be detected as separate problems, they have in common three features: they occur to some degree in all countries; they contain technical, social, economic and political elements; and—most significantly—they interact. Taking the line that the whole is more than the sum of the parts, the members formed an international team of researchers, directed by Professor Dennis Meadows, to examine the five basic factors which 'determine, and ultimately limit, growth on this planet—population, agricultural production, natural resources, industrial production and pollution'. This quote and the report covering these findings was published in 1972 (Meadows *et al.* 1972). Twenty years later three of the authors (D. H. Meadows, D. L. Meadows and R. Jørgen) wrote *Beyond the Limits* (1992).

Using a computer model to project the future, the sequel to *Limits to Growth* outlines a possible range of options, showing that although a sustainable society is technically and economically feasible, it is by no means likely to be secured if present trends continue.

Schumacher, E. F. (1973) *Small is Beautiful*, Blond & Briggs, London

In the 1970s the economist Fritz Schumacher argued the case for a new form of economics based upon Buddhist principles. The optimistic text became a virtual bible for the green movement, exposing the illogicality of the pursuit of profit and progress at the expense of a deteriorating quality of life in terms of environmental pollution and inhumane working conditions. He was one of the earliest economists to recommend smaller workplaces, smaller-scale technologies and the use of local labour and local resources as a means to making economics once again work for real people.

Leggett, J. (ed.) (1990) *Global Warming: The Greenpeace Report*, Oxford University Press, Oxford and New York

In this key text leading scientists and energy analysts from around the world presented the key arguments for taking seriously the scientific evidence that greenhouse gas emissions could be affecting the world's climate. The implications of the scientific findings to date and the issues surrounding them are explored in detail. This was an introductory text and remains a valuable summary of the issues, enabling contemporary reports to be assessed within the broader context.

References and further reading

Aspengreen, A. H. (1994) 'Developing Environmental Opportunities in Industrial Products', in B. Taylor, C. Hutchinson, S. Pollack and R. Tapper (eds) *Environmental Management Handbook*, Pitman, London.

Beaumont, J. R., Pedersen, L. M. and Whitaker, B. B. (1993) *Managing the Environment: Business Opportunity and Responsibility*, Butterworth Heinemann, London.

Bookchin, M. (1962) *Our Synthetic Environment*, Knopf, N.Y.

Brown, L. R. (annually) *The State of the World: Worldwatch Institute Report on Progress Toward a Sustainable Society*, Worldwatch Institute, New York.

Button, J. (ed.) (1990) *The Green Fuse*, Quartet, London.

Calori, R. and de Woot, P. (1994) *A European Management Model: Beyond Diversity*, Prentice Hall, Englewood Cliffs, NJ.

Carson, R. (1962) *Silent Spring*, Hamish Hamilton, London.

Commission of the European Communities (CEC) (1992) 20 February 1992: Green Paper on the impact of transport on the environment, *A Community Strategy for Sustainable Mobility*.

———(1993) *Towards Sustainability: A European Community Programme of Policy and Action in Relation to the Environment and Sustainable Development*, Brussels and Luxembourg.

Department for Education/Welsh Office. (1993) *Environmental Responsibility: An Agenda for Further and Higher Education*, Committee on Environmental and Higher Education (Chairman Peter Toyne), HMSO, London.

Department of the Environment (DoE) (1990) *Amendment to the Montreal Protocol on Substances that Deplete the Ozone Layer*, Cm 1576, adopted at London, HMSO, London.

———(1990) *This Common Inheritance* cmd 1200, HMSO, London.

———(1992) *Amendment to the Montreal Protocol on Substances that Deplete the Ozone Layer*, Cm 2367, adopted at Copenhagen, HMSO, London.

———(1994a) *Sustainable Development: The UK Strategy*, Cm 2426, HMSO, London.

———(1994b) *Climate Change: The UK Programme*, Cm 2427, HMSO, London.

———(1994c) *Biodiversity: The UK Action Plan*, Cm 2428, HMSO, London.

———(1994d) *Sustainable Forestry: The UK Programme*, Cm 2429, HMSO, London.

———(1994e) *Royal Commission on Environmental Pollution Eighteenth Report: Transport and the Environment* , Cm 2674, HMSO, London.

———(1994f) *UK Environmental Business Club Directory*, Business in the Environment (BiE), HMSO, London.

———(1995) *British Government Panel on Sustainable Development: First Report, January 1995*, DoE, London.

Department of Health (Advisory Group on the Medical Aspects of Air Pollution Episodes) (1993) *Oxides of Nitrogen*, HMSO, London.

Department of Trade and Industry (DTI) *Business and the Environment*, constantly updated, HMSO, London.

Ekins, P. (ed.) (1986) *The Living Economy: The New Economics in the Making*, Routledge & Kegan Paul, London.

Goldsmith, J. (1994) *The Trap*, Macmillan, London.

Hawken, P. (1993) *The Ecology of Commerce*, Weidenfeld & Nicolson, London.

Hopfenbeck, W. (1992) *The Green Management Revolution*, Prentice Hall, London.

IUCN, UNEP and WWF (1991) *Caring for the Earth: A Strategy for Sustainable Living*, Gland, Switzerland.

Lang, T. and Hines, C. (1993) *The New Protectionism*, Earthscan, London.

Leggett, J. (ed.) (1990) *Global Warming: The Greenpeace Report*, Oxford University Press, Oxford and New York.

Lovelock, J. (1979) *Gaia*, Oxford University Press, Oxford.

Mannion, A. M. and Bowlby, S. R. (1992) *Environmental Issues in the 1990s*, John Wiley, Chichester.

Massingham, H. J. (1942) *The English Countryman: A Study of the English Tradition*, Batsford, London.

Meadows, D. H., Meadows, D. L., Jørgen, R. and Behrens, W. W. (1972) *The Limits to Growth: A Report for the Club of Rome's Project in the Predicament of Mankind*, Pan, London.

Meadows, D. H., Meadows, D. L. and Jørgen, R. (1992) *Beyond the Limits*, Earthscan, London.

Myers, N. (ed.) (1994) *The Gaia Atlas of Planet Management*, 2nd edn (1st edn 1984), Gaia Books, London.

Pearce, D. W., Markandya, A. and Barbier, E. B. (1989) *Blueprint for a Green Economy* (Blueprint 1), Earthscan, London.

Pearce, D. W., Barratt, S. and Markandya, A. (1991) *Blueprint 2: Greening the World Economy* (Blueprint 2), Earthscan, London.

Pearce, D. W., Turner, R. K. and O'Riordan, T. (1993) *Blueprint 3: Measuring Sustainable Development*, Earthscan, London.

Pearce, D, (1995) *Blueprint 4: Capturing Global Environmental Value*, Earthscan, London.

Reich, C. (1971) *Greening of America*, Penguin Books, Harmondsworth, UK.

Schmidheiny S. (1992) *Changing Course: A Global Business Perspective on Development and the Environment*, BCSD and MIT Press, Cambridge, MA, and London.

Schumacher, E. F. (1973) *Small is Beautiful*, Blond & Briggs, London.

——(1979) *Good Work*, Cape, London.

Tufts University European Centre (1990) *University Presidents for a Sustainable Future: the Talloires Declaration*, Report of the British Panel of Sustainable Development, London, Jan., 1995.

UNCED (1992a) *Rio Declaration*, UN, New York.

——(1992b) *Agenda 21*, UN, New York.

UNEP (1987) *The Montreal Protocol on Substances that Deplete the Ozone Layer*, available from UNEP, ozone secretariat, Nairobi, Kenya.

Worcester, D. (ed.) (1977) *Nature's Economy: A History of Ecological Ideas* (2nd edn 1994), Cambridge University Press, Cambridge.

World Commission on Environment and Development (1987) *Our Common Future*, Brundtland Report, Oxford: Oxford University Press.

ENVIRONMENTAL MANAGEMENT THEORY

A business must have a conscience as well as a counting house.

(Sir Montague Burton)

INTRODUCTION

Throughout the course of the twentieth century the processes of management and the behaviour of organizations, or more accurately, the behaviour of people and groups within an organization, have become the subject of study. As theories of management have evolved, they have served to promote the agenda of industrialists within the broader constraints of the requirements of the wider society, of which an industrial or commercial organization remains a part. The interests of all stakeholders, including shareholders, employees, customers, suppliers and increasingly the ecological environment, are combined by the successful manager's adaptation of the theories of management and organizational behaviour to the requirements of their particular organization. This chapter reviews developments in approaches to organizational theory and management with reference to their potential to take account of the ecological environment.

ORGANIZATION AND MANAGEMENT—HISTORICAL REVIEW

From the inception of management studies writers have adopted a normative approach to organizational planning with an established agenda, to increase market share and to protect the interests of the shareholders. The earliest 'classical' principles of management were based upon the technical requirements of the organization, assuming the co-operation of the worker to be based upon rational and logical behaviour. Since 1966, when the Manchester Business School was first opened, management education has evolved from the simplistic, competitive approach in which the needs of shareholders, staff and the wider community were regarded as intrinsically incompatible, to an acceptance that the requirements of all stakeholders must be satisfied. The following paragraphs trace the evolution of management theories, which are not mutually exclusive. It is possible to draw upon elements from each theory to meet the requirements of a particular organization.

Management theory has evolved to enable the manager to create the most efficient organization. The manager's task is to facilitate the interaction, and mediate the relationship, between:

- The task in hand (the physical manufacture of goods).

- Procurement and sales—mediation with the external environment.

- The board of directors, and the stakeholders.

Although a firm necessarily operates within a wider society and within its ecological environment, early management theory seemed capable of operating in a vacuum. The firm drew from wider society and the environment, but appeared to have no obligation towards either. As management theory has evolved and as ecological concerns have attracted attention within society as a whole, a more responsible approach to the ecological environment has become both possible and necessary. Here the four basic approaches to management, as set out (e.g. by Mullins 1985), are reviewed within this broader context. They are:

- Classical approach.

- Human relations approach.

- Systems approach.

- Contingency approach.

Classical approach

Early approaches to the planning of work to meet the technical requirements of the organization sought to improve efficiency by defining a set of rules as a means to solve common problems in organizations and management. Structural, formal or 'scientific' writers following Taylor (1947) assumed rational and logical behaviour. They have in common a belief in the three basic principles of:

- **Co-ordination** It is necessary to ensure that people act together through the exercise of authority based upon discipline.

- **The scalar principle** An organization is seen as a hierarchy in which duties are graded and delegated from the top down.

- **The functional principle** Specialization is essential, and a distinction is drawn between different types of duties.

The classical approach breaks down into the two subdivisions of scientific management and the bureaucratic model. F. W. Taylor, the early proponent of scientific management, sought the most efficient methods for the control and co-ordination of production. He believed that motivation was dominated by rational-economic considerations, and that workers would pursue their own self-interest even when these conflicted with the interests of their fellow workers. His management principles involved:

1. The development of a scientific analysis of each work task.
2. Scientific selection and training of workers to undertake that task.
3. Close monitoring of workers to ensure tasks carried out according to (2).
4. Clear division of responsibilities between management and workers.

Based on the tested increase in output, measured scientifically and quantitatively, the 'scientific' methods of management led to payment by results to individual workers rather than the general payment for a number of hours at the factory bench. Although the methods were unpopular when first introduced, the practices of work study, organization and methods, time and motion study, payment by results, management by exception and production control have since passed into everyday use. Indeed, it has been argued that workers are only too pleased not to have to think or take any responsibility for their work. They prefer to do exactly as they are told, take the money and leave.

The second subdivision under the classical heading is 'bureaucracy'. Although this approach is slightly less practical and more theoretical, it, too, has given rise to practices which are today considered commonplace elements of management. Unlike previous social forms, a bureaucratic organization establishes permanent administration and work procedures which do not change when the actual person holding a particular post changes. This form of organization is seen as superior, introducing rationality and order into social life, replacing individual judgement and responsibility, or whim as the bureaucrat sees it. Employment in a lifelong career is based upon technical qualifications rather than personality or connections.

Strengths and weaknesses of the classical approach

The classical approach to management marked the formal differentiation between the skilled craft workers of the pre-industrial era and the industrial assembly line workers paid to carry out specific tasks as dictated by a hierarchical management structure. Workers were neither expected to take personal responsibility for their working methods, nor given the opportunity to do so. In the short term, such methods may produce quantifiable improvements in output. Over the long term, the complex interaction of human beings is frustrated, resulting in a loss of efficiency and a failure to co-operate for a common purpose within the organization.

Taylor was concerned purely with the technical question of increasing material output. As ecological consideration become commonplace, the simple quantitative increase ceases to be the most appropriate primary consideration in management terms. In general, the classical approach, whether scientific or bureaucratic, introduced the concept of *limited personal responsibility* as the employee, whether as worker or manager, undertakes the technical function of a particular role as dictated from above in a hierarchical organization. Responsibility always rests with somebody else, while rewards come from following instructions. Whether on grounds of social equity or environmental sustainability, it does not pay to question the orders given for the task in hand. Indeed, there are no mechanisms for such questions to be raised. Within this situation, the informal organization, with its subgroups and subgoals by which individuals do pursue their own strategies within the organization as a whole, is ignored by the formal structures. In the absence of flexible and fluid systems of communication, conflicts can render the system counter-productive, not only in its own terms but also in terms of its social and ecological footprint.

Furthermore, the concept introduced under scientific management of selecting workers according to the requirements of an industry has given rise to more immediate ecological concerns. It is increasingly possible to use the new biotechnologies and genetic engineering to screen out individuals who are susceptible to asthma, allergies or even cancer to determine physical fitness for a task within the chemical or nuclear industries. However, harmful substances remain harmful to the population at large. As the products and waste substances leave the workplace they inevitably pollute the living-space of the wider community.

Human relations approach

Accepting the structures and formal organization established through the classical approach to management, attention was focused upon the behaviour of people *within* an organization. A series of studies known as the Hawthorne Experiments, conducted by Elton Mayo at Western Electric's Hawthorne plant in Illinois, USA (1924-32), (Mullins, 1985) came to be regarded as key social science investigations and gave rise to the human relations approach to management and the formation of personnel departments. The experiments were subsequently criticized for their poor sociological techniques and their failure to identify external social factors and pressures on workers as, for example, in gender power differentials. Nevertheless, these early studies recognized for the first time that people go to work to satisfy non-monetary needs, and operate at an informal level as well as at the formal level heretofore recognized by the formal organizational level. There were four Hawthorne Experiments:

- **Illumination experiment** The intensity of lighting was monitored for its effects upon worker productivity. The results of this experiment were inconclusive.

- **Relay assembly test room** Work assembling telephone relays was repetitive and boring. Leaving a control group, groups of workers were subjected to a series of planned changes to their conditions of work, in terms of hours of work, rest pauses and refreshments provided. Throughout this experiment workers were consulted and kept informed of the changes by a friendly observer. Their opinions were listened to. The higher productivity which resulted was put down to a more sympathetic approach by management.

- **Interview programme** Workers were asked about their general conditions of work and attitudes towards them. As the experiment proceeded, a set list of questions was abandoned in favour of open-ended discussions, with interviewers taking confidential notes. The experience of working with employees in this form of work-orientated interview gave rise to modern personnel management techniques.

- **Bank wiring experiment** A group of men working in a bank-wiring room were observed. It was noticed that the group developed its own structures, with subgroups (cliques) and natural leaders. In these circumstances, although offered financial productivity incentives, the men agreed to a lower level of output, and group pressures ensured individual conformity.

The Hawthorne Experiments gave rise to theories of social organization and motivation of the individual. In the 1950s and 1960s a more psychological 'neo-human relations approach' was adopted. Consciousness of a hierarchy of needs, from physiological needs, safety, love, esteem to self-actualization, arose from Maslow's (1943) more general observations. Within the workplace it became commonplace for Maslow's hierarchy to underpin motivation and satisfaction at work over a range of factors from hygiene through job-satisfaction, group dynamics, motivation, communication and leadership styles.

Strengths and weaknesses of the human relations approach

The classical approach envisaged an organizational structure not unlike an architectural edifice: careful calculations could construct a hierarchical system which would operate like clockwork. This approach failed to recognize that a social organization has more in common with a living organism which evolves in constant interaction with its internal and external environment. The human relations approach enabled management to take reactive measures in view of the realities of human groups, avoiding some of the more obvious negative impacts of the blanket application of classical management techniques. The human relations approach on its own, however, was not sufficiently well developed to allow integration of the goals and concerns of management, workers and the wider stakeholders of the organization. In particular, environmental concerns continued to appear irrelevant to the functioning of the workplace and the wider organization.

Systems approach

The systems approach reconciles the apparent conflict between the classical approach, with its 'systems without people' and the human relations approach, with its 'people without organizations'. Taking account of the systems which operate within a system, the systems approach also places the organization within the wider social environment. General Systems Theory (GST) likens commercial and industrial organizations to biological organisms and observes that any part of an organism's activity affects other parts of the organism. The work of early general systems theorists like Miller and Rice (1967) gave rise to studies of organizations as social systems set within the total environment of society as a whole. Such studies demonstrated that the introduction of technological innovation will disrupt established patterns of social interaction in the workplace as old methods of working are replaced by the new. These observations led to advocacy of a socio-technical approach, using social psychology methodology to develop appropriate social systems when new technology is introduced.

Strengths and weaknesses of the systems approach

The systems approach added the broader social dimension, setting management theory within the context of the wider society of which it remains a part and offering mechanisms capable of reacting to the need for environmental sustainability. It incorporated techniques from social psychology, providing a framework for consideration of the social psychological requirements of employees in respect of adaptation to change. GST enabled the organization to effect internal adaptation in response to pressure for change from external sources including pressures for environmental sustainability. However, as with all early approaches to management, it was limited in its capacity to take account of the requirements of all stakeholders of the organization and hence overlooked social and ecological realities.

Contingency approach

The contingency approach accepts that there is no single optimum state for the operation of the organization. The task in hand and the environmental influences exerting pressures will vary from organization to organization. Contingency theory extends the systems approach to take more account of the actual workings of the organization in practice, seeking to incorporate the informal practices into the formal structure so that all employees are working to the same agenda.

Strengths and weaknesses of the contingency approach

Contingency theory can cover a range of practices designed to meet the operational circumstances of any individual organization. In theory, therefore, it can be used to take account of the interests of all stakeholders, including the local community and the natural environment. In practice, however, contingency theory can also be used by one group of stakeholders to further their own particular interests. For example, where profit maximization for shareholders dominates, 'just-in-time' (*JIT*) procurement policies and 'human resource management' techniques may become vehicles for minimizing the organization's obligations to its suppliers or employees. In this scenario, environmental concerns are incorporated into management practice only in so far as they carry financial implications arising from legislation.

An environmentally sound approach to management can draw upon the best in management techniques in order to create new and environmentally sound organizational methods. It works towards combining the interests of all stakeholders, including finance providers, management, employees, customers, suppliers, the local community and the environment. Elegant and resource-efficient products and services can be produced by substituting engineering expertise, industrial production, consultation and crafts services for energy and raw material imports. By reducing a country's ecological footprint, ensuring peace and social stability at home and abroad, industry can serve its major stakeholder, the wider community upon which it depends for its existence. On a global scale, however, pressures towards the continued evolution of the '*triadic trading system*' may appear to conflict with the quest for ecological sustainability and the social equity upon which it is dependent.

INTERNATIONAL COMPARISONS

Global markets and transnational corporations (*TNCs*) lend credence to the misapprehension that a global corporate management style exists, free from cultural bias and adaptable to the needs of any progressive organization. This is not the case. TNCs have their base in one particular culture or global region, and their management styles reflect their origins. We first look at management styles as they have developed in USA, Japan and Europe.

Management philosophies and practices reflect their sociological settings, and inevitably systems of management are heavily influenced by the cultures in which they originate. Although a global market management style was pioneered by the Americans, Japanese and European firms now compete in the world market for services and manufactured products. The belief that the scientific management system had global application spread when the US economy and American business schools dominated world trade in the 1960s. American business schools continue to teach their particular style of professional management. It has been noted that these schools have perpetuated the notion that a manager with net present value calculations in one hand and portfolio planning in the other can manage a business anywhere.

Since the 1960s, non-American-based TNCs have operated across the globe, with varying degrees of success, the main rivals to the Americans being the Japanese. Although the Japanese use universities for training managers, they give priority to in-company, work-based training programmes. The Japanese value interdependent relationships and favour lifelong worker–firm loyalty. In their overseas operations language and culture have presented barriers to the integration of non-Japanese managers. Hence the Japanese have retained central decision-making and control.

By the late 1960s and early 1970s Japan was recognized across the world, due in no small part to traditional Japanese industrial relations. Japanese culture supports the concept of social contracts. As Japan extended its industrial base, the Japanese worker was guaranteed a lifetime's work with the same firm, creating an exchange of obligation between company and worker. The employee became very much part of the company. Although shareholders have a stake in the company, their interests do not dominate. Hence the worker has an interest, for example, in quality control, and may stay on at work long after hours if there is a minor product fault in manufacture. The worker is the main stakeholder in the Japanese company.

Pascale and Athos (1981) discuss McKinsey's 7S framework which analyses seven characteristics of the successful firm: Strategy, Structure, Systems, Skills, Style, Staff and Shared superordinate goals. US and Japanese firms share similar approaches to the first three—strategy, structure, systems—but differ in the way they handle the 'soft' components—skills, style, staff and shared superordinate goals. While they compete on the world markets, their domestic corporate cultures are very different. Calori (1994) distinguishes between two basic management cultures: Managerial capitalism as followed by American firms and group capitalism as practised by the Japanese.

Managerial capitalism

- **Profit-orientation** The ultimate goal is profit, consumption and the welfare of shareholders. Finance is dominant over industry, with short-term profitability taking precedence over long-term goals.

- **Individualism** The 'self' is the basis of American culture. The firm neither offers loyalty to, nor expects loyalty from, employees over the lifetime.

■ **Intrapreneurship** Professional management focuses on managers rather than workers. The managerial class is the core of the enterprise, rather than the workers. Access to information is retained by managers as a means to control. Managers employ rational tools and strategic planning, and motivation occurs through the managers.

■ **Competition** Anti-trust laws motivate against conglomerates or any form of organized co-operation *within* the US economy.

Group capitalism

■ **Quality-orientated** The search for perfection, with focus on careful implementation.

■ **Long-term orientation** Greater loyalty to the firm, with lifetime employment and stakeholder involvement of workers. Workers are at least as important to the company as shareholders.

■ **Interdependence** The 'self' appears as an obstacle to development. Under the influence of eastern religions, emphasis on group behaviour and interpersonal harmony. Decisions taken in group consultations, with control by peer group. Bottom-up decision-making processes derive from shared loyalties.

■ **Co-operative inter-firm relationships** Tendency to horizontal integration around core companies.

■ **Long-term government protection of domestic industries, with strong supplier–client relationships and transfer of knowledge** Japanese companies see common cause in the promotion of their country as 'Japan Inc.' .

A study commissioned by the European Round Table of Industrialists (*ERT*), an industrialists' think-tank composed of chairs and chief executives of 40 major European companies (Calori and de Woot 1994), identifies three very broad management models to which firms originating in different cultures tend to gravitate:

1. **Anglo-Saxon** US and UK firms tend towards the individualistic form of 'managerial capitalism'.
2. **Capitalism Rhénan** Encompasses forms of 'group capitalism' as in Japan and Germany.
3. **Latin** As observed most notably in the countries of southern Europe, in France, Italy and Spain, with characteristics as below.

Latin management model

■ Frequent state intervention and protectionism: the state may own and manage some industrial companies and financial institutions, and regulations may be biased against international competition.

■ Hierarchical management: management is more personalized, with leadership relying on intuition rather than structures, procedures and written instructions.

■ Tendency to more family businesses, especially in Italy, with more paternalistic community provision.

■ Greater reliance on an elite, especially in France.

Of the three models, the Anglo-Saxon, Capitalism Rhénan and the Latin, the Latin model offers perhaps the greatest scope for the development of a working partnership between business and the environment. However, in the 'triadic' trading system, in which Europe seeks to compete with the two other major trading blocs, based on North America and Japan, the characteristic features of the Latin Model can be more readily identified as defects rather than assets.

TRIADIC TRADE

In the study by Calori and de Woot (1994) the ERT anticipates consolidation of the triadic approach to world trade as Europe develops a distinctive management style to compete with the two other trading blocs, North America and Asia, in a triadic pattern. To date the giants have been the USA and Japan, their success lying in their ability to select and develop products and services capable of standardization for global markets. While electronics and pharmaceuticals are potentially global, food or retail banking are more subject to local differentiation. Nevertheless, even the food business can be successfully standardized, as Coca-Cola and McDonald's testify. ERT identifies Europe's strengths as the ability of its multinational companies to adapt to linguistic and cultural diversity without fragmenting the corporate power structure. ERT seeks to take European management 'beyond diversity' and into a style which will enable Europe's largest companies to compete in the global market-place.

Within the triadic trading system TNCs based within the three trading blocs compete globally, buying in the cheapest markets and selling in the dearest. Since the early 1970s a global system of finance has been founded upon the growth of indebtedness of Third World countries to the developed 'north'. As cash crops force self-sufficient peasants from the land, vast shanty towns provide a source of cheap labour. Factories are built in countries where environmental protection and social legislation are weak or non-existent. The Scandinavian company IKEA designs household goods which are produced in the Far East and sold across Europe. Companies create new products, using biotechnology to develop new strains of food crops to be grown in a monocultural system dependent upon the purchase of agrochemicals. They create demand for standardized products by extending the global cash economy into new markets, regardless of the cultural sensitivity. McDonald's have introduced the beefburger to India, a country where beef has significant religious value for Hindus. Companies export employment and import finished goods, fostering income insecurity and unemployment among the workers of the countries in which their head offices are based. Their power rests in property, not only in terms of land and fixed capital but now of knowledge itself. Patented seeds and processes become the subject of 'Intellectual Property Rights'. Through these means, the ecological footprint of the industrialized world has been extended throughout the Third World.

Despite the obvious dangers of broad generalizations, some culturally determined management characteristics can be detected. Within Europe the UK management model is closest to that of the USA, although there are substantial differences. On the whole, the best British brains have not in the past headed for business training, as have the Americans, and British management generally adopts a pragmatic approach. Germany shares some characteristics with Japan, as do the Scandinavian countries, while a distinctly European transnational management style can be detected in the 'small countries' of Benelux and Switzerland where there is a continuous historic tradition of international trade.

Triadic trade and environmentalism

Firms competing successfully in the triadic trade scenario use local knowledge to promote the global interests of their firm. They promote the ecological sustainability of the locations in which they operate as and when such policies coincide with their global interests. The triadic trade approach holds that big business is needed to tackle big problems. 'Power grows out of the creation of the key resources required to develop it: international teams, technologies, information, networks, relationships, etc. In this respect private power becomes more important and more international.' In this view, the 'immense know-how of our companies (TNCs) can be used to solve environmental mega-problems' such as Seveso, Bhopal, Three Mile Island, Alaska and the problems of the Third World and eastern Europe (Calori and de Woot 1994: 274–5). This faith in the ability of rootless companies to accept full repairing responsibility for the problems which they are largely responsible for generating is genuine, if perhaps mistaken. Capable of moving their operations according to the whims of global trade, TNCs are not always strongly motivated to operate with ecological sensitivity.

During the second half of the twentieth century, management approaches based upon the ecologically unsustainable triadic trading pattern could temporarily afford to ignore the long-term interests of certain stakeholders, including employees, suppliers and the natural environment. Growing awareness of the unsustainability of this approach has given rise to the adoption of environmental management approaches. Initial attempts at grafting environmentalism on to traditional management procedures were, however, cautious and tentative.

To the environmental manager of the global corporation, 'Preserving and improving the environment is never a free option: it costs money and uses up real resources' (Pearce *et al*. 1989: 22). To the ecological manager this is true only if preserving and improving the environment are regarded as activities requiring active management. As Adams (1995) points out, it is obviously wasteful in management terms to spend money on preservation or improvement when the costs of doing so are greater than the benefits. Hence rational decision-making requires that *all* relevant costs and benefits are priced. This leads to the conclusion that environmental protection is best achieved through *less* interference with nature, rather than increased intervention. According to Adams, environmental degradation results from a combination of carelessness and excessive consumption:

> There are two ways a fat person can lose weight. The (orthodox) way—health farms, exercise machines, liposuction—uses up real resources. The (progressive) method—walking or cycling to work, eating less—*saves* real resources. The (progressive's) way of losing weight does not require cost-benefit analysis: he does not need to calculate the cash value of being slimmer and then work out whether or not he can afford it.
>
> **(Adams 1995: 111)**

The ability to respond to a new agenda, be it the need of a person to stay slim or the need of a firm to respect the environment, depends on the degree of commitment to conflicting practice and procedures. A review of predominant management procedures reveals their potential adaptability for ecological sustainability.

A sustainable management style will draw on the best features of traditional management systems while taking account of the culture and physical environment within which the firm is operating. A firm's internal management is also strongly influenced by the legislative framework, a factor which it cannot afford to ignore. Since the early 1970s (globally) the growth in environmental protection legislation has been exponential.

GROWTH OF ENVIRONMENTAL LEGISLATION

Conservative estimates put the annual cost of damage to the environment in Germany alone at around 6–10 per cent of GNP (over DM200 billion or about £67 billion) by the mid-1990s. The figure was arrived at by drawing up a survey and placing a money value on the quantifiable damage. Damage was classified according to the following categories:

- **Atmospheric pollution** Health damage, material damage, damage to crops in the open and to woodland and forest.

- **Water pollution** Damage to rivers and lakes, to the North Sea and the Baltic, and to groundwater.

- **Soil damage** Damage from Chernobyl and 'Chernobyl prevention costs', disposal of 'inherited pollution' conservation costs of habitats and species, and soil contamination.

- **Noise** Loss of residential value, loss of productivity, noise-induced welfare payments.
  (Winter 1988: 18)

Following the introduction of this type of calculation on a national scale in the mid-1980s, the range and scope of legislation and regulation has extended rapidly throughout the developed world. In the UK, the Environmental Protection Act 1990 introduced Integrated Pollution Control (*IPC*), regulating the emissions from '*prescribed processes*' into land, air and water. Liability for pollution was also extended by the Water Resources Act 1991 (see Case Study 4.1). It is now a criminal offence to discharge toxic wastes without consent. The financial effects and adverse publicity of an accidental or deliberate breach of legislation and regulatory requirements may be sufficient to force a firm to cease trading.

Pollution incidents—the accidental or illegal discharge of hazardous substances—may be brought to the attention of regulating authorities through:

- Automatic monitoring systems.

- Inspection by officers.

- The emergency services.

- The public.

CASE STUDY 4.1
Water Pollution

In the UK, under the Water Resources Act 1991, conviction of a water pollution offence at Magistrates' Court can carry a fine of £20 000 or a period of imprisonment. Fines are unlimited in the higher courts, with up to two years' imprisonment a possibility. Shell UK Ltd was fined £1 million for polluting the River Mersey with oil in 1990. In an attempt to minimize the effects of chemical industrial accidents on people and the environment, the 'Seveso Directive' (82/501/EC) was implemented by the passing of the Control of Industrial Major Accident Hazards Regulations (CIMAH) in 1984. Additionally, the Environmental Protection Act 1990 introduced Integrated Pollution Control (IPC) to control emissions from 'prescribed processes' (the most potentially polluting industrial processes) whether to air, land or water.

One-off water pollution incidents may be caused by:

- Effluent treatment plant failure, e.g. power supply interruption, human error, inadequate maintenance.

- Pipe leakage or rupture in underground tanks.

- Spillage of oil or chemicals from tanks or drums, including breakages in transport and failure of hoses. Silage may be disposed of direct into a watercourse, or may be washed there during the clean-up operation.

- Rain may wash materials from the land, e.g. farm wastes, herbicides.

- Fires may lead to the run-off of contaminated waters into water courses.

- Landfill operations can cause pollution by the leaching of pollutants in surface and underground waters.

- Transport accidents by road, rail or air.

- Vandalism.

- Deliberate illegal disposal of effluent and wastes.

One-off pollution events substantiated in England and Wales in 1992 totalled 23 331. A total of 388 (1.7 per cent) of these incidents were classified by the National Rivers Authority (NRA) as being 'major', that is 'causing significant actual damage to the water environment or water abstraction' (Edwards 1995: 31). Oil and sewage caused the most frequent incidents (26 per cent) followed in descending order by organic chemicals, paints and dyes, detergents, pesticides, acids, fertilizers, alkalis and de-icing materials. Hazardous chemicals are transported in vehicles displaying warning signs in case of accidents. However, severe water pollution can occur from non-hazardous substances. Food and drink can cause severe deoxygenation if spilled in water courses. Milk, for example, has a biochemical oxygen demand over 300 times greater than crude sewage. Other 'non-hazardous' products which are potentially hazardous to water courses include detergents and disinfectants.

Source: Edwards (1995)

Pollution incidents of the type described in Case Studies 4.1 and 4.2 have led to projects like *PRAIRE* (Pollution Risk from Accidental Influxes into Rivers and Estuaries). PRAIRE computer software provides a screening exercise for companies holding significant stocks of chemicals. The firm checks local, national and international regulations (such as *EC regulations*) and ensures that it complies with any regulations by acquiring relevant discharge permits. It also ensures that it complies with established codes of conduct. The next stage is to monitor the risk of an accidental spill and implement precautions to contain any spill on-site.

Until the 1990s, for the vast majority of firms in the 'developed north', reactive pollution prevention was the only type of environmental measure implemented. The threat of fines, imprisonment and loss of the firm's goodwill following an accidental or illegal pollution incident remains a predominant motivation for considering the environmental impact of a firm's activities. This '*command and control*' approach to environmental standards regulation has its shortcomings. These include:

■ Inspection and enforcement of legislation is expensive and bureaucratic.

■ Detection can be evaded.

■ Little incentive is available to improve process and technology.

■ There is motivation to 'waste tourism' (cross-border dumping of toxic substances).

CASE STUDY 4.2
Allied Colloids Fire, Bradford

When fire broke out in a warehouse used to store some 400 chemicals at Allied Colloids, Bradford, on Tuesday 21 July 1992, 30 fire engines rushed to the scene. Contaminated fire-fighting water flowed via the firm's drains into the public sewer and also directly into a tributary of the River Spen. An estimated 12–18 million litres (3–4 million gallons) of water were used. As a result, the sewage works were unable to cope and a complex mixture of chemicals, including solvents, detergents and copper, was discharged with the sewage into the Spen. Two residents were taken to hospital suffering from the effects of fumes from the river, and warnings were issued to abstractors along the river system. In total an estimated 8000 fish were killed following the incident, which was classed as a major accident to the environment under the CIMAH Regulations. Ironically, the damage would have been very much greater if the rivers affected had not already been seriously polluted.

Source: Edwards (1995)

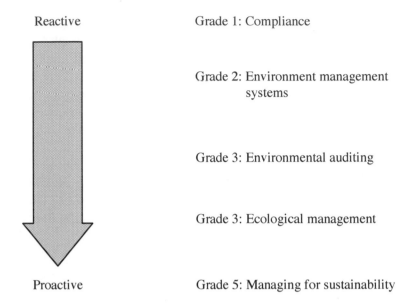

Reactive   Grade 1: Compliance

                                  Grade 2: Environment management
                                          systems

                                  Grade 3: Environmental auditing

                                  Grade 3: Ecological management

Proactive   Grade 5: Managing for sustainability

FIGURE 4.1 *Grades of environmental management (Source: adapted from Welford 1995: 84)*

FROM REACTIVE COMPLIANCE TO PROACTIVE ENVIRONMENTAL MANAGEMENT

By the mid-1990s many firms in the 'developed' world had some form of environmental policy, the minimalist approach being determined by the necessity to conform to environmental legislation. Environmental management policies can be graded on a five-point scale of classification developed from Welford's (1995: 84) scale of *environmental management* techniques (Figure 4.1). Policies range from reactive legislative compliance to proactive management for ecological sustainability. This section explores the motivations and available tools and techniques relevant to each stage of environmental management.

Grade 1: compliance
In the most highly reactive approach, management commitment to the environment is limited to meeting legally prescribed requirements. In view of the extent of legislation and statutory requirements even this minimalist approach requires some input from the firm if it proposes to stay in business.

Grade 2: environmental management systems
The introduction and operation of an environmental management system (EMS) based upon such standards as BS 7750 or the EU Eco-Management and Audit Scheme (EMAS) makes for a continuous systemic improvement. Introduced as pilot schemes following consumer and regulatory pressure in the late 1980s, these programmes of systemic action have been demanded of firms by investors, lenders and insurers seeking to redefine their risk criteria to reflect environmental liabilities. As outlined in Case Study 4.3, an EMS follows the quality

CASE STUDY 4.3
BS 7750 environmental management system

The UK British Standards Institution was incorporated by Royal Charter in 1929 as a non-profit-distributing organization, independent of government, industry and trade associations. In 1990 it embarked on the design of a practical business tool to enable firms to develop an EMS which would meet the requirements of the BSI's standards. Working with government, business and service industries, trade associations, technical committees and environmental organizations, the BSI developed BS 7750 through a pilot programme.

The standard is designed to enable individual businesses to create an EMS tailor-made to suit their own particular activity. It enables a firm to undertake a fundamental review of the environmental strengths, weaknesses, opportunities and threats arising from its operations, products, services and activities. To register to BS 7750, the firm is required to complete five stages of registration. These require the firm to demonstrate how it meets or exceeds legal requirements, how it is monitored, what the firm's objectives are and how the attainment of these is to be measured. Registration offers:

■ Improved operational efficiency and cost reduction in areas such as energy consumption and waste minimization.

■ Effective cost-benefit analysis for environmental compliance beyond legal requirements.

■ Management of a firm's legal liability by demonstrating best management practice.

■ The opportunity to maximize business opportunities by enabling the firm to make credible environmental claims in a competitive market-place.

■ Demonstration to regulators, customers, consumers and the financial community the firm's systematic control and management of environmental effects.

■ Improvement in staff morale by providing measurable environmental improvement targets.

■ Independent third-party endorsement of these claims by BSI, through initial compliance and continuing assessment.

■ Facilitation of registration to future European or international standards.

In addition, BS 7750 was designed to integrate with existing quality management systems that comply with BS EN ISO 9000 (formerly BS 5750).

Published in 1992 and amended in the light of experience in 1994, the standard provided a model for the development of the draft international standard ISO 14001, and is compatible with European Union criteria for an EMS under EMAS.

Source: British Standards Institute BS 7750

management approach, defining policy, specifying process controls, auditing performance and revising policy in the light of the assessment. The mechanics of the EMS process are explored in more detail in Chapter 5.

The key component of an EMS is a company-wide commitment to continuous improvement in environmental performance in terms of specific objectives laid down in a published environmental policy. Although the introduction of an EMS (or compliance with BS 7750) is a rigorous exercise, it sets no absolute standards on the consumption of materials. Neither does it eliminate wastes of polluting emissions to the environment. While standards of this type have been described as 'gravy trains for costly consultants', they do at least provide a basis from which a firm may progress towards the setting of self-determined targets and objectives.

Grade 3: environmental auditing

A firm introducing an EMS reviews its existing management systems from time to time, concentrating on health and safety, contingency planning and direct polluting effects on a reactive basis. At Grade 3 a firm takes a more proactive approach to its total environmental impact, including its impact on the health of employees and the surrounding community. Pollution of air, water and land is reviewed and active measures taken to minimize environmental impacts and costs.

The consumption of all non-renewable sources of energy or materials causes a reduction in that resource and results in pollution of the environment. With this in mind, a firm may seek to conserve the resources it uses by using them more effectively, thus minimizing waste. Advantages accrue from conservation and waste minimization. As NRA manager Tony Edwards has explained: 'Once created, waste cannot be destroyed' (1995: 47). Waste can be diluted or concentrated, or changed in its physical or chemical form to render it 'harmless'. But treatment merely transfers pollutants from one medium to another. For example, treatment may remove waste from water and convert it into a metal sludge requiring disposal in land, or incineration and release as a gaseous emission to the atmosphere. Treatment is expensive, and only rarely provides returns to business through the reuse or resale of recoverable materials. The challenge is to minimize production of waste in the first place, saving real resources while reducing the need for expensive clean-up expenditure.

Indeed, the interests of business and the environment can be seen to coincide over the question of waste minimization. According to a DTI (1992) report, waste minimization can benefit a business through:

- Reduced production costs in the form of on-site waste monitoring and treatment costs, handling, transport and off-site treatment costs, raw material costs, energy and water costs, long-term environmental liability and insurance costs and risks of spills and accidents.

- Improved operational efficiency through the use or resale of reusable waste, increased safety and improved stakeholder image.

Firms are encouraged to incorporate waste minimization within their business strategies through statutory regulations and through consciousness raising programmes. Statutory regulations are regulated by the Environment Agency which incorporates the tasks of the NRA, Her Majesty's Inspectorate of Pollution (*HMIP*) and the waste regulatory authorities. The Aire and Calder Project (Case Studies 4.4 and 4.6) is one of a number of studies designed to be of use for training purposes in order to raise awareness. As the need for cleaner production processes and for waste minimization and pollution prevention techniques has grown, the problems of education have been progressively addressed (see Case Study 3.1). The individual firm faces problems of lack of:

- Commitment.

- Knowledge.

- Information and training.

- Time and human resources.

Addressing these problems, the UK Waste Minimization Projects adopted a 'start-of-pipe' approach, drawing on earlier work by the DTI, the Confederation of British Industry (*CBI*), the Institute of Chemical Engineers (IChemE) and the Dutch *PRISMA* (Project Industrial Successes with Waste Production). All three major projects, the Aire and Calder Project (Case Study 4.4), Project Catalyst (Merseyside) and the Leicestershire Waste Minimization Initiative (*LWMI*), were focused geographically rather than by industry sector (see Case Study 6.4). The primary objective was to 'demonstrate the effectiveness in cost, technical and environmental terms of better waste management rather than costly treatment methods for emissions and waste materials' (Johnson and Stokes, 1995; Atkins 1994). Participating companies tended to be involved in activities with above-average pollutant effects. In all, 35 companies participated in the three projects, representing a wide range of activities (Tables 4.1 and 4.2).

TABLE 4.1 *Project Catalyst. (Source: CEST, 1995: 37)*

Company	Product
Borden Decorative Products	Wall coverings
Chloride Motive Power (CMP)	Batteries
Colgate Palmolive	Body care products
D2D	Computers
Dunlop (GRG Division)	Rubber products
HJ Heinz Company	Food
J Crosfield & Sons	Chemicals
JW Lees & Co. (Brewers)	Brewing
Lever Brothers	Soap products
Manchester Airport	Airport services
Milliken Industrial	Carpet tiles
Pilkington's Tiles	Ceramics
Stoves	Domestic appliances
Royal Mail	Mail services

TABLE 4.2 *Leicester Waste Minimization Initiative. (Source: CEST, 1995: 37)*

Company	Product
CAMAS Aggregates	Quarrying
CAMAS Building Materials	Building materials
Carnaud Metalbox (CMB)	Cans for food and drink
Caterpillar	Earth-moving equipment
Dust Control Equipment (DCE)	Dust control equipment
Everard Brewery	Brewing
KP Foods	Food
RF Brookes	Food
R Smallshaw	Knitwear
Wigston Dyers	Dyeing and finishing

Participating firms were drawn from a range of sectors, predominantly those using productive processes involving toxic emissions to air, land or water. Although original motivation for taking part in the pilot schemes was frequently to achieve cost savings, the process of participation generated heightened awareness of the environmental impact of discharges and the importance of co-operation to prevent environmental deterioration of the local area. The projects relied heavily upon the motivation of key personnel and through them of the workforce as a whole.

Following the 1984 explosion at the Union Carbide plant at Bhopal and other environmental accidents, changes in hazard liability law in many countries have brought the introduction of penalties for the creation of an environmental hazard independent of intention or neglect. These developments have served to focus attention on more integrated approaches to environmental protection, encouraging the adoption of 'environmental risk management' procedures. These include:

- Systematic investigation of *all* potential dangers.
- Appraisal of existing preventive measures.

At this level or grade, however, management remains reactive to external pressures, selecting adaptations to technologies and processes in the light of regulatory pressures and changes in the political and economic climate.

Grade 4: ecological management

Grades 4 and 5 are more holistically proactive. A Grade 4 firm embarks upon an ecological audit. Ecological audits are distinguished from environmental audits by three distinct features:

CASE STUDY 4.4
Aire and Calder Project

A study in 1991 by the Centre for Exploitation of Science and Technology (*CEST*) revealed a lack of awareness of the benefits to be gained from cleaner technology and an apprehension that changes to processes would be more expensive and disruptive than 'end-of-pipe' solutions. As a result of this report a demonstration project was undertaken in the Leeds and Wakefield area of West Yorkshire. The project was initiated by CEST and sponsored by the BOC (British Oxygen Corporation) Foundation for the Environment and Community, Her Majesty's Inspectorate of Pollution, the National Rivers Authority and Yorkshire Water Services Limited.

The 2055 square kilometres of the catchment area of the study has a population of over 2 million. In terms of water management the most important industries are textiles, chemicals, engineering and food and drink. Central to the industrial revolution, the area has a long history of serious water pollution. Most industrial waste water is treated at sewage works. The project was concerned with minimizing effluent discharged both to sewers and direct to rivers.

The objectives of the Aire and Calder Project were:

■ To collect accurate data on costs and benefits of waste minimization.

■ To demonstrate and disseminate the message that 'pollution prevention pays'. Cost saving through waste minimization not only is sound environmental management but also has positive profit-enhancing benefits.

■ To show how waste minimization produces benefits in terms of competitive advantage, compliance with regulations and risk reduction.

■ To focus on procedural changes and cleaner technology, and to identify gaps in supply, technology and science

Working with 11 companies, by November 1994 the project had achieved:

■ Identification of 671 opportunities for reducing waste.

■ Annual cost savings to the companies of £3.2 million.

■ 10 per cent of opportunities cost neutral.

■ 63 per cent of opportunities with a payback of less than one year.

■ Water consumption reduced by 15 per cent and effluent discharge reduced by 22 per cent.

■ Reduction in chemical oxygen demand (*COD*) of 497 tonnes per year.

■ Reduction of settleable solids of 167 tonnes per year

The benefits were achieved by identifying and using people, systems and technology as resources.

- **People** Key people were identified with the project by the firm, and general awareness raised through them.

- **Systems** New procedures, monitoring and targets were introduced.

- **Technology** Appropriate new technologies were introduced.

Source: CEST (1995)

- The mode of assessment is dynamic.

- The firm constantly reviews its indirect as well as its direct impacts on the environment through the use of Life Cycle Assessments (*LCAs*).

- The ecological approach to management accepts that all human activities are grounded in the natural environment.

The environment is not seen as a fixed resource, to be taken from and topped up in a linear process. Ecosystems interact and change over time, requiring a dynamic approach which looks to the avoidance of any cumulative adverse impacts.

Life Cycle Assessment evolved as a tool for powerful multinational companies operating in 'high profile' sectors like packaging and chemicals. The French firm Rhône-Poulenc, for example, features the firm's LCA work in its annual reports, requiring that 'from cradle to grave, each stage in the product life cycle should integrate environmental protection factors, from R&D and production to transportation, packaging, end use, disposal and recycling' (quoted in Business in the Environment *et al.* 1994).

As this practice has become widespread, firms have come to demand that their suppliers produce evidence of having undertaken some form of LCA. This is in part due to the growing realization that in terms of total environmental impacts, SMEs are responsible for the creation of more environmental degradation than the corporate giants. Raw material abstraction, transportation, use and disposal all have impacts which are additional to the production of the goods and services in which the firm is engaged.

A Grade 4 firm rejects the 'business as usual with bolt-on environmentalism' approach.

Grade 5: Managing for sustainability

Managing for sustainability is based on a holistic approach, seeking inter-generational and intra-generational equity as well as social and ecological balance. The application of the reformist systems of Grades 1–4 could, eventually and over the long term, lead to sustainability through a continuous cycle of improvement. Realistically and in practice, however, the momentum necessary to sustain the continuous improvement is unlikely to be maintained. The achievement of a limited number of goals can lead to complacency.

Furthermore, the attractions of long-term environmental sustainability can pall in the light of conflicting short-term demands on the firm's resources.

The total quality management approach relies upon an audit of an existing management system. Although procedures, documents and management are critically reviewed with the objective of reducing the environmental impact of the firm's activities, the firm remains the starting-point. Holistic quality management is environmentally sustainable: it takes the environment as its starting-point. As Welford has explained:

> There is a contradiction which arises when ... organisations commit themselves to sustainable development and then opt for an approach which does not necessarily achieve these fundamental aims. One of the key problems that has arisen is that by adopting a quality-driven environmental management approach, firms believe that they are adopting principles of sustainable development. They seem to be of the view that environmental improvement equates to sustainable development.
>
> (Welford 1995: 88)

As Commoner (1990) and Welford (1994) suggest, there will need to be a 'paradigm shift' in business culture if sustainability is to be achieved in practice. There is today mounting evidence of shifting consumer preferences throughout the 'developed' world towards environmentally sustainable consumption patterns. As polluting processes and products become increasingly unacceptable to the consumer, the ethical and socially responsible firm will survive *because* its sourcing of materials, production methods, distribution, use and disposal of its products are all designed to have negligible environmental impacts. In brief, it is not the management system itself which causes the environmental damage: it is a question of the products and services for which the management system is designed in the first place.

The sustainable firm is not only based upon new products and clean technologies. Conscious of its social and environmental impact, it is also rooted in the community and locality, employing ethical employment practices and housed in aesthetically pleasing buildings. Long-term security replaces short-term profitability as the dominant motivation for the firm's existence.

On a global scale, business awareness of and responsiveness to the environmental impact of business activity has varied from ignorance, through greenwashing to progressive implementation of ecological management principles.

THE WINTER MODEL

The basic components of an ecological or 'environmentalist' management system were pioneered in 1972 by the German manufacturers of diamond tools, Ernst Winter and Sohn. Over subsequent years the company developed the integrated system of environmental business management, known as the Winter Model. By the mid-1980s the firm was celebrated throughout Germany as a model example of an environmentalist company.

The principles of the Winter Model are concisely set out in George Winter's (1988) *Business and the Environment* (see also Winter 1995). According to Winter, no firm has yet achieved perfection in terms of ecological sustainability. The checklist supplies a framework for the manager of any type or size of firm to make a systematic assessment of the areas where improvements can be introduced. The points provide a spur to innovative ecological thinking not only by firms, from SMEs to TNCs, but also to educational establishments, providers of health care, governments and legislative bodies.

The points can be summarized under the following headings.

Company policy
At Winter and Sohn environmentalist considerations underlie all aspects of company policy, from staff training, through materials management, production, recycling and new plant construction to the selection of company vehicles.

Employee relations
To operate effectively, an ecological firm requires workers who are well informed on environmental issues and their implications for the workplace. Winter and Sohn pioneered occupational training through seminars and courses, incorporating environmental management into all aspects of staff relations. Staff committees and consultation schemes encourage constant change and improvement, the firm being seen as a living and dynamic organism. As part of this process the works canteen provision was overhauled to promote healthy and environmentally sound dietary habits; environmental counsellors were made available to offer advice in the homes of employees and neighbouring households. A healthy, well-informed and committed workforce provided the basis of the firm's ecological strategy.

Supply chain pressures
The ecological firm needs to institute an ecologically-orientated purchasing policy. Environmentally hazardous materials need to be replaced, not only in the production processes but also in the production processes of suppliers of materials, furnishings, office materials, canteen food and drink, buildings, company vehicles and all machinery and equipment used by the firm. The pioneer work of firms like Winter and Sohn have led to pressures on firms to institute environmental management systems so that they can secure contracts with firms with a sound environmental management policy.

Marketing and public relations
The ecological firm will work with pressure groups and the local community to promote ecologically sound practice. Avoiding irresponsible and unsubstantiated claims for its products and processes, it will increase its market share as public consciousness of the long-term hazards of polluting activities grows.

Risk reduction
The operation of any installation carries some risk. Liability for environmental damage potentially involving vast sums of money has increased substantially since the 1980s and extends to personal liability of directors, executives and other staff members. The ecological

firm is strongly motivated to comply with environmental legislation and regulations and to ensure that its suppliers follow the same policy.

Profitability

Through a combination of measures, from economical use of materials and energy, recycling and waste minimization to product design and marketing, the ecological firm will secure its place in the market. It will also be attractive to long-term investment.

The 'club' approach

Following from their pioneering work in environmental management, Winter and Sohn recognized the value of the 'club' approach. By setting up an organization of business managers, the introduction of practical environmental protection measures could be encouraged in a wide range of enterprises through an ongoing exchange of information. In Germany, the joint organization was instituted in the form of the German environmentalist society, Bundesdeutscher Arbeitskreis für Umweltbewusstes Management (*BAUM*, the acronym being German for 'tree'). By 1988 the industrial companies comprising the membership of BAUM had identified eight aims:

■ Strengthening the businessperson's sense of responsibility.

■ Passing on environmental business know-how.

■ Organizing exchanges and information from firm to firm.

■ Co-ordinating pilot and research projects.

■ Extending suppliers' environmental liability.

■ Making use of group advantages.

■ Developing a career profile in business ecology.

■ Complementing the work of other institutions.

The 'club' approach has been adopted, in various forms, by businesses and business support agencies across the globe. These include:

■ International Chamber of Commerce (ICC).

■ United Nations Environment Programme (UNEP).

■ Confederation of British Industry (CBI).

■ Industry associations such as the Chemical Industries Association's Responsible Care Programme and the Global Environmental Management Initiative *GEMI* (USA).

The 'club' approach to environmental management can be adopted on an international scale, as in case of the ICC (Case Study 4.5), or at a very local level and focusing on a specific issue, as in the CEST Aire and Calder Project (Case Studies 4.4 and 4.6). The sharing of information and training and the provision of joint facilities are vital in sustaining the efforts of individual managers, particularly in SMEs, to institute ecological policies. This type of organization will be reviewed in more detail in Part 4.

CASE STUDY: 4.5
ICC *Principles for Environmental Management*

The International Chamber of Commerce Business Charter for Sustainable Development exists 'to spread best practice in environmental management as widely as possible among companies of every size, in countries all over the world' (ICC 1994). Founded in response to the forthcoming Rio Earth Summit, the Business Charter committed international business to environmental improvement. In 1994, following an international seminar in the UK, the ICC issued the report *Principles for Environmental Management*, summarizing examples of progress and good practice in implementing the principles since they were first established. Rodney Chase, Managing Director of BP and Chairman of the World Industry Council for the Environment, noted that business should observe environmental good practice because:

- It can be very expensive if anything goes wrong, as with the *Exxon Valdez*.
- Environmental problems can damage a company's reputation, or its products, and sink its management.
- Good practice is part of a company's armoury and can strengthen its competitiveness.
- There are opportunities for cutting costs.
- Recognition of the issues is important for customers and employees.
- The will of society, especially of our own children, cannot be ignored.
- Society will not sign blank cheques for environmental protection—business has to understand this and the trade-offs.
- Some companies, while inviting their customers to buy their products, have to educate people to buy less of them, as in the case of petrol.
- Businesses have to take notice of pressures from their own workforce even more than from campaigners.
- Business has to gain the trust of society—distrust, especially from the media, governments and NGOs, hurts.

(ICC 1994)

Chase stressed the importance of business taking part in public debate on the environment, to present the case for incurring higher costs in order to meet the expense of protection and preventive measures, costs which are inevitably reflected in prices. It is therefore necessary, he maintained, to educate the public by presenting a clear, balanced and technically based case, in co-operation with environmental pressure groups. Confrontation, he noted, is counterproductive. Furthermore, it is important to recognize that employees have environmental concerns, the ignoring of which could lead to poor staff morale. In their report, the ICC stressed the importance of industry taking voluntary initiatives, and called upon statutory bodies to recognize the danger of allowing regulations and economic instruments to check voluntary developments.

Source: ICC (1994)

SUSTAINABLE LIVELIHOODS

Sustainability over the long term will be dependent upon firms capable of providing sustainable livelihoods. These will be locally based and will operate on environmentally and socially sound principles. According to Leigh Holland (1995) this will involve:

■ The provision of secure employment.

■ An equitable level of income from employment.

■ Local needs met by local production.

■ Satisfaction in employment.

■ Local ownership of the means of production.

■ The use of local skills for local benefit.

■ Participation in the community.

■ More democratic management structures, such as co-operatives.

In countries dominated by Anglo-Saxon management systems, SMEs are ideally placed to incorporate ecologically sound practices. Free from the pressures of large institutional investors, the smaller firm can be more adaptive, given the right information and incentives. Environmental innovation can lead to long-term security. For the local firm, self-employment, customer satisfaction and the provision of local employment may be more important than maximizing financial returns for the owners.

THREE LEVELS OF ENVIRONMENTAL IMPACT

Firms can be classified in terms of the environmental impact of their activities. Taylor (1994) has noted that the highest levels of environmental management have tended to be found within the most polluting industries. For sustainability to be achieved the reliance of all industrial, commercial and cultural enterprises upon pollution-generating activity will need to be recognized, and reversed.

Level 1: damaging, dirty or dangerous
These industries have a direct impact on the environment through the production and/or use of highly polluting materials. They are highly motivated to implement environmental management procedures to comply with legislation and regulations. These industries include agriculture and fisheries; armaments; automobiles; chemicals and plastics; coal, gas and nuclear energy; forestry and timber; heavy engineering; metals and mining; road transport; shipping; tobacco; waste disposal; and water.

Level 2: wasteful and polluting
These industries make excessive use of resources, that is, of trees, minerals, energy and/or land. They may cause environmental damage through disposal of waste to air, water or land. They include catering; computers; cosmetics; electrical equipment; electronics; food manufac-

ture; health services; hotels; leisure and tourism; light engineering; packaging and paper; property development; publishing; railways; retailing; telecommunications; and textiles.

Level 3: silent destroyers

Service industries and government bureaucracies appear superficially to be environmentally benign. However, the vast superstructure of these organizations and their employees cause the pollution through their use of cars and commercial vehicles, and their creation of waste through the use and disposal of goods, paper, packaging, office supplies and furniture and so on. Since these industries require roads, offices, car-parks, shops and warehouses, hospitals, services and entertainments, they are indirectly responsible for the bulk of environmental degradation. The silently polluting industries have been slow to consider the environmental impacts of their purchasing, siting and operational policies. They include accounting; advertising; banking; broadcasting; charities (including environmental pressure groups); civil service; education; financial services; insurance; local government; and social services.

A Stockholm Environmental Institute publication (Jackson 1993) demonstrates how the chain of pollution in indoor and outdoor environments operates across the spectrum of the commercial chemical chain as chemicals are used in the course of work and/or generated as waste:

- **Extracting industries** which mine metals, minerals and coal or drill oil or gas.

- **Refining industries** which isolate desired constituents from extracted materials.

- **Chemical manufacturers and processors** who purify and concentrate specific chemicals derived from refineries, and react chemicals together to form a myriad of new substances, such as pharmaceuticals, pesticides, plastics and bulk chemicals.

- **Chemical formulators** who mix and blend manufactured chemicals to form such products as paints, cosmetics and fertilizers.

- **Chemical users** who use chemical compounds to perform certain functions for a variety of businesses, such as dry cleaners, farmers and electronics firms.

- **Individual consumers** who purchase products for use in the home or office.

- **Chemical disposers** who transport, treat and dispose of waste products and by-products from the above stages in the chemical chain.

                                                                      (Jackson 1993: 195)

Not only are the processes hazardous, generating toxic wastes, but also the very products themselves contain persistent synthetic compounds and highly toxic substances. Works of this type indicate the growing awareness of a common responsibility for environmental degradation. The polluting firm does not pollute in isolation from the rest of society. Users and consumers of products are equally responsible for unsustainable activities as are management and employees who seek to meet society's demands through the production process.

CASE STUDY 4.6
Aire and Calder Project Examples

The Aire and Calder Project analysed the impacts of individual firms in terms of their polluting impacts upon their immediate surroundings. All firms were engaged in industrial activities which fell into polluting Levels 1 or 2, as 'damaging, dirty or dangerous' or 'wasteful and polluting'. All provide products and services which are drawn upon by the Level 3 'silent destroyers', as analysis of these projects shows.

Spring Grove

Spring Grove Services is one of the few service industries included in the series of pilot projects. Part of the Granada organization, this large workwear laundry employs 100 people. By reducing the amount of water and chemicals used in the wash service and installing wash-water recycling technology, the firm was able to reduce costs and minimize wastes and resource use.

Horsell Graphic

Horsell Graphic Industries produces lithographic printing plates from anodized aluminium sheet which is coated in special photopolymers. Over 300 people are employed on the 11-acre site, which is a major user of mains water in south Leeds. The project identified wasteful and unnecessary water consumption and effluent generation through losses of acid and alkali and reduced both through alteration of working practices and the provision of basic awareness training to employees.

Rhône-Poulenc

Rhône-Poulenc Chemicals Limited at Leeds produces surfactants for use in shampoos, detergents and a variety of beauty products. The 6-acre site has been used by industry since 1866, with chemical manufacturing beginning in the 1930s. The project enabled the company to take a number of measures to reduce product loss and subsequent releases of chemical oxygen demand (COD) to effluent. As a result of the measures taken to reduce water usage, product loss and effluent volume the company made annual savings of over £50 000 at little or no cost.

Coca-Cola Schweppes

Coca-Cola Schweppes Beverages (CCSB) uses 7500 cubic metres of water per day, one of the largest users of mains water in Yorkshire. Sited at Wakefield, it is one of the largest facilities of its kind in Europe and with a growing market share had doubled its output between 1991 and 1995. Project benefits totalled £1 491 100 per year, necessitating investment of £507 500 with a payback period of four months. The many improvements included removal of the need for lubricants on conveyor belts through introduction of new technology. Conveyor technology in the canning industry enables a machine to fill over 2000 cans per minute.

DuPont Howson

DuPont Howson is the largest producer of lithographic plates in the UK. The plates are made from anodized aluminium sheet coated with a variety of specialist organic chemicals, many of which are made on the site. Improvements to effluent pump design improved use of cooling water, losses of solvent to effluent were reduced and further potential savings were identified.

Croda Colours

Croda Colours Limited of Huddersfield was one of the smallest sites in the Project, employing 25 people. The firm is part of the chemicals division of Croda International plc. The production process was optimized in a number of ways without the need to change it radically. The installation of new meters and subsequent analysis of the data led to tighter control maintenance with savings of £7000 per year. The effluent treatment system was altered to reduce chemical dosing, saving £5000 per year, and a saving of £17 000 was achieved through a change to more concentrated batch mixing using less water.

British Rail

British Rail Neville Hill Depot in Leeds has been used for the maintenance of railway trains for over 100 years. Work on the site includes major maintenance and overhaul of rolling stock and the routine maintenance and cleaning of InterCity and local trains. The Project resulted in cost savings through the installation of new monitoring equipment.

Lambson

Lambson Fine Chemicals is situated at Castleford on the River Aire and employs over 200 people. The site produces speciality organic chemicals including oil additives. The Project led to fewer toxic and noxious sulphur compounds being present in the effluent, which was rendered effectively non-odorous. The COD was also reduced. Odorous liquids from the scrubbers and from the vacuum system were piped to the treatment vessel, avoiding unnecessary release of malodorous materials to the atmosphere. The improvements produced cost savings, improved output, enabled the firm to comply with environmental legislation and reduced the number of complaints about process odours in the neighbourhood.

Hickson

Hickson Fine Chemicals, a division of Hickson International plc, employs over 800 people at a site near the confluence of the Rivers Aire and Calder near Castleford. The site produces organic chemical intermediates and household products including paints, dyes, washing powders and weedkillers. The firm operates an effluent treatment plant to remove contamination before water is discharged to the river. Improvements included the introduction of a new system using 'indirect contact' condensers. These keep cooling water separate from contaminated steam, so that the cooling water can be returned to the river without requiring expensive treatment.

Warwick

Warwick International Specialities manufactures a range of chemicals, mainly for use in the textile industry. The company is particularly active in the manufacture of Speciality Organo Bromite Compounds. This process produces an impure aqueous hydrobromic acid (HBr) solution which has to be drummed and disposed of at a cost of £200 per tonne. Among the Project benefits was the identification of the potential for concentration and reuse of the HBr from off-gases by distillation.

Source: CEST (1995) and authors' research

The realization of the complexity of the problems facing business and industry has given rise to the study of 'industrial ecology', bringing together environmental scientists concerned with climate change, biochemical cycling and heavy metal contamination with specialists involved in industrial policy, economics and the social sciences. In 1994 the Global Change Institute on Industrial Ecology and Global Change published the proceedings of its 1992 conference, calling for improved communications between natural and social scientists studying global change on the one hand, and government and industry decision-makers on the other. The venture is symptomatic of a general appreciation of the complexity of the interrelationship between the natural environment and human social systems (Socolow *et al.* 1994).

THE ENVIRONMENT AND THE SOCIAL RESPONSIBILITIES OF MANAGEMENT

The primary organizational goal, traditionally, has been profit maximization with other goals like providing a service to the customer and employment for the community being secondary goals. Ecologically aware managements note that people have goals, while organizations merely have structures designed to meet these goals. It is the task of management to integrate the personal goals and values of the decision-makers within an organization in such a way that conflicts of aims are minimized. Management seeks to define the objectives and policies of the people who make up the organization so that common objectives can be achieved. In this context profit maximization, therefore, has to be achieved through the acceptance of a number of broader responsibilities towards all stakeholders. Not only do these include social responsibilities in respect of employees, shareholders and finances, consumers and the community at large, but also they include the necessity to take into account the ecological needs of the stakeholders as dictated by the physical realities of the natural environment.

SUMMARY

Legislative change since the mid-1980s has made it necessary for all firms to become increasingly conscious of their environmental impacts with a view to reducing the adverse impacts of their activities upon the environment. Initially, consumer pressures have focused attention on the polluting activities of the 'upstream' sectors such as steel, and metal processing. The growth of supply-chain pressure originating in environmentally aware countries like Germany and the Netherlands, however, has brought consumer pressure 'downstream' to electricity, automobile and chemical sectors (Vaughan and Mickle 1993) and to the 'silent polluters' in homes and offices.

Although the most polluting industries continue to be the most highly motivated to implement environmentally sound procedures, the trend is increasingly towards a holistic approach. Individual firms operate within a given societal framework, and are incapable of taking effective action single-handed. Lateral thinking on the part of far-sighted managers can provide vital inspiration and motivation for change, but in the last analysis business operates in a market situation. Environmental protection and ecological sustainability, therefore, are premised upon the co-operation of all sectors of industry with governments, pressure groups, international bodies, consumers, educational establishments and the general public. Unsustainable practices will not be tolerated where individual consumer citizens, acting through the institutions and organizations within which they live, work and go about their daily business, cease to demand goods and services known to be produced through polluting processes. Hence the development of 'stakeholder capitalism', in which companies accept obligations to employees, suppliers and the local community as well as to share-holders, presents an exciting new range of challenges to management. Part 2 explores the range of tools available to the environmental manager to meet these challenges.

QUESTIONS

4.1 Compare and contrast the Anglo-Saxon managerial capitalism style of management with that of the Winter Model. In your view, is a global management style essential to secure environmental sustainability? Give your reasons.

4.2 A TNC can move its operations across the world according to the cheapest markets for labour and raw materials, and can dispose of toxic wastes in countries with poor legislation. Analyse the tensions between triadic world trading practices and environmental sustainability.

4.3 It has been argued that 'Big is Better', since only powerful and successful firms have the resources to clean up after a nuclear accident or major oil spill. Examine this argument critically.

4.4 Using the products and processes described in this chapter as a resource, draw up a series of guidelines for an environmentally sustainable purchasing policy for your current place of work or study.

REFERENCES AND FURTHER READING

Adams, J. (1995) *Risk*, UCL Press, London.

Atkins, X. (1994) *Project Catalyst*. Report to the Project Completion Event at Manchester Airport.

British Standards Institute (1992) *Specification for Environmental Management Systems*, BSI, London.

Business in the Environment (Bie), SustainAbility, SPOLD and Business in the Environment (1994) *The LCA Sourcebook*, PMC, London.

Calori, R. (1994) 'The Diversity of Management Systems' in R. Calori and P. de Woot, *A European Management Model*, Prentice Hall, Englewood Cliffs, NJ.

Calori, R. and de Woot, P. (1994) *A European Management Model: Beyond Diversity*, Prentice Hall, Englewood Cliffs, NJ.

Centre for Exploitation of Science and Technology (CEST) (1995) *Waste Minimisation and Cleaner Technology: An Assessment of Motivation and the Aire and Calder Experience*, CEST, London.

Commoner, B. (1990) 'Can Capitalism Survive?', *Business and Society Review* 75: 31–5.

Department of Trade and Industry (DTI) (1992) *Cutting Your Losses: A Further Guide to Waste Minimisation for Business*, DTI, London.

Edwards, T. (1995) *The Implications of Water Regulation for Industry*, Stanley Thornes, Cheltenham.

Holland, L. (1995) 'Local Self-reliance and the Role of Small and Medium Enterprises', Paper presented at 1995 International Sustainable Development Research Conference, Manchester, UK.

International Chamber of Commerce (ICC) (1994) *Principles for Environmental Management* (Summary Report of Seminar) ICC Charter, London.

Jackson, T. (ed.) (1993) *Clean Production Strategies*, Lewis, London.

Johnson and Stokes, (1995) *Waste Minimization and Cleaner Technology*, Centre for Exploitation of Science and Technology, 5 Bemers Road, London.

Maslow, A.H. (1943) 'A Theory of Human Motivation', *Psychological Review* 50 (4): 370–96.

Miller, E. J., and Rice, A. K. (1967) *Systems of Organisation*, Tavistock, London.

Mullins, L. J. (1985) *Management and Organisational Behaviour* (1994 edn), Pitman, London.

Pascale, R. T. and Athos, A. G. (1981) *The Art of Japanese Management*, Warner, New York.

Pearce, D., Barbier, E. and Markandya, A. (1989) *Blueprint for a Green Economy*, Earthscan, London.

Socolow, R. H., *et al.* (eds) (1994) *Industrial Ecology and Global Change*, Cambridge University Press, Cambridge.

Taylor, B. (1994) in B. Taylor, C. Hutchinson, S. Pollack and R. Tapper (eds) *Environmental Management Handbook*, Pitman, London.

Taylor, F. W. (1947) *Scientific Management* (includes his writings between 1903 and 1912), Harper & Row, New York.

Vaughan, D. and Mickle, C. (1993) *Environmental Profiles of European Business*, Earthscan, London.

Welford, R. J. (1994) *Cases in Environmental Management and Business Strategy*, Pitman, London.

———(1995) *Environmental Strategy and Sustainable Development: The Corporate Challenge for the 21st Century*, Routledge, London.

Winter, G. (1988) *Business and the Environment: A Handbook of Industrial Ecology with 22 Checklists for Practical Use*, McGraw-Hill, Hamburg.

———(1995) *Blueprint for Green Management*, McGraw-Hill, Maidenhead.

The Internal Environment and Eco- Management

Parts 2 and 3 cover the internal and external business environments respectively. Environment here denotes the sphere of business internally, relating to all aspects of operations and strategy on site, and externally relating the environment within which these operations and strategies work.

Part 2 comprises two chapters. Chapter 5 deals with the strategic side of environmental and ecological management, considering how the proactive strategic planner of the twenty-first century should react to the environmental challenge and why response is so crucial. Chapter 6 covers all aspects of operational management, particularly focusing on specific eco-auditing procedures and environmental impact assessment. Operational management deals with the daily implementation of strategic plans.

INTRODUCTION

Economic activity produces goods and services which people require to improve the quality of their lives. In the process, resources are used up, waste and pollution are produced, and some degree of long- or short-term environmental degradation results. The challenge facing management is to produce a supply of goods and customer services while causing minimal environmental impact.

The central issue is that of cost. Traditionally it has been the least financial cost that has been the motivating factor in corporate decision-making processes. However, as public demand and regulatory pressures increase, companies are under pressure to take the environment into account more seriously. The cost of environmental degradation to future societies, the cost of environmental clean-ups and the cost to nature itself are all significant reasons for the quality company and the corporate strategic planners to take account of the environment.

The biggest challenge to the interests of global business today is the task of reconciling the demands of sustainable development and corporate strategy (Welford and Starkey 1996; Cairncross 1995; Wallace 1995; Fischer and Schot 1993; Welford 1996). Some businesses see the environmental challenge as a red herring. Others see it as contrary to their interests. The proactive forward-looking, competitive businesses, however, see the environmental challenge as a breath of fresh unpolluted air that offers many commercial opportunities, while at the same time offering the possibility of improvement to the welfare of society as a whole as a means to regain any lost public confidence.

As with all changing management scenarios, the challenge of sustainable development has uncovered large-scale commercial opportunities for the proactive company. In Elkington's (1994) 'triadic win scenario' the company, the customer and the environment can potentially all win, with business playing a central role in the movement towards a more sustainable society. Phenomenon such as the greening of the market-place, driven by the green consumer of the 1980s and the emergence of wide-scale acceptance of the long-term importance of the environment to the customer, has led to the development of a 'corporate environmentalism' (Elkington 1994).

Corporate environmentalism appears in a number of shades of green, from a simple greenwashing of the corporate logo to the full implementation of ecological responsibility at all levels within the central decision-making process, with commitments to improve environmental performance through to the implementation of environmental management systems (EMS). With many environmental problems being imported through the supply chain, not only are there horizontal pressures to improve internal environmental performances, but also there are increasingly vertical pressures from the supply chain to adopt the agenda. As a result, corporate environmentalism has escalated over the last 20 years of the millennium. Part 2 explores corporate environmentalism and considers the strategic nature of environmental and ecological management.

ENVIRONMENTAL MANAGEMENT OR ECO-MANAGEMENT?

A useful distinction is made between the terms environmental management and eco-management:

- **Environmental management** deals with environmental concerns on a piece-meal level, the environment being just another strategic issue, an annex to corporate strategy.

- **Eco-management** sees the environment as central to all aspects of corporate operations and strategic planning. It is an integral part of the life of the company and infiltrates to all levels of decision-making.

The two terms are often used interchangeably in business environment literature. Accepting that 'greening' is an ongoing learning exercise for all, from the individual manager to society at large, we note the distinction between the two terms but follow the common practice of regarding them as virtually identical. 'Environmental' concern implies some degree of consideration of ecological impacts.

Stoner *et al.* (1995) puts the environment top of the list of issues that frame the workplace, ahead of ethics, social awareness, globalization, entrepreneurship, culture, diversity, multi-culturalism and quality as management moves towards the new millennium. Stoner's research would suggest that there is an *a priori* case for environmental concerns to be holistically incorporated into all decision-making structures of the firm. Eco-management includes all aspects of environmental management in that the operational procedures discussed under the auspices of environmental management are equally applicable. Eco-management, however, has a rather different focus and philosophy. The environment is not an issue, separate among many, but a central philosophy to be incorporated into all levels of the decision-making process. Chapter 5 will cover the main aspects of strategic eco-management providing an outline model for the proactive company to follow.

REFERENCES AND FURTHER READING

Cairncross, F. (1995) *Green, Inc,–a Guide to Business and the Environment*, Earthscan, London.

Elkington, J. (1994) 'Towards the Sustainable Corporation: Win-Win-Win Business Strategies for Sustainable Development', *California Management Review* 36(2): 90–1000.

Fischer, K. and Schot, J. (eds) (1993) *Environmental Strategies for Industry: International Perspectives on Research Needs and Policy Implications*, Earthscan, London.

Stoner, J., Freeman, R. and Gilbert, D. (1995) *Management*, 6th edn, Prentice Hall, Englewood Cliffs, NJ.

Wallace, D. (1996) *Sustainable Production Systems for Greenfield Economies*, Earthscan, London.

Wehrmeyer, W. (1994) *Environmental References in Business*, Greenleaf Publishing, Sheffield.

Welford, R. (ed) (1996) *Corporate Environmental Management: Systems and Strategies*, Earthscan, London.

Welford, R. and Starkey, R. (eds) (1996) *The Earthscan Reader in Business and the Environment*, Earthscan, London.

CHAPTER 5

ENVIRONMENTAL STRATEGIC MANAGEMENT

The future is purchased by the present.

(Samuel Johnson 1709–84)

INTRODUCTION

An efficient management plan will utilize all available company resources as efficiently as possible so as to minimize costs and achieve the organizational goals most effectively. Minimizing wastage diminishes corporate environmental impact while reducing overall financial costs, achieving congruence between the corporate aims of cost minimization and environmental impact reduction. Strategic management includes the planning and setting of these organizational goals, but has an added action component which includes the implementation of the strategic frameworks, or the establishment of the strategic plans.

In 1962 Alfred D. Chandler defined strategic management as 'The determination of the basic long term goals and objectives of an enterprise and the adoption of courses of action and the allocation of resources necessary for carrying out these goals' (Chandler 1995: 16). Strategic management is all about staying ahead of the competition, and requires lateral thought. Fannin and Rodrigues (1986: 84) define it as 'a stream of decisions that a) guide the organization's ongoing alignment with its environment and b) shape internal policies and procedures'. There are five fundamental stages of strategy development a company must go through to be engaged in strategic management (Jauch and Glueck 1988). It must:

1. Develop a mission statement.
2. Set its objectives.
3. Undertake an external environmental analysis.
4. Undertake an internal environmental analysis.
5. Implement a relevant strategic programme suitable to the company.

This process is then revised and fed back constantly to update procedures.

Effective eco-management requires a well-considered strategic response, in which environmental concerns are at the centre of corporate strategy. To assess the extent to which environmental concerns can be integrated into the strategic process it is necessary to delineate some of the major strategic management theories.

Johnson and Scholes (1989: 6–8) define corporate strategy as 'the direction and scope of an organization over the long term, ideally which matches its resources to its changing environment and in part its markets, customer or clients so as to meet stakeholder expectations'. Clearly, if stakeholders change their values and expectations, companies have to modify their strategic management processes to satisfy the new corporate strategy direction.

Essentially the strategic management process is three-fold:

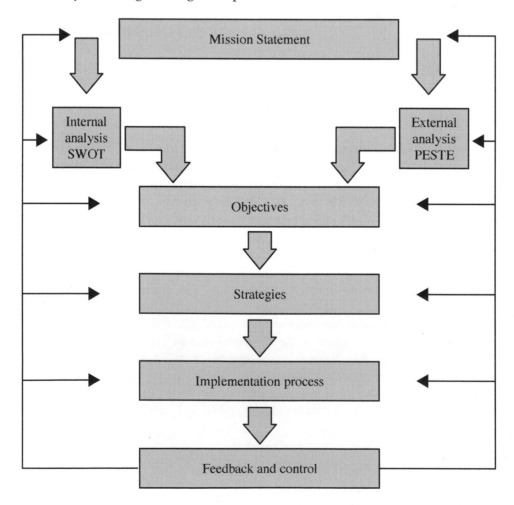

FIGURE 5.1 *Strategic management*

1. To decide upon a mission statement.
2. To analyse the internal capacity to satisfy the mission statement.
3. To develop the business objectives and strategies to satisfy the mission statement.

This chapter will take the Figure 5.1 model as the basis for analysing strategic eco-management. The main focus of the chapter will be on the objectives, strategies and implementation side of the strategic planning process, leaving the internal environmental (eco-auditing) details to Chapter 6 and the external environmental analysis to Part 3. (The word 'environment' is used in the general business sense here to mean all internal aspects of the company. It is also used to denote the general external surroundings in the external environment.) The objectives, strategies and implementation elements will include a brief analysis of the traditional theory followed by an applied environmental analysis where the authors develop new models of strategic eco-management. The feedback and control element is self-explanatory. Feedback and control involves an ongoing process of revision and will, therefore, not be covered as a separate section.

MISSION STATEMENT

If a company is aiming to develop a credible and long-term strategy for the environment it is essential that top management accept the need for an environmental pledge within the auspices of the mission statement. The mission statement is essential, laying out what the organization wants to achieve and who it wants to be. It can also be seen as a 'visionary projection' (Richards 1978). Any proactive forward-looking organization of the twenty-first century must include environmental variables within this forward-looking projection.

INTERNAL ANALYSIS

The internal environment (i.e. within the company, not including external factors such as economic policy, technical developments and political changes) is usually characterized and analysed through what is known as the *SWOT* analysis. SWOT stands for Strengths, Weaknesses, Opportunities, Threats. The idea is that through a systematic analysis the internal capacity of the company or organization can be assessed and the potential for satisfying the mission statement objectively judged. One regularly used tool is the ecological value chain which has been developed by Smith (1992) specifically for environmental purposes (Figure 5.2).

The Value Chain (originally developed by Porter 1985) allows the use of resources to be strategically assessed by linking it to the process of environmental auditing. The green value chain stresses the need to focus the environmental microscope on all aspects of the management process and not just the more publicly sensitive areas such as marketing or advertising. The idea is to sustain a strategy throughout all aspects of the value chain.

Another well-used model in strategic management is the 7S concept (Waterman *et al.* 1980), which links Structure, Systems, Strategy, Style, Staff and Skills with the internal Shared values

Support activities	PRIMARY ACTIVITIES		
	Inbound logistics	Operations	Outbound logistics
Procurement	Transportation impacts Storage modes	'Green consumables' Clean technologies Recyclable packaging	Storage modes Transportation modes
Technology development	Waste minimization through source reduction Alternative raw material resources	Clean technologies Pollution minimalization and control	Finished product recyclability
Human resource management	Staff selection Supplier selection	Corporate culture Training programme Corporate environmental awareness	Subcontractual arrangements
Management systems	Inventory reduction Recyclability	'Just-in-time' processes	Cradle-to-grave recycling and recovery infrastructure

FIGURE 5.2 *The ecological value chain (Source: Smith 1992)*

(Figure 5.3). This model helps our understanding of strategic eco-management. All elements of the company are to be assessed through the internal value of sustainable development and the ethic of social responsibility. The effects of this are felt throughout every aspect of the company's operations and strategy. The 7S eco-framework provides an excellent holistic eco-model for placing green issues right at the centre of all internal decision-making.

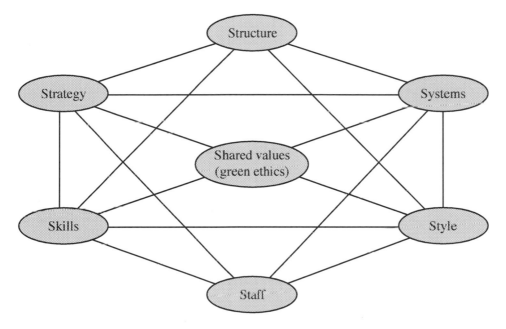

FIGURE 5.3 *The 7S eco-framework (Source: adapted from Waterman* et al. *1980)*

EXTERNAL ANALYSIS

PESTE analysis

The PESTE or STEEP acronyms are the most commonly used models within the field of strategic management to explain and analyse the external environment. PESTE stands for Political, Economic, Social, Technological and Ecological (rearranged to form STEEP). PESTE is used to analyse all possible external market opportunities and threats. Since the early 1980s all aspects of PESTE have placed significant pressure on the competitive global company to become more environmentally aware. Pressure to conform to excellent environmental practice has come not only from the threat of political and economic pressure but also from the opportunities that have opened up to companies keen to exploit another major change management situation. This is particularly so from the angle of the technical market.

OBJECTIVES

After having considered the internal and external environments, the next phase of the strategic planning process is to develop objectives. Assuming that the organization has developed its mission statement, the objectives (in the light of the internal and external analyses) are simply a development of the general philosophy stated in the mission statement. The objectives aim to point the direction in which the strategy should go. At this stage the strategic planner should be looking to delineate specific environmental components and he or she will require significant information. This information can be collated through the process of the initial environmental review.

After the initial review companies can undertake fuller environmental reviews and set objectives and develop targets through external and internal environmental analysis.

Initial environmental review

To make an informed decision regarding commitment to the environment, senior management require information. This includes both external information (socio-economic and political data) and internal information (company or organizational details). The kinds of questions that senior management usually ask are:

- How much is it going to cost and over how long?

- Why is the environment important to us?

- How important a priority is it?

To answer these questions and satisfy senior management of the need to consider environmental issues holistically in corporate strategy, the first requirement is to undertake an initial environmental review. This exploratory stage may take the form of asking a few preliminary questions about operations, processes and relevant regulations. The types of questions that could be posed at this stage fit into the following 10-point model.

Statement and policy

- Has somebody senior been given responsibility for overseeing the task?

- Has anyone done anything like this before?

- If yes, do you have access to the results?

- Does your company have an environmental policy/statement/strategy?

Managing the improvements

- Are the top management committed to making the change?

- Has the desire been indicated to every member of staff (have staff been included in developing the vision)?

- Has someone been given responsibility for overseeing the programme?

- Has environmental improvement been covered in the company budget?

- Is your product designed to be environmentally friendly?

- Are you aware of any major restrictions to improvement?

Materials used

- Do you keep an inventory of all the materials used?
- Do you know where they come from and how they are produced?
- Have you considered using any alternative materials?
- Are all the materials stored properly?
- Are you aware of all the relevant regulations relating to your company and environmental protection?

Waste management

- Do you know how much waste you produce and what it consists of?
- Do you know what happens to your waste and how it is treated?
- Could you reuse or recycle any of your waste?
- Do you keep careful records of your waste?

Pollution control and monitoring

- Do you know what your company discharges to the atmosphere or into local water courses?
- Do you know what limits have been placed on these?
- Do you know how much is discharged?
- Can you monitor this?
- Are all the discharges properly licensed?
- Have the potential environmental effects of these discharges been noted by the company?
- Would your staff be able to recognize a pollution incident?

Energy use

- Could you list all the forms of energy you use?
- Do you know how much you use?
- Is this monitored?
- Do you think your company could save energy?

Transport

- Do you operate a transport fleet of some kind?
- If so, are the vehicles selected to reduce environmental impact?

Historical use and contaminated land issues

- Does your site leak potentially hazardous substances?

- Are you aware of the site's historic use?

- Has it been used to manufacture anything dangerous?

- Do you know if this may affect your company today (legislation, health and safety etc.)?

- Is this historic use recorded anywhere?

- Could your site pose a risk to others?

- Is your site kept clean and tidy?

Visual image

- Does your site fit in with the local landscape?

- Could you identify any improvements that could be made?

Environmental strategy

- Can you identify the most important environmental issues affecting your company?

- Will you be doing this on your own?

- Can you identify who might be prepared to form an environmental committee?

- Do you know where to find local sources of help?

(Gaylor and Young 1994)

Action plan

Environmental consultants offer the type of service outlined in the 10-point model above. In a 'Green Health Check' of this type, the consulting company provides an initial environmental overview to assess whether further investment in the environment is required. Following an initial review of this type, the company is in a more informed position from which to decide the action priorities.

It is often at this stage that organizations will begin to develop specific objectives and targets that would be desirable. This can be collated in the form of an action plan. The action plan is simply a set of objectives that aim to move in a particular direction. The direction should of course be towards satisfying the criteria laid out in the mission statement. An action plan includes timescales of objectives, targets to be set and amounts of resources to be mobilized.

It may be the case that after having undertaken this overview the company decides it is necessary to commission a full environmental review before finalizing its policy and strategy to accommodate green concerns.

STRATEGIES

Having considered the initial material, the next major phase of the strategic management process is the strategy phase. This considers how to satisfy the goals and how to get there. Strategy represents the decision process that links the capability of the organization with the general opportunities and threats it faces. An effective strategy requires the prediction of general trends in order to reduce long-term risk and minimize possible loss of market share. There are numerous traditional strategies and models to achieve optimum return including the application of Ansoff's Matrix (Ansoff 1956), the Boston Consulting Group and the Gap analysis among others (Johnson and Scholes 1989: 177–8; 204). One central strategic management model for strategies, however, includes Porter's Generic Model. The Three Generic Strategies that Porter (1985) suggests a company can choose are:

1. **Cost leadership** Where companies find a reduction of costs through experience and economies of scale and aggressive construction of efficient-scale facilities.
2. **Differentiation** Where added value to products and services distinguishes them from the competition.
3. **Focus** Where the strategy focuses on a particular group, segment of product line or geographical market. This strategy can be followed on the basis of differentiation or cost leadership.

(Porter 1985)

Strategies 2 and 3 are both significant to the environmental agenda. Being environmentally aware, active and engaged is an essential strategy focus for the twenty-first century business. The question is how to become aware enough to make a rational well-argued case for strategic environmental implementation. The environmental review (which can provide the necessary information), therefore, is a critical strategy component of eco-management.

Environmental review

Environmental reviews can provide a series of indicators to show potential for improvement of environmental efficiency over time. Reviews are an assessment of current environmental performance within a specific company. The environmental review is usually undertaken by an external consultancy prior to the implementation of an EMS. Reviews can, however, be undertaken internally as an initial step by smaller and medium-sized companies (SMEs). There is sufficient written material presently available to companies to exercise their own initial review, providing an overview of the company's environmental position. More rigorous reviews are often beyond the resources and expertise of most companies requiring more detailed scientific operational analyses to be undertaken by scientists, lawyers, management systems experts and operational analysts.

The following blueprint for an environmental review draws from BS 7750's environmental effects inventory (British Standards Institute 1992) and the BiE's *Executive Guide* (Business in the Environment (1990).

The review should consider the following issues:.

- The level of management commitment to environmental issues, including specific tasks and responsibilities.

- Compliance to relevant legislation and regulations and opportunities for compliance plus strategies.

- Specific products and processes, their design, production and distribution channels.

- Capacity for the expansion into new markets to take advantage of environmental opportunities, i.e. new product innovation and increased competitive advantage from new green operations.

- Competitor strategy observation.

- Technology checks—comparisons to BATNEEC (see Chapter 10).

- Investments in auditing, waste, energy and systems.

- Analysis of current monitoring procedures (raw materials, storage, energy usage, etc.).

- Environmental health and safety procedures and enforcements.

- Accident contingency plans.

- Centrality of the environmental agenda at all levels of management decision-making.

- Communication and information diffusion to all staff and stakeholders (including the local community) of ongoing corporate environmental performance.

- Operational management reviews and assessments, including site locations, buildings, office environment, furniture, supplies and catering, products, production processes, emissions (air, water, land), marketing, distribution and transport, finance and investment, community relations, education and training.

- Continual assessment of auditing procedures and future possibilities of EMS implementation.

- Regular policy updates and a continual review process.

The environmental review uncovers information which allows senior management to make an informed decision regarding long-term commitment to the environment.

A typical environmental review will:

- Help companies develop environmental policies, objectives, and management systems which take into account the existing and evolving standards, legislation and regulations as well as the needs of the company.

- Help management in the improvement of their own environmental performance.

- Pinpoint areas which need further consideration.

- Heighten environmental awareness within the company.

- Encourage the company to improve its relationships with its suppliers, contractors and agents with the local authorities, and agencies with the local communities and most importantly with its customers.

Environmental reviews provide the information for directors to develop the necessary strategic plans. The environmental review is sometimes called the baseline audit. It differs from traditional auditing procedure in that it does not check and verify the performance of a company: rather it defines the starting-point and measures the basic environmental performance. The review is an initial SWOT analysis, in which the team looks at the strengths, weaknesses, opportunities and threats which provide the foundation for the implementation of a thorough and holistically applicable environmental management system. It encompasses a systematic analysis of company operations and environment impacts with respect to current legal compliance and regulatory standards.

Benefits of an environmental review

- It establishes the basis upon which effective environmental management can be built.

- It identifies current and forthcoming demands from environmental legislation.

- It identifies possible cost savings.

- It identifies potential market opportunities.

- It identifies and prioritizes areas of significant environmental damage.

- It provides management information relating to strategic problems.

- It provides information that allows management to fine-tune its policies and focus its response.

- It provides the basic information required for constant reappraisal of environmental performance via the environmental audit.

- It provides the basic information of risk evaluation which is increasingly needed by investors and insurers.

(Welford and Gouldson 1993: 62)

The baseline review provides the foundation for future comparison of change. As the company undertakes further environmental audits over time, the initial review is often used as a measuring point by which change and improvement of performance can be measured. The review itself may well be a process of self-education, an awareness exercise in itself, enlightening the company to issues involved in the greening of business and to the opportunities available for reduced costs and increased market shares. Until a review is undertaken, a business's awareness of its impact on the environment is often limited. A review undertaken by an independent consultancy provides third party verification of a company's initial commitment towards environmental improvement. The results from the initial review can then be consolidated in the development of a company policy.

Ansoff Matrix

When deciding on the overall policy to combat the change management challenge of the environment, the Ansoff Matrix can be employed (Ansoff 1965). Figure 5.4 shows the possibilities for new product development and the possibilities for the exploitation of new markets emerging from the environmental challenge. In Hong Kong the government plans to have spent US$4 billion to 5 billion for environmental clean-up and development between 1989 and the end of 1999. With the World Bank estimating that the demand for environmental technology products and services will be in excess of US$300 billion by the year 2000, there is a powerful commercial incentive to consider product development and diversification strategies as well as an ecological one.

Having secured the policy direction it is then the job of the strategic eco-planner to devise a policy document. If the organization has plumped for a 'do nothing' strategy the policy for the environment could well be little more than a few greenwashed annexes to the existing corporate policy. If, however, the organization decides there is a requirement to develop new policy contents to take account of the green challenge their documents could be similar in nature to the Ansoff Matrix (Figure 5.4).

PRODUCT

	Present	New
Present	'Do nothing' Withdrawal Consolidation Market penetration	Product development
New	Market development	Diversification

MARKET

FIGURE 5.4 *Ansoff Matrix (Source: Ansoff 1965)*

Environmental policy

A critical first stage in the process of the greening of business is to secure senior level management commitment to the initial consideration of environmental issues within corporate strategy. Having secured this commitment and undertaken an initial overview in the form of a review the next stage is to write a policy document which will include corporate aims and objectives on the environment. Since workforce commitment and co-operation is an essential component of successful policy, it is common practice to establish an environmental committee at an early stage. This may be done by extending the remit of the health and safety committee, in co-operation with union representatives.

The policy should act as a statement of intent. It can be used to inform the world, to pre-empt any legislative requirements for reporting and to communicate company ethics and intentions to staff, who stand to benefit in the first instance from improved working conditions. The following elements could be included:

- Environmental mission statement.

- Policy.

- Environmental policy statement.

Environmental mission statement

The directors, senior management and all employees are committed to the following environmental policy and to the minimization of company impact on the environment through a continuous improvement programme.

Policy

- To set environmental guidelines and standards that meet and where appropriate exceed current national and local statutory requirements, and where regulations do not exist provide in-house performance targets.

- To review and develop these guidelines and standards in the light of developments in technology and industrial practices and trends of legislation.

- To minimize waste and to reuse and recycle materials and products.

- To improve energy use through conservation measures and increased efficiency, and to design energy efficiency into new services, buildings and products.

- To minimize or eliminate the use of toxic materials and chemicals and to minimize wherever possible harmful emissions.

- To assess the actual and potential environmental effects of all existing or planned products and projects and to mitigate impacts in all cases.

- To inform all employees of their responsibilities for policy implementation and to provide appropriate training to ensure that policies are implemented effectively.

- To carry out monitoring through environmental audits, to ensure policy implementation.

- To ensure that contractors and suppliers are informed of and comply with the company's environmental guidelines and standards and to help them implement their own environmental policy as an integral part of a quality purchasing policy.

- To make available information about the company's environmental guidelines and standards to all stakeholders, including the local community, who have an interest in the company and its environmental performance.

- To establish and maintain a dynamic community relations programme that emphasizes the protection of the local environment.

- To include environmental issues in discussions with unions and to incorporate environmental ethics into all training programmes.

- To monitor progress and evaluate targets and to publish environmental performance reports on an annual basis.

The annual report should clearly state how the company affects the environment and how it aims to reduce its overall environmental impacts. The reported information can be laid out in executive format at the beginning for quick look reference but should also include more substantial exposition within the main body of the report.

Environmental policy statement

The statement below encapsulates what an environmental policy could look like:

Our Business Will . . .

- Adopt and aim to apply the principles of sustainable development—that is development which meets the needs of the present without compromising the abilities of future generations to meet their own needs.

- Strive to adopt the highest available environment standards in all countries of operations.

- Adopt a total cradle-to-grave assessment (see Chapter 6) and responsibility for our products and services.

- Aim to minimize the use of all materials, supplies and energy. Wherever possible we will use renewable or recyclable materials and components.

- Minimize waste produced in all parts of the business and aim for 'waste free' processes.

- Expect similar environmental standards to our own from all third parties involved with our business—suppliers, vendors, contractors.

- Publish our environmental position.

- Encourage employees involvement in environmental action.

- Liaise on a continuous basis with the local community.

- Adopt an environmentally sound transport strategy.

- Aim to include environmental considerations in investment decisions.

- Assess on a continuous basis the environmental impact of all our operations.

- Assist in developing solutions to environmental problems, and support the development of public policy.

(BiE 1990)

Large-scale chemical operations and companies with significant deleterious effects on the environment would find it hard to greenwash their company's image if they adopted and publicly reported this type of policy. As regulatory pressure increasingly dictates the environmental agenda, the more likely it will be that companies will be required to publish their environment performance data. A policy like the one delineated here goes a long way towards setting the standards required to satisfy current regulatory demands. Case Study 5.1 illustrates B&Q's policy.

CASE STUDY 5.1
B&Q

Statement

'B&Q is committed to the minimization of environmental damage caused by the day-to-day running of the business and the securing of raw materials, production, packaging and disposal of its product range'.

General policy

B&Q recognizes that every business operation has an impact on the environment and that it is impossible to totally eliminate environmental impacts. However, its aim is to reduce as far as possible environmental impacts by considering the way it operates, buys and sells. The responsibility that B&Q holds towards the environment applies to its suppliers as well. It starts with companies extracting the materials from the ground to the processing of the materials and through to the consumer's use of the finished product. B&Q also feel that it is its responsibility to inform customers how to dispose of the goods they buy.

Strategy

B&Q has:

1. Appointed a full-time scientifically qualified environmental co-ordinator to report to the board of directors and to undertake any relevant environmental research.

2. Required the environmental co-ordinator to diffuse information to staff, and stakeholders, monitor environmental developments and act as spokesperson for the company.

3. Undertaken to publish a high quality magazine called *Talking Environment* which is circulated to staff and other interested parties to keep all stakeholders informed of the developments within the company.

This effective strategy is a part of its overall green marketing policy connecting all company operations with concern for the environment. An effective holistic environmental management system of the type developed by B&Q offers benefits from reduced waste and energy costs, is beneficial to customer relations and makes for a well-developed green marketing strategy.

Supply chain policies

In additional to having a general overall policy, B&Q has subject-specific policies. Under its 'Timber Policy', B&Q resolved to purchase timber from managed sources by the end of 1995, and to set new targets on completion.

B&Q also required every timber supplier to have implemented its own environmental policy and undertaken an environmental audit. This audit not only is a general environmental audit but also includes the requirement for suppliers to undertake a cradle-to-grave assessment of all the products supplied to B&Q. B&Q also checks compliance with this policy aim through its own supplier environmental audit (*SEA*) which includes regular visits to supplier sites and a commitment to regular improvements in environmental performance over time, although B&Q does work with suppliers to help them achieve these stringent goals.

Non-manufacturing suppliers are required to ensure compliance with B&Q's policy by their own suppliers. This includes distributors, importers and buying agents. All suppliers are expected to assess the environmental performance of their suppliers. It is also its policy to de-list suppliers who show no commitment to improving their environmental performance.

B&Q places less stringent environmental restrictions on the operations of suppliers from developing countries. The argument is that basic health and safety and other ethical considerations are more urgent and for these B&Q does require self-auditing, dates established for improvements and open information flows.

B&Q has statements within its environmental policy covering all areas of business operations and strategy. They include sections on financial auditing, marketing, operations management, packaging, personnel training, and logistics (which includes transport impacts).

Source: B&Q; Author's research

IMPLEMENTATION PROCESS—ENVIRONMENTAL MANAGEMENT SYSTEMS

This section focuses primarily on the application of systems theories to the satisfaction of the environmental objectives. The implementation phase is really how to make the strategies work and to ensure that the movement of the company is consistent with the overall philosophy delineated in the mission statement.

One of the main focuses of a proactive strategy for the environment to be included in the targets set is the establishment of an EMS. Environmental management systems are the major tool used to implement environmental objectives. Although there has been a tendency to overplay the importance of the EMS framework where there has been little actual change in corporate values, the procedure can be a valuable process in the movement towards sustainability both for large and smaller companies.

Having undertaken and completed the process of an environmental review, revised policy aims and written a corporate environmental action plan, the next step towards holistic ecological management is to establish an EMS. Used correctly this exercise can be the most rewarding undertaking for a company dedicated to improving its environmental performance. Used incorrectly it can be just another bureaucratic paper-pushing exercise. An integrated EMS should draw together all aspects of management decision-making and workforce operations with the ethical objectives of the company. The implementation of an EMS is central to any long-term quality commitment.

Although in the long term, investment in ecologically sound measures invariably pays dividends, in the short term a period of initial outlay may be required. Investment demands payback. The establishment of an EMS provides momentum towards gaining competitive advantage by communicating the changes that are being made through an effective green marketing strategy. Sound green marketing (covered more extensively in Chapter 6) requires the customer to be convinced of the green claims that are being made within the marketing campaigns. EMS and their associated standards are one way of validating these claims (Rothery 1995).

Environmental management systems include the Winter Model (see Chapter 4), the British Standard BS 7750, the EU Eco-Management and Audit Scheme (EMAS) and the International Standard ISO 14000 Series on the environment. A number of environmental management programmes preceded these standards; Canada, South Africa, France (X 30-200), Ireland (IS 310), Spain (UNE 77-801) and Finland all have regulations relevant to their national statutory requirements. Here, the focus will be on the BS 7750 and the European-wide system, EMAS. None of the systems demands the attainment of environmental performance levels, although all require companies to satisfy registration requirements, including commitments, where applicable, to reduction of toxic emissions on a continual basis.

BS 7750

In 1992 the British Standards Institution drafted BS 7750, which was derived from the quality standard BS 5750 (ISO 9000), refined through commercial consultation over a two-year period and launched in January 1994 (Figure 5.5). BS 7750 is essentially a means of establishing an EMS in a company, and it meets most of the requirements for registration to the Europe-wide EMAS scheme. Although it is a voluntary scheme and does not demand environmental performance, target setting, dates for change to take place, or open access information, the standard has drawn considerable interest to the commercial–environmental agenda.

Performance measurements are not required and accreditation is achieved through the satisfaction of individual corporate goals. The implication of this is that standards are not actually standardized. The environmental quality achieved could be a poor environmental quality set by a decision-maker within the company as an easily attainable goal. This does not, however, decry the importance of the EMS in the quest for environmental excellence. The concept of the systems approach provides the company with a useful focus for raising environmental standards.

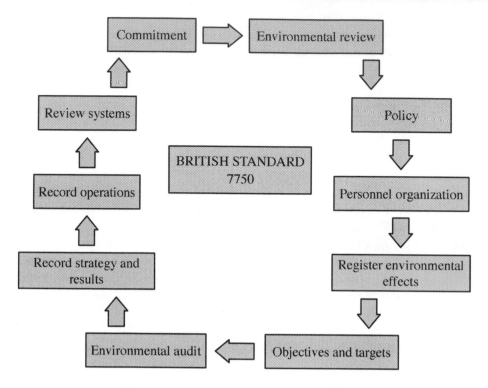

FIGURE 5.5 *BS 7750 (Source: British Standards Institute 1992)*

BS 7750 has a dual function:

1. It provides assurance for the company of appropriate control measures to achieve its defined environmental objectives.
2. It provides a mechanism for public demonstration of this compliance.

The standard is a positive feedback loop control system which includes continuous improvement over time. Development of an environmental policy is based on a thorough emissions and impact review of the company's operations. A cycle of monitoring audits and reviews allows the policy to be continually reassessed. Prepared under the direction of the Environmental and Pollution Standards Committee and piloted in 1992, BS 7750 is accepted to some degree as an initial measure of environmental quality. The BS 7750 was intended to complement the quality standard BS 5750 with which it shares common systems principles.

EMAS

Like BS 7750, the Europe-wide Eco-Management and Audit Scheme (EMAS) recognizes that effective environmental management is an integral part of sound management practices (Figure 5.6). Introduced in April 1995, EMAS is voluntary and is ratified by European law although the administration of the scheme is held by the individual member states.

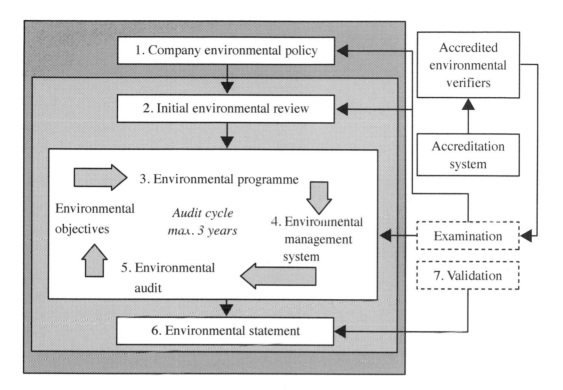

FIGURE 5.6 *EMAS (Source: EMAS: A Practical Guide, and Hillary, 1995)*

EMAS is designed to provide recognition for those companies who have established a programme of positive action to protect the environment, and who seek continuously to improve their performance in this respect.

(DoE 1995)

EMAS was originally an auditing scheme designed to be mandatory for over 50 industrial sectors, requiring companies to undertake an annual environmental audit, the results of which were to be published in the form of a statement (Welford 1995). The standard was then modified to include eco-management principles. The revised EMAS scheme was launched in 1993 (see DoE 1995; Hillary 1995). EMAS requires companies to develop policies and systems on a site-specific basis. It is designed to provide the customer with evidence of an active involvement in environment improvement rather than requiring any compliance to legislation or best practice. Validation of the standard is external and independent.

To gain accreditation, companies are required to publish their strategy for environmental management which must include quantified objectives. It differs from BS 7750 in that information about achievements and audits must be open to public scrutiny although the scheme does not go so far as to demand performance targets. This significant requirement makes the exercise public property and mitigates spurious exercises, increasing the demand for satisfactory performance measurement generation.

The following are questions generally asked in preparation for EMAS registration.

About your product
Can you . . .

- Reduce the material input?

- Select alternative materials with less significant effects on the life-cycle?

- Improve the efficiency and useful life of the product?

- Improve the recyclability of a product?

- Use less or alternative packaging?

- Use more efficient distribution?

About your process
Can you . . .

- Use cleaner technologies which are more efficient in their use of resources?

- Recover and reuse materials, saving on resources, raw materials and energy?

- Recycle materials within the process?

About your use of natural resources
Can you . . .

- Use renewable energy sources?

- Use less damaging fuel sources.

- Recover and reuse energy and water?

- Do more to protect and conserve the natural environment?

- Decontaminate and use surrounding land?

(DoE 1995)

Having considered these preliminary questions companies are required to go through the following seven stages.

Environmental policy
To register with EMAS, companies are required to draw up a company-wide environmental policy. The policy is designed to communicate company intentions to all stakeholders. Including compliance with relevant regulations and a commitment to continuous improvement, the policy has to be adopted at the most senior management level. It is also suggested that the policy is continuously reviewed and reassessed over time as environmental performance within the company changes and as new products and processes are innovated.

Environmental review

The second stage involves a thorough company-wide operational review. This involves measuring and reporting all environmental impacts from the pre-production stage through to distribution. Companies are also expected to list all relevant legislation and identify compliance and non-compliance. The environmental review aims to develop or compile a register of significant environmental effects associated with the site's activities and all the relevant statutory pollution controls with which the site is to comply.

Environmental programme

The programme is ideological and methodological in nature. It is intended to delineate company goals and objectives for the site and then to describe how they are to be satisfied and achieved. The programme flows from the policy and review stages.

Environmental management system

The EMS stage aims to create the management structure within which the environmental programme can be satisfied. For example, management may be given new responsibilities and titles or placed in new groups to attain the objectives. The EMS is the framework which can facilitate regular auditing of company operations and procedures. The system aids the plan of strategies to achieve continual environmental improvement. Procedures and responsibilities are to be clearly defined and delineated. The system normally includes:

■ Training and education programmes.

■ A plan of how targets are to be attained.

■ Evidence that records are being documented.

■ Evidence that environmental effects inventories are in existence.

The last item includes product, external releases, and stock controls as well as legislative requirements. An EMS should also include an explanation of the lines of communication to staff and stakeholders and a timescale for events and for review of the systems. The amount of resources to be dedicated to the task should also be stated. Initial registration under EMAS requires that an environmental review has been undertaken and that an EMS is fully operational.

Environmental audit cycle

This is an extended environmental review flowing from the earlier processes establishing the EMS. The audit is a more detailed measurement of environmental practices and performance. The audit procedure has to be continuous in nature and repeated at least every three years. Practices are compared with policies, incongruity is highlighted and progress assessed.

Environmental statement

The statement is to be written on an annual basis for each site under registration. The statement is to be public property to ensure freedom of information regarding the company's environmental claims. It is on this fundamental issue that EMAS differs from BS 7750. The statement includes information regarding objectives, timescales for achievements (eliminating over-ambitious claims), and environmental impacts being made by the company and management systems being used to overcome them.

Validation

The policy programme, management system, audit procedure and the environmental statement all have to be verified by an independent, accredited verifier at the end of each year (see Case Study 5.2 on Akzo Nobel Chemicals).

CASE STUDY 5.2
EMAS and Akzo Nobel Chemicals

Akzo Nobel Chemicals Limited, Gillingham, UK, is part of the business unit Polymer Chemicals, within the chemicals Group of Akzo Nobel. The site was officially opened as Novadel Ltd in 1938 for the production of white lead, associated paint products and additives for the flour-milling industry.

The 18 acre site on the banks of the River Medway in Kent is one of four major organic peroxide producing locations within the EU operated by Akzo Nobel's Chemical Group; it employs 140 personnel. These are five major manufacturing units, with several minor units producing speciality chemicals including organic peroxides for the plastics and rubber industries and a monomer for the production of an organic glass for the optical industry. The site also serves as a UK distribution centre for other Akzo Nobel products produced outside the UK.

Akzo Nobel is one of the first companies to gain EMAS accreditation in the UK (Registration no. UK-S-0000004) progressing from BS 7750 approval which was independently assessed by Bureau Veritas Quality International Ltd (a *UKAS*-accredited organization—see p. 137). Their objectives (which predate EMAS registration) are as follows.

Environmental objectives 1995

- To meet the 1995 Waste Water Consent limits.

- To reduce Site Energy Consumption by selective energy reduction projects.

- To eliminate landfilled waste from the Perkadox 14 Plant by on-site treatment of the waste water from the process.

- To improve process yields and efficiencies through defined waste minimization projects on the site.

- To register the site to EMAS by the end of 1995.

- To set site housekeeping standard and to set up an audit system to improve standards.

Source: Akzo Nobel Chemicals (1995)

ISO 14000 Series

The Geneva-based International Standards Organization (ISO), the leading developer of voluntary standards for the private sector, is currently developing a range of environmental standards in the form of the ISO 14000 Series. The process which was started in 1990 by the European Standardization Committee (*CEN*) and the ISO was designed to include standards on environmental management and performance including EMS, auditing, labelling, and Life Cycle Assessment (LCA). The plan was to develop over twenty environmental standards, starting with an initial batch of eight. For our purposes three are considered in detail here:

1. **ISO 14001** Environmental Management Systems—Specification with Guidance for Use.
2. **ISO 14004** (previously drafted ISO 14000) Environmental Management Systems—General Guidelines on Principles, Systems, and Supporting Techniques.
3. **ISO 14040** Life Cycle Assessment—General Principles and Practices.

ISO 14001

ISO 14001 is an environmental management standard, available to International Standard countries from late 1996–7 (Figure 5.7). The standard provides most of the necessary management systems element required by EMAS and is designed to supersede BS 7750 (and any other national environmental management systems) in this respect as the accepted route to EMAS accreditation. It is necessary for a company planning on gaining EMAS accreditation to fulfil further additional criteria than the requirements of ISO 14001 (primarily on the reporting side) (Rothery 1995).

The standard has five key points:

1. Environmental policy.
2. Planning—environmental aspects, legal and other requirements, objectives and targets and environmental management programme.
3. Implementation and operation—structure and responsibility, training awareness and competence, communications, environmental documentation, document control, control procedures for routeing operations and emergency preparedness.
4. Checking and corrective action—monitoring and measurement, non-conformance and corrective and preventive action, records, EMS audit.
5. Management review.

(ISO 1995a)

ISO 14004

Recognizing the importance of small and medium-sized enterprises, ISO 14004 is a general introduction and guide to the implementation and maintenance of environmental management systems. It is a practical standard following the format:

■ How to start.

■ Defining a purpose and establishing a plan.

■ Implementation of an EMS.

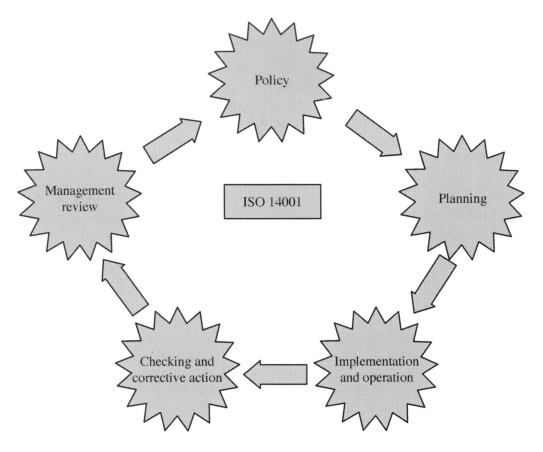

FIGURE 5.7 *ISO 14001—(Source: International Standards Organization 1995a)*

- Measuring and assessing an EMS.
- Reviewing and improving an EMS

(ISO 1995b)

ISO 14040

Containing information on limitations of LCA, goals of the procedures, how to collect data and calculate impact assessments and validate them, ISO 14040 is an attempt to standardize the rapidly expanding and controversial area of Life Cycle Assessments. Although ISO does acknowledge the need to develop alternative and more specific life-cycle standards this is a start to achieve harmonization within a muddy area (ISO 1995c).

ISO—an industrial escape route?

The developments are, however, not without their problems. Developed by industry for industry, there is concern that the standard will supersede other environmental management standards and weaken industry's resolve to respond to the holistic environmental challenge. For example the ISO standard requires companies to comply only with local legislation, again allowing companies a hoop to jump through. If a company is located in a country with undeveloped environmental legislation, the standard could be awarded to a company who would not gain ISO recognition elsewhere in the globe.

Harris Glueckman (1995) argues that the ISO standard has a number of significant failings. It could remove the desire to become accredited to EMAS and can be seen as a sufficient stamp of environmental excellence without touching on many of the Agenda 21 principles agreed at the Earth Summit in Rio 1992. ISO could in theory override the EMAS system, cheapening the price of accepted excellence in the environment. ISO 14001 is a management systems standard, not a reporting standard, therefore, ISO has argued, it should not require open public information flows. It will also not require independent verification, making the standard little more than a self-assessment exercise for industry.

BS 7750 and ISO 14001—the differences
The United Kingdom Accreditation Service (*UKAS*) agreed in principle that BS 7750 accredited organizations could in theory be awarded the ISO 14001 (as it presently stands in draft format) if the following points were taken into account. Although it is clear from UKAS that the ISO 14001 will not be seen as an annex to BS 7750 as it will most probably replace it, this list does highlight some of the central elements of ISO 14001 that are required to be considered.

■ Commitment to 'prevention of pollution' is included in the policy (clause 4.1b).

■ Commitment to 'comply with relevant environmental legislation and regulations, and with other requirements to which the organisation subscribes' is included in the policy (clause 4.1c).

■ The system is designed to take due regard of the requirements for preventive action set out in clause 4.4.2 of ISO 14001.

■ The system is designed to control environmental aspects over which the organization can be expected to have an influence in order to determine those which have or can have significant impacts on the environment (clause 4.2.1).

■ The management review is undertaken by top management (clause 4.5).

■ The EMS audit programme must be based on the environmental performance of the activity concerned (clause 4.4.4).

■ Monitoring and measurement (clause 4.4.1) must also include recording of information to track performance, relevant controls and conformance with the organization's objectives and targets.

■ Monitoring and measurement (clause 4.4.1) must also include establishment and maintenance of a documented procedure for periodically evaluating compliance with relevant environmental legislation and regulations.

■ The system must provide that the organization consider process for external communication on its significant environmental aspects and record its decision (clause 4.3.3).

- Training must include awareness of roles and responsibilities including emergency preparedness and response requirements (clause 4.3.2.c).

- Management representative(s) must have a defined role, responsibilities and authority for reporting on performance of the EMS to top management for review and as a basis for improvement of the EMS (clause 4.3.1).

- Objectives and targets to be consistent with the environmental policy and include the commitment to prevention of pollution (clause 4.2.3).

- Regard must be paid to the concepts as defined (clauses 3.3 and 3.4) of environmental aspects and environmental impacts (see clause 4.2.1).

- The environmental policy must support the organization's intentions and principles in relation to its overall environmental performance which provides a framework for action (clause 3.9).

- The environmental performance to be achieved by the management system must be defined in line with the definition in clause 3.8

SCEEMAS

SCEEMAS is the Small Company Environmental and Energy Management Assistance Scheme in the UK. In most countries the SME sector carries more 'economic weight' than any other sector. Employing the vast majority of people in a developed country, SMEs are the foundation of most international economies. 'In Germany they produce just over half the net economic output, employ two thirds of all workers and train more than 80 per cent of all new employees.' (Davis 1992: 54). With an economic input as large as this, sustainability cannot be considered plausible without the heavy involvement of the SME sector owner managers. Because of their shorter lines of managerial communication and flexibility within niche markets, SMEs are in fact ideally placed to adopt the environmental agenda. The main obstacles to involvement include time, cost and motivation from lack of information flows (Hutchinson and Hutchinson 1995). It is clear, however, that some sort of response is required from the SME sector if sustainability is to be achieved.

On the whole, SMEs have been slow to become involved in strategic eco-management. In general they require easily accessible, cheap, practical advice on how to improve environmental performance without severely affecting their bottom line. This information has not been readily available to date. Additionally, heavy capital investments are not generally feasible to the small company with limited resources. The key to inducing SME involvement therefore is labour involvement. Staff training and education is essential if the SME sector is to become more involved in the move towards sustainability.

Although recognized by the UK Advisory Committee on Business and the Environment (ACBE 1993) as an essential and underestimated industrial sector in the environmental debate, no real concrete incentives designed specifically for the distinctive nature of the sector were developed until SCEEMAS.

The SCEEMAS initiative is the first large-scale attempt within Europe to include the SME sector in eco-management. Launched in the winter of 1995, SCEEMAS is an attempt to make the EU EMAS scheme accessible to the small and medium-sized enterprise sector and is complementary to BS 7750. Grants available from the UK Department of the Environment (DoE) help meet the costs of implementing an EMS. Assistance is targeted to firms with up to 250 employees within Great Britain (Northern Ireland operates the Environmental Audit Scheme) and they are also restricted to the industrial activities delineated by EMAS Regulation no. 1836/93 (manufacturing, power generation, recycling and waste disposal). It is to be open to SMEs with more than one site. Grants of up to 50 per cent are to be made available for consultancy advice only; equipment costs do not qualify.

SCEEMAS assistance covers three main areas, as follows.

Environmental review, policy and programme
This covers the work that a firm needs to undertake in order to establish a register of the significant environmental effects associated with the site's activities and all the relevant statutory pollution controls with which the site must comply; identify the scope for savings and improvements; initiate a site programme and introduce an EMS or adapt an existing management system. This work attracts a 40 per cent grant.

Establish an environmental management system
Firms may need outside help in establishing or modifying an EMS tailored to the requirements of the site and operations which conform to the requirements of EMAS and/or BS 7750. This work also attracts a 40 per cent grant. Case Study 5.3 describes the work of a commercial environmental consultancy, ACER Environmental.

Publication of an environmental statement
To register under SCEEMAS the firm must establish an appropriate mechanism for reporting their progress and achievements (i.e. policies, audit results and management system proce-dures, etc.). The company should make these findings publicly available as well as ensure that they are consistent with the requirements of EMAS. Registration triggers not only the payment of the full 50 per cent grant on this stage but also the balance from any previous stages to produce an overall grant of 50 per cent consultancy costs (Thomas 1995).

On a global scale, initiatives of the SCEEMAS type make available essential support to enable SMEs to respond to the environmental challenge.

BS 7750, EMAS, ISO 14001 and SCEEMAS registration

Reasons for registration
It is advantageous to register for one of the above-named schemes for the following reasons:

■ Market-place advantages.

■ Improved stakeholder relations.

CASE STUDY 5.3
ACER ENVIRONMENTAL

ACER Environmental, a commercial environmental consultancy which is a wholly owned subsidiary of Welsh Water plc, was awarded a European Commission contract to assist small and medium-sized enterprises to implement EMAS. Formally launched in Wales in July 1995 the initial project was to last 18 months. The Commission provides half the cost of running the scheme and ACER provide the professional consultancy for the participants to prepare EMS and assisted self-reviews. The cost to each company is approximately £500 and includes:

- A step-by-step workbook produced by Coopers and Lybrand Deloitte.

- Supplementary information packs containing information on what is required for the scheme, the timetable, and EMS case studies.

- Five interactive workshop sessions to include details of the requirements of EMAS, with practical examples.

- Full consultancy support for progress reporting as the project evolves.

- Company site review undertaken by the consultants which will provide unbiased accounts of environmental performance at each site.

- A telephone helpline service operated by the consultants.

Source: ACER Environmental (1995)

- Financial benefits.

- Waste minimization.

- New product developments.

- Litigation mitigation.

- Insurance hedging.

- Lower clean-up costs.

- Reduced transport, storage and packaging costs.

- Improved staff working conditions and higher productivity.

- Quality management attainment.

Reasons against registration
Inevitably, there may be a number of drawbacks to registration. These can include:

- Time.

- Cost.

- Lack of available resources.

- Lack of interest.

Environmental management systems accreditation—UK

As a result of a merger between two accreditation bodies, the United Kingdom Accreditation Service (UKAS) was established on 1 August 1995. It accredits independent third party certification bodies in the fields of calibration and testing laboratories, product, personnel and quality systems certification as well as certification of environmental management systems and of the environmental verifiers for EMAS.

Accredited bodies (to date: italicized names are EMAS accredited)

- Aspects Certification Services Ltd.

- British Approvals Service for Electric Cables.

- *British Standards Institution.*

- *Bureau Veritas Quality International Ltd.*

- Construction Quality Assurance Ltd.

- Det Norske Veritas Quality Assurance Ltd.

- Electricity Association Quality Assurance Ltd.

- Intertek Services Corporation.

- Japan Audit and Certification Organization for Environment.

- *Lloyd's Register Quality Assurance Ltd.*

- Professional Environmental & Caring Services (QA) Ltd.

- *SGS Yarsley International Certification Services Ltd.*

- *TRADA Certification Ltd.*

SUMMARY

Effective eco-management requires a well-considered strategic response. This includes the development and implementation of an initial environmental review, an environmental action plan, an environmental review, a policy statement document and the implementation of an environmental management system. The initial 'visionary projection' is followed by analysis of the internal pressures for and against adopting an eco-friendly strategy (SWOT), together with consideration of the external pressures (PESTE). Review of the results of this process enables a set of objectives to be drawn up. Following from this, appropriate strategies are devised. These can then be implemented in the final stage of the process.

Chapter 5 has covered the details of each of these stages and has included brief descriptions of the major management and auditing regulations available to organizations in the UK. Strategic plans require consolidation in the form of associated operational procedures. It is through the design and implementation of strategic plans that corporate value changes occur through active staff involvement in the sustainable agenda. It is towards those operational initiatives we turn in Chapter 6.

QUESTIONS

5.1 Outline the strengths and weaknesses of voluntary environmental management schemes such as BS 7750, EMAS and ISO 14001.

5.2 Critically assess B&Q's environmental policy (Case Study 5.1).

5.3 Drawing upon material from Case Study 5.3 on ACER Environmental, discuss the case for and against SCEEMAS registration.

BIBLIOGRAPHY

Key texts

Davis J. (1991) *Greening Business*, Blackwell, Oxford
This is a well-argued, intuitive book that approaches the greening of business from a holistic angle within the broad context of sustainable development.

Taylor, B., Hutchinson, C., Pollack, S. and Tapper, R. (eds) (1994) *Environmental Management Handbook*, Pitman, London
This text covers real case studies and offers practical advice on how to improve environmental performance.

Welford, R. and Gouldson, A. (1993) *Environmental Management and Business Strategy*, Pitman, London
This text is easy to read, clear and definitive for the UK context on strategy and environmental management.

References and further reading
ACBE (1993) *Advisory Committee on Business and the Environment: Third Progress Report*, DTI and DoE, London
Acer Environmental (1995) *Environmental Management Audit and Risk Capability Profile*. Beacon House, William Brown Close, Llantarnam Park, Cwmbran, Gwent, NP44 3AB, UK.
Akzo Nobel Chemicals (1995) Environmental Report, Gillingham Site, Pier Road, Gillingham, Kent, ME7 1RL, UK.

Ansoff, I. (1965) *Corporate Strategy*, McGraw-Hill, New York.

B&Q, Portswood House, 1 Hampshire Corporate Park, Chandlers Ford, Eastleigh, Hants, SO5 3YX, UK.

British Standards Institute (BSI) (1992) *British Standard 7750* HMSO.

Business in the Environment (BiE) (1990) *Your Business and the Environment: An Executive Guide*, 8 Stratton Street, London, W1X 6AH.

Chandler, A. (1995) *Strategy and Structure*, reprinted in J. Stoner, R. Freeman and D. Gilbert (eds) *Management*, 6th edn, Prentice Hall, Englewood Cliffs, NJ.

Davis, T. (1992), *Towards a Business Implementation of Agenda 21—Guest editorial*, The Centre for our Common Future, August/September, INEM main Secretariat, Bahnhofstrasse 36, D-22880 Wedel (Holstein) Germany.

Department of the Environment (DoE) (1995) *Eco-Management and Audit Scheme: An Introductory Guide for Industry*, DoE, HMSO, London.

Fannin, W. and Rodrigues, A. (1986) 'National or Global? Control V Flexibility', *Long Range Planning* 19(5).

Gaylor, J. and Young, J. (1994) *Going Green the Easy Way*, Payback publishing, Plymouth, UK.

Glueckman, H. (1995) *ISO 14000: An Uncommon Perspective*, European Environment Bureau (*EEB*), Benchmark, Brussels.

Hillary, H. (1995) 'EMAS: A Practical Guide', in DoE, *Eco-Management and Audit Scheme*, DoE, London.

Hutchinson, A. and Hutchinson, F. (1995) 'Sustainable Regeneration of the UK's SME Sector: Some Implications of SME Response to BS 7750'. *Greener Management International* 9: 73–84.

International Standards Organization (ISO) (1995a) *ISO 14001 Draft—Environmental Management Systems—Specification with Guidance for Use*, BSI (cash office), Lynford Wood, Milton Keynes, MK14 6LE, UK.

———(1995b) *ISO 14004 Draft—Environmental Management Systems—General Guidelines on Principles, Systems, and Supporting Techniques*, BSI (cash office), Lynford Wood, Milton Keynes, MK14 6LE, UK.

———(1995c) *ISO 14040 Draft—Life Cycle Assessment—General Principles and Practices*, BSI (cash office), Lynford Wood, Milton Keynes, MK14 6LE, UK.

Jauch, L. and Glueck, W. (1988) *Business Policy and Strategic Management*, 5th edn, McGraw-Hill, Maidenhead.

Johnson, G. and Scholes, K. (1989) *Exploring Corporate Strategy*, Prentice Hall, Englewood Cliffs, NJ.

Porter, M. (1985) *Competitive Strategy and Competitive Advantage*, The Free Press, New York.

Richards, M. (1978) *Organisational Goal Structure*, reprinted in G. Johnson and K. Scholes (1989) *Exploring Corporate Strategy*, Prentice Hall, Cambridge.

Rothery, B. (1995) *ISO 14000 and ISO 9000*, Gower, Basingstoke, Hampshire.

Slater, J. (1992) *Directors' Guide to Environmental Issues*, Director Books, Hemel Hempstead.

Smith, D. (1992) 'Strategic Management and the Business Environment: What Lies Behind the Rhetoric of Greening?', *Business Strategy and the Environment* 1(1): 1–9.

Thomas, C. (1995) *Small Company Environmental and Energy Management Assistance Scheme—Sceemas*, The UK Competent Body for the EC ECO-Management and Audit Scheme, unpublished.

Waterman, R., Peters, T. and Philips, J. (1980) 'Structure is not Organization', *Business Horizons* June: 14–26.

Welford, R. (1995) *Environmental Strategy and Sustainable Development: The Corporate Challenge for the 21st Century*, Routledge, London.

Welford, R. and Gouldson, A. (1993) *Environmental Management and Business Strategy*, Pitman, London.

Wheatley, M. (1993) *Green Business: Making it Work for your Company*, Pitman, London.

CHAPTER 6

ENVIRONMENTAL OPERATIONS MANAGEMENT

Cleanliness is indeed next to godliness.

(John Wesley 1703–91)

INTRODUCTION

The next step for business and industry, one year after the Rio Earth Summit, is to operationalise their role towards achieving Sustainable Development by creating an Industrial Agenda 21, which includes quantifiable and measurable objectives.

(International Network for Environmental Management (*INEM*) 1993)

Chapter 6 covers the operational processes involved in eco-management. Practical examples of energy efficiency, waste minimization, environmental impact assessments (EIAs), eco-auditing procedures, Life Cycle Assessment (LCA), supply chain management, green marketing and the range of tools available to implement environmentally sound strategies are assessed, using case study examples to illustrate the concepts.

ENVIRONMENTAL AND ECOLOGICAL AUDITING

The environmental audit has evolved from regulatory and customer pressure to quantify, analyse, measure and disclose a company's environmental performance. It provides an in-depth procedural analysis of performance measurements and targets, offering a management approach to deal strategically with environmental issues primarily as a means to meet legislative requirements. Environmental auditing can be defined as

the evaluation of a site, plant, or production and processing system in relation to the laws, regulations, policies and good practices that directly or indirectly affect the environment. It is used to compile and report all pertinent information related to the environment, as well as occupational health and safety where appropriate.

(Cockburn 1990: 52–4)

Ecological auditing extends the remit. The Elmwood Institute argues that the task of the eco-audit 'is not only to verify compliance with fixed standards but also to minimise environmental impact' (Callenbach *et al.* 1993: 26–7). The degree to which this strategy is successful is dependent upon the extent to which the auditors can balance economic and ecological goals. Eco-audits attempt to consider environmental performance from a holistic angle. Rather than viewing green issues as purely a risk management issue, ecological auditing measures and analyses all aspects of company policy and operations with respect to their environmental impact and consequences.

The environmental auditing procedure is an integral part of implementing an EMS. Audits can be:

- Process specific (i.e. covering one particular aspect of production).

- Product specific.

- Issue based (i.e. on health and safety or compliance to legislation) or cover one particular environmental concern like energy or waste management.

There are a number of different approaches to audits: one can undertake a product audit covering all environmental impacts of the product, process audits that look specifically at the environmental impact of the production process, and issue audits which cover specific issues in isolation (e.g. health and safety, legislative compliance or investments). The eco-auditing procedure, however, extends the parameters to include environmental impact measurements for the local community and implications for all stakeholders of the company. The eco-audit is holistic in nature and covers all of the aspects of possible environmental impact within a company. This chapter will, therefore, explain the process of the eco-audit under the following headings:

- Site history.

- Production process.

- Product and communications.

- External environment.

Environmental transport strategies are also briefly introduced as they are becoming an increasingly dominant factor in the move to environmental sustainability.

SITE HISTORY

The first step is to acquire a clear understanding of where the company has come from and what activities have been undertaken on the site under review. The normal procedure is to conduct an environmental impact assessment (EIA) on the site. This process is usually undertaken when a company buys new land to meet conditions for insurance cover against future environmental litigation or health and safety risks arising from previous activities on the site.

Environmental impact assessment

EIAs are also undertaken when a company wants to extend or modify its existing production processes. The EIA assesses all significant direct and indirect environmental effects on the surrounding environment as well as any possible socio-economic impacts that may accrue.

An EIA is a systematic gathering of all relevant quantitative and qualitative information by experts in consultation with informed parties in order to enable informed decision-making to occur. The process includes a wide-ranging consultation process with statutory and non-statutory institutions in order to understand all implications of expansion or purchase, and to assess the benefits or drawbacks of any mitigating measures proposed. When undertaken by an independent third party, the process gains credibility and provides excellent information for the auditing team to use to begin an eco audit on site. (Case Study 6.1 describes an EIA carried out by SGS Environment for Severn Trent Water Ltd.)

Slater (1992) suggests that the following four points should be included in the final EIA statement:

1. The description of the development, local environment and local baseline conditions.
2. The identification and evaluation of the impacts.
3. Alternative solutions, proposals and mitigation of impacts.
4. The communication of results, developmental consequences, end-product effects.

PRODUCTION PROCESS

Energy

> Energy is the lifeblood of industry and we need to use it wisely.
>
> (European Round Table of Industrialists 1992: 13)

Although in some areas the green agenda and the corporate agenda have been a marriage of convenience where domestic dispute has been rife, the energy efficiency debate has not been one of them. Energy efficiency has been pinpointed by environmentalists as a key area where the green agenda of saving the earth's resources, and the business agenda driven by financial cost reduction, overlap. A more efficient use of energy reduces corporate costs and minimizes raw material depletion. This section considers energy efficiency from the perspective of a company undertaking an eco-audit and attempting to minimize its environmental impact. An environmentally sound energy policy requires minimization of energy usage coupled with selection of the most environmentally appropriate energy source. Energy generated from renewable resources, such as wind power, is ecologically sounder than energy derived from a non-renewable fossil fuel source. It generates less pollution and minimizes resource depletion.

Energy usage

Implementing a well-designed energy efficiency programme remains the most effective way of reducing CO_2 emissions and saving energy. Although the European chemical industry reduced its average consumption of energy per tonne of product by 35 per cent from 1974 to

CASE STUDY 6.1
SGS Environment EIA of Severn Trent Water

SGS Environment was commissioned by Severn Trent Water Ltd to undertake an EIA for a proposed replacement Sludge Destruction Plant at Coleshill, North Warwickshire, UK. SGS Environment is an independent environmental research and consultancy company which was responsible for the preparation of the Environmental Statement.

The Environmental Statement which was to accompany Severn Trent Water's planning application was to be voluntarily submitted to inform the planning authority of any possible environmental effects which may arise from the development of a replacement sewage sludge incinerator. The aim was to avoid adverse environmental effects at the design stage.

Consultations were undertaken with a wide range of statutory and non-statutory consultees to obtain a range of diverse views on the development. Consultation with statutory authorities included:

- Her Majesty's Inspectorate of Pollution (HMIP).
- English Nature.
- Countryside Commission.
- Warwick County Council.
- North Warwickshire Borough Council.

After undertaking a baseline assessment, a full air quality assessment exercise (which included the implementation of the stringent German air quality standards) and a risk assessment (which included accident scenarios for failure of the gas cleaning system and power failures) were all carried out. The following impact areas were considered:

- Landscape and visual amenity.
- Water quality: effluent emissions and effects on river and groundwater quality.
- Air quality and dust: emissions to the atmosphere and effects arising from changes in air quality.
- Noise from the incinerator.
- Solid waste disposal effects.
- Traffic generated by the project.
- Ecology.
- Socio-economic factors.

Landscape and visual amenity

The landscape and visual amenity assessment covered the replacement of the existing 92 m stack with two 40 m stacks which would significantly improve the visual quality of the site as well as the development of a new, lower incinerator. The Severn Trent Water Ltd (STWL) plans were for the temperature plume to be controlled and made visible 5 per cent of the time. This was considered acceptable by all parties to the consultations. The assessment also covered landscaping including screen planting to reduce visual and landscape effects, because the planning authority required the new buildings to blend into the existing landscape.

Water quality

Liquid effluents were to be treated in a waste water treatment plant before transfer to the Minworth sewage works. The EIA found that there would be no significant changes to recent effluent discharge rates from Minworth sewage works.

Air quality and dust

The adoption of stringent standards for emissions to the atmosphere from the incineration plant stack, and the design of the 40 m stack, were agreed with HMIP. An agreed requirement was for a scheme of monitoring these emissions, to be agreed with the county planning authority. The assessment found that emissions from the new incinerator would be less than the existing one. Hence improving air quality in the locality would improve over the long term, once initial increased dust levels from the demolition work had subsided.

Noise from the incinerator

Work hours were to be agreed with the local planning authority, bringing noise level pollution in line with BS 4142 and BS 5228 noise requirements. Before the incinerator building was to be used for the treatment of sewage sludge, the building was to be enclosed with sound insulating materials in accordance with the county planning authority regulations. Noise level monitoring was required to be undertaken during construction and operation of the project. The assessment concluded that it was unlikely that any noise nuisance would occur due to the isolated nature of the site. The replacement incinerator was expected to be quieter than the existing one and noise levels were expected to be below ambient levels.

Solid waste disposal effects

The ash generated would contain heavy metals and would therefore need to be deposited in an appropriately licensed landfill site. Liquid wastes were to be treated in an industrial water treatment plant prior to input to Minworth. It was concluded that there would be no change to effluent quality.

Traffic generated by the project

The project would incur a maximum increase of 15–20 vehicles per weekday during the 22-month construction period. During the operation of the project, the expected increase was one heavy goods vehicle (*HGV*) per week to transport ash to landfill. This was seen as environmentally insignificant.

Ecology

The development would have no significant impact on local Sites of Special Scientific Interest (*SSSIs*) which lay in the maximum zone of impact identified by the air modelling procedure. Indeed it was concluded that as air quality in the local area was to be improved through the development, the project would have positive impacts on the ecology of the surrounding area.

Socio-economic factors

Although the new plant would lead to a reduction in STWL staff numbers, it would not involve compulsory redundancies.

On the basis of the information provided by the EIA, an environmental statement was submitted to the county planning authority by STWL.

Source: Kevin Leather, SGS Environment

1989, significantly reducing CO_2, and the European cement industry reduced its fuel consumption by 35 per cent between 1960 and 1990, reducing CO_2 emissions by 20 per cent, there is still a major global catastrophe looming from the expulsion of carbon gases in the form of the greenhouse effect. Each individual company can undertake an energy audit, reduce its costs and mitigate its overall environmental effects.

An energy audit measures the usage of energy including the potential for reduction. There are a number of ways a company can reduce its energy usage:

- Thermostats and controls can be introduced to use energy more conservatively.
- More efficient lighting systems can be installed by using low energy light bulbs.
- Simple staff training can inform and educate regarding energy usage.
- Heat recovery devices can be installed into ventilation systems.

Industry has a considerable role to play in the reduction of CO_2. Industry needs, therefore, to:

- Improve its energy management by minimizing fuel and material inputs.
- Innovate in research and development with the aim of investing in newly developed equipment with lower environmental impacts.
- Develop products which will use less energy in the production process, e.g. solar powered insulation materials, cars with electric motors and thermal engines and compact fluorescent lamps.

Case Study 6.2 gives examples of municipal energy efficiency measures in Germany and the USA.

CASE STUDY 6.2
Innovative Municipal Finance: Some Examples

A number of municipalities across the globe have noted that energy efficiency measures can reduce pollution and energy use. These measures can save money, attract private finance capital and be largely self-financing. Pioneering co-operative schemes of this type indicate directions of progress towards sustainability on a multisectoral basis.

Solar Rooftop Programme

The German city of Saarbrücken has instigated a programme to install solar voltaic cells of 1 megawatt on the rooftops of all buildings. The cells are expensive. Therefore the scheme was introduced in two stages.

1. A loan programme was set up with local savings banks for home owners to introduce energy efficiency measures at low rates of interest.
2. As the savings from energy efficiency exceeded loan payments, the scheme was extended to cover the higher costs of the solar cells, with a small government subsidy.

The scheme aided a new local solar cell industry while reducing greenhouse gas emissions.

School Energy Bank Programme

A scheme in Iowa, USA, instituted by the Iowa Department of Natural Resources in the late 1980s, was designed to install energy management improvements in all public and non-profit facilities by 1995. Iowa's 3500 schools were targeted as the first part of the programme. The department identifies the improvements, the school district costs them, and private banks provide the finance through a 'lease purchase' mechanism. The scheme creates jobs while saving energy costs, which are ploughed back into the local economy.

Source: International Council for Local Environmental Initiatives (*ICLEI*) (1995)
***Cities for Climate Protection Newsletter*, 1, March.**

Energy can also be saved by employing an effective recycling system. If a company recycles its materials effectively it can reduce the use of energy significantly and satisfy its ethical objectives. British Steel for example operates a recycling scheme that is estimated to include the recycling of approximately 1 billion cans a year, saving more than 12 million gallons of oil in the production process.

Since 1973 industrialized countries have achieved:

■ About 25 per cent less energy consumption per unit of industrial production.

■ From 30 to 75 per cent saving in the heating of new houses and buildings.

- Increase in the energy efficiency of domestic appliances.

- Improvement in energy efficiency of vehicle engines.

- Almost 50 per cent less fuel per passenger kilometre used by aircraft.

(European Round Table of Industrialists 1992)

Case Study 6.3 gives examples of energy efficiency measures by international companies.

CASE STUDY 6.3
Energy Efficiency Measures: Some Examples

Energy efficiency is one environmental area capable of yielding large paybacks from investments. It is in the interest of the environment, the company and its stakeholders that energy use is minimized and efficiency gains achieved. Increasingly, large companies have started to invest in energy efficiency measures to achieve any possible cost savings and to satisfy the growing legislative and stakeholder pressures to be green.

Hoffmann-La Roche

Hoffmann-La Roche decided to invest 340 million *ECU* (542 million Swiss Francs) amounting to 3.8 per cent of its sales, on safety and environmental protection in 1993. A part of the programme involved the conversion of the use of coal to natural gas to cut CO_2 emissions and eliminate sulphur dioxide emissions.

ICI

The ICI group records a 12 per cent improvement in energy efficiency 1990–3 and over the same period a real 18 per cent reduction in energy used. Between 1980 and 1990 the oil industry in the EU achieved an underlying 30 per cent improvement in refinery energy efficiency through energy conservation investments.

Pilkington

Pilkington has saved over 30 per cent of its energy use since 1970 by insulating its furnaces. Some of the more progressive companies in Europe have recognized the challenge to business survival coming from the environmental lobby and have begun to build their site units well ahead of current legislation.

Pirelli

Pirelli has established a co-generation plant which produces electricity and steam for tyre curing and domestic heating. The plant is fuelled by natural gas and CO_2 emissions are, therefore, minimal. A holistic energy efficiency strategy will include investment not only in new technology but also in new capital equipment

Source: European Round Table of Industrialists (1994)

Renewable energy sources

Renewable energy is energy which occurs naturally and repeatedly in the environment and can be harnessed for human use without depleting precious, finite resources. Sources include the sun, waves, wind, wood, straw and waste (Yorkshire Environmental Project BWEA 1995: 1). The Montreal Protocol committed world industry and political leaders to stabilizing CO_2 emissions at 1990 levels by the year 2000. Alternative sources of energy supply have been earmarked for technological development and research because the majority of CO_2 emissions emanate from fossil fuels burning to create electricity. The conventional sources of energy include coal, oil, gas and nuclear power. In the UK the target set by the Major government is that 5 per cent of the country's electricity be generated by renewable sources by the year 2000.

Waste minimization

Waste minimization has been subject to a whole host of international interest in terms of legislation and regulation since the mid-1980s. The UK government ended 1995 by introducing financial measures to encourage environmental responsibility including a landfill tax and grants for SME environmental improvements. The government also released its White Paper called *Making Waste Work* (Department of Environment 1995) laying out its strategy for sustainable development and setting targets for waste control, recovery and recycling. This is on top of the waste regulations within the Duty of Care part of the Environmental Protection Act 1990. Pressures to develop an integrated waste management strategy in business are stronger today than they have ever been and, if legislation is anything to go by, these pressures are more likely to increase significantly over the next few years than to diminish.

There are two central waste strategies that companies can adopt in their pursuit of a green waste minimization. The first is to deal with the waste after it has been generated and to mitigate its effects on the environment. The second is to minimize the amount of waste generated in the first place, thereby reducing the amount of mitigation required at the end of the pipe.

Once waste has been generated it cannot be destroyed without some environmental impact. Waste has to be recycled, diluted, dispersed or dumped, all of which have a deleterious effect on ecosystems. The cost of waste treatment to the environment and to industry in many cases makes the whole process of waste management a costly exercise. The optimum waste management strategy is, therefore, waste minimization at source.

Waste can be prevented by a reduction at source, product changes, and on-site recycling of waste and material recovery. There are to date many examples of proactive companies who have reaped the benefits of a well-managed waste minimization strategy. For example, 3M, with its 'Pollution Prevention Pays' programme, was one of the first major companies to recognize the advantages of environmental protection measures (see Case Study 3.1).

After 15 years the programme is estimated to prevent annually the production of 126,000 tonnes of air pollutants, 16,000 tonnes of sludge, 6,600,000 litres of wastewater and

409,000 tonnes of solid and hazardous waste plus an energy saving equivalent of 210,000 barrels of oil. During the period 1975–1990 the programme has saved the company $506,000,000.

(Edwards 1995: 3)

Cost savings on this scale are incentive enough to consider an integrated waste management strategy. However, companies are often slow to appreciate the potential benefits and savings that can accrue from an integrated waste management strategy.

Site operations
Companies interested in waste minimization usually begin by asking a few generalized questions regarding site operations. This gives the senior management some initial information from which to judge the necessity for a waste minimization strategy. Questions will reflect the following sentiments:

1. Do you know how much waste you produce and what it consists of?
2. Do you know what happens to your waste and how it is treated?
3. Could you reuse or recycle any of your waste?
4. Do you keep careful records of your waste?

Having generated some initial information, senior management is now in a position to establish a full waste minimization strategy. The following strategy is based on information from the March Consulting Group (1994) which was developed as a result of the research in the Aire and Calder Project (see Case Studies 4.4 and 4.6).

A waste minimization strategy
The strategy (Figure 6.1) involves six stages.

Commitment to action
Companies need to have a policy commitment to waste minimization, senior management support, clear objectives and a strategy with targets and timescales.

Organization for action
Organization for action covers the need for the establishment of a multidisciplinary team, appropriately trained, led by the project champion and reporting to senior management. The production staff should be involved at the outset.

Audit and review
The waste audit involves a review of process and ensuring that there are comprehensive and up-to-date process diagrams. Waste streams have to be identified and quantified with accurate baselines determined. There needs to be a good understanding of site utilities—the consumption costs of water, electricity and other fuels plus waste generation and disposal costs. Examination of the site, storage areas and foul surface water drainage systems, air pollution and noise mitigation with the production of good plans is essential for assessing the reduction of risk. Past and present compliance with environmental regulations should also be reviewed.

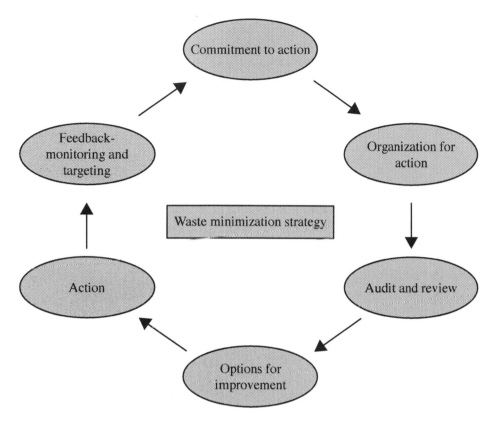

FIGURE 6.1 *A waste minimization strategy*

Options for improvement
Options should be costed and prioritized. Some may involve simple procedural changes and good housekeeping while others require capital investment and/or research and development.

Action
This covers the implementation of the programme of changes with the setting of targets and timescales.

Feedback—monitoring and targeting
Review of the results of the changes and the identification of further opportunities. Waste minimization is a journey rather than a destination with monitoring and targeting being a feedback loop for continually assessing performance.

What are the benefits of a waste minimization strategy?
The Dutch PRISMA (Project Industrial Successes with Waste Production), which ran from 1988 to 1990, involved 10 companies in the Netherlands. Like the Aire and Calder Project, PRISMA has set a high level of expectancy for a number of follow-up demonstration projects within the UK. These projects seek to build on the weighty body of research supporting the development of integrated waste management strategies on a regional level. Projects include

Project Catalyst in the Mersey catchment area (Atkins *et al.* 1994) as well as one project based in Leicestershire (see Case Study 6.4). Although the implementation of an effective strategy like the Aire and Calder Project can be expected to lead to cost savings in the traditional sense, the payback period may occasionally be longer term. However, even where financial returns are not immediate, most waste minimization exercises are as cost-effective as treatment or disposal. The dividends of a prevention strategy as opposed to an end-of-pipe approach to waste management are summarized in a report (Department of Trade and Industry 1992).

Reduced

- Production costs.

- On-site waste monitoring and treatment costs.

- Handling, transport and off-site treatment costs.

- Raw material costs.

- Energy and water costs and consumption.

- Long-term environmental liability and insurance costs.

- Risk of spills and accidents.

Improved

- Operational efficiency.

- Income through the sale of reusable waste.

- Safety.

- Company image in the eyes of shareholders and other stakeholders.

(DTI 1992)

No products are totally environmentally friendly, since all productive processes have some impact on the environment. This leads some environmentalists to the conclusion that the only truly green business is no business at all. Nevertheless, it is possible to assess the life cycle of any product in order to reduce its impact on the environment reduced. To make an informed and rational decision regarding waste levels and impacts on the innovation of new technologies, and the implementation of new ecological management practices, companies require an evaluation of the impact of their products on the environment. To this end, a Life Cycle Assessment (LCA) can be undertaken.

Life Cycle Assessment
The LCA, commonly referred to as 'cradle-to-grave' assessment, examines all aspects of environmental impacts associated with the life of a product from the extraction of the raw materials through the pre-production process to the distribution and final disposal.

Central to the understanding of LCA is the realization that production is cyclical in nature. Raw materials are taken from the earth, processed, used and returned to the earth as waste. Although materials may be returned to the production process as recycled/reused materials, this merely delays final disposal. LCA measures the continual process of extraction, use, disposal and extraction. Although the final stage of the LCA appears difficult to regulate due to consumer disposal decision-making apparently being beyond the jurisdiction of the company, companies may educate consumers to recycle or reuse products and gain a higher 'green' profile in the process.

LCA analyses all environmental impacts related to product development and permits the comparative analysis of the environmental impacts of similar products. The assessment is of the product rather than the system, as in EMS, but does include the impacts of the processes involved, such as energy usage. Due to the holistic nature of the assessment from cradle-to-grave, LCA can not be restrained to just one site or indeed to one company. It requires significant co-operation down the supply chain to produce a product LCA.

LCA has been described as 'a tool which can more directly measure progress towards sustainability' (Welford 1995: 101). The LCA process brings issues of futurity and equity into the product design process. As designers seek to minimize long-term environmental impacts, the design process itself comes under the spotlight. Since the vast majority of environmental implications flow causally from the initial product choice, the issue of product choice has implications for sustainability.

Essentially a tool by which companies can assess the environmental impact of the product, LCA is an integral part of an ecological auditing procedure. The LCA is used as the framework for the EU *eco-labelling* scheme, providing an objective measurement of product impact. LCA often leads to the redesign of products to reduce environmental impact, and provides a systematic framework for impact analysis and the continual updating of procedures. As LCA has developed as a procedure it has gained credibility.

There are three main stages of LCA, as developed by LCA practitioners at the Society of Toxicology and Chemistry in Vermont 1990 (Faur *et al.* 1991).

1. Life cycle inventory (or data collection).
2. Impact assessment (or environmental evaluation).
3. Improvement analysis (or company response).

Following the initial initiation phase where objectives are established and project targets set, the process moves on to the inventory phase.

1. **Inventory phase** Provides a detailed picture of the raw material and energy inputs used by a system—and of the solid, liquid and gaseous wastes produced as outputs.
2. **Impact assessment phase** Involves linking inventoried inputs and outputs to real-world environmental problems. This phase includes classification of problems, characterization and valuation of their impacts.

3. **Improvement phase** Focuses on changes to the system to improve its overall environmental performance and flows from the valuation phase of the LCA process.

(**Business in the Environment** *et al.* **1994: 20–1**)

Although one could run each stage sequentially, independent of each previous stage, it is more usual for the LCA programme to run all three of the phases together due to the iterative nature of the process.

A typical LCA covers the following areas:

- Raw material sources.

- Transport.

- Energy.

- Production.

- Usage and disposal.

Environmental impact assessments are integral to each stage of the LCA, and have significant implications for the supply chain. Once a company begins to consider the LCA implications for its products or services, its suppliers will be subject to increased scrutiny. If less environmentally damaging raw material sources or energy sources can be found, companies will turn to alternative sources of supply.

Raw material sources

An initial question facing the proactive company of the twenty-first century relates to the supply of raw materials. Are they taken from renewable sources? If they are not, are there possibilities for alternative raw material sourcings that will allow the production of the product to be sustainably maintained? For example, B&Q's policy decision to source its timber from managed renewable supplies by the end of 1995 rules out timber industry suppliers taking timber from non-renewable sources (see Case Study 5.1).

It is equally important to consider the impact that the raw materials used have on the environment, in order to assess any long-term detrimental environmental impact. Initially, companies have found this a difficult area to assess, since in many cases extraction is far removed from the production process. For example, a carpenter who uses varnish on completed woodwork may be unaware of the impact that the extraction of the oil had on the environment. However, it has become increasingly necessary to check sources of supply as supply chain pressure has been adopted by an increasing number of major companies.

Transport

Transport is covered in more detail in Chapter 12; however, there are LCA implications. Transport has two major environmental aspects attached to it in LCA terms: energy used and emissions produced. An effective LCA analyses these two elements and assesses the implications of alternatives for the overall environmental impact of the product. There are clear macro-policy determinants attached to this area of LCA. If government ideology is committed to reducing carbon emissions, rail and water transportation will be encouraged and long-distance road haulage penalized. If this is the case, the incentive to reduce road transport may have a strong bearing on company strategies. Legislation may take the form of resource taxes, making a significant impact on company policy regarding transportation. The more legislation attempts to regulate carbon emissions the more companies are likely to consider alternative forms of transportation.

Energy

Every commercial operation uses energy in some form, making it a central dimension to LCA. The LCA process measures the environmental impacts of the energies used not only at the production stage but also from source. This may present problems in terms of information flow, particularly for the SME, requiring new technologies to assess the environmental impact of the energies used within the production process and the relative merits of alternative sources of supply. It is important for all companies to assess how energy and waste can be reduced within the production process, and to acquire the necessary assistance to follow this process through.

Production

> Everybody's dream in LCA is to be given a piece of software that will enable them to plug in the values for the product, press a button, and be told if their product is more environmentally acceptable than their competitors.
>
> **(Richards 1993: 11)**

As the LCA process develops, more freely available information regarding databases for most primary raw materials will become available. The LCA process is an invaluable process to go through for the company committed to sustainable development and seeking to produce a sustainable product for its customers.

Where problems occur with LCA they are logistical. It is important to set boundaries and targets to be attained, despite the difficulties of defining the limits to an LCA in terms of the component parts of the raw materials and their environmental impact. Since all areas of production have environmental impacts, each stage needs to be analysed back to the source to fulfil the rigorous requirements of the LCA process. This includes the life history of the capital equipment and the environmental impact of all the operational life cycles. As the technology and capabilities for accurate LCA develop, more effective information diffusion channels regarding LCA results also emerge. An initial phase within this process is the eco-labelling procedure which displays a company's green credentials for consumers to make informed choices regarding their purchasing decisions.

Usage and disposal

Crittenden and Kolaczkowski (1995) argue that waste minimization techniques can be split between waste reduction at source and various recycling initiatives. They suggest that waste can be reduced at source through the implementation of a four-fold model which includes good practice, technological changes, input material changes and product changes. Good practice techniques can accrue fast payback over short periods of time with little investment, being achieved through regular auditing procedures and accreditation to quality standards.

Case Study 6.4 describes two waste minimization projects.

CASE STUDY 6.4
Waste Minimization

Leicestershire Waste Minimization Initiative (LWMI)

Launched in January 1994, LWMI is a demonstrator project like the Aire and Calder Project. The aim is to demonstrate the cost-effectiveness, technical efficiency and environmental performance of an effective regional waste minimization project.

Stressing the bottom-line cost of reactive waste treatment and disposal, the project was established and funded by the East Midlands Advisory Group on the Environment. Comprising Leicestershire County Council, the Leicestershire Training and Enterprise Council, the Department of Trade and Industry, the National Rivers Authority, the BOC Foundation for the Environment and Severn Trent Water, the LWMI required participating companies to meet only 25 per cent of the project costs. After six months potential costs savings of £2.6 million a year had been identified.

Project Catalyst

Project Catalyst (in the North West of England) was one of the largest waste minimization projects in the UK, costing almost £1 million and involving fourteen companies. Managed by three consultancies and funded by the DTI, the BOC Foundation for the Environment and the participating companies, £2.3 million a year savings had been achieved after one year, and a further £8.9 million was identified as possible cost savings if the recommendations from the on-site audits were implemented. Almost £2.5 million of savings involved zero cost, and almost £3 million had a payback of less than one year.

The project identified opportunities for reducing emissions and discharges into the environment by tackling the cause of waste and its reduction or avoidance at source. Of the total value of opportunities identified, 55 per cent involved technology modifications, 19 per cent were good housekeeping, 23 per cent involved recycle/reuse and 3 per cent were from product modifications. The results demonstrated the value of a co-operative, regional waste minimization project.

All participants claimed a range of benefits from participation in the initiative. Not only did participants identify significant cost savings and improvements in environmental performance but also they implemented many operational and behavioural changes leading to improved managerial performance as a result of the project.

Source: Atkins (1994)

Technical investment involves a more substantial outlay, but can accrue significant cost savings over time. Investments of this kind generally apply to capital equipment innovation within the production process and can include modification of existing equipment as well as additional replacement investments. Input material changes include the replacement of hazardous raw materials and the auditing of all substances used in the production process that are potentially hazardous to health.

The fourth dimension of their model relates to the possibility of changing the product. This includes packaging minimization and associated design issues as well as considerations of product line diversification to less harmful products.

Waste reduction at source is the optimum ecologically sensitive waste strategy. Companies do, however, have to consider what to do with the waste that has been generated. Therefore although companies should not replace a minimization at source strategy purely with a recycling strategy there is a place for an integrated recycling strategy within the over-aim of a waste management policy.

Waste treatment and disposal to landfill can be a costly business. It makes good economic sense to attempt to reduce output waste and to reclaim the benefits available by recycling waste into the production process wherever possible. Recycling should be considered only if resources have been reduced as far as possible and reused where ever appropriate.

One of the major problems of an efficient commercial recycling scheme is the separation of recyclable and non-recyclable materials. To have an integrated recycling strategy companies also have to consider the implications of post-production recycling. These two issues are central to the success of this part of the waste management strategy. Materials can be recycled on and off site. Off-site recycling is generally undertaken when there is not the on-site technology to recycle, the materials are not suitable for process reintroduction or where there are not enough materials on site to make the job worth while (Crittenden and Kolaczkowski 1995).

Case Study 6.5 is taken from Project Catalyst.

CASE STUDY 6.5
Pilkington's Tiles Ltd

Identification of the problem

The first stage in the production of ceramic wall tiles involves dispersing the finely ground raw materials in water to form a clay 'slip', followed by removal of oversized and metal particles by sieves and magnets. The slip is eventually spray dried to produce a powder suitable for pressing into tiles.

The equipment used could produce a slip only with a high proportion of water. Since it was uneconomic to remove the spray drying, water was first removed by a filter press in order to increase the solids concentration.

The water removed at this stage contained solids at too high a level to permit discharge into the river. Treatment was therefore required which involved flocculation and filtration. The recovered solid was sent to landfill and the water discharged to the river.

Changes made

Equipment obtained from elsewhere within the organization was installed which could produce high density slip, i.e. with high solids content, at the initial stage. This eliminated the need to subject the slip to a filtration stage prior to spray drying.

Savings, costs and payback

■ Reducing solids loss by 50 per cent saved £42 500 per year.

■ Reducing operating costs by 43 per cent saved £80 000 per year

■ Total savings were £122 500 per year.

■ Installation of vessels and ancillary equipment cost £186 000.

■ Payback was achieved in 18 months.

Source: Atkins (1994)

PRODUCT AND COMMUNICATIONS

This section covers the risk of not considering the implications of environmental pressure on product choice, how to green a marketing strategy and how to communicate and report the results.

Crisis management and risk assessment

Corporate decision-makers face the constant risk of media attention following an environmental crisis. With the growth and speed of modern communications, focus on an environmental issue, accident or disaster involving their company can present managers with unwelcome communications problems. The Union Carbide Bhopal explosion and the *Exxon Valdez* Prince William Sound oil spill (see Chapter 2) are two examples of environmental crises which called for immediate management reactions. Crises have the following characteristic elements:

■ **Surprise** By their very nature, crises result from problems which were not anticipated and at times when they are least expected.

■ **Immediate pressure** Answers are demanded immediately from employees, worried relatives, the local community and local newspapers, radio and television.

- **Factual uncertainty** Managers require facts and figures, both to assess the situation and to answer the immediate questions coming from internal and external inquiries.

- **Speculation** Well-informed 'experts' seek to interpret the unfolding situation, setting the seal on perceptions and consolidating rumour.

- **Glare of publicity** Management becomes aware that each decision it makes is being rigidly scrutinized from outside.

- **Bunker attitude** Management may react by seeking to withdraw from external communications in order to focus on solving immediate problems. This can lead to the company being reported on solely by hostile interests.

In order to retain control in the immediate aftermath of a crisis, management must be in a position to:

- Define the problem.

- Allocate key management to speak out consistently.

- Anticipate worst case scenarios.

Journalists demand verifiable facts. If these are not supplied by the firm, journalists will turn elsewhere, to a disgruntled ex-employee or a whistle-blowing pressure group able to claim that management was warned but took no action. As the *Exxon Valdez* oil spill and its aftermath indicate (see Chapter 2) attempts to batten down the hatches and ride out the storm attract adverse media attention and succeed in communicating negatively with key stakeholders, including employees, shareholders, customers, suppliers and the general public.

In order to forestall the adverse publicity resulting from an environmental crisis, a risk assessment procedure is advisable. Typically, a team consisting of experts in management, finance, operations and communications provides assessments of:

- Areas of risk and business vulnerability.

- Analysis of operational and management procedures.

- Development of crisis management plans.

The aim of these procedures is to facilitate effective implementation of remedial procedures in the event of an environmental crisis, coupled with the ability to communicate effectively with employees, the media and the wider public.

Crisis management strategies have become essential to business survival in those industries where the product or service rendered involve the use of potentially hazardous materials. When the type and quantity of substances used pose a potential threat to employees, customers, the local community and/or wildlife resources, that is water courses, land or air, management must remain on constant alert and precautionary measures will require constant review. In the light of the growing threat to a firm's viability posed by potential adverse media publicity, companies are under increasing pressure to seek out alternative products and production processes and to build the new features into their marketing strategies. Product durability, designs for reuse and repair and technologies designed to reduce the strength and quantities of toxic substances in, for example, timber preservation or dry cleaning processes, offer greater security, both environmentally and financially. An essential part of this process is dependent upon effective communication with the company's stakeholders.

Marketing

Strategies and policies need to be communicated to be effective in operation. Customers, stakeholders and staff require a supply of current information about the implementation of policies, results generated as well as any awards and successes achieved. Effective and open communication of corporate environmental information is a central part of a holistic ecological strategy. It substantiates claims regarding improvements, encourages staff and stakeholders and provides critical information for potential investors. Without a well-developed communication strategy, companies lose many of the commercial benefits of a newly established environmental management system.

Social change marketing

> Social marketing involves the design, implementation and control of programmes aimed at increasing the acceptability of an idea in one or more groups of target adopters. It utilises concepts of market segmentation, consumer research, product concept development and testing, directed communication facilitation, incentives and exchange theory to maximise the target adopters response. The sponsoring agency pursues the change goal in the belief that they will contribute to the individual's or society's best interest.
>
> **(Kotler and Roberto 1989: 24)**

The literature argues that the changing of behaviour patterns through social marketing necessitates a re-evaluation of beliefs, attitudes, intentions, values and behaviour (Elliot *et al.* 1994; Kotler and Roberto 1989). Environmental issues have been (and continue to be) one of the most significant social change issues. The problem has been that although people are unquestionably concerned about the environment they find it difficult to see how small changes in individual lifestyles will affect the macro-picture. Social change marketing, therefore, has to do with increasing public awareness regarding lifestyle changes.

Green marketing

Green marketing (which can be classed as a dimension of social change marketing) was initially highly effective in the evolution of consumer attitudes on green issues, and there is still much to be learnt from the practices of efficient and effective green marketing strategies. Marketing is central to the understanding of commercial progression towards a more sustainable society.

'Marketing has contributed to the current environmental crisis, because of its central role as a driving force behind the unsustainable growth in consumption (or what could be termed over-consumption)' (Peattie 1995: 24). Peattie holds that marketing has promoted the adoption of unsustainable global lifestyles. Hence marketing will be central in the evolution of new ethically conscious products, processes, companies, lifestyles, values and ideas. Essentially marketing is the key mechanism for communication of a 'new' ethical morality towards the earth's resources.

The scope of green marketing is considerable, relating to issues from conservation, through to fair trade and humanitarian concerns. With the development of market research in order to understand consumer wants, marketing has been defined by Kotler as 'a social and managerial process by which individuals and groups obtain what they need and want through creating and exchanging products and value with others' (Kotler 1994: 13). In this sense, marketing has moved beyond the promotion of producer wares and values, to the research and investigation of consumer intentions in order to supply their wants and needs. The deciphering of needs and wants over the long term has become increasingly problematical. Hence the proactive forward-looking company requires a strong element of futurity in their marketing analysis of customer needs.

It is clearly in the long-term interests of the global consumer that there are enough resources to go round and to supply a relatively high quality of life, in terms of a decent standard of education, food provision and health care. If the resources being used to provide the present level of quality of life are finite then it is in the interests of the consumer to provide goods and services with the lowest environmental impacts. However, if marketing analyses are based upon short-term options, they may uncover short-term consumer wants, as opposed to long-term needs. This is due to the fact that the consumer has limited knowledge of future environmental conditions as well as to the fact that future needs are far less tangible than present wants.

Catering for the green consumer

Hidden or explicit, there is always an inherent implicit value judgement attached to analysis in market research on consumer wants, values and needs. Wants, which are infinite, can be clearly distinguished. Identification of needs, which are finite, requires a degree of values understanding. Heroin addicts want more heroin but they do not need it unless they want to die. Similarly, the global consumer may want three cars, but if it is unsustainable for all who want three cars to have them, this is not what the global consumer needs. In the progressive market-place of the future, green marketing will become 'the holistic management process responsible for identifying, anticipating and satisfying the requirements of customers and society, in a profitable and sustainable way' (Peattie 1995: 28). Satisfying the demands of the market with the more general ethical elements within this statement will remain a delicate task.

In some ways it is difficult to distinguish between environmental management in the general sense and environmental or green marketing, since sound environmental marketing occurs as the outworking expression of effective environmental management. The two concepts are mutually dependent. Environmental or green marketing involves the view that all the activities of the company are a part of the product that is consumed. As with all ecological holistic management concepts it is impossible to segment and isolate concepts and practices. They are interrelated and mutually dependent.

During the 1980s and 1990s, however, the global market has been flooded by green claims of differing validity. Spurious claims and false or misleading statements have been made by companies keen to cash in on the new 'green consumer' seeking to achieve mere marketing advantage. Company images were 'greenwashed' in an attempt to deceive the public about green credentials. Logos were greened as practices continued as business as usual. Companies sold paper as 'recyclable' and products were labelled as free of toxic substances which have never formed any part of that particular product. Such actions drew a legislative backlash.

In the UK, the Advertising Standards Association (1995), for example, moved to quash misleading and unqualified advertising claims. Words such as 'environmentally friendly' and 'wholly biodegradable' now require substantiation. However, the dubious terms 'greener' and 'friendlier' are still permitted if the company can prove that its product or service is relatively more friendly or green than that of its competitors. The central problems of information and accuracy continue to face the *green consumer* in a fluid situation.

Even if consumers have the time and desire to weigh up green claims, they may still not have all of the necessary information required to make an informed decision. In the face of a growing number of spurious claims the general public or green consumer has largely been disenfranchised during the 1990s, giving rise to demands for credible labelling schemes or more rigorous deterministic legislation.

Strengths and weaknesses of green marketing
Despite growing consumer suspicion of facile green marketing claims, there are important reasons for considering green marketing. The most important reason is to diffuse information to:

- Staff.
- Stakeholders.
- Investors.
- Media.
- Regulatory authorities.

If a company is to invest significant amounts of capital and time to improve its environmental performance, it should clearly communicate these improvements to all stakeholders, encouraging others to do the same and informing stakeholders of the priority of ethical management in the new millennium. If information is to be diffused one has to consider the content of that information. An effective green marketing strategy requires effective environmental management back-up. Although it is possible to mislead the public for a certain amount of time regarding spurious claims regarding environmental performance, in the long run the unethical practices are unearthed, leading to unwanted negative publicity which counteract the gains initially made. If a green marketing strategy is to be successful it needs to be backed up by concrete evidence. Changes to practices based on facts of substance are more cost-effective than superficial, image tinkering in an attempt to continue with 'business as usual'.

Charter (1992) considers seven aspects of green marketing: price, product, promotions, place, people, process and physical evidence. Full-costs accounting, packaging, advertising and claims, eco-labelling, transport, personnel, and employee commitment, awareness and training are essential elements in progressive green marketing. Like Peattie (1995), Charter (1992) covers a wide area of topics but draws together the importance of having an integrated green marketing strategy that conveys the progressive ideals of the company.

Product choice, design and packaging

The choice of product or service dictates the parameters within which the audit is carried out. Although the job of the auditor is to inspect the environmental performance of a particular company, and to neutrally report the findings, an eco-audit can be used to recommend changes and to draw attention to potential impact reducing measures. In this process, analysis of product design or service is essential, since product choice and design determines the production process. One question that needs to be considered is, could the product be produced using less raw materials by design modification?

Design decisions affect:

■ Raw material usage.

■ Production processes.

■ Energy efficiency levels.

■ Transportation policies.

■ Recycling decisions.

■ Landfill policy.

An eco-audit should therefore include an initial analysis of the product or service itself considering if any diversification of production or modification of product design could significantly reduce environmental impact. Skippingdale Paper Products (Scunthorpe, UK), part of the Aire and Calder Regional Environmental Management Project, have shown how a fresh consideration of the product design can reduce environmental impact at source, removing the necessity to mitigate impact further down the production line at greater cost. By removing unnecessary padding and condensing the product, they redesigned their product in order to reduce waste output and raw material usage. For an investment of £150 000, nappy packs were reduced in size by 60 per cent. The smaller, more compact product required less transportation space on the lorries saving 600 000 km transportation a year. Over nine months the payback per year was estimated at £195 000 (March Consulting Group, 1994).

New energy-saving products

Product design often dictates customer energy usage. Fiat, for example, are developing a range of urban vehicles that use methane-powered engines that have low emission exhaust systems. In Italy methane-powered buses and methane-powered refuse collection trucks are being used in Madrid, Ravenna and Rome. Philips have also developed the low energy compact fluorescent lamp that lasts eight times as long as the ordinary filament light with obvious cost saving implications.

In traditional business practice, built-in obsolescence has been an attractive option as a means for companies to sustain their markets, particularly for producers of automobiles, audio-visual equipment, computers and 'white goods'. The green consumer, aware of the environmental implications of this practice, has come to demand product durability. German manufacturers have led the way in offering substantially longer guarantees, and it is reasonable to anticipate that guarantees for most household products will last for 10 years and will cover labour as well as spare parts (Cooper 1994).

Product choice can affect the overall sum of material and energy consumption and waste generation. Refinement in product design or diversification can significantly reduce energy usage. By altering the design of the packaging to include recyclable materials, for example, a company can reduce energy costs simply by using less primary materials in packaging.

Packaging

Packaging is an important element in the design and marketing of the product. Packaging has valuable functions to perform:

- It displays essential legal and consumer information.

- It protects the product.

- It avoids unnecessary spillage in transit.

- It presents the brand image.

The volume of single-use packaging has given rise to problems of disposal, giving rise to legislative pressures, forcing reconsideration of the amount and type of packaging employed. Companies are therefore required to assess the environmental impact of the packaging materials and to seek out more sustainable designs and materials, including assessing the potential for recycling and reuse of packaging materials. It is estimated that of 50 million tonnes of packaging waste generated within the EU only 19 per cent is currently recycled (Business in the Environment and Coopers & Lybrand Deloitte 1991). The EU Directive on Packaging and Packaging Waste (EU 1994) has increased pressures on companies to reduce packaging and to consider the implications of their packaging, and reusable and recyclable packaging has emerged as an increasingly attractive option. The Directive required member states to implement a national policy on packaging by 30 June 1996.

The Directive states that member states must prevent the formation of packaging waste wherever possible. However, where packaging waste is generated the following targets are to be attained:

- By no later than 20 June 2001, between 50 per cent and 65 per cent by weight of packaging waste is to be recovered (rather than burying it in landfill).

- Within that general target and timescale, between 25 per cent and 45 per cent by weight of packaging materials contained in packaging waste is to be recycled (i.e. reprocessed for original or other use, but not including energy recovery) with a minimum of 15 per cent by weight for each packaging material.

(EU 1994, A10: 40)

These targets are subject to review every five years, and the aim is to substantially increase the targets set. Member states are also encouraged to set targets in advance to meet the new strategic requirements. The EC has reserved the right to employ economic instruments to promote the implementation of the Directive's objectives, if required.

Commercially, therefore, companies under the auspices of European legislation will be required very soon to consider their packaging policies strategically. Although the reclamation and recycling of packaging is clearly a major issue within the Directive, the reduction of packaging at source is the real long-term aim.

Eco-labelling

Ecolabels are seals of approval given to manufactured products deemed to have fewer impacts on the environment than functionally and competitively similar products. But far from encouraging industry to strive for higher environmental standards, voluntary eco-labelling schemes are rapidly degenerating into a means whereby industry can set the standards it likes. Whilst some products and processes have undoubtedly been improved, overall ecolabelling is proving to be an extremely blunt instrument for environmental protection.

(West 1995: 16)

The concept of eco-labelling originated in the German Blue Angel Scheme in 1978. By the early 1990s 80 per cent of households in Germany were aware of the scheme and its implications (Welford and Gouldson 1993), and the idea had spread throughout the developed world. However, the very popularity of the idea proved an initial problem, as spurious green advertising claims were becoming commonplace. In the UK, the plethora of false green claims led to 350 companies being nominated for the Friends of the Earth Green Con Awards in 1990.

Applicable to all member states of the European Union the EU eco-labelling scheme was established during 1991 and launched in the summer of 1993 after an initial conceptual launch in March 1992. The aim was to ameliorate the growing number of corporate environmental claims and to protect consumer interests. Designed to inform consumers about the environmental excellence of a product and to amalgamate the increasing number of individual country environmental labels, the EU label was intended to offer consumers the ability to make valid choices between different and competing products in the same category of objective environmental criteria.

The EU-wide eco-labelling scheme which emerged due to the consumer pressure in the late 1980s has been slow to capture the imagination of industry. With an initial application fee of £500 and a licence fee levied as a percentage of annual turnover of the product at factory

HOW THE SCHEME WORKS

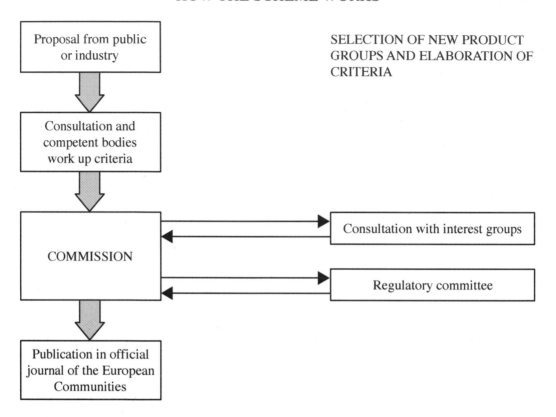

FIGURE 6.2 *Eco-label system*

gate prices set at 0.15 per cent, the standard remains voluntary. Criteria and assessment procedures are somewhat arbitrary, and to date only a handful of companies have been awarded a label.

Furthermore, the label (Figures 6.2 and 6.3) is not available to all commercial goods. The EU initially decided to concentrate on a few specific product groupings. Each grouping was assigned to a competent national body to develop the specific criteria necessary to achieve the award. The product categories include:

■ Paper products, textiles and insulation materials (Denmark).

■ Batteries, paints/varnishes and shampoos (France).

■ Laundry detergents, dishwater detergents, household cleaning products (Germany).

■ Floor/wall tiles, packaging materials, refrigerators (Italy).

■ Cat litter, shoes (Netherlands).

■ Antiperspirants/deodorants, dishwashers/washing machines, soil improvers/growing media, hairsprays, hairstyling aids, light bulbs (UK).

AWARD OF ECO-LABEL TO INDIVIDUAL PRODUCTS

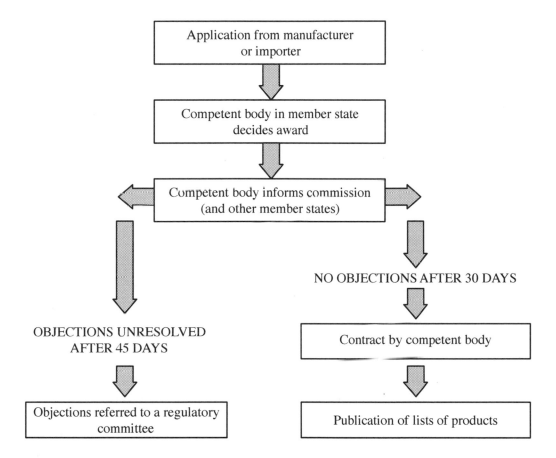

FIGURE 6.3 *Eco-label award process*

The criteria for award of an eco-label to a product type are based on a matrix as shown in Table 6.1.

Basically the company has to undertake a Life Cycle Assessment of the product. An LCA or 'cradle-to-grave' approach is a systematic analysis of a product's affect on the environment at all stages of production, from consideration of the raw material used in manufacture, through the product's production to its distribution and disposal. The problem with cradle-to-grave assessment to date has been that the industry-wide variation of assessment and measurement has not been standardized. Therefore individual industries who have become involved with LCA have tended to determine their own individual standards. LCA is a complex concept, involving intricate scientific analysis of environmental impact and subjectivity of assessment criterion. This has led to variation of opinion on the impact of the concept to date.

Food, drink and pharmaceuticals are specifically excluded from the scheme, weakening any claim to offer consumers a comprehensive set of guidelines for green purchasing. From the

TABLE 6.1 *The EC Eco-labelling Scheme: indicative assessment matrix*

Environmental fields	Product life cycle				
Waste relevance					
Soil pollution and degradation					
Water contamination					
Air contamination					
Noise					
Consumption of energy					
Consumption of natural resources					
Effects on ecosystems					

launch in 1992 the media were not slow to pen the headlines, 'Eco-label Still Not Sticking', and the EU label has been heavily criticized from all sides. For example, environmentalists have criticized the fact that 'effects on ecosystems', one of the product category criteria, did not include animal testing. While the Eco-labelling Commission can claim that other EU laws covered the animal testing subject area, the many omissions have served to reduce the credibility of this particular scheme. Nevertheless, the experience gained from schemes of this type has served to strengthen knowledge and expertise in handling green marketing issues.

In particular, it emerges that a holistic environmental audit requires an analysis of a company's marketing and advertising strategy, while an ecological audit includes ethical considerations to provide substance to an ethical green image. By establishing an overall EMS undertaking an environmental audit and gaining accreditation to an acceptable labelling scheme, a company can systematically consider its green performance and gain strong competitive advantage from the exercise.

Environmental reporting

In tandem with the recognition of industry's new role as a partner in the sustainable development process, there is rising public demand for fuller accountability by industry, which must display proof of responsible environmental stewardship to justify self-regulation.

(Spencer-Cooke 1994: 4)

Greater corporate environmental disclosure of information is a critical variable in the strive for sustainability and has been one of the main reasons for the development of the Corporate Environmental Report (*CER*). As more and more companies have discerned the times and seen the growing pressures to become more environmentally honest or open about their activities, companies have become increasingly aware of their requirements to disclose information.

Pressure for disclosure of environmental information has steadily increased, and can come from a number of sources, and may come in a number of forms. Disclosure may be necessary in order to:

- Be seen to stay in line with environmental policy aims.

- Provide the information for effective partnerships working towards sustainability.

- Adhere to the requirements of *Agenda 21* (UNCED 1992) and the European Fifth Action Programme (EC 1993).

- Meet public pressure to be more environmentally accountable.

- Take account of the increasing possibilities of industrial licence being tied to CER publications (adherence to accepted standards).

- Adhere to more stringent regulatory requirements.

- Meet green marketing pressures, for example advertising image.

- Search for excellence and quality.

- Stay ahead of the competition.

- Meet pressure from financial capital investment markets.

While green reporting remains on a voluntary basis, industry is ideally placed to participate in the evolution of regulation. Pressure for increased environmental disclosure can come from employees, shareholders and public authorities, with an increasing trend towards interest coming from the capital investment markets. If a company has a questionable environmental prospect or history, the threat of costly litigation renders them bad investment risks. To date the CER is being seen as a concrete symbol of corporate commitment and a failure to disclosure information will come to be seen as a negative investment variable, as financial analysts come under increasing pressure to verify the environmental credibility of investments.

> Much work needs to be done to convince business and governments that environmental protection is not a burden but a necessary investment, not only to allow us and our children to live a materially decent and healthy life but also to be at peace with our consciences. A sobering example is that of Peru, which did not invest in an adequate water supply infrastructure because it cost too much, thus losing thousands of people to cholera and billions of dollars in lost export and tourism; a sum greater than the cost of the infrastructure, which still has to be built.
>
> **(Davis 1992: 54)**

There is a clear link between indigenous population health and the health of the local economy. Although the information requirements of the financial analysts in the capital markets are, on the whole, still limited to financial data (environmental expenditures, operating costs, fines, write-offs, environmental liability provision and cost savings), there is an increasing trend for companies to disclose non-financial information into the public domain, for example market and product-related environmental trends, incidents, permits and suspensions, company position relative to EC legislation, risk and environmental management systems, environmental measures taken or envisaged and linkage of figures on environmental spend with expected pay-offs and management benefits (Owen 1992; Spencer-Cooke 1994). Environmental reporting has become a key factor within the process of environmental management.

Report contents

Reporting can take a number of forms, from written reports to informal disclosure of information. Decisions regarding communication and means of dissemination need to be considered concurrently within the environmental management strategy. Elements of reporting can be categorized under the following headings:

Qualitative

- Forward by a senior person.
- Profile of the enterprise.
- Environmental policy.
- Environmental targets and objectives.
- Views on environmental issues.
- Community relations.

Management

- Environmental management systems.
- Management of environmental risks.
- Office and site practices.

Quantitative

- Environmental indicators and targets.
- Use of energy and natural resources.
- Compliance with regulations and permits.
- Financial indicators.

Products

- Products, processes and services.
- Additional information.

(World Industry Council for the Environment 1994)

Before the World Industry Council for the Environment (*WICE*) joined with the Business

Council for Sustainable Development (BCSD) in 1995 to form the World Business Council for Sustainable Development (WBCSD), it developed guidelines for companies to prepare an environmental report (WICE 1994). The work includes an environmental reporting matrix which enables organizations to consider the audience of the report and what to include.

Full-costs environmental accounting, where the price of the product reflects the full cost of production, including any associated environmental clean-up costs or energy costs, flows from the corporate environmental reporting procedure. As the full-cost accounting agenda gathers pace, all sizes of corporations can expect increased investor pressure to clean up their operations to reduce the potential liabilities.

EXTERNAL ENVIRONMENT

The final section in this chapter will cover two elements of the external environment with respect to operational eco-management, the supply chain and transport implications. Although there are many other aspects of the external environment they are covered in detail in Part 3.

Supply chain management

> Environmental pressures are forcing organisations to take stock of the way they operate. When making purchasing and supply decisions, the environment is taking its place alongside the issues of price, quality, delivery, security of supply and other criteria.
>
> **(Business in the Environment 1993: 1)**

Supply chain management involves the integration of the corporate goals and targets for the environment into the purchasing and supply side of the company's operations. A company can achieve only so much in isolation, particularly in the implementation of LCA. Raw material supplies and initial processes involved earlier on in the supply chain need to be assessed if full environmental information disclosure is to be achieved. Hence any integrated waste management policy and LCA has to take account of the whole supply chain. Inputs from suppliers generate waste and must, therefore, be monitored, measured and recorded.

Pressure to consider product ingredients and process operations is increased as environmental clauses begin to be written into contracts. Coupled with legislative change, these pressures force recognition of the need for an integrated strategy to include vertical forward and backward movement along the supply chain, in order to hedge against any unforeseen litigation within the chain that will threaten market position. Business in the Environment (1993) has published a strategic document that delineates a supply chain strategy. The model is explained in three main stages that include:

1. **Issues** Explaining the need for the principle and identifying the relevant issues.
2. **Action points** Explaining the steps which could be considered to meet the criteria for the principle.
3. **Guidance** Offering advice and information to help meet the action points.

Issues

There are a number of costs and benefits attached to supply chain environmental management. Costs include investments in time and human resources to assess suppliers' performances, as well as costs incurred in supporting suppliers' improvement programmes. Increased prices may accrue from suppliers due to the more stringent requirements, and these need to be taken into account. There are four main benefits attached to an integrated supply chain policy, as follows.

Compliance with legislation and regulation

An integrated supply chain management policy can assist in meeting legal requirements for good environmental management. Additionally, it may be used to extend the terms of practice of the organization beyond current requirements, keeping the organization ahead of its competitors and the regulatory stick. This strategy also satisfies the requirement for an internal risk management strategy by reducing the possibility of litigation due to deleterious practices, increasing the long-term investment attraction of the company.

Security of supply

By auditing a supplier's policy a proactive company reduces the possibility of supply chain disruption. Suppliers could be jeopardized at any time by legislation requirements and a sound long-term supply chain policy mitigates this possibility.

Market opportunities

As customers are increasingly demanding ethically produced goods and services, any company failing to proactively consider their responsibility towards the environment is running the risk of losing custom. This has dual-directional implications. Adoption of ethical principles along the supply chain reduces the possibility of unexpected litigation and supply failure, while a forward movement reduces the chance of lost custom due to the organization's incapacity to keep up with the customers' ethical demands.

Benefit versus cost

Just as companies in the 1980s recognized that in the long term the initial costs of becoming a 'quality managed' operation would pay, so in the 1990s the forward-looking organization sees that the initial costs of greening business operations (which includes the supply chain) will eventually pay dividends far in excess of initial investment levels.

Action points

1. Identify the legislative pressures and understand the operational implications.
2. Identify those suppliers where environmental risks are important enough to represent a threat to security of supply.
3. Identify the main market opportunities and pressures where environmental policy in purchasing has a role to play.
4. Identify resource needs and evaluate the costs and benefits of building the environment into purchasing and supply.
5. Identify those suppliers (including contractors) who contribute to the organization's performance and therefore image in the community.

Guidance

If the company has an internal environmental department it is beneficial for the purchasing manager to work with them on developing a sound supply chain strategy. This includes being aware of present legal requirements or future legislative developments. The committed ethical company of the twenty-first century will have an integrated EMS, including a supply chain policy and strategy which guides and facilitates the purchasing managers' decision-making process.

There are a number of operational implications of an effective supply chain policy. Having undertaken a supplier audit, a company may decide that to be consistent with the overall environmental aims, suppliers should be required to modify their practices. Alternatively, the company may decide that there is a need to find alternative sources of supply, if negotiations with existing suppliers to modify practices prove difficult. The increased demands incurred by the implementation of a holistic EMS may dictate the necessity for the generation of new suppliers of machinery and services to satisfy new technological demands within the organization. Effluent control and monitoring equipment and cleaner technologies in general may all require new supply links to be made for which a thorough supplier audit should be undertaken.

Supply chain environmental management offers an ideal opportunity for information diffusion and technology transfer. As pressure increases from along the chain, more and more organizations are recognizing the need to audit their operations in a holistic manner to keep up with the competition and to keep existing customers. An integrated environmental supply chain management strategy by necessity includes an increase in co-operation between organizations. As companies seek to satisfy ever increasing customer and legislative demands co-operation between organizations within the supply chain becomes standard practice. The benefit of increased co-operation is clear. There will be an increase in the transfer of environmental commitment as the customer enables the supply to attain to the new requirements (Gouldson 1994). Table 6.2 summarizes business implications and supply chain implications of UK and EU legislation.

Environmental transport strategies

The global transportation of goods and people is one of the most significant environment issues facing us today.

> Transport contributes around 20% of the UK's total CO_2 emissions, and most of this comes from road transport. In addition, vehicle emissions also contain nitrogen oxides (NO_x) and hydrocarbons (which contribute to the formation of ground level ozone), carbon monoxide and lead. Reducing vehicle usage and vehicle emissions is, therefore, a key environmental issue.
>
> (BiE and Coopers & Lybrand Deloitte 1991: Annex V)

Pollution from transport leads to many diverse human ailments including respiratory diseases like asthma, lung diseases and other circulatory disorders.

TABLE 6.2 *Operational implications of legislation for supply chain environmental management. (Source: Business in the Environment, 1993: 8)*

Legislation	Business implications	Supply chain implications
Eco-labelling scheme (1993) (EU)	Reduce product impact in use	■ Collaboration with suppliers in product development, materials design, and recovery/recycling systems
Environmental Protection Act 1990 (UK)	Reduce emissions to air	■ Purchase emissions control and monitoring equipment ■ Select alternative fuel ■ Purchase alternative solvents/cleaner technology
Duty of Care/EC Waste Directives 1990 (EU)	Reductions in solid waste volumes and toxicity, and improvement in treatment/disposal practices	■ Develop raw material specification to reduce toxicity ■ Monitor treatment and disposal ■ Service contractors (to auditable standards) ■ Purchase recovery/reuse-use technology
Water Industry Act 1991; Water Resources Act 1991	Lower concentrations, elimination of prescribed substances in discharges to sewer/water	■ Monitor contractors to conform to company procedures and standards ■ Purchase effluent control and monitoring equipment ■ Select alternative materials to reduce traces of heavy metals
Green Paper on Environmental Liability 1980 (EU)	Remediation /clean-up of land contamination	■ Purchase new services
Packaging and Packaging Waste Directive 1995 (EU)	Reduce/replace packaging	■ Select new suppliers/alternative materials ■ Collaborate with suppliers to recover/recycle

Reprinted with kind permission of Business in the Environment (BiE), the National Environment Unit and KPMG Peat Marwick.

EC Directives have already pushed through new emissions standards for cars in the 1990s (concerning particulate expulsion and carbon monoxide) as well as the obligatory design of catalytic converters for all cars. This trend is set to continue in the search for a less polluting transport system. Additionally the UK government has increased the previously lax taxation on company cars, making their usage more costly and placing yet another pressure on companies to consider carefully their transport policy with regard to the environment.

As pressures to conform to legislative standards increase, cost will rise. These costs can, however, be minimized through a well-designed holistic environmental transport policy. The following areas are analysed in a transport audit and need to be considered in the development of an holistic environmental transport policy:

■ Modes of transport.

■ Storage and packaging for transportation.

■ Product destination.

■ Employee incentives/education.

■ Site access.

■ Health and safety hazards in transportation.

■ Alternatives to travelling, e.g. teleconferencing.

■ Noise levels.

For an initial overview of the requirements of maintaining and operating an efficient transport fleet, see Winter (1995: 159–60). Winter considers all aspects from tyre pressures, carburettor adjustments and the disposal of oil in a manner fitting to an efficient holistic environmental transport policy.

SUMMARY

This chapter has focused on the holistic application of eco-auditing. Eco-auditing requires an unblinkered total quality philosophy which recognizes that environmental concerns are an integral part of all areas of production, product development, communications, supply chain management and all other external environmental considerations. It also looked at the positive and negative side of green marketing and advertising from the perspective of both the local and the global consumer, drawing the conclusion that companies require environmental management systems to be in place before claiming green success. Transport, introduced briefly here, is of strategic importance in eco-management and is reviewed in more detail in Chapter 12.

QUESTIONS

6.1 Elaborate upon the distinction between 'environmental' and 'eco-' management.

6.2 Draw up an outline 'cradle-to-this-room' environmental impact assessment of the material resources and production processes upon which you are dependent in order to be studying at this moment. You should include: furniture and furnishings, equipment, clothing, food consumed over the previous 24 hours, building, and energy sources. Are there any less environmentally damaging options available to you?

6.3 Explain how and why a green marketing strategy differs from traditional marketing practice.

BIBLIOGRAPHY

Key texts

Peattie, K. (1995) *Environmental Marketing Management*, **Pitman, London**
This text is an excellent and thorough presentation of most marketing elements of environmentalism. Peattie also takes a holistic and lateral perspective in his analyses that encompasses the majority of elements of eco-management within marketing.

Welford, R. (1995) *Environmental Strategy and Sustainable Development: The Corporate Challenge for the 21st Century*, **Routledge, London**
There is a significant section in this book on eco-management and it deals with sustainability and management in a holistic manner.

Welford, R. and Starkey, R. (eds) (1996) *The Earthscan Reader in Business and the Environment*, **Earthscan, London**
A collection of first-class readings covering R&D and techniques for environmental improvement.

References and further reading

Advertising Standards Association (ASA) (1995) *British Codes of Advertising and Sales Promotion*, Committee of Advertising Practice, ASA, London.
Atkins, W. S. (1994) *March Consulting Group, Aspects International Report on Project Catalyst*, Birchwood Boulevard, Birchwood, Warrington, WA3 7QU, UK.
Business in the Environment (BiE) (1993) *Buying into the Environment: Guidelines for Integrating the Environment into Purchasing and Supply*, BiE Publications, 8 Stratton Street, London, W1X 6AH.
———(1994) *SustainAbility and SPOLD and Business in the Environment* (1994) *The LCA Sourcebook*, London.
Business in the Environment and Coopers & Lybrand Deloitte (1991) *Your Business and the Environment: A D-I-Y Review for Companies*, Legal Studies and Services (Publishing) Ltd, London.
BWEA (1995) *Wind Energy 'The Facts'*, British Wind Energy Association, Yorkshire Environmental Project (YEP) (*c.*1994) Yorkshire Environmental Limited, ARBRE, 2 The Embankment, Sovereign Street, Leeds, LS1 4BG, UK.
Callenbach, E., Capra, F., Goldman, L., Lutz, R. and Marburg, S. (1993) *EcoManagement: The Elmwood Guide to Ecological Auditing and Sustainable Business*, Berrett-Koehler, San Francisco.
Charter, M. (ed.) (1992) *Greener Marketing*, Greenleaf Publishing, Interleaf Productions Limited, Sheffield.
Cockburn, D. (1990) 'How Green was my Audit?', *CA Magazine* November, 52–4.

Cooper, T. (1994) *Beyond Recycling: The Longer Life Option*, New Economics Foundation (*NEF*), London.

Crittenden, B. and Kolaczkowski, S. (1995) *Waste Minimization—A Practical Guide*, Institution of Chemical Engineers, Rugby, UK.

Davis, T. (1992) *Business Associations for Environmental Management*, Ecodecisions, London.

Department of the Environment (1995) *Making Waste Work: A Strategy for Sustainable Waste Management*, DOE, HMSO, London.

Department of Trade and Industry (DTI) (1992) *Cutting Your Losses: A Further Guide to Waste Minimization for Business*, DTI, London.

EC (1993) *The European Fifth Environmental Action Program*, EC, Brussels, Belgium.

Edwards, T. (1995) *Waste Minimization: Pollution Prevention Pays for Industry and the Environment*, Sixth Annual Conference on Industrial Wastewater Treatment, 20–21 February, Ramada Hotel, Manchester.

Elkington, J. (1994) 'Towards the Sustainable Corporation: Win-Win-Win Business Strategies for Sustainable Development', *California Management Review* 36 (2): 90–100.

Elliot, G., Unsworth, D., Gomel, M., Saunders, J. and Mira, M. (1994) 'Social Marketing: Conceptual and Pragmatic Observations from a Current Australian Campaign', *Journal of Marketing Management* 10: 581–91.

EU (1994) *EU Directive on Packaging and Packaging Waste* (OJ L365, 31.12.94), in *Commercial Environmental Law*, Rel 4, 1995 A10.

European Round Table of Industrialists (ERT) (1992) *The Efficient Use of Energy: Looking into the Future*, Discussion Paper, Rue Guimard 15, 1040 Brussels.

———(1994) *The Climatic Change Debate: Seven Principles for Practical Policies*, Rue Guimard 15, 1040 Brussels.

Faur, J. A., Denison, R., Jones, B. (eds) (1991) *A Technical Framework for LCAs*, Society of Environmental Toxicology and Chemistry, 1010 North 12th Avenue, Pensacola, Florida 32501–3307, USA.

Gouldson, A. (1994) 'Co-operative Advantage and Strategic Alliances in Supply Chain Environmental Management', Paper presented at *Third Greening of Industry Conference*, Copenhagen, 13–15 November.

International Network for Environmental Management (INEM) (1993) *'The Tokyo Appeal': Towards an Industrial Agenda for Sustainable Development*, INEM, Tokyo, 10 September.

Kotler, P. (1994) *Marketing Management* (8th edition), Prentice-Hall, New Jersey.

Kotler, P. and Roberto, E. (1989) *Social Change Marketing: Strategies for Changing Public Behaviour*, The Free Press, New York.

March Consulting Group (1994) 'Reducing Costs and Improving Environmental Performance through Waste Minimization: the Aire and Calder Experience—a Brief Management Guide', in T. Edwards (1995) *Waste Minimization: Pollution Prevention Pays for Industry and the Environment*, Sixth Annual Conference on Industrial Wastewater Treatment, 20–21 February, Ramada Hotel, Manchester.

Owen, D. (ed.) (1992) *Green Reporting*, Chapman & Hall, London.

Peattie, K. (1995) *Environmental Marketing Management*, Pitman, London.

Richards, T. (1993) 'Courtaulds Research UK' in BiE, SustainAbility and SPOLD *LCA Sourcebook*.

Slater, J. (1992) *Directors' Guide to Environmental Issues*, Director Books, Hemel Hemp-
    stead.
Spencer-Cooke, A. (1994) *'Where Silence is not Golden'—Towards the Strategic Use of
    Corporate Environmental Reporting for Company Valuation*, ACCA, Certified Accoun-
    tants Educational Trust, London.
UNCED (1992) *Agenda 21*, UN, New York.
Welford, R. (1995) *Environmental Strategy and Sustainable Development: The Corporate
    Challenge for the 21st Century*, Routledge, London.
Welford, R. and Gouldson, A. (1993) *Environmental Management and Business Strategy*,
    Pitman, London.
West, K. (1995) 'Ecolabels: The Industrialization of Environmental Standards', *The Ecologist*
    25 (1): 16.
Winter, G. (1995) *Blueprint for Green Management*, McGraw-Hill, Maidenhead.
World Industry Council for the Environment (WICE) (1994) 40 Cours Albert 1er, 75008
    Paris.

CONCLUSION TO PART 2

The following model outlines the ten steps a company should go through to improve its environmental performance and sums up the details of Part 2.

TEN STAGES TO GREENING A BUSINESS

1. Secure commitment of senior management.
2. Undertake an initial environmental review.
3. Develop objectives and policy aims and an action plan.
4. Develop an environmental management system.
5. Implement the system.
6. Undertake an environmental audit/eco-audit.
7. Gain independent verification and standard accreditation.
8. Market and communicate the changes.
9. Continuously review procedures and progress/assess target attainments set.
10. Consider new innovations in strategy and operations.

By following these principles and acknowledging the need for a radical environmental overhaul of company strategies and operations, the proactive company can stay ahead of potential environmental litigation while satisfying increasing customer demand for green business ethics. An integrated holistic eco-management understanding of corporate environmental strategy will be an essential prerequisite to maintain competitive advantage in the twenty first century.

The External Environment and Eco-Management

INTRODUCTION

A corporation is subject to many external pressures, and its success depends upon its ability to respond with acumen to these pressures. Pressures may be Political, Economic, Social or Technological, forming the subject of a PEST analysis of the company's external business environment. In this sense 'environment' refers to all external considerations arising from the surrounding social institutions.

Part 3 deals with political questions, involving not only the state and its formal regulations but also the entire complex of relational power and authority. Each chapter covers different aspects of the green political framework within which the firm must operate. The topics covered in Chapter 7 on Green Politics are those conventionally viewed as 'political', involving formal elections or some form of delegation and pooling of resources to a common end. These include the work of such bodies as the United Nations, European Union, national governments, trade unions and pressure groups. Chapter 8 on Green Economics covers the emerging green political economy through which the costs of pollution are being shifted from society as a whole and to the individual polluter. Chapter 9 on Green Society reviews concrete social developments arising from growing political demands for sustainability. These include socially directed investment, ethical approaches to employment, bioregion-alism and permaculture. Chapter 10 on Green Technology also arises from the political. Tools and processes do not arise through biological evolution. Science and technology are tools developed by their makers to serve ends selected by their masters. The selection of ends is a political act. The topics covered in the chapters in Part 3 are interlinked. Legislation, as covered in Chapter 7, may be economic in its motivation and effect. Ethical investment in Chapter 9 arises from social motivations but will again impact upon the subject matter of Chapter 8.

CHAPTER 7

GREEN POLITICS

Politics is the art of preventing people from becoming involved in affairs which involve them.

(Paul Valéry 1871–1945)

INTRODUCTION

Politics in all its forms is an expression of public opinion backed up by some degree of power or authority. Public opinion can be assessed through market research and surveys, but it has its effective expression through legislation and regulation. National and international legislation and regulation are normally determined by elected representatives in consultation with business networks and organizations, trade unions and pressure groups. These groups also work directly with firms to promote the concerns of their membership. This chapter provides examples of the types of environmental pressures and measures which are impacting upon firms.

WORLD-WIDE PUBLIC OPINION

In 1992 the George H. Gallup International Institute conducted a survey of public opinion on environmental issues. The survey, entitled *The Health of the Planet Survey: A Preliminary Report on Attitudes to the Environment and Economic Growth Measured by Surveys of Citizens in 22 Nations*, (Gallup 1992) concluded that 'concern about the environment has become a world-wide phenomenon'. On a world scale:

- The environment was rated as one of the three most serious problems in half of the 22 countries surveyed.

- Majorities in 20 of the 22 countries were prepared to risk slowing economic growth to protect the environment.

- Majorities in most countries considered that the environment was affecting their health, and was even more likely to affect the health of their children.

■ In the majority of countries over half of the respondents had acted as 'green consumers', avoiding products that are harmful to the environment. High scoring countries included Canada, Chile, Finland, Norway, (West) Germany and the United Kingdom.

Pressures for change in business attitudes towards the environment come from consumers who are also citizens, voters, employees and members of the complex variety of institutions which make up society.

CORPORATE ENVIRONMENTALISM

Corporate environmentalism has appeared in international trade agreements like the North American Free Trade Agreement (*NAFTA*) in the form of specific policy commitments to sustainable development. In this context, sustainable development is defined as striking a balance between environmental and economic issues. According to this view, industrial development remains essential if poverty is to be eradicated in developing countries. Corporate environmentalism accepts that economic growth cannot occur at the expense of the environment, upon which growth itself depends. Corporate environmental goals include:

■ Reduction of all toxic wastes and emissions, working towards an ultimate goal of zero adverse effects.

■ Reduction of potential risks to the public.

■ Investment in sustainable agriculture.

■ Co-operative research programmes.

Corporate environmentalism seeks to incorporate these principles in international agreements and to establish them on a global scale through the growth of global corporate environmental organizations. In the run up to the Earth Summit in Rio de Janeiro in June 1992, Stephen Schmidheiny, UNCED's adviser for business and industry, organized the Business Council for Sustainable Development (BCSD). Drawn from 26 countries and 5 continents, the 48 corporate chief executives who formed the BSCD initially co-operated to create a consensus position on global environment and development issues. *Changing Course:* (BCSD 1992), prepared for Rio, was the first attempt by a global business organization to indicate the direction of future developments. Prepared in conjunction with environmental pressure groups, and using a range of case studies, publications in the mode of *Changing Course* highlight the growing recognition of the central role of business in achieving the goals of sustainable development strategies. A strong motivation is the recognition that customers are no longer prepared to ignore the life-cycle impacts of the products they buy or to tolerate the risk of environmental disasters like Bhopal or the *Exxon Valdez*.

In 1995 the BCSD merged with the World Industry Council for the Environment (WICE) to form the World Business Council for Sustainable Development (WBCSD). Close institutional ties were established between WBCSD and the International Chamber of Commerce (ICC), providing for joint projects and public relations. ICC, with its 2000 signatories, works with the International Bureau of Chambers of Commerce (*IBCC*), using their extensive communications networks to reach businesses across the world. The Charter Bulletin is an important tool of communication. Additionally, the ICC has produced a number of environmental publications.

The global environmentalists pursue a policy of promoting 'eco-efficiency', by minimizing the environmental impact of creating goods and services. The operation of market forces is central to their thinking. The use of environmental resources and processes (e.g. the absorption of waste) which have been regarded as 'free goods' can be regulated only if they are prices at 'full cost'. When this happens, markets will work for, rather than against, environmental protection. It is the task of the coalition of global environmental organizations to present information and generate public awareness in order to gain political support for the unpopular fiscal and legal changes which such pricing policies will necessarily entail. Policies of this type are implemented by elected representatives of governments.

ENVIRONMENTAL LAW

For the most comprehensive analysis of UK and European law see Ball and Bell (1995) and Garner's Environmental Law updates (Garner 1995)

Environmental legislation within a state may take three forms:

1. **Criminal law** Certain actions which damage the environment (or represent a threat to the environment) may be designated as criminal offences. Prosecution by the state (or occasionally by private individuals in private prosecutions) of a person found guilty of such an offence may result in penalties such as a fine, a term of imprisonment and/or payment of costs of reparation. Corporations and individuals can face official criminal proceedings.
2. **Administrative (public) law** This takes the form of a challenge to the legality of official decisions. For example, a planning decision might be challenged on grounds that it was environmentally detrimental and therefore illegal. Normally, however, the grounds on which official decisions may be reviewed are limited and would not allow the courts to reconsider the issue on its merits.
3. **Civil law** Civil law imposes legal obligations on the dealings between different corporations, individuals and interest groups in society. Where rights and interests are infringed, compensation for those aggrieved may be secured in the form of damages. In addition orders may be made (often called injunctions) preventing future environmental harm or requiring remedial steps to be taken. The introduction of civil liability for damage to the environment flows from the European Community Fourth Environment Action Programme. Civil law is seen as an effective way to implement EC policy on the environment. It can put into effect the 'polluter pays principle', and has the potential to secure prevention and rectification of pollution at source.

No text can provide a business with precise information on all specific legislation relevant to its operations. Legislation is constantly being updated in the light of events, new scientific research and pressure from interest groups. Although new legislative proposals can take years to become enshrined in legislation, long-term strategic decision-making must take account of general trends in future legislation. Professional legal advice is therefore indispensable. The following section describes the regulatory and legislative frameworks in the UK.

EC Directives and Regulations

UK business practices are increasingly strongly influenced by developments within the EC. Until the Single European Act (SEA 1986) environmental issues were not specifically required to be considered in EC legislation. However, when the need for an EC policy on the environment became apparent in the 1970s the European Court of Justice (*ECJ*) declared in its rulings that protection of the environment was one of the essential objectives of the EC. This enabled the EC to introduce legislation under related Articles of the Treaty of Rome.

The Single European Act 1986 was a major development. It confirmed the ability of the EC to legislate on environmental issues and laid down specific powers for action. Additionally, the EC is now obliged to make environmental protection requirements a component part of its other policies under Article 130r of the Treaty of Rome. Objectives laid down for the EC in the SEA 1986 include:

- Protection and improvement of the quality of the environment.

- Protection of human health.

- Conservation and rational use of natural resources.

The principles of EC environmental law as established by the SEA 1986 are in close accord with those adopted by corporate environmentalism. They include:

- Prevention.

- Rectification of environmental damage at source.

- Polluter pays principle.

Environmental protection was also laid down as one of the basic objectives of the European Union, in the Treaty on European Union signed by the EU member states in Maastricht in February 1992. The legislative framework within the EU is complex and subject to constant change.

EU environmental legislation

Environmental quality measures can take three basic forms:

1. The so-called 'command and control' measures with specific legal penalties for breach of regulations.

2. Market-based instruments, e.g. a *carbon tax*.
3. Voluntary systems, e.g. eco-labelling and EMAS (see Case Study 7.1).

By 1992 the EC had issued 445 legislative texts relating to the environment. Environmental protection is also secured through legislation which is not specifically designed for this purpose. EC legislation takes the form of regulations, Directives and decisions.

Regulations
These have immediate effect in all member states, requiring no alteration in the laws or regulations of the member states. (Some examples are described in Case Study 7.3.) According to Article 189 of the EC Treaty, regulations confer rights or impose obligations on individual citizens and are immediately binding. Regulation 93/259 on 'the supervision and control of the shipments of waste within, into and out of the EC' completed the monitoring system on waste transfers.

Directives
Member states are bound to achieve the objectives of a Directive, but they are free to select the methods by which they do so. This may involve incorporation of the individual points of the Directive in their national legislation, or production of evidence that existing legislation meets the targets. Directives do not apply immediately, but do carry deadlines for achievement of the required effects. In practice, the Directive is the most common instrument used by the Council and the Commission. For example, Directive 85/337 specified that Environmental Assessment (*EA*) statements must be prepared for major developments at the planning stage (see Case Study 7.2). The Directive was implemented in England and Wales by the Town and Country Planning (Assessment of Environmental Effects) Regulations 1988. If a member state fails to comply with a Directive within a certain time limit it may be taken to the European Court of Justice. In addition, individuals may also have recourse in the national courts of law if they have suffered loss as a result of the delayed implementation.

Decisions
Decisions are taken by the European Union, normally the Commission but sometimes the Council. They apply to particular cases, often individual firms, and are not aimed at the general public. EEC Decision 76/431 set up a committee on waste management.

CASE STUDY 7.1
EC Regulation 93/1836: EMAS

European Council Regulation 93/1836 of 29 June 1993 allows 'the voluntary participation by companies in the industrial sector in a community eco-management and audit scheme (EMAS).' Designed to encourage industry to combine economic growth with environmental protection, the regulation is based on Article 130s of the Treaty of Rome. EMAS (sometimes referred to as 'the Eco-Management and Audit (EMA) Scheme) is designed to give practical implementation to the EC's policy regarding the protection of the environment through sustainable growth. In particular it seeks to 'prevent, reduce and as far as possible eliminate pollution, particularly at source, on the basis of the polluter pays principle, to ensure sound management of resources and to use clean or cleaner technology.' It calls for:

- Continuous improvement of environmental performance.

- Environmental management systems incorporating environmental auditing procedures.

- Awareness and training of workers in the establishment.

- Provision of information to the public on the environmental aspects of their activities.

- Production and dissemination by companies of periodic environmental statements.

As an international standard which can be met by the recognition of existing standards in member states, most EMAS requirements are met by BS 7750. Each member state is required to designate a competent body to maintain the register of sites. In Britain this is undertaken by the British Standards Institution (BSI).

EMAS is directed specifically at companies in the mining, quarrying, power and waste disposal sectors. It applies to industrial sites only, not the whole organization, with non-industrial participation permitted only on an experimental basis, although member states may make provision for non-industrial sectors, e.g. the UK has introduced a scheme for local government. The emphasis of EMAS is on the measurable performance of the company, rather than on the management tools, as is the case with BS 7750. For EMAS the core issue in the verification process is continuous measurable improvements.

Accreditation from schemes which meet the EMAS criteria can be used to satisfy banks, financial institutions and customers of a firm's achievement of standards in environmental performance. It can provide incentive to imaginative proactive lateral thinking in improving a firm's environmental performance and profitability simultaneously. For example, following a BS 7750 accreditation exercise, Renlon, a small UK firm in the property preservation business, substantially reduced its use of toxic substances. This reduced Renlon's costs while minimizing risks to the environment and to employee and customer health. The process of publicity proved helpful to the firm's marketing image. On the other hand, accreditation can be sought as an end in itself, proving a disincentive to further improvement (see also Chapter 5).

Department of the Environment 1995

CASE STUDY 7.2

EC Directive 85/337 Environmental Assessment for Major Projects

All member states were obliged to implement legislation to standardize identification and analysis of the environmental impacts of major developments. Environmental Assessment (EA) statements must be prepared for all new 'dirty neighbour' industrial developments. These include major petrochemical, iron and steel and chemical works, processes involving asbestos, thermal power stations, disposal of radioactive waste, heavy metals and other toxic substances. The regulations cover major infrastructure works, canals, railways, roads, ports and airports. In addition, EAs may be required for a wide range of agricultural, industrial, waste disposal and infrastructure schemes, including salmon hatcheries and glass manufacturing, if the planning authority consider that the development will have a significant effect on the environment.

The specific elements of the environment to be evaluated through the EA process are laid down in the EC Directive. They include impacts upon:

■ Human beings.

■ Flora and fauna.

■ soil.

■ Water.

■ Air and climate.

■ Landscape.

■ Material assets.

■ Cultural heritage.

The EA regulations provide a standardized and systematic framework for decision-making. All major impacts of major new developments are identified and analysed, so that decision-makers can act in the light of evidence and can communicate their findings to the public.

Authors' research

CASE STUDY 7.3
EC Regulations: Some Examples

The inevitable tensions within the legal framework between environmental principles and economic considerations is demonstrated by the 'Danish Bottle Case'.

The Danish Bottle Case

Danish national legislation bans the use of metal cans for beer and soft drinks and stipulates their sale only in returnable bottles with a compulsory deposit. The legislation stimulates reuse and effectively rules out plastic bottles, and the scheme has succeeded in achieving a return rate of 95 per cent. Article 30 of the EC Treaty, however, bans national rules which have the effect of impeding the free movement of goods within the Community. Since the refilling of bottles is most practical where transportation is minimized, the Danish legislation was considered by competing foreign brewers to have the effect of benefiting home producers. Reflecting this pressure, the Commission brought a case against Denmark to the European Court of Justice (ECJ). The ECJ ruled in favour of Denmark, on the grounds that protection of the environment is a legitimate justification for national legislation, and that the practice had not been introduced in order to protect domestic industries. It remains to be seen, however, whether this rule will apply generally to national standards which are stricter than the environmental standards laid down by EC legislation.

Waste disposal in Germany

The escalating economic costs of waste disposal coupled with the shortage of suitable landfill sites, particularly in Germany, has given rise to far-reaching proposals for EU legislation to harmonize environmental laws in general and packaging waste management in particular. Solutions, in order of priority, are:

1. Minimization of packaging.

2. Recovery and reuse.

3. Recycling.

4. Disposal to landfill sites.

In 1990, 80 per cent of packaging waste in Europe was incinerated or disposed of in landfill sites. Pressure to reduce the total volume of waste has come in particular from Germany. The German domestic Waste Packaging Ordinance established the *Grüner Punkt* or 'Green Dot' programme which places a responsibility for collection, recycling and disposal of packaging on producers and retailers. Consumers can return all packaging materials at the point of sale, and producers must accept all returned packaging. This 'Topfer Law,' so-called after the German Environmental Minister who saw the proposals through, is unpopular with Germany's competitors as it is seen as putting importing firms at a disadvantage. Through its taxation system Belgium also penalizes corporations which do not recycle their packaging products.

Reuse and recovery

The aspiration in the EU is to reduce incinerated or disposed waste to 10 per cent of levels in the early 1990s, with the bulk of the reduced packaging being reused or recycled. Reuse is accompanied by the concept of 'recovery'. This may include the recovery of energy from the packaging through incineration, a concept more popular with the packaging industry than reduction and reuse. As a detailed American study has shown (see Case Study 10.5), the environmental implications of the reuse and recycling of packaging materials is one highly complex subject in a sea of complexity. In the negotiation of legislation the combination of environmental and economic considerations, scientific evidence and the competing interests of industrial sectors and national interests ensures that there are no easy answers.

Authors' research

UK national legislation

The British approach to pollution control has always involved a pragmatic balance between environmental and economic considerations. Hence environmental protection legislation has been strongly influenced by the necessity to meet EC requirements.

Background

Most environmental law sources are statutory as opposed to judge-made law and those statutes generally require detailed 'fleshing out' by statutory instruments and environmental protection regulations. Environmental protection is, however, also supported in part by common law, e.g. the law of nuisance or rules on restrictive covenants (Ball and Bell 1995). Prior to the Environmental Protection Act 1990, there was no unifying concept of 'environment' underpinning statute law. Relevant legislation was designed to deal with specific symptoms and related problems arising from industrialization. Hence:

■ Public Health Acts, starting in 1875, sought to redress insanitary living standards in industrial towns.

■ Housing Acts maintained housing standards.

■ Clean Air Acts sought to eliminate smoke from towns and cities.

■ Control of Pollution Act 1974 was designed to 'make further provision with respect to waste disposal, water pollution, noise, atmospheric pollution and public health.'

Public health legislation sought to establish standards in public health in respect of housing, atmospheric pollution (domestic and industrial), offensive and foul-smelling trades, water, waste, sewage drains, smoke and noise. Enforcement was by central agency and local authorities:

■ The Industrial and Clean Air Inspectorate, formerly the Alkali Inspectorate, was centrally administered.

■ Environmental health departments of local authorities were locally administered.

In practice, industrial manufacturing processes were monitored by the central agency. This restricted the powers of local authorities, who were normally entitled to enforce only legislation applying to commercial and domestic premises. The Public Health Acts created the concept of 'statutory nuisance' under which local authorities and individuals could take legal action (including ultimately prosecution) for a variety of environmental problems including noise, smell, dust, smoke and fumes.

Environmental Protection Act (Parts 1 and 2) 1990

The pre-existing legislation on air pollution (under the Alkali Acts and Health and Safety at Work, etc. Act 1974) was swept away and incorporated within the Environmental Protection Act 1990 (EPA 1990), the provisions of which were implemented gradually between 1990 and 1995. Part 1 of the Act introduced a new system known as Integrated Pollution Control (IPC) in relation to industrial processes. IPC is a scheme whereby processes capable of causing pollution to the environment are brought under a unified system of control, authorization and enforcement, in respect of emissions to all environmental media. It also introduced a similar system controlling only atmospheric pollution from less polluting processes. Processes subject to IPC requirements must be prescribed by the Secretary of State, and may include any process capable of causing harm to humans or to any other living organism supported by the environment. Regulations under the EPA 1990 were initially enforced by:

■ Her Majesty's Inspectorate of Pollution (HMIP) for major industrial processes, including chemicals, pharmaceuticals, incineration, chemical waste treatment, animal and plant treatment.

■ Local authorities for other processes (in respect of air pollution).

All processes controlled under Part 1 of the EPA 1990 are subject to utilization of Best Available Technology Not Entailing Excessive Cost (BATNEEC) having regard to the Best Practicable Environmental Option (*BPEO*) with regard to released substances. These terms are used in international standards and have the effect of strengthening economic arguments for moderating pressures on management to secure environmental protection.

Part 2 of the EPA relates to the generation, management and disposal of waste. The first Act in the UK which related to waste was the Deposit of Poisonous Wastes Act 1972. This was replaced by the Control of Pollution Act (*COPA*) 1974 which introduced a more regulated system of waste licensing for landfill or incineration which had previously not existed. Although a significant step forward COPA proved to be limited in its scope and in 1990 waste regulation moved away from purely disposal towards 'management'. Part 2 renders control over usage and disposal from cradle-to-grave which also includes transportation.

Water Resources Act 1991

Legislation for control of water pollution in England and Wales is broadly covered by the Water Resources Act 1991. The Act controls discharges of wastes to rivers and streams, lakes, canals, estuaries, underground waters and territorial sea waters within the three-mile limit. All discharges to these waters require consent from the regulating authorities (Environment Agency in England and Wales; River Purification Board in Scotland) and must comply with set conditions. It is an offence to cause or allow any polluting matter to enter those waters. If pollution occurs, whether through accident or deliberate action, the authorities have powers to instigate legal proceedings and to recover the costs of remedial works. Until the setting up of the Environment Agency in 1995 the Act was administered by the National Rivers Authority (NRA) in England and Wales.

Water Industry Act 1991

Industries may discharge trade effluent to sewers only with the approval of the appropriate sewage undertaker. Discharges are subject to the terms and conditions of trade effluent consents as issued under Section 18 of the Water Industry Act 1991.

Environment Act 1995

The Environment Act 1995 established two new agencies, the Environment Agency for England and Wales and the Scottish Environment Protection Agency. Both agencies are independent, non-governmental, corporate public bodies operating through a board appointed by the government. These *quangos* (quasi-autonomous non-governmental organizations) are constitutionally very similar to the NRA. The Act also established an Advisory Committee for Wales and a series of regional advisory committees for protection of regional environments, local fisheries and flood defences.

The Environment Agency for England and Wales incorporates the NRA, HMIP and the Waste Regulatory Authority (*WRA*). Its duties are:

■ Integrated pollution control.

■ Control of radioactive substances.

■ Regulation of waste and waste carriers.

■ All the functions previously carried out by the NRA, including water resources management, land drainage, fisheries, and pollution control.

The new agencies cannot provide truly integrated environmental protection since they do not cover all environmental matters. Environmental assessments for town and country planning, which have important preventive roles, the regulation of discharges to sewers, the control of noise and smells and the use of market instruments remain outside their remits (Ball 1994).

The second part of the Environment Act deals with contaminated land liability updating Part 2 of the EPA 1990. Contaminated land is defined here as land in such a condition by reason of substances in, on or under the land that:

■ Significant harm is being caused; or

■ There is a significant possibility of such harm being caused; or

■ Pollution of controlled waters is being or is likely to be caused.

(Payne 1995: 36)

The contaminated land issue here relates to people's liability to contribute to the cost of cleaning up contaminated sites. The direction given by the regulatory body (Environment Agency or the local authority) to the recipient can involve site assessments, site clean-ups and restoration to the state before contamination and post-clean-up monitoring. Failure to comply to a notice given by the regulatory body (without due reason) can be viewed as a criminal offence with one-off fines of £20 000 and £2000 per day for each day of non-compliance (Payne 1995: 36).

The UK has a number of environmental legislations that affect commercial operations other than the EPA 1990 and the Environment Act 1995. There are also the Radioactive Substances Act 1993 and the Clean Air Act 1993. Due to the continually changing and dynamic nature of environmental legislation, the reader is advised to consult Garner's Environmental Law updates for a complete reference of environmental legislation in the UK (Garner 1995).

Environmental legislation: some examples in practice

Integrated Pollution Control (IPC) in the UK covers certain aspects of atmospheric pollution, water use and discharge and solid waste disposal. The excellent *DIY Environmental Review for Companies* (Business in the Environment and Coopers & Lybrand 1994) classifies the environmental impacts as follows:

- **Atmospheric emissions** Acid rain, air pollutants, CFCs/ozone layer depletion, global warming, solvents, vehicle emissions.

- **Water use/discharge** Effluent discharges, water supply.

- **Solid waste** Packaging, paper, recycling, waste management

The process of production may entail a wide range of processes which are subject to environmental legislation.

Solvents

The production of paints, degreasing agents and other substances can involve the use of solvents which, when released into the atmosphere may be toxic, carcinogenic and persistent. They may cause air pollution through emission of volatile organic compounds (*VOCs*) which lead to ozone creation at ground level, causing photochemical smog. Production and use of these substances is controlled under the Environmental Protection Act 1990, the Environmental Protection (Prescribed Processes and Substances) Regulations 1991 (CSI 1991/472), the Water Resources Act 1991, and, in respect of the health and safety aspects, by the Control of Substances Hazardous to Health (*COSHH*) Regulations 1988.

Effluent discharges

Discharges of effluent from industrial sites to sewers and natural water courses are regulated under the Water Industry Act 1991, the Environment Protection Act 1990 and the Environmental Protection (Prescribed Processes and Substances) Regulations 1991 (CSI 1991/472). Discharges of effluents to water courses require registration and consents. It is a criminal offence to discharge without consent or to breach the conditions attached to one.

Magistrates courts may impose fines of up to £20 000 or three months' imprisonment. Conviction on indictment may carry an unlimited fine or up to two years' imprisonment. On the 'polluter pays principle' funds for monitoring water quality and pollution control in England and Wales come from application and annual charges for consents, and costs recovered from polluters for the cleaning up of pollution.

Packaging

The mountains of waste resulting from the production and disposal of metal, plastic, glass, paper, cardboard, and wood packaging has attracted increasing attention across the industrialized world. Waste results from use of scarce raw materials and energy, and pollution results from disposal to landfill sites. Further, PVC (polyvinyl chloride) plastics have been the subject of legislation in respect of the release of hydrogen chloride and dioxins when incinerated. Two EC Directives (89/369 and 89/429) control emissions from municipal waste incineration and set stringent emission standards for the two toxic substances. In more general terms, the EC Packaging Directive OJ L365 (31.12.94) requires each member state to ensure that 25-40 per cent of all packaging waste output by weight is recycled and encourages the use of reusable packaging. France is committed to the recycling or incineration of all household packaging by 2003. The Netherlands plans to eliminate packaging disposal without energy recovery by 2000. Germany had already achieved 80 per cent level of reuse and recycling of packaging by 1995.

Effects of pollution

The effects of pollution through disposal of toxic wastes, whether to the air, to land or to water courses, can be seen to impact directly upon human health and can therefore be most readily monitored and controlled. Impacts upon the visual landscape, flora and fauna, and the atmosphere over the long-term are more difficult to assess.

Energy efficiency

Legislation in respect of energy efficiency and the natural environment has been introduced. Concern over emissions resulting from energy production has given rise to proposals to harmonize EC fuel taxes in order to reduce emissions of CO_2, S_2 and NO_x while increasing energy efficiency. The moves are reflected in EC Directives, (e.g. 75/716, 85/377, 87/36) relating to the sulphur content of certain fuels. The EPA 1990 in the UK also makes reference to this problem. Companies are encouraged through advisory bodies and grants to explore means to control energy costs through new technologies, such as combined heat and power (CHP) systems, small-scale hydro-electric and wind-power schemes, landfill, gas waste and refuse-derived fuels.

Environmental impact assessments

DOE Circulars 13/88 and 1/92 give guidance on EIAs. EC pressures are increasing for more dynamic assessments of all new developments.

Pollution prevention guidelines

The NRA produces an excellent series of Pollution Prevention Guidelines designed to provide guidance and practical advice on measures to prevent damage to the environment, including information on technology and equipment. These guidelines are obtainable from the NRA as these leaflets are constantly updated. **Address: National Rivers Authority, (now part of the Environment Agency,), Rio House, Unteside Drive, Aztec West, Almondsbury, Bristol BR12 4UD.** The guidelines clarify the legal framework and legal terminology and provide contacts for further information. The guidelines include:

- General guide to the prevention of pollution of controlled waters.

- Above ground oil storage tanks.

- Use of oil separators in surface water drainage systems.

- Disposal of sewage where no mains drainage is available.

- Works in, near, or liable to affect water courses.

- Working at demolition and construction sites.

- Fuelling stations: construction and operation.

- Safe storage and disposal of used oils.

- Prevention of pollution of controlled waters by pesticides.

- Pollution from highway depots.

- Industrial sites.

- Prevention of pollution of controlled waters by sheep dip.

- High pressure water and steam cleaners.

- Inland waterways: marinas and craft.

- Retail foodstores and similar sites.

- School and educational establishments.

- Pollution prevention measures for the control of spillages and fire-fighting run-off.

Landfill Tax

In the spirit of making 'the polluter pay', proposals for a Landfill Tax were introduced in the UK in autumn 1994. The intention was that waste disposal companies would pass on the additional costs to waste producers. The resulting rise in awareness among producers of the true costs of their activities would provide motivation to reduce waste and recover more of the waste for reuse and recycling. The Landfill Tax proposal is linked to the setting up of private sector environmental trusts, financed from forgone tax income and water regulatory authorities. Their role might include restoration of landfill sites where responsibility is unclear, or research into more sustainable waste management practices.

The British government favours an *ad valorem* tax, based on a percentage of the charges being made by operators. These charges reflect differing land values in the locality of the landfill sites. This method has the advantage of ease of administration, and hence lower costs. However, a weight-based tax, with different bands according to the nature of the waste, would benefit companies which are prepared to set higher environmental standards. An *ad valorem* tax would force wastes into cheaper and less environmentally sound landfills, and would encourage the transportation of wastes over long distances.

Strengths and weaknesses of environmental legislation

The precautionary principle would indicate that dispersal of toxic substances to land, water and air can result in unquantifiable multiplier effects along food chains and ecosystems. However, in the absence of scientific proof of specific damage or cause for concern relating to a particular practice, especially over the long-term, it can be argued that there is no specific justification for altered practice. Hence the temptation to frame legislation in terms of BATNEEC or BPEO. Individual firms capable of drawing on their own scientific and legal advisers are unlikely to be forced into acceptance of strict environmental standards through 'command and control' mechanisms of this type.

Further, where the monitoring system itself is dependent upon the 'polluter pays principle', pollution is necessary in order to pay for the monitoring and clean-up processes. The most polluting industries will have the greatest incentive to employ costly consultants in order to continue their operations, rather than switching to products and production methods which are almost entirely environmentally neutral in effect. The argument that no industrial process can be entirely environmentally benign from-cradle-to-grave obscures the reality that many industrial processes are fundamentally environmentally disastrous and can be only super-ficially 'greened'.

However, legislation expresses the general tenor of social expectations from industry. The necessity to meet public expectations and avoid public retribution in the event of substantial breaches of the law provides industry with the motivation to enter into dialogue with public authorities, business 'clubs', the media and environmental pressure groups. The first wave of environmental legislation has provided smaller companies with little guidance, resulting in apathy or negative attitudes towards the environment. This problem has been tackled by a series of projects designed to promote environmentally sound practices within industry in general, and within SMEs in particular.

Enforcement is one of the main stumbling blocks to effective environment regulation in the UK. It requires huge amounts of capital funding and immense administrative management. Tracking down and dealing with all environmental infringments in SMEs for example is an administrative nightmare and logistically impossible with the current funding supply. There are three main enforcement agencies:

■ Regulators.

■ Pressure groups.

■ Individuals.

The regulators (primarily the Environment Agency) form the major enforcement bodies, with pressure groups and individuals bringing a handful of cases to the courts every year. Most people think of prosecutions when they think of enforcement. By far the most significant action taken, however, is far less draconian in nature and often takes the form of persuasion, advice and guidance about how to clean up and where to go for professional services. The NRA (who previous to the Environment Agency dealt with the most prosecutions) undertook only 300–500 prosecutions a year.

GREEN BUSINESS ORGANIZATIONS

Businesses with the necessary expertise have come together with statutory authorities to provide guidance for firms seeking to meet marketing and legal pressures on environmental issues. Such organizations include the following.

Business in the Environment (BiE)

Set up in 1990 in order to support progress towards sustainable development in the UK, Business in the Environment has co-operated with Coopers & Lybrand and, with the support of the European Commission, produced a DIY workbook entitled *A DIY Environmental Review for Companies* (1994). Carefully designed, it offers practical advice on environmental legislation and management with particular reference to the requirements of SMEs. Written 'by business for business' the DIY guide is regularly updated, and has proved a valuable resource.

Other publications

Buying into the Environment
Produced in association with KPMG and the Chartered Institute of Purchasing and Supply, this provides an excellent résumé of the rationale and practicalities of supply chain pressures. Illustrated with practical examples from leaders in the field, including IBM UK, B&Q, BT, Skippingdale Paper Products, Suffolk County Council and HD Plastics, the text supplies information on the supply chain implications of environmental legislation.

LCA Sourcebook
The LCA Sourcebook, produced with SustainAbility and its European counterpart SPOLD (Society for the Promotion of LCA Development), includes a valuable 'Life-Cycle Directory' of firms and statutory and non-statutory organizations throughout Europe with relevant resources and expertise.

Grime Goes Green
This video, featuring HRH the Prince of Wales and the actor John Cleese, illustrates the contribution which staff can make in the environmentally friendly workplace.

Networks and partnerships

BiE uses environmental networks to support SMEs, sharing information through 95 regional groups. It has offered advice on good environmental practice to 10 000 companies. The Welsh Arena Network has worked with a further 200 companies.

Additionally, BiE has worked in partnership with the Open University to develop a distance learning pack on environmental review processes, and, in conjunction with the Chartered Institute of Purchasing and Supply, it has encouraged companies to influence the environmental management practices of suppliers. Together with Extel Financial, BiE has raised awareness of environmental issues in the City of London through a review of the attitudes of analysts.

Address: BiE, 8 Stratton Street, London, W1X 5FD.

Centre for Exploitation of Science and Technology (CEST)

CEST works with industry, the public sector, academia and government policy-makers to identify new approaches to existing problems through commercial and technological innovation. CEST is a not-for-profit organization which is funded by industry and by the UK government. Sponsored by the BOC Foundation for the Environment, CEST undertook a series of waste minimization projects, including the Aire and Calder Project, in conjunction with HMIP, the NRA and Yorkshire Water, Project Catalyst in conjunction with the DTI, and the Leicester Waste Minimization Initiative (LWMI) under the umbrella of the East Midlands Advisory Group on the Environment.

Publication

The initial report on these projects, *Waste Minimization and Cleaner Technology: An Assessment of Motivation*, was published in 1995. The report demonstrated the value of the 'club' approach, in which firms meet at local level, sharing expertise and generating motivation for change.

Address: Centre for Exploitation of Science and Technology (CEST), 5 Berners Road, London N1 0PW.

CBI Environmental Policy Unit

This provides a focal point for British industry in general, and SMEs in particular, on environmental policy and associated legal developments. Its first action plan focused on climate change, waste management, recycling and litter. The CBI works to promote environmental issues in co-operation with its membership, NGOs and statutory authorities.

Address: CBI, 103 New Oxford Street, London, CW1A 1DU.

Publications

It has produced a series of publications in its 'Environment Means Business' series, including a guide to environmental management systems entitled *Setting the Standard* (1995).

Business in the Community (BiC)

Business in the Community (BiC) works to involve communities in business practices. Although environmental issues were not its primary concern, it includes environmental projects within its programme.

Address: Business in the Community (BiC), 8 Stratton Street, London, W1X 5FD.

Institute of Business Ethics (IBE)

The *IBE* was founded by the Christian Association of Business Executives. Its patrons are the Archbishop of Canterbury, the Cardinal Archbishop of Westminster, the Moderator of the Free Church Federal Council, the Moderator of the General Assembly of the Church of Scotland, the Chief Rabbi and the Iman of the London Central Mosque. It seeks to clarify ethical business issues and to establish 'common ground between people of goodwill of all faiths'.

Publications

Ethics, Environment and the Company: A Guide to Effective Action
Although now dated (published in 1990) it includes examples of environment policy statements from John Laing, Rohm and Haas Company, 3M UK, ICI, KPMG Peat Marwick McLintock, Iceland Frozen Foods and Sainsbury's.

Benefiting Business and the Environment (1995)
This contains the results of interviews with over 40 companies, and covers over 70 different environmental initiatives. These include projects for energy saving, reduction of waste, recycling, reduction of transport and water use.

Address: IBE, 12 Palace Street, London, SW1E 5JA.

Society for the Promotion of LCA Development (SPOLD)

Established in 1992, SPOLD is an association of 20 large companies in Europe formed to promote the development and application of LCA.

Publications

LCA Sourcebook
The *LCA Sourcebook*, commissioned in conjunction with Business in the Environment and SustainAbility, contains a 'Life-Cycle Directory' giving details of 96 groups, organizations and consultancies working in the field throughout Europe, together with a comprehensive list of their publications.

Feasibility Study
SPOLD has also commissioned PA Consulting to produce a *Feasibility Study for Developing an Open Database for Life-Cycle Inventory Analysis* (1993) on commodity chemicals.

Address: SPOLD, Avenue E Mounier 83, Box 1, 1200 Brussels, Belgium.

SustainAbility Ltd

This is an environmental consultancy working on corporate environmental management and strategy. It assists corporate clients to take a life-cycle perspective in their strategic thinking.

Its members have participated in consultative committees involved in the preparation of the UK eco-labelling scheme and environmental assessment schemes through the Building Research Establishment Environmental Assessment Method (*BREEAM*) consultative committee.

Services
Since its inauguration in 1987, SustainAbility has become one of Europe's most influential environmental management consultancies. It provides environmental management, research and internal and external communications services to leading companies across a range of sectors, including biotechnology, chemicals, electronics, finance, fast-moving consumer goods (*FMCG*), food and drink, health care, plastics, office supplies, packaging, retailing and tourism. Its other services include:

- Corporate strategy.

- Stakeholder analysis.

- Policy reviews.

- Environmental management systems.

- Environmental audits.

- Supplier challenges.

- Environmental action plans.

- Communications.

- Corporate environmental reports.

- Training.

- Market research.

- Product life-cycle management.

Advisory councils
In addition to working directly with corporations, the public sector and NGOs, Sustain-Ability is represented on many advisory councils and committees. These include:

- BioIndustry Association.

- Building Research Establishment Environmental Assessment Method (BREEAM).

- Institute of Environmental Managers.

- UK Eco-Labelling Board.

- US National Wildlife Federation.

- World Resources Institute (*WRI*).

Corporate clients

- B&Q
- Bank of Scotland
- Body Shop
- British Airways
- British Airways Holidays
- British Gas
- British Petroleum
- British Telecom
- Building Design Partnership
- BUPA
- Dow Europe
- Gardner Merchant
- Glaxo
- Grand Metropolitan
- IBM UK
- ICI (Fibres, plc, Polyurethanes)
- Lever Brothers
- Manweb
- Midland Bank
- Monsanto
- Novo Nordisk (Bio-Industrial, Healthcare)
- Procter & Gamble
- Reed Exhibitions
- Shell (International, International Chemicals UK)
- Stanhope Properties
- TSB Bank
- Universal Offices Supplies (John Menzies Group)
- Volvo Concessionaires
- Welsh Water
- W H Smith

Public sector and NGO clients

- Business Council for Sustainable Development
- Commission of the European Communities
- Department of the Environment (DoE)
- Department of Trade and Industry (DTI)
- Joseph Rowntree Foundation
- OECD
- UNEP
- US Agency for International Development
- World Resources Institute
- Worldwide Fund for Nature (WWF)

Publications

- *The Green Consumer Guide* 1988.
- *The Green Business Guide* 1991.
- *The Corporate Environmentalists* 1991.
- *The LCA Sourcebook* 1994.
- *The EPE WorkBook* 1994 (see Case Study 7.4).
- *Who Needs It? Market Implications of Sustainable Lifestyles* 1995 (see Case Study 7.5).

Founders

A founder member of the Association of Environmental Consultancies, SustainAbility's founders John Elkington and Julia Hales were elected to the United Nations Global 500 Roll of Honour for their 'outstanding environmental achievements' in 1989.

Address: SustainAbility Ltd, The People's Hall, 91–7 Freston Road, London W11 4BD.

CASE STUDY 7.4
SustainAbility's *EPE WorkBook*

The *EPE (European Partners for the Environment) WorkBook* produced by Sustain-Ability in conjunction with the EU and the French Environment Ministry provides an example of the successful co-operation of companies, government agencies and environmental organizations in promoting a shared sense of responsibility for the environment.

Taking the five key sectors in the Fifth European Environmental Action Programme *Towards Sustainability*, agriculture, energy, industry, tourism and transport, the *WorkBook* presents three scenarios or alternative visions of the future designed to guide constructive thought. The key assumptions are summarized in three scenarios.

Scenario 1: No Limits

Environmental concerns prove to have been greatly overstated. Global environmental degradation has not materialized and economic growth based on new, clean industries has generated the wealth to pay for a clean and safe environment in Europe. Liberalization and privatization have continued apace with world-wide free markets driving innovation and growth. Today's environmental challenges are met with high-tech solutions. The emphasis is on maximizing quality of life.

Scenario 2: Orderly Transition

Environmental problems are recognized as serious, but can be solved with strong, integrated economic and environmental policies. The result: a growing role for the European Union in co-ordinating and integrating policies. Centralization and optimization are favoured. Top-down management and stewardship are the norm, with regular government intervention to ensure strict and evenly applied standards. The priorities: attaining environmental and social goals and delivering the best possible world for the greatest number of people.

Scenario 3: Values Shift

New scientific evidence following a series of environmental disasters, shows that environmental problems are truly serious, requiring radical industrial and economic change. Growing dissatisfaction with government and business catalyses a bottom-up approach. Social and ecological concerns are paramount, as people recognize the value of caring, fairness and community life. Major changes in consumption patterns occur so as not to exceed environmental limits and share global environmental space equitably. Local economies and self-sufficiency are central and non-market activities increasingly important, with business and industry focused on meeting needs rather than producing goods.

Prognosis

The authors of this report stress the need for constructive thought about the future. Clothed in dispassionate language and lacking in rhetoric, the prognosis to be derived from the scenarios is gloomy. The first two scenarios, which stand highest on the probability stakes, offer the options of choking on the debris of high-tech super-growth or the loss of civil liberties in a mass of statutory enforced green tape.

Source: *SustainAbility News Annual Review* 1994 6: 7

CASE STUDY 7.5
SustainAbility's *Who Needs It?*

Subtitled 'Market Implications of Sustainable Lifestyles', the report extrapolates from an international survey of the business implications of the predicted shift to more environmentally sustainable production and consumption patterns. Backed by Dow Europe and WWF, the research provides an example of co-operation between industry and environmental pressure groups in developing a sound and rational approach to the environment. The report outlines the emergence of the 'Age of the World Citizen', which follows from the 'Age of the Global Consumer'. It offers the 'Needs Test' to enable businesses to plan ahead, and bases its strategic and practical advice on its review of trends in consumer behaviour. This type of material is becoming increasingly valuable not only to management and industry but also to trade unions, ethical and green investment groups, marketing consultants, pressure groups and media professionals.

Groundwork Foundation

The majority of business associations and NGOs are nationally based, with international connections. The Groundwork Foundation has promoted environmental developments at local level through establishing Groundwork Trusts throughout Britain and in mainland Europe. Its primary focus has been on derelict industrial areas, seeking to attract new businesses and engage local people in environmental action. Groundwork works with the private sector locally and nationally, forming partnerships between companies, statutory authorities and community groups. Developed in partnership with ESSO UK and Television South Education, its Greenlink initiative has, with government approval, established a long-term partnership between schools and local industry based upon a shared concern for the environment.

Address: Groundwork Foundation, 85–7 Cornwall Street, Birmingham B3 3BY.

ECO-LABELS

The rise of 'green consumerism' led to a proliferation of unsubstantiated 'green' claims by companies eager to cash in on the new market. A rash of products were described as 'eco-friendly,' 'environmentally safe,' 'ozone-friendly,' 'safe for incineration' and 'recyclable'. Spurious claims exaggerated the eco-friendliness of products, including:

- Statements that a product was free of a particular toxic substance which it never contained in the first place.

- Claims that packaging was 'fully recyclable' where the company had no facilities to reclaim and recycle.

- Unsubstantiated claims that the product was 'eco-friendly'.

An eco-labelling scheme offers the facility for a product to be objectively assessed by an independent body in order to assess its eco-friendliness. If the product meets an agreed list of criteria, it is awarded an eco-label as a seal of approval, enabling the customer to make an informed choice. In this way, market forces may be harnessed to promote better industrial practices by reducing product-related environmental impacts (see Case Study 7.6).

World-wide over 30 eco-label schemes sprang up in the decade 1985–95, adapted from the original German Blue Angel scheme established by the German Federal Environment Agency in 1978. The name originates in the scheme's emblem, adopted from the logo of the United Nations Environment Programme. In the German scheme profit-making organizations are not permitted to participate directly in the definition of criteria. Originally, the scheme was intended as an adjunct to an evolving regulatory process for environmental quality standards in products and processes.

Subsequent eco-labelling schemes have been less successful in establishing rigorous standards. Although eco-labelling boards in the EU, for example, are theoretically expected to guarantee independence and neutrality in the establishing of criteria through drawing on expertise from industry, consumer organizations and pressure groups, in practice the demands of industry take precedence. Hence industry in the EU scheme has succeeded in limiting the environmental effectiveness of the scheme by confusing the issue in two ways. First, by narrowing and manipulating the categories of products to be assessed: compact fluorescent light bulbs are roughly six times as energy efficient as the standard incandescent variety, which account for over 90 per cent of the EU market. The eco-labelling scheme obscured this fact from consumers by creating two separate product categories, eligible for two separate eco-labels. Products differentiated in this way include cars with catalytic converters, kitchen paper with a high percentage of recycled fibre and CFC-free refrigerators. Second, by excluding from Life Cycle Assessment many of the most severe impacts: disposable paper products account for 35-40 per cent of domestic waste by volume, yet the impact of waste on the environment is not considered relevant.

In practice, the criteria selected for award of eco-labels has been limited to those which industry has found the easiest to quantify and address, including material use, energy consumption and waste disposal. Issues such as soil erosion, loss of biodiversity, long-term impacts of material abstraction, product durability and ethical questions such as animal testing have been excluded. The result is a scheme which offers minimal information to enable consumers to adopt ecologically sustainable lifestyles.

CASE STUDY 7.6
EU Eco-label Scheme

Eco-labelling is a market-orientated environmental policy which seeks to influence consumer behaviour by identifying the relevant environmental impacts of different products. Eco-labelling was first introduced in 1978 in the form of the German 'Blue Angel' scheme, which covered 3500 products. Most schemes are administered by the public sector, although the United States 'Green Cross' and 'Green Seal' are both administered by private sector organizations. Schemes also exist in Norway, Sweden, Canada and Japan.

EC Regulation 92/880 established an EC eco-label award scheme entitling companies to use the logo for products which meet the criteria of the scheme. EC Decision 93/326 established the guidelines for the fixing of costs and fees for the scheme, and EC Decisions 93/430 and 93/431 established the ecological criteria for washing machines and dishwashers, the first products to be covered by the scheme. The impacts of individual products are assessed from the cradle to the grave. The scheme is administered by the EC Directorate-General XI (Environment, Nuclear Safety and Civil Protection) in Brussels, and in the UK by the UK Eco-labelling Board.

The first step is to establish criteria for eco-labelling of product groups.

Laundry detergents

These are defined as products, whether in powder, liquid or any other form, designed for use in washing machines for the washing of textiles. Criteria focus on: 1. The dosage per wash (heavy and low duty). 2. The ingredients—in terms of total chemical content, long-term aquatic toxicity, phosphates, non-biodegradable organics and biological oxygen demand. 3. The packaging and its potential reuse. The criterion for phosphates is included to take account of the potential of detergents to contribute to eutrophication (water pollution).

Paints and varnishes

Criteria for indoor paints and varnishes for DIY and professional use focus on: 1. Fitness for use. 2. White pigments. 3. VOC content. 4. Volatile aromatic hydrocarbon. 5. Water pollution when tools are cleaned. 6. Solid waste residues, including the container. 7. Pigments and other substances—cadmium, lead, chromium V1, mercury, arsenic, dibutyl and dioctyle—must not be used.

Light bulbs

Criteria for single-ended light bulbs focus on: 1. Energy efficiency. 2. Mercury content. 3. Packaging—no laminates of composite plastics. 4. Product use information—low temperatures, dimmer switches. 5. Lifetime must exceed 8000 hours. In the early stages only compact fluorescent lamps were capable of meeting the criteria.

Shared responsibilities in the EU

Responsibility for developing product group criteria have been shared among the countries of the EU.

- *UK-led studies* include hairsprays, soil improvers, growing media, hairstyling aids, antiperspirants and deodorants, light bulbs (single-ended and double-ended) and furniture care products.

- *German-led studies* include detergents and cleaning agents.

- *Danish-led studies* include textiles, insulation materials, toilet rolls, kitchen towels and fine paper.

- *Commission-led studies* include refrigerators.

- *Italian-led studies* include floor and wall tiles, building materials and packaging materials.

- *French-led studies* include shampoos, batteries, paints and varnishes.

- *Dutch-led studies* include cat litter and shoes.

- *Greek-led studies* include mattresses and tourist services.

- *Portuguese-led studies* include ceramic tableware.

The Commission provides competent bodies with a set of guidelines on Life Cycle Assessment to be applied when developing criteria for the Eco-labelling Scheme. LCA compares different products on the basis of their common function, relates environmental impacts from the cradle to the grave to both market changes and technological improvements and identifies well-founded ecological criteria.

Source: Authors' research

TRADE UNIONS AND ENVIRONMENTAL ISSUES

Trade unions have a long history of involvement in health and safety in the workplace and in the local community. The urban living environment has impacted particularly strongly upon the lives of workers, giving rise to trade union pressure for improved standards in housing, water and sanitation, clean air and parks and open spaces. Trade unions are ideally placed to work for the protection of the environment in which all live, work and raise their families. Environmental policies adopted by the Trades Union Congress (*TUC*) and individual unions can provide the educational basis necessary for worker co-operation with the ecologically conscious firm. Since workers also have a vested interest in the long-term survival of the firms for which they work, the combination of income security and environmental sustainability offers fertile ground for development of ecologically sound policies.

Co-operation between workers and management on ecological issues requires a systematic approach if it is to be successful. As the CEST study (Johnson and Stokes 1995) on waste minimization showed, merely requesting suggestions from the workforce, with or without a financial reward, was unproductive. Workers had little interest in creating cost-savings or increasing profitability for a firm which failed to recognize them as individuals. On the other hand, where companies formed teams focusing on operations and led by a project champion, new projects were supported with enthusiasm. This was found to be particularly true in smaller firms (under 100 employees). Co-operation between workers and management is more typical of German industrial relations than Anglo-Saxon. However, such co-operation is emerging as a key component of an ecological management style.

ENVIRONMENTAL PRESSURE GROUPS

Another component of ecological management is the ability to work with environmental pressure groups. The growing appreciation of common interests between industry and environmental pressure groups is reflected in the increasing incidence of joint projects and mutual support. The Body Shop, frequently quoted as an example of an ecologically sound management, was one of the 1991 recipients of the Better Environment Awards, jointly sponsored by the Environment Foundation, the Department of the Environment and Shell UK. Body Shop joint poster campaigns with Greenpeace and Friends of the Earth have been designed to educate consumers and potential customers on green issues, including acid rain, recycling and the ozone layer.

Greenpeace

Greenpeace, the largest international pressure group, campaigns non-violently in defence of the natural world. Its campaigns for the causes and effects of pollution and wildlife destruction are based upon extensive research and reports. Publications and leaflets are made available to businesses and the general public.

As Case Study 7.7 on Shell UK versus Greenpeace shows, there is today even more reason for both industry and pressure groups to work together in the co-operative aim of ecological sustainability. In the case study one can see how both parties suffered severe publicity from a position that could have been averted.

CASE STUDY 7.7
Greenpeace and Brent Spar

Towards the end of 1994, Greenpeace, the largest international environmental pressure group, became aware of the fact that the UK Department of Trade and Industry (DTI) was conducting an internal review of the options for decommissioning redundant offshore installations. It emerged that Shell UK's Brent Spar oil rig was likely to be the first of a number of installations which it was proposed to be dumped at sea.

Although inshore structures in the North Sea were required to be brought ashore under International Maritime Organization guidelines, installations in the central and northern part of the North Sea could be dumped in situ. In the UK sector the dumping of the Brent Spar could have created a precedent which could have smoothed the way for the dumping of 50 to 60 other installations, and contaminated items from other industries. Aware of this, Greenpeace were concerned that Shell's Best Practicable Environmental Option (BPEO) was operating only on a case-by-case basis, ignoring the cumulative effects of dumping more than one installation.

Shell's decision in June 1995 to dump the platform in the Atlantic Ocean 150 miles west of the Hebrides in 6000 ft of water was therefore met by a spectacular, well-planned Greenpeace campaign. Helicopter-borne campaigners defied water hoses and attempts to evict them from the oil rig, watched by a barrage of media photographers. Meanwhile, condemnation by several governments and the threat of a petrol station boycott, which could have cost Shell £5 million a week in lost profits, forced Shell to order the two tugs towing the 66 000 tonne rig to turn around and head back to shore.

The incident raised the question of the lack of public awareness of environmental issues in the UK in comparison with other European countries. Shell countered with accusations that Greenpeace were emotional, alarmist and scientifically naive, arguing that decommissioning on land would be both more hazardous and more expensive than dumping at sea. The whole episode highlighted the potentially volatile nature of the relationship between commerce and pressure groups. It also, however, led to harmful publicity for both parties that could have been averted if there had been closer dialogue between the two groups.

Authors' research

Worldwide Fund for Nature (WWF) '95 Group

The '95 Group is made up of companies who have committed themselves to obtaining wood and wood-derived products from sources abiding by forestry Stewardship Council Standards. Homebase (Sainsbury's DIY subsidiary and a founder member of the group) has worked to create a detailed database on sourcing world-wide. The firm uses supply chain pressure to ensure that all its suppliers can provide evidence of sound environmental practice, and was the recipient of WWF's 1995 award (see Case Study 7.8).

European Environment Bureau (EEB)

Environmental pressure groups may co-operate not only with industry and statutory bodies, whether at local or national level, but also with each other. At national or international level such pressure groups are normally referred to as 'non-governmental organizations' (NGOs). Within Europe the European Environment Bureau (EEB) forms a particularly powerful federation of NGOs. Formed in December 1974, the Federation of 150 NGOs includes 4994 organizations with 826 regional branches, representing 10 million citizens as individual members. Formed two years after the Stockholm Conference on the environment, the primary objective of the EEB is to work for sustainability in the EU through seeking the better use of human and natural resources throughout the EU. The EEB seeks to ensure that the international commitments entered into by the EU and its member states are fulfilled, this with special reference to the Rio Earth Summit and the Global Summit in Copenhagen. The EEB seeks to work in partnership with regional authorities, companies, trade unions, consumer organizations and agricultural groups. Common approaches have been sought on environmental impact assessments, ecological water quality and air quality management. A further object of the EEB is to promote access to information in order to foster increased acknowledgement of the role of citizens and NGOs in the practical implementation of sustainable development. At international conferences EEB has supported maintenance of environmental standards through EC policies threatened by the globalization of the economy and the effects of the General Agreement on Tariffs and Trade (GATT) agreements. EEB has been a source of proposals for new policies the aims of which are to promote an 'eco-industrial revolution'. To this end it seeks to ensure NGO participation in the framework formal consultation bodies for eco-labelling and EMAS, and has issued position papers on these topics. Its many publications include *Low Electricity Europe: Sustainable Options* by J.S. Norgaard and J. Viegand (1995), *Who Needs Biofuels?* by Karola Taschner (1995), *The Time is Ripe: A Binding Community Emission Register is Overdue* by Ralph Ahrens (1995) and *An Activity Report on Eco-labelling* by Karola Taschner (1995). These publications are available from the European Environment Bureau (EEB), Rue de la victoire 26, B-1047 Brussels, Belgium.

Further, in co-operation with the French Ministry for the Environment, EEB organized a series of international meetings to heighten the awareness of NGOs of the negotiation of the Convention on Desertification. Through a process of publication of reports, conferences, statements, position papers, press releases and newsletters it works to implement its strategic five-year plan adopted in 1991. There are four points in this plan:

1. To follow up the implications of the Maastricht Treaty and any future Treaty Reviews.
2. To play an active role in the discussion about the future of the EU and its role in international environmental debates.
3. To enforce the key strategic environmental policy statements of the EC, especially the Fifth and subsequent Action Programmes.
4. To influence specific environmental initiatives in each of the following areas: (a) Key sectoral issues, e.g. transport, energy, agriculture; (b) Key cross-sectoral issues, e.g. economic instruments, freedom of information; (c) Key instrumental issues, e.g. policy integration, Environmental Agency, implementation/enforcement.

(EEB 1995: 30)

CASE STUDY 7.8
Worldwide Fund for Nature (WWF)

While acknowledging that 'all companies are profit driven, and every industry has a detrimental effect on the environment', the leading environmental pressure group WWF has developed a longstanding partnership with the corporate sector. WWF works closely with industry for three interconnected reasons:

■ Fund-raising.

■ Expanding awareness of WWF.

■ Encouraging improvements in business practice.

Co-operation between the environmental pressure group and industry takes a number of forms. For example WWF has worked with the following companies.

■ *Continental Tyres*, the second largest tyre manufacturer in Europe, donated £10 000 towards the costs of running the London to Cambridge Pedal for the Planet bike ride.

■ *ICI/Tioxide* helped to develop educational material for 11 to 16 year olds focused on pigment manufacturing. The pack includes data, information and film from ICI archives 'to demonstrate the industry's difficulties in weighing up consumer expectations and commercial profit against the cost to the environment'.

■ *Shell Education Service* sponsored *The Past Speaks Out*, the WWF history and environment competition in schools in 1991.

■ *Tesco Stores* pledged £100 000 to WWF's Vanishing Species Campaign while printing examples of conservation work on the packaging of their children's breakfast cereals. Tesco customers were given a special offer to join WWF at half price.

WWF has worked with a large range of firms, notably BT, B&Q and National Westminster Bank, to develop supply chain pressures through environmental audits and Life Cycle Assessment. It has promoted the '95 Group which seeks to eliminate wood derived from non-renewable resources from all their products. Additionally, WWF has produced an extensive catalogue of educational materials for schools and colleges which includes over 400 publications, including *Beyond the Green Horizon* (in association with Green Tourism), *Green Business* (in association with Pitman Publishing and the Institute of Management) and *Environmental Management Handbook* (in association with Pitman Publishing).

WWF permits the use of its logo alongside the corporate name in these co-operative ventures. Although the use of the panda logo appears to endorse the product as an eco-label, WWF states that it means no more than that the company has made a financial contribution and is 'probably benefiting from increased awareness of WWF's mission. The panda label is not an eco-label or endorsement, either of a product or of a company's environmental status.' However, as a result of the co-operation, corporate partners often commit themselves to ongoing environmental improvements. As WWF points out with some justification,

> very few individual supporters of WWF can claim to lead completely sustainable lifestyles. Most drive cars, for example, and many work for companies and organisations which inevitably have a detrimental effect on the environment. By working with responsible companies, WWF can help raise awareness of the environment in industry and encourage long-term investment in the improvements needed
> (*WWF News*, Autumn 1995: 18)

Last but not least, WWF argues that co-operation with business and industry enables it to raise vital funds to continue its work as an environmental campaigning group.

Source: Adapted from WWF publicity material

The EEB has identified the 'three deadlocks' of agriculture, energy and transport, arguing in favour of resource taxation and against labour-intensive taxation systems. Its 1992–7 Plan focuses on the agricultural sector, considering both EU internal and external policies, and working in close relationship with networks in the field of transport and energy.

UK EEB member organizations include: Aviation Environment Federation, Campaign for the Protection of Rural Wales (CPRW TY GWYN), Chartered Institute of Environmental Health, Civic Trust, Council for the Protection of Rural England (CPRE), Environment Councils Fauna and Flora Preservation Society, Friends of the Earth (FoE England & Wales), Friends of the Earth Scotland, Green Alliance, Media Natura, Mersey Basin Trust, National Society for Clean Air and Environmental Protection (*NSCA*), National Trust, Plantlife, Pesticides Trust, Royal Society for Nature Conservation (*RSNC*), Royal Society for the Protection of Birds (*RSPB*), Scottish Civic Trust, Scottish Environment Education Council (SEEC), Town and Country Planning Association, Wildlife Link, WWF-UK.

This powerful combination of pressure groups, each group with its research, networking and publicity machine, is mirrored throughout the member states of the EU, and has become a valuable mechanism for the determination and expression of public opinion in the EU, and its translation into legislation.

Eco-sponsoring

'*Eco-sponsoring*', the sponsoring by industry of an environmental pressure group or a specific conservation project, has developed from the more traditional practice of sponsoring sporting events or charities. As with the more traditional form of sponsoring, the firm enhances its advertising profile while the recipient organization is enabled to work more effectively towards its chosen goals. Co-operation may be founded upon bonds of sympathy, as in the German Lufthansa sponsoring of the protection of cranes through the German Association for Bird Protection. Most often, funds are advanced to an environmental pressure group for a specific project following careful negotiation. The temptation for a pressure group to accept funds from any source is moderated by the realization that sponsors may be seeking to relieve a guilty conscience. Indeed, acceptance of funding from firms with unsound environmental policies may be counter-productive for both parties to the sponsoring through the effects of adverse publicity.

On an international scale, WWF has accepted funding and donations from many different organizations (see Case Study 7.8), while Greenpeace has been wary of accepting any large donations from industry. Business in the Environment has been sponsored by AEA Technology, Birds Eye, BT, Cawoods, East Midlands Electricity, General Utilities (part of the Générale des Eaux Group), Lloyds Bank, National Power, North West Water, Nuclear Electric and Welsh Water. Sponsoring can prove a mutually useful educational exercise between a pressure group and an industrial firm, regardless of the specific terms or projects involved. For SMEs, sponsoring of a local wildlife area or schools education project can prove particularly productive.

In the UK privatized public utilities have also found it useful to focus their sponsoring and community involvement on environmental projects. Wessex Water recruited the scientist and television personality David Bellamy to their environmental advisory committee and sponsored environmental projects which involved the use of water in the surrounding countryside. Manweb, the regional electricity company based in Chester, has spent £2 million on community projects and £5.5 million on energy efficiency projects over a four-year period. It has jointly funded a survey of the prospects for renewable energy, with the Department of Trade and Industry, and has a 45 per cent stake in two windfarms, one of the sources of renewable energy. The progress of small local projects provides information and expertise for use on a wider scale.

SUMMARY

The complex networking of business organizations and NGOs gives rise to the legislative framework within which industry operates. Their work gives rise to the legal mechanisms of command and control laws, market-based instruments such as a carbon tax, or voluntary regulatory schemes like EMAS and eco-labelling through which environmental protection may be guaranteed.

Corporate environmentalism has increasingly begun to appear on international trade agreements. The increased interest from this economic perspective has fuelled the concern and need for more and more environmental legislation (criminal, administrative and civil law). There have also been significant developments since the early 1980s of voluntary environmental regulations which are briefly covered within this chapter. In addition to the regulatory and legislative developments, the chapter also considered the importance of some of the green business organizations and environmental pressure groups of interest within the UK.

QUESTIONS

7.1 Bearing in mind the problems of enforcement, examine the view that legal penalties are the most effective means to reduce pollution.

7.2 The three scenarios in SustainAbility's *EPE WorkBook* have been developed through a collaborative European initiative involving industry, governmental organizations and environmental pressure groups. In your view, which is the most likely scenario to emerge in future? Base your answer on available evidence.

7.3 Examine the strengths and weaknesses of the argument that co-operating between corporations and environmental pressure groups is capable of making a positive contribution to long-term sustainability.

REFERENCES AND FURTHER READING

Ball, S. (1994) 'The Environment Agencies Bill', *Integrated Environmental Management* 35: 4.

Ball, S. and Bell, S. (1995) *Environmental Law: The Law and Policy Relating to the Protection of the Environment*, 3rd edn, Blackstone Press, London.

Business Council for Sustainable Development (BCSD) (1992) *Changing Course: A Global Business Perspective on Development and the Environment*, BCSD, London.

Business in the Environment and Coopers & Lybrand (1994) *A DIY Environmental Review for Companies*, BiE, London.

Department of the Environment (DoE) (1995) *Eco-management and Audit Scheme: An Introductory Guide for Industry*, see, HMSO, London.

European Environment Bureau (EEB) (1995) *Annual Report of Activities* (April), EEB, Rue de la Victoire 26, B-1047 Brussels.

Gallup (1992) *The Health of the Planet Survey: A Preliminary Report on Attitudes to the Environment and Economic Growth measured by Surveys of Citizens in 22 Nations*, Gallup, London.

Garner, J. F. (ed) (1995) *Garner's Environmental Law*, Butterworth, London.

Johnston, N. and Stokes, A. (1995) *Waste Minimization and Cleaner Technology: An Assessment of Motivation*, Centre for Exploitation of Science and Technology (CEST), London.

Payne, S. (1995) '*Environment Act 1995*', *Student Law Review* autumn: 36–8.

GREEN ECONOMICS

The purpose of studying economics is not to acquire a set of ready-made answers to economic quotations, but to learn how to avoid being deceived by economists.

(J. Robinson 1903–83)

INTRODUCTION

Traditionally, managers have been guided in their decision-making by economists, who have drawn their analysis of the economy from pure and applied economic theory. By forecasting the effects of change upon market forces the economist seeks to provide an assessment of the likely outcomes of alternative courses of action which may be of use to business leaders and in government policy formation. This chapter explores the potential for environmental or 'green' economics to regulate the exploitation, pollution and loss of species diversity. Accepting that economic systems are underpinned by ecological systems and not vice versa (Turner 1993), definitions are examined regarding the processes and purposes of economics.

Four approaches adopted by economists to tackle the problems associated with the impact of economic activity on the environment are considered. The four approaches are:

1. The traditional market forces approach.
2. The market failure approach.
2. The property rights approach.
4. The holistic (ecological) approach.

First, however, it is necessary to examine some of the assumptions underlying neo-classical economic theory, starting by looking at the relationship between economists and the environment.

THE ECONOMIST AND THE ENVIRONMENT

The attempt to incorporate environmental considerations within the study of economics arises from two basic types of concern:

1. Environmental degradation has real economic costs as land is degraded and agricultural production falls, as the costs of providing safe drinking water rise and as health costs rise with air pollution.
2. The aesthetic or ethical values people place on the environment, on its landscapes, flora and wildlife, cannot be registered against continued environmental degradation.

(Hamilton 1994: 71)

The assumption that an economy can continue to function regardless of the total sum of detrimental effects is one of a series of assumptions which devalue economic theory as a guide to practical action. The core problem is the means by which economic theories are derived. Within any discipline, theories are derived from a series of observations and premised within an existing paradigm. Thus, econometrics, the branch of economics placing particular emphasis on numerical calculations, is defined as the 'application of mathematical and statistical techniques to economic problems'. The economist formulates an economic model.

Then, using the best data available, statistical methods are used to obtain estimates of the parameters in the model. Methods of statistical inference are then used to decide whether the hypothesis underlying the model can be rejected or not. Econometrics is thus concerned with testing the validity of economic theories, and providing the means of making quantitative predictions.

(Bannock *et al.* 1986: 135–6)

The process of formulating economic theory through the use of econometric techniques gives rise not only to theories which may have practical application but also to a range of theories about the particular problems associated with applying statistical methods to economic theory and data. Hence the distinction between 'econometric theory' and 'applied econometrics'.

Like any science, econometrics, whether theoretical or applied, is incomprehensible to the lay reader. However, unlike other sciences, many econometric theories cannot be explained in lay language. This severe limit to their value in policy formation arises from the assumptions which underlie the selection of data to be measured and the construction of the models to be verified. The selection and analysis of data for the econometric process is so heavily dependent upon assumptions that the translation of the findings back into the language of the real world becomes a problem. This can have its amusing side.

Legend has it that a chemist, a physicist and an economist were marooned on a desert island with nothing but a stack of tinned baked beans; there was no can opener. They first asked the chemist to try his hand to keep them alive. He attempted to extract salt from the ocean to corrode through the tin. When this failed, they decided another option was in order. So the physicist attempted to angle the can between the other cans in such a way as to direct the sun light on to the top of the can to burn through it. By tea time they were rather hungry and in a last-ditch attempt (suspecting the move would be futile) they turned to the economist who had been sitting watching their efforts all afternoon with a rather annoyingly smug face. Immediately when consulted he had the answer, 'Assume a can opener. Then there is no problem.' Like all parables, the story touches the heart of the matter. A training in neo-classical economics enables the economist to assume that there is no conflict between the environment and economics.

This phenomenon gives rise to real concern when the advice of economists is sought and accepted *as if* the assumptions adopted could be taken as fact. Economists study a particular form of decision-making, for example that relates to market activity in the allocation of scarce resources. In assuming, for the sake of theoretical argument, that exchange on the market is the only relevant mechanism, economists proceed to assume that *in fact* human decision-making is not only guided by considerations falling within the subject area of economics but also *best* guided by the market. Ethics or altruism may contribute to decision-making, but the bottom line is the determining and relevant consideration. Economic theory is premised upon the assumption that if it is counted, it counts. The extension of this principle beyond the market-place, to take account of environmental considerations appears at first glance as a logical possibility. As Waring explained:

> [New Zealand's] pollution-free environment; its mountains, streams with safe drinking water, the accessibility of national parks, walkways, beaches, lakes, kauri and beech forests; the absence of nuclear power and nuclear energy—all counted for nothing.
>
> (Waring 1989: 1)

The extension of economic principles beyond the market-place, putting a value on goods which are not normally traded, indeed could never be traded, has been welcomed as a useful measuring device. It is, however, merely an extension of the fundamental flaw of using economic theory to guide action, in isolation from ethical and ecological considerations. Real-life problems are inevitable when the fundamental operating principle of economic theorists is premised upon a series of assumptions that can be used to illuminate a real-life situation *without referring back to the assumptions upon which the theory* is premised. We look now at some of the assumptions upon which economic theories are premised.

ECONOMISTS' ASSUMPTIONS

No system stands on its own feet. As Schumacher has argued in *Small is Beautiful*, 'it is invariably built on a metaphysical foundation, that is to say, upon man's basic outlook on life, its meanings and its purpose' (Schumacher 1973: 201). Although a successful business manager requires training in economics, the subject of study is based upon a series of assumptions about human interactions with the social and physical world. The economics we learn as we pass through the education system encompasses a sequence of concepts, from supply and demand, through price elasticity, markets, quantity theory of money, oligopoly, aggregate demand and aggregate supply, rent, interest and profits, to theories of comparative advantage. Be they micro or macro, economic theories come dressed in sophisticated tables, equations and graphs which, to the uninitiated, appear little short of incomprehensible.

Nevertheless, though impressive to the outsider, economic theories remain firmly based upon this set of prior assumptions. Those theories, and the assumptions necessary to sustain them, have (it would appear) evolved and been selected to meet the needs of industrializing economies. The five basic assumptions can be summarized as follows:

■ **Assumption 1: Markets** Neo-classical economists assume that markets exist for goods and services such that trade will produce all the necessary regulation via positive and negative feedbacks.

■ **Assumption 2: Externalities** Occasionally there may be some external effects from production or consumption. These can be identified and internalized.

■ **Assumption 3: Infinite wants and infinite resources** Although humans have infinite wants, the capacity of the earth to supply raw material and energy and to absorb the waste from human activity is also infinite.

■ **Assumption 4: Absence of institutionalized interventions in markets** Markets are free to adjust mechanistically in response to the realities of consumer demand and resource scarcity.

■ **Assumption 5: Rational Economic Man** All scenarios depicted by pure and applied economics are premised upon the assumption that the human agent in the economy is Rational Economic Man.

Markets

Neo-classical economists argue that all goods are rationed through price. In the free market, individual firms and consumers make millions of decisions which in total add up to an overall economy thus providing the best of all possible worlds. From Adam Smith's suggestion (Smith 1776) that general prosperity will result despite the fact that it was not directly sought by each individual, the existence of the 'Invisible Hand' has become a fundamental assumption underlying economic theory. Deviations from it are by definition deemed exceptions to a rule and require special pleading. In this respect, environmental goods are no different from any other goods and services. As depletion of a particular resource occurs, the price system will ensure that a substitute is found. Therefore the initial assumption of the invisible hand is based upon the further assumption of infinite substitution. Hence, it is argued, resource depletion and environmental degradation cease to be analysed from a realistic perspective.

The substitution assumption is based on the theory that within the free market individual actions are guided by knowledge of causes and effects. The homely ring of the term 'free market' is misleadingly reminiscent of the country fair where individuals trade with known individuals and have reputations to win or lose. The notion of a market as a 'spacious public place' containing crowds, stands and baskets has been replaced by 'market shares', 'price fluctuations' and 'equilibrium' (Sachs 1992: 7). In the process, the right to pollute someone else's stretch of coastline, whether through negligence or ignorance, the right to plough a motorway through someone else's back yard, has come to be accepted as an integral aspect of market freedom.

Externalities

To economists, 'externalities' are spillover effects on the welfare of other firms or individuals arising from production. These effects, whether good or bad, are external to the market and therefore to economic theory. For example, a company may discharge toxic waste into a landfill site, contaminating a local stream. The costs of this pollution will not appear on the company's balance sheets, but may be met by local residents suffering a loss of amenity or by communal expenditure via taxation to clean up the stream. Economists argue that these costs (they are rarely benefits) should be 'internalized' by adjusting prices so that the consumer pays the full cost of the production of the product, enabling the firm to pay compensation or to clean up the damaged resource. Costs internalized in this way may render the damaging processes uneconomic.

Infinite wants and infinite resources

This third assumption is linked to Assumption 1. Although the study of economics is defined as the allocation of scarce resources, it is assumed that wants are infinite and that resources are infinite over time. An excess of demand over supply at one point in time will, in theory, give rise to an increase in supply over time. Economists are trained to recognize and measure 'more' and 'less' but they have no concept of 'sufficiency'. Therefore, although economic theory purports to be in the business of efficient resource allocation, the notion of scarcity is overridden by belief in the permanent potential for economic growth. Neo-classical economics has no mechanism for distinguishing between resource *use*, defined as living off the interest, and resource *depletion*, defined as living off the capital. Theory is based on the assumption that there is no need to differentiate between the two.

Absence of institutionalized interventions in markets

Another debatable assumption relates to the theoretical convention of basing economic measurement and analysis in a particular point in time and covering the whole with the ubiquitous 'other things being equal'. This facilitates the disregarding of any weighting of the legislative or fiscal framework in favour of a particular combination of the factors of production, land labour or capital. Underlying this assumption is the further assumption that it is the duty of government to 'provide the legal framework in which unfettered markets allocate resources' (Hamilton 1994: 39). In this scenario, economists advise governments on what 'can' and 'cannot' be achieved by disregarding a whole swathe of apparent irrelevancies.

The tax system provides a number of examples of non-environmentally neutral interference in the economy. In assumption-free theory, the invention of a device to produce twice as many pins in half the time should (theoretically) allow the workers in a factory to be paid the same amount for half the hours of employment, and additional leisure. In economic theory, technological innovation is 'assumed' out of the equations. However, in reality taxation of labour, savings and value added and subsidies for capital investment can have a surprising result. The labour force is cut, saving the cost of wages to the employer. The element of income tax allowed for indirectly in the wages plus the direct payment of the employers' national insurance contribution are no small factors in this decision.

Additionally, continued escalation of production will enable investment to be made in further labour-saving machinery, encouraged by a taxation system which favours capital investment. In this way, the seemingly 'free' market dictates high unemployment alongside high energy consumption and high resource depletion. Ironically, constantly expanded production requires new markets for the stream of manufactured goods, bringing 'cheap' land and labour in the developing world into the cash economy, with further negative implications for environmental sustainability.

Rational Economic Man

Underlying all other assumptions is the convention of belief in *Homo economicus*, Rational Economic Man. As a useful starting-point for studies requiring measurements and calculations, belief in the existence of an individual, autonomous, rational agent has a lot to offer. The problem is that theories based upon the assumption of the existence of a rational, fully informed, self-interested maximizer of utility are limited in their application value. The American economist Thorstein Veblen described *Homo economicus* in his infamous attack at the turn of the nineteenth century:

> The hedonistic calculator of man is that of a lightning calculator of pleasures and pains, who oscillates like a homogenous globule of desire and happiness under the impulse of stimuli that shift him about the area, but leave him intact. He has neither antecedent nor consequence. He is an isolated, definitive human datum in stable equilibrium except for the buffets of the impinging forces that displace him in one direction or another. Self-imposed in elemental space, he spins symmetrically about his own spiritual axis until the parallelogram of forces bears down upon him, whereupon he follows the line of the resultant. When the force of the impact is spent, he comes to rest, a self-contained globule of desire as before.

(Veblen, quoted in Lutz and Lux 1988: 57)

Despite denials, professional economists are fondly attached to this comic character, who springs from nowhere and has no duties or responsibilities beyond a role as the key agent in determining market forces. Environmental economics is an attempt to adapt theories based upon the above five assumptions to the realities of environmental degradation and its attendant social injustices.

ENVIRONMENTAL ECONOMICS

Neo-classical economic theory relies upon the concept of the free market as the ideal mechanism for the distribution of scarce resources. The objective of economic activity has been the creation of wealth through the competitive, and hence profitable, combination of land, labour and capital. In practice, a theory which dismisses social, ethical and environmental considerations as irrelevant has considerable limitations. In theory, rational optimizing agents may use their fixed preferences to select from a range of options as, unfettered by legal restrictions, a free market tends towards equilibrium, a state of Paretan optimality where none can be better off without others becoming worse off. In practice, 'new', 'green' or 'environmental' economists have sought means to adapt economic theory to take account of the realities of environmental issues.

As Pearce *et al.* (1989: 132) observe, economic analysis is based on the assumption that 'economic value' reflects people's preferences. 'Those preferences exhibit themselves in market and non-market situations, and there is no rational basis for designing economic policy as if only *some* preferences mattered, i.e. those expressed in the marketplace.' Hence economists have adopted three basic stances on the environment. The three are not mutually exclusive.

1. The market forces approach.
2. The market failure approach.
3. The property rights approach.

We examine these reactions of economists to the sustainability debate in more detail.

The market forces approach

The normative Austrian School approach is to seek to incorporate the market into the market exchange mechanisms without resort to planning. Economic forces will ultimately act to ration scarce resources and force production into entirely environmentally friendly modes. This argument carries some weight, in the sense that the economy and the functioning of the business sector are perceived as closely interlinked. The accounting 'bottom line' has long been the central justification for business activity. Yet changes in the economic climate are a primary focus of attention for management in both the short and the long term strategic development. Increasingly, economic pressures which have impacted upon firms have derived from environmental sources. While this highly theoretical approach *might* succeed in protecting the environment in the long run, it could equally well result in massive environmental degradation before the market learns to rectify itself. Recognition of the need for a more proactive approach has spread across different schools of economic thought.

The market failure approach

More enlightened economists seek mechanisms to ensure that consumption needs are met without damaging the environment's capacity to supply resources and absorb waste, that is to forestall depletion of 'free' resources. As society comes to recognize the environment as a consumption good rather than a mere resource set, the right to profit from environmental degradation, whether from negligence or ignorance, will come under increasing attack.

Until the 1990s, however, the 'prisoner's dilemma' (see Case Study 8.1) suggested that firms acting in isolation to clean up their acts were unlikely individually to make much impression. While 'cleaner' operations certainly incurred costs, they also served to put the 'dirty' firms at competitive advantage.

CASE STUDY 8.1
The Prisoner's Dilemma

The study establishes fairly conclusively that Rational Economic Man pursuing his own self-interest is paradoxically unlikely to be acting in his real self-interest. 'In order to realise the self-interested outcome one has to let go of self-interest. . . . Only if men were actuated by moral self-sacrifice, could they serve the interest of the whole human race.' Lutz and Lux (1988) came to this conclusion following from their review of the 'prisoner's dilemma'. In 1950 a mathematician and two social scientists told the following parable:

> Secret police hold two political prisoners who are suspected of belonging to an illegal opposition party. Each prisoner is held and interrogated in an individual cell. The police need a confession for conviction, otherwise they will be held for one year and then let go. In the case that both of them confess, their co-operation will be taken into account and they will each get five years. On the other hand, if only one of them confesses, thereby implicating the other, the confessing one will immediately be set free while his tight-lipped partner is put into the slammer for eight years. The prisoners can either confess or not confess, but since they are kept in separate confinement, neither knows what the other will do or does.
>
> **(Lutz and Lux 1988: 79)**

Prisoner A faces the following options. He can:

1. Confess, assuming that B will not confess, and that a sentence of zero is less than a term of one year in jail.
2. Confess, assuming that B will confess. If he does not confess and B does, he faces eight years. If both confess he receives only five years.

In sum, whether B confesses or not, it is in A's rational self-interest to confess. Since the same holds true for B, both will confess and be locked up for five years. The optimum solution would have been for them both to confess. Apparent self-interest, however, worked against them. The logic of the parable is that self-interest imprisons.

Self-interest does not produce optimal results when the outcome of an individual's actions depends upon the actions of others. Most human activity takes place within the social context in which this rule invariably holds true.

Adapted from Lutz and Lux (1988: 79–82)

This occurs because the market system fails to take account of environmental costs and benefits over the short and the long term. A firm's freight vehicles may cause pollution in the form of noise and emissions, the effects of which may degrade the natural environment of members of the public who are not associated with the firm. The market failure approach seeks to impose taxation on road or fuel use with a view to reducing these 'externalities' by making the 'polluter pay'. The costs appearing on the balance sheet may alert the firm to the need to reduce negative impacts on the environment, and give the financial incentives to do so.

The 'market failure' approach of applying pollution charges is particularly limited in its effectiveness where the source of pollution is less easy to identify as the responsibility of a single firm or individual. The individual component of the total sum of noise and toxic emissions from freight transport are particularly difficult to identify. Affecting the price of resources through taxation (e.g. a carbon tax) also has its limitations. Equilibrium prices can be adjusted through the price mechanism in such a way that external costs associated with consumption choices are reflected in prices. This type of measure may well produce a new equilibrium level of consumption, with less environmental degradation.

Taken as a whole, however, taxes like these tend to be regressive. Their primary impact is usually upon lower income groups, either directly through rising fuel costs or indirectly through rising prices of essential consumer goods. They may therefore be politically unsustainable. Tradable pollution discharge permits, as introduced by the US Clean Air Act, have proved equally inept and ineffective.

The property rights approach

A second neo-classical approach is to blame environmental degradation on inadequately defined property rights. Over-grazing of land and over-fishing of seas occur because restraint on the part of one person will not significantly alleviate pressure on the scarce resource. With property rights over particular sections of rivers or the sea vested in a particular owner, those individuals could seek recompense through the legal system for pollution caused to their property.

In his seminal work *The Tragedy of the Commons* (Hardin 1968) Hardin described the problem of unfettered individualism, using the hypothetical example of a piece of common grazing land. No individual farmer wants resource depletion to occur. This is, however, the collective result of rational economic behaviour. In the absence of regulation, each farmer will seek to maximize individual returns. If one farmer places an additional animal on the common the total impact will appear small and the farmer stands to receive an increase in income. When all farmers take similar action, the effects are magnified and the land becomes degraded and unproductive. Some mechanisms to plan access to 'free' resources appear essential for the common good.

Neo-classical theory is constructed on the assumption that all economic resources and goods are the property of rational economic agents—individuals. These individuals are assumed to be well informed about the range of options open to them and as to the full range of potential results of their actions. The right to own property, and to trade that property in the free market, is defended by laws. These laws include the right to redress in the event of damage to that property. Often, however, the ownership of the polluted source cannot be located in a single firm or individual: for example, who owns the sea? (See Case Study 8.2.) Indeed, the effects of pollution may cross national boundaries, negating legislative measures of the country affected.

CASE STUDY 8.2

Canada's East Coast Fishery

For 450 years Newfoundland's fishery industry operated as an informal system of private property. Using fixed gear techniques, largely handlining and stationary cod traps, they did not actively pursue the fish or disturb their habitat. Fluctuations in fish abundance were reflected in catches, which served as indicators of fish abundance and ensured sustainability. Within the industrialized world, this provided an example of a highly successful community-controlled fishery. Each of the five communities studied had its own system regulating access to the fishing grounds to prevent over-fishing, and to resolve conflicts. Cod-berths, the sites where cod-trap nets could be set, were allocated in varying methods by the communities studied and monitored by respect for customary observance. As the Committee on Federal Licensing Policy, a group of Newfoundland academics (University of Newfoundland, 1994) explained in 1974:

> entry to the inshore fishery, far from being wholly uncontrolled (as is often assumed) has long been regulated according to customary rules and regulations emanating from the local level.

By the 1970s the smaller boats faced competition from 'longliners' of greater size and sophistication and from offshore draggers or trawlers. Both were assisted by refrigeration and by the technical ability to pursue and abstract vast stocks from the sea. In the late 1970s, when cod stocks had reached an all-time low, the Canadian government, informed by Canada's scientific fisheries bureaucracy, ignored the advice of the fishermen. Instead of restricting the size of boats or the methods of fishing, they reduced the numbers of fishermen permitted within the 200-mile fishing zone. Their espousal of *Tragedy of the Commons* rhetoric favoured the offshore trawler industry with its more 'efficient' technology, with disastrous consequences.

In 1992 the cod fishery closed, forcing the redundancy of 25 000 fishermen and a further 10 000 related redundancies. Furthermore, the inshore fisherman's knowledge of fish stocks and movements was dismissed as unscientific mumbo-jumbo by fishery scientists at the Canadian Department of Fisheries and Oceans (DFO). Working in co-operation with two offshore trawler corporations, PFI and NatSea, who consistently lobbied for higher quotas, they vastly overestimated cod populations on which their Total Allowable Catch (TAC) and Maximum Sustainable Yield (MSY) were based. By 1992 studies confirmed that scientific predictions of cod stocks were seriously flawed, and a total moratorium was placed on cod fishing. The effect on the local Newfoundland fishing communities has been devastating, and has alienated these citizens from central government. With hindsight, a more environmentally sustainable policy would have been for the government to work with the larger number of inshore fishermen to regulate fishing through a locally regulated property regime.

Source: Matthews (1995)

Market and property rights solutions rely heavily on the assumption that 'transaction costs' are minimal. In many cases, the costs of establishing the cause of damage and the ownership of the damaged resource may outweigh any potential financial benefit to be derived from making the claim. We now examine a number of economic instruments designed to create a more sustainable economy. These draw upon the 'market failure' or 'property rights' solutions, or contain elements of the two approaches.

Economic instruments

Economic instruments are, in the strictest sense, the political means to intervene in the 'free' workings of an economy based upon the 'market failure' approach. If economic theory is taken to be a series of observations about the working of economic mechanisms, as the Austrian School would hold, intervention can be justified only in defence of the free market. According to this philosophy, no intervention, whether for social reasons as argued from a Keynesian standpoint or for environmental reasons, can be justified *on economic grounds*. Although logical at one level, this stance has been recognized as not being particularly rational. Hence the introduction of a range of economic instruments designed to enhance environmental protection.

The polluter pays

A number of measures fall under the 'polluter pays' category, which derives from the market failure approach. When the costs of the deterioration of environmental resources from production and consumption are observed not to be adequately reflected in the price system, it may be necessary to resort to public measures to reduce pollution. Such measures are designed to ensure a better allocation of resources by reflecting environmental costs in the prices of goods which cause pollution in the process of their production or consumption. According to the OECD (1976), pollution damage costs fall into two broad categories, those reflected in direct financial costs and those reflecting loss of amenity, upon which a price needs to be set.

Direct financial costs include:

■ Human health, such as loss of productivity, health-care costs, research into pollution avoidance.

■ Animal loss, in terms of fish and animal resources.

■ Plant loss, as in reduced crop production, reduced forest growth, increased pest attack.

■ Natural resource depletion, as in lost production from contaminated water or soil, increased clean-up costs.

■ Materials reduced in quality, with increased repair costs.

■ Climate and weather changes, including reduced agricultural yields from air pollution, smogs, shift in rainfall patterns.

Loss of amenity through risk aversion includes:

- Human health in terms of bereavement, distress at loss of amenity.

- Loss of flora and fauna, reduced pleasure in fishing, observing wildlife and landscapes.

- Material deterioration of soils and buildings.

The idea of using taxation or pollution charges as an alternative to regulation is not new. Arthur Pigou (Pigou 1932), the Cambridge economist, put forward the idea of a tax as a means to bridge the gap between private cost and social cost as early as 1920. Until the 1990s, however, most taxes or charges on polluters were designed to provide revenue to meet the costs of regulation, most usually on water but also on aircraft noise. Although early taxes were not designed to eliminate environmentally damaging behaviour, economic instruments have increasingly been designed with a view to combating resource depleting and polluting activities. Measures include the following.

Resource taxes

The purpose of resource taxes is to discourage undesirable activities and to encourage desirable ones. Hence taxes are placed on less desirable activities, such as pollution and resource depletion. Since the purpose is to reduce negative effects, such taxes can replace other forms of tax, or they may be used to subsidize research and development into ecologically sound alternative technologies. These taxes are normally introduced gradually, and with due publicity, in order to minimize economic disruption. (See Case Study 8.3 on Landfill Tax.)

Charges

The imposition of charges is a useful way to regulate access to scarce resources by seeking to ensure that the polluter pays. Pollution charges per unit of pollution are set higher than the costs of removing that unit in an environmentally sound way. Charges for tourism in protected areas, or for water for irrigation, fall into this category. As with resource taxes, the aim is to provide motivation to avoid the damaging activity and incentive to find environmentally sound alternatives.

Deposit/refund schemes and performance bonds

A deposit is charged on environmentally unfriendly products or inputs, and refunded once the product has been disposed of appropriately. The scheme enables the full social and environmental costs to be fully reflected in the economic costs of a product. So long as the deposit is sufficiently high, it reduces the risks of illegal dumping. Further, it provides a means of identifying the origins of toxic wastes. In a similar way, a performance bond recognizes sustainable resource management. For example, a timber company may be required to pay reforestation bonds, redeemable once the replanted forest has reached a certain age. This type of scheme can work at different levels, from the individual to the community or a particular industry.

Assurance bonds

Assurance bonding is a variant on the deposit refund system. It requires would-be users of society's resources to post a bond, equal to the worst case damage to the environment, in advance of the activity. Deposits on glass bottles encourage users to dispose of the packaging in an environmentally sound way (through return for reuse or recycling) and it discourages disposal as litter or unsorted waste. Similarly, with the assurance bond system, the worst case scenario is evaluated by the regulatory authority, and bonds calculated on this basis. Bonds are refunded if, over time, resource users can demonstrate that damages to the environment were less than the amounts predicted. The system ensures that funds are available to protect the environment, and provides incentive for firms to introduce cleaner technology.

Tradable permits
Permits to pollute or use resources are sold by auction or on the basis of existing use. These permits can be resold. The system has severe limitations as a permanent solution to pollution problems, particularly where pollution costs are a very small proportion of the total costs of the product, or in the case of highly toxic wastes. However, in some circumstances, as for example in the case of discharges to water courses, they can be used during the transition to more sustainable techniques. Money raised can be given in compensation, or can be used to clean up the system or restore degraded ecosystems. Tradable permits are used where it is important to maintain a maximum level of resource use or polluting emissions.

CASE STUDY 8.3
Landfill Tax

The UK government's introduction of a Landfill Tax in 1995, one of the first in Europe, is an example of a resource tax designed to cut pollution and encourage waste minimization. At the time of the introduction of the tax, about 100 million tonnes of waste were produced annually in the UK. These wastes arose from households (18 million tonnes), commercial (13 million tonnes), construction and demolition (20 million tonnes) and 'other industrial wastes' (49 million tonnes).

The scheme was designed to raise landfill charges from £10 a tonne to £15 a tonne through imposing a 50 per cent tax estimated to raise £500 million annually. The plan was to encourage industry to recycle wastes, reduce the amounts created and find alternatives to landfill such as incineration.

Revenue raised in this way is available to restore old landfill sites and contaminated land. Additionally, the revenue can be used to reduce employers' national insurance contributions, with the effect of simultaneously increasing the cost of pollution and reducing the cost of employment. According to the Environment Secretary, the tax was intended to deter disposal of batteries, car tyres and plastics while encouraging schemes for recycling wastes. Incineration for electricity generation is also encouraged by a resource tax of this type.

Adapted from press reports 1995

Alternative evaluations

A number of measures designed to build environmental considerations into the economic decision-making process flow from the 'property rights' approach. These include:

Cost benefit analysis (CBA)

Cost benefit analysis is a tool which can be used to integrate environmental and economic goals in policy formation. The method attempts to put a monetary value on both costs and benefits so that they are expressed in the same units. In road-building projects estimated costs in terms of noise, pollution, disruption to neighbourhoods and loss of countryside may be added to costs of labour and materials. Costs are weighed against benefits of increased accessibility. Shorter journey times are also calculated in monetary terms. Proponents of CBA regard it as a simple and practical device for making the decision-making process more objective and rational. All decision-making involves some assessment of costs and benefits, however intuitive. CBA provides a conceptual framework for making policy formation more systematic and explicit.

Cost benefit analysis can be used to ascertain whether an investment project, for example a new trunk road, can be justified on the basis that its overall benefits outweigh its overall costs. To the normal course of planning (stage 1) are added environmental and social considerations (stage 2). In order to evaluate stage 2, a money value is placed on environmental and social costs and benefits (stage 3).

- **Stage 1** Identification of economic costs and benefits. Economic costs include costs of labour, costs of materials, including purchase of land, and costs of construction. Benefits include time saving, reduced accidents on other roads and increased efficiency of vehicle operation.

- **Stage 2** Identification of environmental costs. This is done through an environmental impact assessment process. Factors considered include noise, visual impacts, air pollution, effects on agriculture and ecological impacts. Since these items are not normally traded, a monetary value has to be ascribed to them.

- **Stage 3** Evaluation of the total costs and benefits of the project.

This neat approach to incorporating environmental values within decision-making processes has its detractors. It is argued that loss of beautiful countryside cannot be evaluated in monetary terms. The value of scenery is, like the value of a human life, priceless. Nevertheless, even human life is given a monetary value in everyday commerce, for insurance purposes. Indeed, it is not inconceivable for the insurers of an aircraft to place a higher value on the craft than on the human life of its passengers. In the event of mechanical failure, in certain circumstances it could make economic sense to ditch the passengers and save the aircraft. As a matter of course, road construction CBA exercises build in estimates for the increase or decrease of loss of life predicted to occur through the lifespan of the project.

Problems associated with CBA include:

- **Identification** It may not be possible to assess indirect or unexpected effects on the social or natural environment.

- **Objectivity** The assigning of a monetary value is necessarily subjective. In practice the preselection of alternatives, the vital element in the CBA process, is undertaken by the organization wishing to promote its plans.

- **Distribution** CBA totals the costs and the benefits and disregards the distribution of benefits or costs. A small group may benefit considerably, while society as a whole carries the costs.

- **Ethics** CBA may be used to avoid considering the moral implications of a decision. Slavery, for example, can appear cost-effective. Without political checks and balances, decision-making based on monetary values alone appears flawed.

- **Time** Future costs and benefits may be discounted in favour of the present, discriminating against future generations.

Contingent valuation

Contingent valuation is the general descriptive term for attempts to value items which are not normally traded or have no economic value. The building of a road through a piece of 'unproductive' land destroying an ancient woodland is economically attractive. Although the monetary valuation of environmental assets is put forward as a case for preservation, it is also a tool used by advocates of projects which are likely to be opposed on non-economic grounds.

Since people are not willing to pay infinite sums of money to save a life, economists assume that a monetary value can be put on virtually anything. Contingent valuation exercises ask people to state how much they would be prepared to pay to protect a species of wildlife or a local beauty spot. Answers to this hypothetical line of questioning are statistically analysed and weighed alongside other considerations and result in a conclusion.

Questions as to the value of an 'environmental good' may be framed in two ways: as 'willingness to accept' (*WTA*) or as 'willingness to pay' (*WTP*). WTA is an indication of the amount a person would be prepared to accept in compensation, for example, for the extinction of a rare species. In reality, the subject may reject the very idea of benefiting from the extinction of a species. The design of the questionnaire will, however, discourage the answer 'nothing', since this would place a low value on the species, giving the opposite message to that intended. The subject will therefore select a high value from those on offer in the questionnaire (from which infinity will be excluded as a matter of course). It is therefore argued that WTP is more realistic. Since WTP guestimates bear some relationship to ability to pay, they are invariably considerably lower than WTA, often by a factor of five or six times.

Contingent valuation techniques can be recognized in courts of law. The $1 billion compensation paid out by Exxon in respect of the *Exxon Valdez* oil spill disaster was made following contingent valuation surveys showing public demand for compensation.

Hamilton (1994) quotes an example of the contingent valuation survey conducted by Stoll and Johnson. The survey estimated the value of endangered whooping cranes at $573 annually. This conclusion was reached by measuring the recreation, option and existence values placed on the cranes from a survey of visitors to Arkansas National Wildlife Refuge in Texas and from postal surveys of the residents of Texas, Chicago, New York, Atlanta and Los Angeles:

■ Recreation values were estimated from the willingness of visitors to pay.

■ Option values, indicating willingness to pay to preserve the option to see the cranes in future, were obtained from visitors and the postal surveys.

■ Existence values, indicating willingness to pay to know that the species continues to exist.

Contingent valuation techniques can result in high values being placed on the environment. As Hamilton explains:

> This has led to the peculiar situation in which business people and economists who work for them oppose the use of the technique even though they are ideologically predisposed to accept the application of hard-nosed economic techniques. Conservationists, on the other hand, are very suspicious of any attempt to place dollar values on the environment but often find that the results of applications of the technique support their case. Thus business favours the technique but rejects the results, while conservationists reject the technique but favour the results.
>
> (Hamilton 1994: 69)

The ability of these methods to produce statistical 'evidence' for and against a particular project is highly dependent upon the prior assumptions underlying the initial modelling framework. Some aspects of an environmental asset, for example its aesthetic value, may be unique and irreplaceable. Like a human life they are not exchangeable for money. Others, like its ecological significance, are very difficult to evaluate in monetary terms through inadequacies in people's knowledge. Yet others are public goods, like clean air, which can be consumed only collectively. While statistical calculations *can* be made as to people's preferences, one evaluation of an environmental asset as 'infinite' renders the statistical approach unworkable. The decision to ignore or exclude infinity as a valid response is itself a value judgement and cannot be dismissed as 'objective reasoning'.

Discounting

Economists note that individuals express preferences about *when* costs and benefits accrue. Normally, the further into the future the cost or benefit, the less value is placed upon it. This is because:

■ There is positive capital productivity. A unit of currency now can be used to purchase capital which will generate more worth, adding, say 10 per cent to the unit's value in a year's time.

■ People have a time preference. They are impatient, preferring a bird in the hand. They might be very rich or dead at the later date.

To economists, therefore, a unit of currency this year is worth 1 + r (the discount rate) next year. One unit next year is worth less than one unit this year. The discount rate is the obverse of the interest rate. The *private* discount rate is familiar to most people. It corresponds to the rate of interest earned on savings. The *social* discount rate is the rate at which future costs and benefits are discounted by projects which have social benefits, e.g. public investment projects. It is argued that government has inter-generational responsibility and is able to take responsibility for collective provision for future generations which is impractical for isolated individuals.

People act differently as private economic agents compared with their role as citizens. Hence the social discount rate will be lower than the private discount rate. The lower discount rate is used to calculate the benefits to society of alternative investments which will have large environmental benefits. Even so, the use of any positive discount rate means that the present value of the natural environment declines over time. After a period of 50 years it is generally insignificant.

Daly and Cobb (1989) therefore reject the idea of discounting the effects of resource depletion and environmental degradation on the future. This rejection of the idea of 'benign neglect toward the future' is not new. In 1924 Pigou pointed out:

> There is wide agreement that the state should protect the interests of the future in some degree against the effects of our irrational discounting, and of our preference for ourselves over our descendants. The whole movement for 'conservation' in the United States is based upon this conviction. It is the clear duty of government which is the trustee for unborn generations as well as for its present citizens, to watch over and if need be, by legislative enactment, to defend exhaustible natural resources of the country from rash and reckless spoliation.

> **(quoted in Daly and Cobb 1989: 411)**

The 'rash and reckless spoliation' arises from the continued failure of the economic system to create mechanisms designed to offer the consumer a series of balanced choices. As Galbraith demonstrates in the 'Dependence Effect' (see Case Study 8.4), there is a need for reliable indicators of wealth, with increases balanced by depreciation, as a means to more enlightened decision-making by policy-makers and consumers.

The three approaches to environmental economics, the market forces approach, the market failure approach and the property rights approach, provide examples of attempts to incorporate environmental considerations within the economic framework. We turn to one further approach which attempts to incorporate the value of the environment in an economic system which has evolved from the prior assumption that the environment and society have always been there, and so will always continue to provide the economy with the resources it requires for growth.

The holistic approach

The holistic or 'institutionalist' approach to economics recognizes at the outset that human needs may be expressed as 'individual utility functions' by economic agents. Individuals are

CASE STUDY 8.4
Dependence Effect

However uneasily, the economist remains doggedly attached to the notion of independently determined wants, and the need to find means to satisfy these wants, ignoring the fact that economic wants are usually dependent upon advertising. A hungry person does not have to be told of his or her need for food. Yet a new consumer product requires an advertising campaign based on modern techniques of salesmanship. In effect, the producer not only creates the goods, but also creates the desire for them by bringing into being wants that never existed. 'One cannot defend production as satisfying wants if that production creates the wants [and] the urgency of the wants can no longer be used to defend the urgency of the production. Production only fills a void that it has itself created.'

Galbraith draws a parallel with a socially concerned individual, collecting money to increase hospital facilities in the town, ignoring the fact that round the corner the local doctor is mowing down pedestrians to keep up trade in the hospital. He argues that private affluence and public squalor does not enhance overall economic welfare. Old and overcrowded schools, underfunded police, sanitation and transportation systems and lack of non-toxic supply of air are high prices to pay for the satisfaction of newly generated wants arising *from* the productive system itself.

Adapted from Galbraith (1984)

immersed in a social culture which determines actions, for example the moral rules and values which dominate compliance with legislation. These codes of values reject the use of terrorist tactics to pursue individual self-interest to its logical conclusion. Acts contributing to the destruction of the environment, threatening the viability of sustainability over the long term, are increasingly being classed as acts of global eco-terrorism. However, the mainstream economic system continues to endorse as economically viable many activities which are environmentally unsustainable. Ameliorative measures of the type outlined above are useful learning aids in a period of transition towards social recognition of the necessity to preserve the environment proactively.

As individuals recognize the limits to environmental degradation, their insights give rise to alternative and less environmentally damaging forms of growth. Unlimited growth, both in population numbers and in the average propensity to consume finite resources of any given population at a point in time, have become the focus of concern. Although everyday patterns of production, distribution and exchange in industrialized countries are slow to reflect change, the evolution of tools for sustainability maintains a constant momentum of change.

Sustainability indicators
Traditional indicators of economic growth can transform failure into success. GNP rises in the wake of a production process that disregards the environment, and it rises still further

when the resulting environmental damages are mitigated through further economic activities (e.g. the clean-up operation). Although the economic system is deemed to exist to create wealth, it has no mechanisms to distinguish realistically between wealth and waste. Rational Economic Man acts in the market-place from a position of almost total ignorance as to the true outcomes of the choices being made.

Before the 1980s attempts to measure wealth were based on crude financial statistics. Starting in 1942, the chief western economic indicators have been gross domestic product (*GDP*) and gross national product (*GNP*). GDP is defined by the World Bank as 'all goods and services ... rendered by residents and non-residents of a country.' GNP measures the sum of incomes, including net incomes from overseas investments. National accounting measures *economic* success, and GNP per capita is often taken as an indicator of individual welfare.

Such measurements provide only crude indicators of welfare. An increase in production may, however, cause deterioration in environmental quality and increased debility in the work-force. These externalities will not be reflected in the figures indicating economic growth. A further problem arises if increases in welfare due to unpaid housework and voluntary work are not included in the calculations as increases in economic welfare. Aggregated measurements may offer misleading indicators of individual welfare if wealth is unevenly distributed. Vast inequalities in wealth can threaten economic stability by leading to social disintegration and environmental degradation (e.g. the over-fishing of seas and deforestation).

Ecological economists have noted that GNP measures wealth and waste indiscriminately. A car accident involving serious injury, for example, appears as a plus in national income accounting terms. It provides employment for the ambulance drivers, health workers, fire brigade, garage repairs, insurance industry and car salesforce and manufacturers. The *Exxon Valdez* disaster in 1989 and the Braer disaster in 1993 added their enormous costs *to* GNP measurements. Spectacular accidents are dwarfed, however, by the day-to-day costs of damage associated with routine industrial and domestic waste emissions. GDP as yet fails to account the negative value of degradation of air, water, soils, biodiversity and non-renewable resources. A more accurate measure of wealth requires establishment of a meaningful ratio of inputs (costs) to output (value).

Valuing the environment

In calculations of net domestic product (*NDP*) national accounting accepts that stocks, as well as flows, must be accounted, since income derived from depreciation of capital is no indication of economic success. At the Rio Earth Summit in 1992, 178 nations committed themselves to further 'expand existing systems of national accounts in order to integrate environmental and social dimensions in the accounting framework, including at least satellite systems of natural resources in all member states' (Department of the Environment 1994). Although countries are not required by the UN to fully integrate environmental concerns into their core accounts, the suggestion is that they prepare 'satellite' accounts to show both physical and monetary units consistent with the core accounts. The need for indicators to measure and evaluate the complex trends in the state of the environment, as acknowledged in *Sustainable Development: The UK Strategy* (Department of the Environment 1994) requires the development of the indicator as a tool. To this end, the World Bank has collaborated with the UN Statistical Office and national authorities in a pilot scheme to develop a new methodology. Two sets of 'environmentally adjusted net domestic product' (*EDP*) calculations were devised to derive a more realistic net domestic product (NDP). These showed:

- **Depletion** estimates of resource depletion, e.g. oil, mineral and timber extraction.

- **Degradation** monetary estimates of environmental degradation, e.g. air and water pollution, waste disposal, soil depletion and groundwater use.

(**Lutz 1993**)

Early attempts in countries such as Norway and France to construct physical accounts of natural resources in order to provide 'satellite' national environmental accounts (Pearce *et al.* 1989) provided the impetus for further research into methodology. In *Towards Sustainability* the Commission of the European Communities (1993) accorded high priority to research on 'the state of the environment, appropriate indicators and tolerance capacities', and the New Economics Foundation report *A Green League of Nations* (NEF 1993) provided a 'preliminary set' of environmental indicators for 21 OECD countries. Early studies of this type suggested that good indicators should:

- Be drawn from information which is readily available.

- Be relatively easy to understand.

- Be about something measurable.

- Measure something believed to be important in its own right.

- Be available within a short space of time from the collection of data.

- Be based on information which can be used to compare different geographical regions.

- Preferably be internationally comparable.

(**NEF 1993**)

According to Lutz (1993) the experience of early methodological work on indicators of sustainability points the need for investment in further research into:

- Basic data collection.

- The relationship between such data and human welfare/economic development.

- The derivation of policy relevant indicators at different levels of aggregation.

Despite the problems associated with the development of indicators, international policymakers accept the requirement for finer definitions of welfare and sustainability than the crude 'single ruler' of conventional accounting.

Index of sustainable economic welfare (ISEW)

The Stockholm Environment Institute has developed an *ISEW* based upon the initial work of Daly and Cobb (1990). In rough terms, the index can be summarized as follows:

ISEW = Personal consumption + non-defensive public expenditures − defensive private expenditures + capital formation − costs of environmental degradation + services from domestic labour − depreciation of natural capital.

(Jackson and Marks 1994: 5)

The index takes the standard economic measure of consumer expenditure as used to calculate GNP on a 'personal consumption' basis. These measures are adjusted to take account of:

- Defensive expenditures which are subtracted and include expenditures on health, education and lifestyle maintenance (e.g. costs of commuting) along with certain environmental externalities. Government expenditures are included in the index only in so far as they are not defensive.

- Man-made (non-human) capital is included in the form of a 'net capital growth' adjustment (a net national product (*NNP*) element), together with an indicator of the sustainability of the economy in international terms.

- Environmental degradation relating to the non-monetarized loss of environmental quality.

- Additions to welfare through the contribution of domestic labour.

- Loss of natural capital through the depletion of natural resources and loss of natural habitat.

Defensive expenditures

Defensive expenditures are 'expenditures necessary to defend ourselves from the unwanted side-effects of production' (Daly and Cobb 1990: 70). Leipert, the German economist, has constructed a typology of defensive expenditures, that is of measures taken to clean up damage or prevent it from happening (Ekins 1986: 135–7). Expenditures fall into four categories.

- Investment and current costs of environmental protection by manufacturing industry and government, including R&D and compensation for damage caused by environmental pollutants.

- Costs induced by spatial concentration of production associated with urbanization, including cost of commuting, housing and recreation.

- Costs of increased risks and insecurity of industrial society, including crime prevention, accident prevention and national defence.

- Costs arising from unhealthy living and working conditions, including unhealthy diets, industrial disease, alcohol and drug abuse and psycho-social health effects arising from unemployment.

Production may generate not only wealth but also various forms of damage to the social and environmental framework in which production takes place. Leipert suggests that measurement of 'defensive expenditures' will enable them to be deducted from GNP in order to arrive at a net product. The exercise is a valuable indicator of the scale and complexity of measuring environmental and social costs of production. The work of measuring the sustainability or otherwise of national economies has been carried forward through the establishment of Indices of Sustainable Economic Welfare (ISEWs).

The study provides 'a basket of results' which can be presented as 'a *preliminary attempt* to provide an index of sustainable economic welfare for the UK' (Jackson and Marks 1994: 6, emphasis original). It would appear from these results that while GNP has increased over the period of study, welfare has not improved to the same extent. Indeed, sustainable welfare appears to have declined in the UK since the mid-1970s. Through the manipulation of a complex of variable parameters the UK-ISEW and similar studies provide a useful addition to the methodology necessary to provide an economics of sustainability. Cobb and Cobb (1994) and Diefenbacher and Habicht-Erenler (1991) have published further work on the development of ISEW. Studies of this type provide the basis for an informed reaction to the growing evidence of environmental degradation. However, they need to be accompanied by progressive measures at local, national and international levels if they are not to merely add to statistical overload. Case Study 8.5 describes some environmental measures in the UK.

CASE STUDY 8.5
Environmental Measures

The report of the Environmental Challenge Group (MacGillvray and Kayes 1994) on indicators for the UK environment provides decision-makers, policy analysts and the general public with a valuable range of indicators of human pressures on and responses to the environment. The report further highlights the need to develop good 'state' of the environment indicators in addition to these 'pressure' indicators.

Indicators should have three essential qualities:

- Simplification.

- Quantification.

- Communication.

It is these qualities which make them increasingly useful, outside the financial area, for public consumption when dealing with the complexities of the environment and sustainable development.

Indicators, actual and potential, examined in the report fall under the following headings:

Fundamental concerns

- **Biodiversity** Extinct species, SSSI damage, farmland species index, declining species, habitat status, land under active conservation management, species action plans.

- **Quality of life** Sustainable economic welfare, asthma cases reported by family doctors.

- **Footprints abroad** Timber imports from sustainable sources, cotton imports from sustainable sources.

The state of the UK environment

- **Atmosphere** Emissions of CO_2, NO_x, SO_2, areas of SSI at risk from acid rain, HCFC production, critical load exceedance, population exposed to poor air quality.

- **Land** Hedgerow loss, land use, tree health survey, rates and types of new tree planting, soil condition.

- **Fresh water** Nitrates in ground water, water consumption, water pollution incidents, water quality measurements.

- **Coastal and marine waters** Bathing beach standards, coast watch litter, oiled seabirds, fish stocks and catches, oil spill incidents, eutrophication.

Pressures on the environment

- **Agriculture** Decline in farmland bird species, expenditure on agri-environment, applications of fertilizers/pesticides per farmed hectare.

- **Energy** Energy consumption by fuel type, energy intensity of the economy.

- **Industry** Special waste intensity, toxic releases, contaminated land.

- **Transport** Transport km by mode, length of motorways/trunk road lanes, journey length/time.

- **Waste** Toxic waste trade.

Statistics gathered under the above headings are drawn from existing measurements taken by government and other research bodies. As indicated in the appendices to the report, this type of non-financial measurement is being adopted by statutory bodies such as the OECD and the Canadian government. These attempts to create meaningful indicators highlight the scale of the problems and the difficulties of interpretation and comparison, particularly on an international scale. They also reflect the inadequacies of policy formation based upon simplistic financial calculations.

Adapted from MacGillvray and Kayes (1994)

Locally intensified economies

Sachs is one of a growing group of economists to link ecological sustainability with local economic regeneration. The argument is that global sourcing causes social as well as ecological damage and that it is entirely possible, indeed socially and ecologically profitable, to supply as many goods and services as possible locally. Global sourcing of goods and services cause the following (Sachs, 1992).

- Local and regional unemployment, as centralized forms switch production on a global scale according to lower labour costs. As Goldsmith (1994) explains, global free trade theoretically supplies consumers with cheaper imports. However, 'the real cost of apparently cheaper goods will be that people will lose their jobs, get paid less for their work and have to face higher taxes to cover the social cost of increased unemployment' (Goldsmith 1994: 104).

- Increased distances between producer and consumer. Flowers are brought from Kenya, shoes from Taiwan, and car manufacturers obtain parts from all over the world. Even the assembled elements of a yoghurt carton have travelled 9000 km. The transportation involved in covering these vast distances is economical only because fuel costs do not take into account the real scarcities. Transporters place the social and ecological costs on the public purse, as the land between the destinations is degraded, concreted over, subject to noise, and poisoned at will.

- Increased distances between the consumer and the waste disposal location. Electricity generation by nuclear or fossil fuels, and the dumping of toxic wastes appear to have no direct connection to the consumer.

Ecological economists recommend the forging of business links at local and regional levels in order to enforce

- Ecologically realistic prices.

- Long distance transportation taxes.

- Local customs charges/regional free trade.

- Local knowledge informing local decision-making on the subsidiarity principle.

In the course of these developments the boundaries of economic theory are shifting away from the conventions of micro- and macro-theory premised upon the nation-state as the sole macro unit, and recognizing the realities of international and subnational agglomeration.

SUMMARY

The short-term inability of market forces to supply an infrastructure adaptable to changing circumstances is a serious flaw in the link between economic theory and economic practice. Together with the neo-classical assumptions of perfect knowledge in relation to the results of actions, this flaw limits the individual's ability to make rational decisions in the light of that knowledge. In short, the range of options available to an individual is limited by the existing socio-economic and technical framework. Recognition of the failure of traditional economic conventions has led to the development of new tools and approaches in order to achieve sustainability.

As the authors of *Blueprint for a Green Economy* declare,

> We can summarise the necessary conditions for sustainable development as constancy of the natural capital stock; more strictly the requirement for non-negative changes in the

stock of natural resources, such as soil and soil quality, land biomass, water biomass, and the waste-assimilation capacity of the receiving environments.

(Pearce *et al.* 1989: 173)

If the given stock of resources is not to decline, decision-making, whether by individuals as consumers or citizens, or by firms or governments, needs to be informed decision-making within an economic system which does not reward resource depleting and polluting activities.

In the short term, physical assets may be substituted for natural ones and as technology advances, increased efficiency in use and recycling will prolong the availability of supplies. While this may be the case for some resources, 'No technological fix (not even dark glasses and sunblock) is a satisfactory substitute for a damaged ozone layer. Nor does it make sense to talk of substitutes for extinct species' (Cairncross 1991: 48). The irreversible depletion of unrenewable natural resources is unfair to future generations. Cairncross raises the question of who, in the present generation, are the most appropriate decision-takers. This chapter has reviewed the options, tools and information available to all potential actors in the economic decision-making process. These include the truly rational individual acting as consumer, manager, producer, voter and legislator. The chapter has attempted to show how economic decisions can be made by a wider spectrum of interested and informed parties than simply the accepted central actors through participation and enlightened economic understanding.

QUESTIONS

8.1 Neo-classical economic theory provides all the tools necessary for a comprehensive understanding of the economy. Discuss.

8.2 Outline the extent to which the availability of alternative indicators overcomes Galbraith's 'dependence effect', as described in Case Study 8.4.

8.3 Summarize the strengths and weaknesses of sustainability indicators as guides to policy formation.

BIBLIOGRAPHY

Key texts

Pearce, D., Barbier, E. and Markandya, A. (1989) *Blueprint for a Green Economy*, Earthscan, London
Blueprint originated as a report for the UK Department of the Environment under the title *Sustainable Development, Resource Accounting and Project Appraisal: State of the Art Review*. Popularly known as the Pearce Report, the book represented the first attempt to

present the UK government with a series of practical proposals for financing measures to secure a sustainable environment. The authors refer to Kenneth Boulding's seminal work *The Economics of Spaceship Earth*, first published in 1966 and reprinted in Daly (1973) (see under Daly and Cobb 1989), which points out that according to the First Law of Thermodynamics energy or matter cannot be destroyed. Energy or matter can only be converted or dissipated, and must end up somewhere in the system.

Pearce, D. W. and Turner, R. K. (1990) *The Economics of Natural Resources and the Environment*, Harvester Wheatsheaf, London

This covers the history of the development of environmental economics, leading on to the question of the evaluation of resource depletion and the ethical issues surrounding the incorporation of environmental values into economic affairs. As with the selection of the title *Blueprint*, these authors are not modest in their claims to provide answers to exceptionally tricky questions. See also Pearce, D. W. and Watford, J. (1993) *World Without End: Economics, Environment and Sustainability*, Oxford University Press, London.

Daly, H. E. and Cobb, J. B. (1989) *For the Common Good*, Beacon Press, Boston, MA

This critique of traditional economics follows from the classic text H. E. Daly (ed.) (1973) *Towards a Steady State Economy* (W. H. Freeman, San Francisco). As senior economist in the Environment Department of the World Bank, Herman Daly was well placed to explore the potential for liberating the discipline of economics from its abstract strait-jacket, enabling it to take account of physical and biological realities. The book provides an excellent introduction to new economic thought.

Further reading

For a review of contingent calculation methodology see Bateman and Turner (1993).

For a full introduction to research on environmental indicators, see MacGillivray and Kayes (1994). It is an example of the growing trend for economic research to be undertaken as a collaborative venture between pressure groups (see Case Study 8.5). The research was commissioned by the Environmental Challenge Group, representing Friends of the Earth, the International Institute for Environment and Development (*IIED*), the New Economics Foundation, the Royal Society for Nature Conservation, the Royal Society for the Protection of Birds, WWF-UK, and Wildlife and Countryside Link. It was co-ordinated by the Wildlife and Countryside Links of England, Northern Ireland, Scotland and Wales, and the Climate Action Network. A further 14 organizations supported the report, including United Nations Environment and Development— UK.

References and further reading

Bannock, G., Baxter, R. E. and Rees, R. (1986) *The Penguin Dictionary of Economics*, Penguin, Harmondsworth.
Bateman, I. J. and Turner, R. K. (1993) 'Valuation of the Environment, Methods and

Techniques: the Contingent Valuation Method', in R. K. Turner (ed.) *Sustainable Environmental Economics and Management*, Belhaven, London and New York.

Cairncross, F. (1991) *Costing the Earth*, The Economist Business Books, London.

Cobb, C. and Cobb, J. (eds) (1994) *The Green National Product*, University of America Press, New York.

Commission of the European Communities (CEC) (1993) *Towards Sustainability: A European Community Programme of Policy and Action in Relation to the Environment and Sustainable Development*, Brussels and Luxembourg.

Daly, H. E. and Cobb, J. B. (1990) *For the Common Good*, Beacon Press, Boston, MA.

Department of the Environment (DoE) (1994) *Sustainable Development: The UK Strategy*, Cm 2426, HMSO, London.

Diefenbacher, H. and Habicht-Erenler, E. (eds) (1991) *Wachstum und Wohlstand: neuere Konzepte zur Erfassung der Sozial-und Umweltverträglichkeit* Metropolis-Verlag, Marburg.

Ekins, P. (ed) (1986) *The Living Economy: New Economics in the Making*, Routledge, London.

Ekins, P. and Max-Neef, M. (eds) (1992) *Real-Life Economics*, Routledge, London.

Galbraith, J. K. (1984) 'The Dependence Effect', in M. W. Hoffman and J. M. Moore (eds) *Business Ethics: Readings and Cases in Corporate Morality*, McGraw-Hill, Maidenhead.

Goldsmith, J. (1994) *The Trap*, Macmillan, London.

Hamilton, C. (1994) *The Mystic Economist*, Willow Park Press, Fyshwick, Australia.

Hardin, G. (1968) 'The Tragedy of the Commons' in Daly, H. E. (ed) (1973) *Towards a Steady State Economy*, W. H. Freeman, San Francisco.

Jackson, T. and Marks, N. (1994) *Measuring Sustainable Economic Welfare: A Pilot Index: 1950–1990*, Stockholm Environment Institute/New Economics Foundation, Stockholm.

Lutz, E. (1993) *Toward Improved Accounting for the Environment*, World Bank, New York.

Lutz, M. and Lux, M. (1988) *Humanistic Economics: The New Challenge*, distributed in the UK by Jon Carpenter Publishing, Apex Press/Bootstrap Press, New York.

MacGillvray, A. and Kayes, R. (eds) (1994) *Environmental Measures: Indicators for the UK Environment*, RSPB/WWF/NEF, London.

Matthews, D. R. (1995) 'Commons versus Open Access: The Canadian Experience', *The Ecologist* 25 (2/3): 86–96.

New Economic Foundation (NEF) (1993) *A Green League of Nations*, NEF Working Paper, London.

OECD (1976) *Economic Measurement of Environmental Damage*, OECD, Paris.

Pearce, D., Barbier, E. and Markandya, A. (1989) *Blueprint for a Green Economy*, Earthscan, London.

Pigou, A. (1932) *The Economics of Welfare*, Macmillan, London.

Robinson, J. (1960) *Exercises in Economic Analysis*, Macmillan, London.

Sachs, W. (1992) 'Economics Knowledge and Reality' in P. Ekins and M. Max-Neef (eds) *Real-Life Economics*, Routledge, London.

Schumacher, E. F. (1973) *Small is Beautiful*, Blond & Briggs, London.

Smith, A. (1776, 1970, 1974) *The Wealth of Nations* (ed. Andrew Skinner) Penguin, Harmondsworth, UK.

Turner, R. K. (ed.) *Sustainable Environmental Economics and Management*, Belhaven, London.

University of Newfoundland (1994) *Report of the Committee on Federal Licensing Policy*, University of Newfoundland, St. John's, Newfoundland.

Waring, M. (1989) *If Women Counted*, Macmillan, London.

9 GREEN SOCIETY

Where society requires to be rebuilt, there is no use attempting to rebuild it on the old plan.
(John Stuart Mill 1806–73)

INTRODUCTION

Over the decades since the publication of *Silent Spring* (Carson 1962), the mass media have shifted focus from the isolated symptoms of environmental degradation towards appreciation of the underlying interconnections between environmental problems and their causes. This chapter explores the growing awareness of the need for a holistic approach to sustainable development and its reflection in the financial mechanisms of ethical investment, insurance risk assessment and bioregionalism.

DATELINE MEDIA FOCUS ON ENVIRONMENTAL PROBLEMS

Changing business practices, as outlined in Chapter 4, have on the whole been reactive to particular perceived problems, with the most polluting industries being identified as problematical and hence being pressurized into remedial ecological measures. However, as the following analysis shows, causes for concern have escalated, and there is little evidence that remedial ecological measures taken by individual firms or particular sectors have done any more than ameliorate some of the symptoms. Meanwhile, the underlying causes of an overarching problem await a more systematic approach.

Although it was not until the 1980s that serious attempts were made to reduce the environmental impact of industry, specific concerns were highlighted by the media in campaigns which varied considerably in the degree of urgency and persistence. Table 9.1 outlines the broad categories of media attention to environmental problems occurring in each decade.

TABLE 9.1. *Dateline media focus on environmental concerns*

1960s	1970s	1980s	1990s
Quarrying and mining	Quarrying and mining	Quarrying and mining	Quarrying and mining
Detergents	Detergents	Detergents	Detergents
Water (dams)	Water (dams)	Water (dams)	Water (dams)
Pesticides	Pesticides	Pesticides	Pesticides
Air pollution	Air pollution	Air pollution	Air pollution
	Packaging	Packaging	Packaging
	Whaling and deep sea fishing	Whaling and deep sea fishing	Whaling and deep sea fishing
	Biotechnology	Biotechnology	Biotechnology
	Transport	Transport	Transport
	Chemicals	Chemicals	Chemicals
	Waste/by-products	Waste/by-products	Waste/by-products
	Armaments	Armaments	Armaments
	Nuclear power	Nuclear power	Nuclear power
		Forestry	Forestry
		Incineration	Incineration
		Landfill	Landfill
		Plastics	Plastics
		Power generation	Power generation
			Tourism
			Electrical
			Office supplies
			Catering

The 1960s

The 1960s was still an age of innocence, in which problems of noise and the visual impairment of the countryside were noted but tolerated as a necessary stage in the development of a strong economy which would provide riches for all. Like the building of dams for power and irrigation, the quarrying and mining of minerals, metals and materials for buildings and roads were spotlighted as individual and isolated problems. They were a price worth paying for a 'better world'. Pesticides and the spread of monocultural farming methods, reliant on agrochemicals, were tolerated in moderation on the grounds that technological developments would in time provide 'clean' alternatives. Equally, it was thought, air pollution would be solved by the discovery of new technologies. The latter view was reinforced by the success of the Clean Air Acts in the UK in 1956 and 1968. Aimed at all coal-burning sources, the Acts succeeded in replacing domestic coal-burning with cleaner gas and electricity, and in reducing industrial smoke through new furnace design.

The 1970s

The 1970s saw the introduction of new problems and hence new causes for concerns. The introduction of disposable one-way packaging, of sliced bread in plastic wrappers, of beer and soft drinks in non-returnable bottles, created for the first time a mountain of useless waste. Pre-packaged food and drink offered to open distant markets to the producer, who sold the concept of ease and cleanliness to the consumer. Few gave a thought to the long-term implications of the escalation of these practices. The mountain of non-reusable waste was different in character from previous packaging, when beer was bought directly from the barrel in the pub, or carried home from the side door in a covered jug. Bottles, baskets and jars were discarded only after a lifetime of reuse; clothes, bags and sacking were eventually converted into rugs and dusters before their final disposal on the universal garden compost heap. The 1970s saw both the virtual end of sustainable packaging policies in the 'developed' world, and the first protest by the newly formed Friends of the Earth at the introduction by Cadbury Schweppes of the non-returnable soft drinks bottle.

Coal-burning in homes and power stations was replaced by the generation of electricity which promised to be 'too cheap to meter' in nuclear power stations. This was the decade of the growing division between environmentalists, voicing concern at the increasing production of nuclear power stations, nuclear weapons, armaments, and toxic chemicals, and the scientific advisers to industry who dubbed environmentalists starry-eyed 'alarmists.'

This decade also saw the growth of the motorway system, with its attendant noise, air pollution, visual impairment and social disruption not only along the lengths of motorway but also through the towns and villages linked by the new infrastructure. However, concern at heavy goods vehicles thundering through their neighbourhoods did not prevent people turning their backs on the local grocer, greengrocer and butcher and buying the goods brought to the new 'supermarkets' supplied by heavy lorries from distant suppliers.

The 1980s

By the 1980s the problems of air pollution, water pollution and soil contamination, coupled with the major problem of noise, could no longer be dismissed as mere hiccups on the way to a wealthier society. Nevertheless, waste minimization was assumed to imply minimizing waste while maximizing production. The production and distribution of packaged food, consumer 'durables' and clothes designed to be limited in their durability, created new problems of disposal of wastes to landfill sites and incineration. The increasing use of plastics also compounded problems of waste generation and disposal. Armaments, the most disposable of consumer durables, continued to be a top earner in the export markets.

As the scale of causes for concern grew, reflected in mounting media coverage, research into alternative technofix solutions to individual symptoms of the overarching problem started to provide scientists and consultants with dazzling and lucrative career prospects. Collaboration between science and industry continued to promote the view that environmental degradation was a temporary and remedial problem worth tolerating in the pursuit of material growth, while environmentalists proposing a radical rethink of the whole strategy of industrial production continued to be labelled 'alarmist'.

During this period television provided a visual portrayal of:

- The decline in whale populations.

- The decline in deep sea fish stocks.

- The rapid erosion of tropical forests for ranching, the extraction of tropical hardwoods and fuel.

- The threat to the ozone layer.

- The growing concern of the 'greenhouse effect'.

- The increasing extinction of species and consequent genetic loss.

Biotechnological research and the increasing use of animals for experimentation in human food production and for health purposes also attracted considerable adverse publicity. Nevertheless, the scientific community continued to accept lucrative rewards from industry in return for advances in these fields.

The 1990s

Earlier concerns focused specifically upon the polluting process, primarily of the manufacturing industry, and the media were broadly supportive of the idea that the polluter should pay for any environmental costs. The 1990s, however, brought the dawning realization that service industries were generating pollution through their demands for, and use of, the products of the heavily polluting industries. Banking and insurance offices, educational establishments (including colleges and universities, the civil service, local government, accountancy, advertising, local government, broadcasting, social services, charities and NGOs (including green pressure groups) were dependent upon an environmentally unsustainable industrial system for their very existence. The housing, clothing and supply of food to their workers, the transportation of employees to work in cars and other vehicles, the fuels for cars and for heating, lighting and computers, the office supplies, including paper, inks and electrical goods, the works catering, even the hospital and cremation facilities for the sick and the dead, required rising amounts of environmental inputs and generated escalating amounts of waste. Even the leisure time of staff became the focus of media attention, as golf courses and hotels destroyed small, local and sustainable cultures across the world, generating further use of road and air transport systems.

By the 1990s it was becoming increasingly apparent that the whole 'development' process required a thorough overhaul. The economic system which counted the creation of waste as wealth, and the clean-up of pollution incidents as an addition to GDP, no longer appeared convincing. Nevertheless, individuals were caught up in a system of education and employment which took the 'development' scenario as both normal and necessary. Change could only follow from experimentation in new holistic approaches followed by teaching from the example of good practice. Such developments took place throughout the 1980s and bore fruit in the 1990s. They include ecologically sound practice in ethical investment, permaculture and bioregionalism.

ENVIRONMENTALLY RESPONSIBLE INVESTMENT

Ethical investment has evolved in recognition of the fact that finance is the driving force in the global economy. Hence, investors can influence industrial development by avoiding industries which are socially damaging or ecologically unsound. The practice has arisen through the growing awareness of the illogicality of the green consumer avoiding ecologically unsound products while their Personal Equity Plan (PEP) or pension fund is investing their money in the very products they are avoiding as consumers. Churches, local authorities and charities also have funds to invest which can be used to support ecologically sustainable outcomes.

Ethical investment has its origins in the USA in the 1960s when socially conscious investors sought to avoid chemical companies producing Agent Orange for use in the Vietnam War and companies based in South Africa; it has grown rapidly since. By the 1990s ethical and ecological approaches to investment became synonymous, since environmental sustainability was unlikely to be sought by a company rejecting the concept of human equity. Organizations working in the broad field of ethical investment share a common aim: to make socially responsible investment financially acceptable. There is nothing socially responsible about losing money.

The process is heavily dependent upon information flows. While some investors may accept lower than average returns when they support projects with high ethical or ecological profiles, the early trend has been for investors to seek returns which compare favourably with the rest of the market. This latter Socially Responsible Investment (*SRI*) approach may lead on to Socially Directed Investment (*SDI*) in which ethical or ecologically sound outcomes are recognized as a non-monetary benefit or 'income'.

Positive criteria for ecologically sound investment may include:

■ Mass transportation systems.

■ Renewable energy generators, e.g. wind power.

■ Companies with sound waste management policies.

■ Companies applying the same standards in their overseas operations as in their home bases.

■ Organic farming projects.

Typical exclusion criteria may include:

■ Armaments and the arms trade.

■ Exploitative working conditions.

■ Nuclear power.

■ Oppressive regimes.

- Tobacco and alcohol.

- Animal experimentation.

- Non-renewable energy sources.

Evaluation techniques
There are two approaches to evaluation: issues approach and systems approach.

Issues approach
The issues approach involves selection of a checklist of specified criteria which may be selected or avoided, for example animal welfare, tropical rainforest products, recycling, carbon dioxide generation, ozone depletion, nuclear power or acid rain. Checklists of this type are compiled by research organizations from issues commonly raised by ethical investors. Since a company either is, or is not, using the techniques or products in question, such checklists are easy to use. However, they may lead to anomalies, where a company has some environmentally sound policies but not others.

Systems approach
The systems approach avoids such anomalies by considering the company as a whole in the context of the range of issues relevant to the industry as a whole. However, it does require heavy research investment.

Different funds and investment managers may apply different criteria, often relying heavily upon specialist research organizations. These may apply varying combinations of the two evaluation techniques.

Investment funds owners and managers
During the 1990s there have been attempts to oblige pension fund managers and trustees to vote their shares at company meetings, in order that pension funds, which hold the savings of the citizens, become active and interested shareholders in UK industry. The intention is to ensure that the long-term implications of investment decisions are taken into consideration, not so much on detail but on matters of principle, paying particular attention to environmental issues, ethical questions and policies towards employment. According to Pat Conaty of the UK Social Investment Forum (*UKSIF*), there is considerable confusion over the question of ownership and control of the shareholdings.

Ownership of a pension scheme's assets is vested in the trustees of a pension scheme, who act in the interests of the beneficiaries. The management of the schemes is, however, handed over to investment managers who are based in the City of London or Edinburgh and have many billion pounds of pension fund money under their control. These investment managers own comparatively little. Barings, for example, had a net asset value of only £400 million but nearly £12 billion under its management. The rapidly growing PDFM had 300 pension fund clients and managed over £32 billion by 1995. These giants of investment management hold effective control over what happens in the markets. Although they are not the owners, they act as if they were. Left to themselves, their sole criterion is short-term profitability. This is changing slowly, as the numbers of pension funds voting regularly rises. By 1995 only 26 per cent of pension funds, which hold 35 per cent of the UK equity market, were voting regularly. Pension funds and the long-term funds of insurance companies together account for over £500 billion. As consumers and beneficiaries become more aware of the combined impact of their investments, interventions can be expected to increase. Initially, social equity issues pave the way for ecological concerns. A growing number of funds have arisen based upon ethical and ecological criteria (Sparkes 1995).

ORGANIZATIONS AND FUNDS

By the mid-1990s there were over 20 green unit trusts in the UK alone. All funds use some in-house research and some 'buy in' research from specialist organizations. However, funding practices and legislation vary from firm to firm and country to country. Tennant (1994) distinguishes between environmental technology funds which may support, for example, waste management projects in firms which are not necessarily environmentally responsible in total performance. Such 'environmental technology funds' are legal in Germany, while ethically responsible funds as such are not. Interest in social, ethical and environmental investment has given rise to a proliferation of research and campaigning groups, independent financial advisers (*IFAs*), ethical bankers and green and ethical investment funds.

Research and campaigning groups

UK Social Investment Forum (UKSIF)
The UKSIF was launched in 1990 to provide a contact point for the socially responsible investor, and a forum for diverse social and community groups. Like similar ventures in the USA, it seeks to represent the broad spectrum of social investment, from the more traditional socially responsible social investment funds to community-based and socially directed investment projects, including community banking and neighbourhood initiatives. One of its primary functions is to act as an educational resource, providing information to the investor about the existence of ethical investment opportunities. It produces an annual directory of organizations and individuals working towards social, ethical and environmental sustainability, ranging from the Allchurches Investment Management Services Ltd, through the Co-operative Bank plc, National Westminster Bank, PIRC (Pensions and Investment Research Consultants), Surfers Against Sewage, TSB Unit Trusts to SG Warburg Enterprise Fund Ltd.

Address: 318 Summer Lane, Birmingham, B19 3RL.

Ethical Investment Research Service (EIRIS)
EIRIS provides information for investors seeking to apply positive or negative criteria to their investments. It identifies forms of investment which meet the criteria of an investor, and works to promote a wider understanding of the issue of corporate responsibility. EIRIS was founded in 1983 with financial support from the Church of England Board of Social Responsibility, The Church in Wales, the Joseph Rowntree Charitable Trust, The Methodist Church World Development Fund, the Presbyterian Church in Ireland and the Society of

Friends (Quakers). It vets all companies quoted in the *Financial Times* (FT) All-Share Index, and some companies in the secondary markets. EIRIS are a major source of research information and offer a wide range of advice on various ethical investments (EIRIS 1996). They provide lists, factsheets and a quarterly newsletter, but do not make moral judgements or offer financial advice. Ethical funds in the UK commonly rely upon information from EIRIS.

Address: 504 Bondway Business Centre, 71 Bondway, London, SW8 1SQ, Telephone: 0171 735 1351.

International Association of Investors in the Social Economy (INAISE)
INAISE is based in Brussels and has over 35 banks and socially directed investment funds as its members.

Address: Rue D'Arlon 40, B-1040 Brussels, Belgium.

Investor Responsibility Research Centre (IRRC) USA
The IRRC provides detailed environmental profiles of 500 companies. Quantitative data for emissions efficiency and compliance are provided by special indices.

Address: Available from the UK Social Investment Forum, 318 Summer Lane, Birmingham, B19 3RL.

Council on Economic Priorities (CEP) USA
The CEP supplies concise, factual information profiles.

Address: Available from the UK Social Investment Forum, 318 Summer Lane, Birmingham, B19 3RL.

Franklin Research and Development Corporation (FRDC)
FRDC, the largest ethical research group in the USA, summarizes qualitative ratings. The value of 'socially responsible investment' in the USA is roughly 100 times the value of the UK market.

CERES
The American Coalition for Environmentally Responsible Economics (CERES) was formed by the US Social Investment Forum and a group of environmental groups in 1988. Its set of 10 principles, launched at the time of the *Exxon Valdez* disaster, and sometimes referred to as the Valdez Principles, seeks to establish the responsibility of corporations for the environment. A number of large corporations, including General Motors, have signed up to CERES. In doing so they have committed themselves to the 10 principles:

1. Protection of the biosphere.
2. Sustainable use of natural resources.
3. Reduction and disposal of wastes.

4. Energy conservation.
5. Risk reduction.
6. Safe products and services.
7. Environmental restoration.
8. Informing the public.
9. Management commitment.
10. Audits and reports.

Address: Available from the UK Social Investment Forum, 318 Summer Lane, Birmingham, B19 3RL.

Pensions and Investment Research Consultants (PIRC)

PIRC advises trade unions and local authorities on ethical investments, enabling pension funds to exercise their influence and raise environmental standards. PIRC has established a Code of Practice, and has acted in particular campaigns, bringing City influence to bear alongside Greenpeace and Friends of the Earth, for example in the campaign to stop Fisons from damaging wetlands by the company's peat extraction. In this campaign, pressure from investors was the decisive factor. By 1994 pension funds worth £16 billion had backed the PIRC Code. PIRC conducts research and publishes a monthly bulletin covering corporate responsibility and ethical investment.

Address: Available from the UK Social Investment Forum, 318 Summer Lane, Birmingham, B19 3RL.

Ethical Consumer

This magazine is a regular collation of information from previously published sources, including NGOs, business directories, newspapers and magazines. It encourages readers not only to buy ethically, but also to let the companies know of their decisions and the reasons for them. To this end it publishes a list of addresses of the companies it has covered. Like the consumer magazine *Which*?, it considers a wide range of products in each issue. Typical issues include magazines, fresh fruit and vegetables, rice, watches, hand tools, outdoor leisure equipment, seeds, bicycle accessories, ethical unit trusts, petrol, and washing machines. It covers reports of involvement or malpractice within a company over the past five years in the following categories: oppressive regimes, trade union relations, wages and conditions, land rights, environment, irresponsible marketing, nuclear power, armaments, animal testing, factory farming, and other animal rights. It includes a symbol to indicate if a boycott of the company has been called somewhere in the world.

New Consumer

Now defunct, New Consumer produced a regular news journal and other publications making comparative evaluation of the social, ethical and environmental policies of companies. It explored areas of work which contributed to a sustainable future, and provided independent information against which social and environmental claims could be assessed. Its research was used by the press, by campaigning groups and by companies themselves.

Independent ethical advisers (IEAs)

Holden Mehan
Holden Mehan are independent financial advisers specializing in Socially Responsible Investment (SRI). As members of the Financial Intermediaries, Managers, and Brokers Regulatory Association (*FIMBRA*), their services cover investments, pensions, school fee planning, protection, mortgages and estate planning. They advise companies, partnerships, co-operatives, charities and individuals on the full range of ethical and environmental funds. Their *Independent Guide to Green and Ethical Investment Funds*, providing a mine of information on the subject, is available free of charge.

Address: 55–7 High Holborn, London, WC1V 6DX.

KPMG
The Environmental Services Department of the London-based accounting and management consultancy service KPMG monitors the progress of FT-SE 100 companies in environmental reporting. By 1994 over one-third produced separate environmental reports (compared to 20 per cent in the previous year) of which six were independently verified. The environmental reports include details on emissions and environmental costs and benefits and performance measurement targets. However, only 12 per cent of the top companies had set quantifiable environmental performance targets.

Global And Ethical Investment Advice (GAEIA)
GAEIA was the first independent financial adviser in the UK to set up a home page on the World Wide Web (http://www.ukinfo.gam.com/about/euro.htm.

Ethical bankers
Ethical banking brings together depositors, banks and borrowers in a partnership for progress towards ecological and social sustainability. Ethical banks are founded on the belief that investment and industrial development require the infusion of new banking values, in which banks must help businesses to develop modes of ownership and financial techniques to encourage sustainable entrepreneurship. The ethical banking movement has grown on a world-wide scale. It includes GLS Community Bank in Germany, the Free Community Bank in Switzerland, Triodos in the Netherlands, Belgium and UK (the result of the merger between the Dutch bank and Mercury Provident) as well as a network of smaller banking organizations in Australia, Austria, Belgium, Denmark, France, Germany, New Zealand, Norway, Sweden and the United States.

Mercury Provident Bank
Mercury Provident is an early example of a social bank lending to projects offering social or environmental benefits. The bank's default rate on its loans proved 'so low as to be embarrassing to your typical high street bank.' Established in 1974, the bank provided a meeting-point for people, ideas and money, and to 'get rid of the mystique of the bank.' Its

projects include community schools, organic farms, waste recycling ventures, health care and local retailers, providing examples of the efficacy of the voluntary principle in practice. According to one financial commentator, Danyal Sattar, 'No laws were passed to bring this to pass, no taxes were raised, no headline news has been made. Yet quietly and softly, examples of social and environmental development have been financed and developed.' (conference speech).

Triodos Bank

In 1995 Triodos, the Dutch ethical bank, merged with its sister organization Mercury Provident, offering their customers the benefits of a larger organization and internationalization. The bank is a social bank, lending only to organizations and businesses with social and environmental objectives. The work of Triodos has been assisted by the fiscal Green Regulation which came into force in the Netherlands on 1 January 1995. These regulations recognize that the existing economic order is not capable of translating sustainability into realistic prices. Products which impose heavy burdens on the environment are under priced because the costs of pollution are passed on. Hence the Green Regulation provides fiscal encouragement for investment in the 'green' sector. In the debate, Triodos's Het Windfonds (The Wind Fund: see Case Study 9.1) was used as an example. Triodos is also concerned about the relationship between the west and developing countries, and has moved the debate on from 'development aid' to 'development partnership.' They argue that lending, rather than giving, has an important part to play in that it creates both a relationship and mutual responsibility. Lending stimulates a business-like approach which makes repayment possible, because value is created. The value added remains in the country to add to its prosperity. Triodos supports the Fair Trade Organization, a wholesale company which has carried out fair trade with the Third World for 35 years, and supports alternative technologies, for example renewable energy projects. The principle of partnership ensures that investors are committed to monitoring and encouraging the companies in which they have invested. See Case Study 9.2 for examples.

Okobank

Germany's 'hippy bank' opened in 1988 to meet the needs of green campaigners who were aware that established banks were lending money to people and causes they considered unacceptable. The bank has mixed ecological and social awareness, refusing to lend to projects which damage the environment or trade in weapons. From small beginnings of DM7 million, their ability to comply with German banking licence criteria has depended upon support from sympathetic bankers who sit on their advisory board. Their lending policy gives equal weight to ethical and commercial considerations, and the bank retains close links with the Dutch Triodos and the Alternative Bank Schweiz.

Co-operative Bank

This UK bank was founded in the nineteenth century as part of the Co-operative Movement. Its ethical policies continue to be customer-led, in the belief that commercial organizations should make a positive contribution to the community. The Co-operative Bank uses both negative and positive pressures. Its refusal to invest in certain types of business is complemented by support for environmental schemes and community initiatives. A pro-gramme of consultation with the bank's customers consolidated the bank's ethical policy in the mid-1990s. In particular, it requires business customers to take a pro-active stance on the environmental impact of their own activities.

Ecology Building Society

Although not operating as a bank, this building society has similar functions to the ethical banks (see Case Study 9.3).

CASE STUDY 9.1
The Wind Fund

The Triodos/Mercury Provident Wind Fund was launched in 1995 with the intention of raising £10 million for wind-powered electricity generation projects and other small-scale renewable energy schemes. Alongside environmental questions, its criteria for selection of projects include the social context. The Fund will expect a project to have a strong degree of accountability to the local community, including part-ownership by local people, with opportunity for participation in management and decision-making. The Fund provides an example of a holistic approach to investment.

Source: Chitty (1995)

Green and ethical funds/ethical unit trusts

Friends Provident Stewardship Unit Trust

The first ethical unit trust, Friends Provident Stewardship Unit Trust accounts for over 50 per cent of all socially responsible funds invested in the UK. Its ethical products include unit trusts, pensions and insurance funds. Companies in which it invests must have ethically sound policies on labour relations, pollution control and environmental protection. Companies involved in environmental degradation, nuclear power, CFCs, water pollution, or the exploitation of animals, for example through production or distribution of furs, intensive farming or animal-tested cosmetics, are avoided.

NPI (Global Care Fund)

NPI (National Provident Institution) is a mutual pensions, investments and life assurance company managing funds of over £7 billion on behalf of over 500,000 policy holders. Originally founded in 1835, NPI launched Global Care Unit Trust in 1991 to provide investment in companies whose products and practices are not considered to adversely affect the environment or the community.

CASE STUDY 9.2
Ecologically Sound Investments supported by Mercury Provident and Triodos Bank

Iris Water and Design has developed a natural sewage system for large and small dwellings, using flow forms and reed bed TREATMENT (*RBT*). With the aid of a Mercury Provident loan, the firm bought a workshop which it has converted to expand its work.

Little Pencoed Farm in Dyfed has been supported by Mercury Provident in converting to organic agriculture. It provides pesticide-free vegetables to the local market and runs a residential centre to offer people experience of farming life.

Tower Hamlets Environment Trust is a pioneering development working to bring environmental and social improvement to inner cities. It has completed more than 250 environmental improvement projects since its foundation in 1979.

Cafédirect Coffee is grown by farmers working together in co-operatives. It is the first fair trade product to be sold by major supermarkets in the UK. Cafédirect guarantees the producers a fair deal, paying them more while keeping the price to the consumer competitive.

Roggeplaat Wind Park is located on a former construction island near the East Scheldt Barrage. The park can produce at least 400 kilowatts of sustainable energy and has the best production of all the wind parks in the Netherlands.

Source: Triodos (1995)

Capitalist market theory assumes perfect knowledge of the market-place. In practice this unwarranted assumption can be only partly approached through specialist information services. Environmental funds provide vital information, enabling the economy to achieve near to perfect markets. The size of the environmental investment industry in the UK, Europe and the USA is difficult to estimate; it has been suggested that more than £51 billion of investment in the UK has been screened for social responsibility, with the figure in the USA being estimated at $500 billion. The influence of green investment, operating alongside supply chain pressures and green reporting, is unlikely to diminish, given growing awareness of both investors and consumers. In 1994 a Walker Group Survey in the USA reported that 70 per cent of consumers would not buy from a company which they regarded as socially irresponsible, while 25 per cent of investors agreed that business practices and ethics are 'extremely important to investment decisions'. Inevitably, growing consumer awareness that their purchasing decisions can affect their children's future in environmental terms will impact upon investment decisions.

CASE STUDY 9.3
Ecology Building Society

The Ecology Building Society (*EBS*) defines ecology as 'the link between the Natural and the Social Sciences'. Founded in 1981, to provide a means of finance for the purchase of ecologically sound properties, the society grew from its original assets of £5000 to assets of over £16 million by March 1994. According to its promotion, 'Advances shall be made to persons or on property which, in the opinion of the Board, are most likely to lead to the saving of *non-renewable resources*, the promotion of self-sufficiency in individuals or communities, or the most ecologically efficient use of land.' Investors with the society are enabled to make their investments become a 'Statement of Concern' about the earth, about people and animals and their interdependence.

In the 1970s it was impossible to obtain a mortgage to turn a run-down property into a family home or to develop an ecologically sound project without embarking upon extensive 'modernization'. Conventional mortgages required extensive 'renovation', including replacement of windows, asphalting of floors, re-timbering, re-tiling, roofing in modern materials, installation of damp-proofing, compulsory woodworm treatment and other 'improvements' which could completely ruin the character of the property. Most building societies remain unwilling to lend on such properties except on highly disadvantageous terms, and the EBS remains the only society prepared to lend up front on the current value of such a property. It is also prepared to make further advances at the same rate based on a revaluation once initial work has been completed. This enables borrowers to carry out work in stages at their own pace.

Loans may be made for:

- Small-scale workshops.

- Back-to-backs, which are by their nature energy-saving, often located in inner cities.

- Homes for people running small businesses with an ecological bias, including paper-recycling, organic horticulture, craft workshops.

- Derelict but sound houses which would otherwise have been abandoned.

- Renovation and construction of houses which incorporate special energy-saving or energy-efficient features.

- Organic smallholdings and farms, even where agricultural restrictions apply.

- Properties, the use of which will help to promote the life of small communities.

This small, specialist building society operates only on the margin between the rates of interest received from borrowers and those paid to investors. Unlike most other lenders, the EBS is not tied to any insurance company, and so does not receive vast sums of money by way of commission. Nevertheless, it has been able to meet the requirement of the European Directive for financial bodies to have capital (reserves) of at least £1 million. Members receive a regular newsletter containing factual information on ecological issues and examples of original design projects, and are encouraged to attend the interactive annual general meeting.

The EBS has been a leader in the field of ethical finance, meeting the needs of its members and being responsive to their views, making policy changes where appropriate. It operates on the principle of mutuality, whereby the organization is controlled by its members, the original essence of building societies. In this its operations contrast with other major building societies who are intent on conversion to plc status.

Address: 18 Station Road, Cross Hills, Nr Keighley, West Yorkshire, BD20 7EH.

ENVIRONMENTAL RISK

A further source of pressure on companies to adopt environmentally sound strategies come from the investment implications of environmental risk.

German sociologist Ulrich Beck (1988) has labelled post-industrial society the 'Risk Society'. Awareness of environmental risks has created a new pattern of consciousness, uniting all sectors of society in a set of common concerns. While previous generations battled with concepts of class division and the inequitable distribution of wealth, the universal nature of environmental risks has shifted the focus of attention. Nuclear accidents, pollution of the air and the seas, and holes in the ozone layer have effects which know no territorial boundaries, and affect rich and poor alike. The growing awareness of the implications of environmental hazards has increasingly impacted upon investment decisions through its insurance implications.

Schmidheiny (1992: 257) has outlined the problems which environmental risks are creating for commercial lenders on a global scale. He cites the example of the Australian company, Burns Pillips & Co., who bought two pharmaceutical plants in Italy and were subsequently liable for clean-up costs for problems created before the purchase in 1987. The remedial costs were more than the price of the original purchase. Investors are becoming increasingly wary of the implications of environmental risk, since borrowers may be unable to repay their loans and in some circumstances liability may extend to the lender.

As Schmidheiny (1992) points out, environmental risks differ from traditional insurable risks on three counts:

1. Environmental risks have a potential for almost unlimited liability. Unlike traditional insurance risks, problems created by an individual incident may not be limited in their effects in terms of space or time. Recognizing a potential problem, the US nuclear power industry sought to limit its liability to a fixed amount, leaving the costs of a catastrophe to be borne by the government. Beyond a limited amount of insurance offered by Lloyds of London, lending institutions have no guarantees against liability for environmental hazards.

2. Environmental risks may impact upon all policy holders at the same time. In normal insurance, a large pool of the insured helps to spread the risk. However, if a substance previously regarded as safe is discovered to be toxic, all manufacturers and users of the substance may become liable. 'It is as though a single accident by one insured motorist could trigger claims for insurance coverage from every policyholder.'

3. Proper actuarial tables depend upon a large number of small, well-defined incidents to create a viable insurance business. The potential for a few catastrophic incidents renders comprehensive environmental risk coverage impracticable.

As a result, lending institutions find themselves under increasing pressure to protect themselves and their borrowing clients by assessing potential environmental risks. This trend is reinforced by national legislation and by the defensive reactions of the insurance industry. In Germany in 1991 hazard liability law was introduced, establishing liability independent of neglect or intention, with the stated intention of introducing a more integrated approach to environmental protection. As the concept spreads through the EU, firms in all sectors of industry are drawn into the process of examining the environmental impact of the products and processes they use and the waste they generate.

In 1991 the UK Association of British Insurers deleted the clause relating to gradual pollution and contamination from all liability policies. The same clause was deleted from all risk policies unless caused by fire or peril. Losses by insurance companies compounded their general reluctance to provide environmental cover, resulting in a 'Catch-22' situation for companies. Companies requiring risk insurance must provide a site-specific detailed audit which, if it shows contamination, may result in refusal of the request by the insurers. A site which does not show contamination is more than likely to find insurance cover unnecessary. Environmental risk insurance provides one of many examples of the failure of traditional management strategies to adapt to changing environmental circumstances.

Traditional management approaches to policy and strategy have been shown to have limitations in their ability to assimilate the full implications of environmental hazards (see Case Study 9.4). As Frank Fischer (1993) has pointed out, environmental risk analysis has been based on the engineering model, in which the objective probabilities of technical failure are isolated and measured in terms of intrinsic and extrinsic physical properties. Managers have systematically sought to evade the social and political implications of industrial decision-making processes. Hence risk is expressed as the 'the product of the estimated degree of harm (death or damage) a given technical failure would cause, and its probability of occurrence.' For a complicated system this involves four stages:

1. Identifying the various separate components—materials, pipes, pumps, coolants, seals and fail-safe devices.

2. Measuring the statistical probability of failure of each component, using past experience.

3. Evaluation of environmental factors which might contribute to a technical failure, (e.g. geological faults), and/or exacerbate the effects of failure, e.g. weather conditions influencing the spread of toxic substances.

CASE STUDY 9.4
Limitations of Bolt-on Environmentalism

The 'Just-in-time' logistics philosophy from Japan, employed by many companies today, requires more frequent deliveries, generating increased pollution from the added traffic levels. Commercial transport companies, therefore, such as Exel Logistics and BOC Distributive Services, have been forced to adapt their operations in the light of environmental pressures. The list of problems they have identified indicates the shortcomings of the bolt-on environmentalism approach. The list includes:

■ Reduction of fuel consumption through driver training, the use of speed limiters and the monitoring and use of improved aerodynamic vehicles.

■ Reduction of noise through the use of air break silencers and plug-in points for refrigerated vehicles at site.

■ Trials with fuel additives to reduce particulate emissions and improve fuel consumption.

■ Cab communications to tackle congestion problems.

■ Reduction of water pollution by designing all new vehicle washes to incorporate recycling facilities and environmentally friendly cleaning materials.

■ Reduction of noise to residential areas through replacement of vehicle floors, ramps and tail lifts to reduce noise in loading and transit.

In addition, the Dutch have explored the potential for fuel and weight/distance taxes to encourage energy efficiency in design and driving of vehicles and reduce the practice of empty-loading. The pressure group Transport 2000 has suggested that the incentive to shift to rail or water for transport over 200 km would reduce the number of large vehicles by 20 per cent. The environmental problems associated with transport indicate that the siting of factories and depots has environmental implications which may suggest a reversal of policies of centralization.

Adapted from Paveley (1992)

4. Integration of the foregoing factors through chains of probabilities to provide an overall estimate of systems failure and its long-term and short-term effects.

The result is a mountain of data which fails to reduce the mutual distrust between business on the one hand and the pressure groups and the public on the other.

HOW CLEAN IS CLEAN?

Social pressures on companies for action on environmental protection have shifted rapidly through three stages from a focus on:

1. The most polluting industries.
2. Green consumerism.
3. Sufficiency production.

Stages 1 and 2, necessary though they were, gave rise to a bonanza of scientific research and consultancies more concerned with securing an extension for 'business as usual' than with providing long-term ecologically sound solutions. Firms, industries and governments attempted to monitor the environmental impacts of materials, processes and wastes by assuming expansion of material output as a necessary given. In the process it has become increasingly clear that all technologically based activity has multiple and long-term outcomes in terms of environmental impact.

Attempts to tackle pollution through the imposition of 'clean-up' measures is, on the whole, successful only in transferring pollution from one medium to another and does little to reduce overall levels of pollution. The reduction of atmospheric pollution from fossil fuel power stations has been achieved by the use of desulphurization filters, or by a switch to nuclear power. Both result in hazardous wastes which require disposal to landfill sites. The processing of sewage and the disposal of the resulting sludge has the same effect.

In addition to the transfer of problems from one medium to another, there is the growing recognition of the inequity of inter-generational transfer. Virtually all technology-rooted activities pose risks to future generations and are likely to impact significantly upon their quality of life. The impact of waste disposal and other industrial activities upon the health and quality of life of future generations has received relatively little attention in terms of scientific and policy research, with regulation being primarily in respect of the disposal of radioactive materials. The effects of disposal of hazardous non-radioactive materials on future generations has received less attention, despite the knowledge that many hazardous substances are dangerous at trace levels. If non-radioactive carcinogens, for example, were subject to legislation ensuring that they were to be treated and disposed of in a similar manner to nuclear wastes, costs and procedures, this could prove prohibitively burdensome. Yet this raises fundamental questions relating to the long-term viability of an individual business or industrial sector.

Who needs it?
The third phase of pressure on companies to adopt ecologically sound policies is encapsulated in the 'Sustainability Vectors' developed by SustainAbility and outlined in their report *Who Needs It?* (1995). The authors of the report argue the case for sufficiency production based on growing interest in 'sustainable lifestyles' based upon the ancient concept of human needs taking priority over other requirements in the market. They quote the Greek philosopher Socrates, who puzzled his friends by viewing the local market but never buying anything. Asked why he came to market, he replied, 'I am always amazed to see how many things there are that I don't need.' The issue of need is back on the agenda, because of the apparent impossibility of satisfying the infinite desires of a population of 8 billion to 10 billion.

The logic is simple. The more we consume, the more raw materials and energy have to be produced, the more products have to be transported and the more wastes have to be disposed of.

(SustainAbility 1994: 4)

The *Who Needs It?* report sketches out the implications of this logic for specific products, processes and industrial sectors and applies a 'needs test' to a number of products. Its 10 'Sustainability Vectors' cover questions of:

■ **Ethics** Including inter-generational and intra-generational equity.

■ **Socio-cultural factors** Conservation of sociological, cultural and biological diversity, with an emphasis on quality of life rather than material standards of living.

■ **Technological factors** Dematerialization will require investment in sustainable technologies.

■ **Macro-economic factors** 'Eco-infrastructure' projects, from state-of-the-art sewage treatment to transport planning and reformed financial systems, will be necessary to support individual companies in the developed and developing countries.

■ **Political factors** Change will be dependent upon evolution of a political economy capable of fostering the visions and values of sustainability.

(SustainAbility 1995)

SustainAbility anticipates an escalation in 'sustainable lifestyle' pressures for change on a global scale, pressures which will inevitably have implications for the policies and strategies of companies of all sizes and in all industrial sectors.

BIOREGIONALISM

Considerations of the type outlined above have led to a recognition that all forms of economic activities impact upon people and the locality in which they live. The direct connection between economic activity and environmental degradation suggests a holistic approach premised upon the concept of 'bioregionalism'. Originating in the USA with 'deep ecologist' Kirkpatrick Sale (1985) and others, bioregionalism is based upon an ecological consciousness of self and place which is compatible with sustainable living. The concept of a bioregion is based on a particular part of the earth's surface which has identifiable natural characteristics and catchment areas. As Welford (1995: 183) explains, the 'bioregional model puts more emphasis on local activity, on local development and on the protection of the environment in a proactive way by all those living in certain areas.'

Conventional terminology does not lend itself readily to the explanation of certain aspects of the bioregional concept. In conventional terms a region is a place defined by geographical boundaries in the form of lines on maps drawn up in order to define political 'ownership'. The concept of *place* is central to the definition of bioregionalism, in that economic activities are conducted in a particular spot. However, bioregionalism accepts that human activities impact beyond the local spot or boundary, as rivers flow from the mountains to the sea and

weather systems carry rain and pollution from one specific location to another. Bioregionalism is therefore based less on the concept of politically defined rights than on the concept of
ecologically defined duties or obligations. As Welford explains:

> Bioregional economies must conserve resources and systems of the natural world and have
> a stable means of production and exchange. Within bioregions there must be co-operation
> and participation and growth must be seen as organic. Bioregionalism means living within
> the natural limits to growth. Moreover, it stresses social and ecological processes as being
> one and inseparable. Thus there is a role for spatial reorganisation into small-scale
> communities (Sale, 1985) as the key to an ecological society.
>
> **(Welford 1995: 185)**

Welford (1995) has identified three principles of bioregionalism:

1. Liberating the self from impersonal market forces and bureaucracies, opening up local
   political and economic opportunities through communitarian values of co-operating,
   participation, reciprocity and the recognition of roots.
2. Developing the potential of a region towards self-reliance through small-scale, appropriate production, local markets and shared responsibility for sustainable development.
3. Developing an understanding of the natural environment and replacing exploitation with
   sustainable lifestyles.

The principles of bioregionalism run directly counter to globalization and the concept of the
global market-place based upon increasing size and centralization. They are premised upon
the concept of diversity, and cannot therefore be encompassed within a universal model or
blueprint. Bioregionalism encompasses the principle of subsidiarity, devolving decision-
making to the lowest practicable level and setting it in a particular place. In the process, it
engenders respect for the living space of neighbouring and more distant bioregions and their
communities. The ability to think and act locally has global implications which are explored
more fully in Part 4.

SUMMARY

As different pressures on industry to consider the environmental angle have increased, so the
opportunities to profit from a well-planned long-term finance strategy have also evolved. The
perceptive investor will see the movement of society towards a more ethical socio-economic
outlook as positive, investing in those areas that will have the least impact on the
environment, sustaining the investment potential over time and reducing the chances of
sudden costly litigations against the investment areas.

There is strong socio-economic and cultural evidence from the USA and Europe, to suggest
that environmentalism is here to stay and that we are liable to move further towards a more
localized economic fabric over time where goods and services are produced, as far as possible
locally, where companies are locally accountable and where people demand an increasing
share in their environmental welfare. Inward, local environmental investments are, therefore,

liable to become more and more significant over time and are worthy of more serious consideration by the forward-looking investor of the twenty-first century.

QUESTIONS

9.1 Hairdressing salons have become highly polluting businesses, with their aggressive dyes and environmentally contaminating rinses. What problems are likely to be encountered by hairdressing, or any other small service business, seeking to operate on sound ecological principles could be alleviated through green investment funds?

9.2 Explore the strengths and weaknesses of the argument that financial pressures on companies will continue to fuel the greening of industry.

9.3 Examine the pressures on a company to locate in a developing country any of its operations involving toxic substances. Illustrate your answer with topical examples and material from this chapter.

9.4 Compare and contrast the role of investment in initiating production on the proverbial desert island with that in a developed country.

BIBLIOGRAPHY

Key texts

Schmidheiny, S. (1992) *Changing Course: A Global Business Perspective on Development and the Environment,* Business Council for Sustainable Development and MIT Press, Cambridge, MA and London
Over 50 leading multinational companies have combined their experience and expertise in environmental issues to present this guide to the twin goals of environmental protection and economic growth. The book provides case studies of best practice from across the world, introducing innovations such as the recycling of the car, sustainable forestry and pulp production and a host of similar examples. The author is a Swiss industrialist, and former Chairman of BCSD (now WBCSD) and Principal Advisor for Business and Industry to the United Nations Conference on Environment and Development.

Sparkes, R. (1995) *The Ethical Investor,* HarperCollins, London
Written for the UK market, this book introduces the general principles of investor activism and offers an indication of likely future trends. Sparkes argues the case for the use of ethical investment to force change towards environmental sustainability, using techniques similar to those used to force change in South Africa's apartheid regime. He examines the evidence of the growing trend to use investment constructively as a mechanism to reduce adverse environmental impacts. As a review of the potential trend away from unqualified demands for financial returns from investors, this book is likely to be the first in a series of resources on green investment finance for the environmental manager.

Smith, D. (ed.) (1993) *Business and the Environment: Implications of the New Environmentalism*, Paul Chapman, London

This collection of essays from international experts in the field of economics, politics, law and the social sciences presents an excellent introduction to the environmental issues being faced by corporate managers and provides an excellent resource for students. The emergence of an environmentally aware business culture is documented with contributions on the greening of accounting, risk assessment and biotechnology. A valuable resource.

References and further reading

Beck, U. (1988) *Riskio Gesellschaft*, Surkamp, Frankfurt/Main.

Carson, R. (1962) *Silent Spring*, Hamish Hamilton, London.

Chitty, G (1995) 'Business Diary', *Resurgence* 170: 9.

EIRIS (1996) *Money and Ethics–a guide to Pensions, PEPs, Endowment Mortgages and other Ethical Investment plans*, Ethical Investment Research Service (EIRIS), 504 Bondway Business Centre, 71 Broadway, London, SW18 1SQ.

Fischer, F. (1993) 'The Greening of Risk Assessment', in D. Smith (ed.) *Business and the Environment: Implications of the New Environmentalism*, Paul Chapman, London.

Paveley, H. (1992) 'Logistics and the Environment', *Logistics Today* 11(5).

Sale, K. (1985) *Dwellers in the Land: A Bioregional Vision*, Sierra Club, San Francisco.

Schmidheiny, S. (1992) *Changing Course: A Global Business Perspective on Development and the Environment*, BCSD and MIT Press, Cambridge, MA and London.

Sparkes, R. (1995) *The Ethical Investor*, HarperCollins, London.

SustainAbility (1994) *Annual Review of 1994*, SustainAbility, London.

———(1995) *Who Needs It? Market Implications of Sustainable Lifestyles*, SustainAbility, London.

Taylor, B., Hutchinson, C., Pollack, P. and Tapper, B. (eds) (1994) *Environmental Management Handbook*, Pitman, London.

Tennant, T. (1994) 'The Growth in Environmentally-responsible Investment' in Taylor *et al.* (1994) *Environmental Management Handbook*, (pp. 85–102), Pitman, London.

Triodos (1995) Triodos Bank Publicity pamphlet, Brunel House, 11 The Promenade, Clifton, Bristol, BS8 3NN.

Welford, R. (1995) *Environmental Strategy and Sustainable Development: The Corporate Challenge for the 21st Century*, Routledge, London and New York.

CHAPTER 10

GREEN TECHNOLOGY

One machine can do the work of fifty ordinary men. No machine can do the work of one extraordinary man.

(Elbert Hubbard, 1856–1915)

INTRODUCTION

The need for industry to install cleaner technologies to minimize waste, pollution and resource depletion is taken as self-evident in much of the literature on business and the environment. The likelihood that cost is an inevitable barrier to the rapid introduction of new technologies appears equally self-evident. Hence the use of BATNEEC (Best Available Technology Not Entailing Excessive Cost), BPEO (Best Practicable Environmental Option) and other such acronyms in official literature on the business and the environment. This chapter explores the potential for 'new' and 'old' technologies to contribute to sustainability within the political, economic and social framework which underpins all commercial activity.

New developments in biotechnology, energy-use and waste minimization technology are explored through some practical examples. The necessity for technology to be appropriate to the needs of society and the wider community is explained through the examples of the 'Green Revolution' and the 'Flavr Savr' tomato, and an attempt to reconstruct nature in the form of 'Biosphere 2' is considered in the light of environmental reality. The chapter concludes that appropriate technology must be rooted in the concepts of efficiency and sufficiency, which lead to ecological, long term security.

NOVELTY AND SUSTAINABILITY

Recognition of the strains placed upon the environment through all forms of industrial activities has led to acceptance of the need for a complete reorientation of technology. From research and development, plant design, the manufacture, purchase, transportation of goods and the size and siting of manufacturing units, novel engineering will be employed to give the competitive edge for the progressive enterprise. As Saemann explains:

> Rather than meeting only the traditional objective of technical elegance and economic success, technology will have to fulfil two additional objectives: Societal acceptance and environmental compatibility. Meeting these new objectives or responsibilities requires new technological solutions ('novel engineering').
>
> (Saemann 1992: 180)

In the new scenario, traditional preoccupation with profits must cease to dominate decision-making in commerce and industry. Instead, profitability and growth will weigh in as one of three equivalent responsibilities alongside environmental sustainability and growing non-material quality of life. In this scenario, BATNEEC and BPEO may be viewed as useful conceptual jumping-off points for the ultra-cautious industrialist.

BATNEEC and BPEO

In the UK the Environmental Protection Act 1990 gave Her Majesty's Inspectorate of Pollution (HMIP) the duty to ensure that the employment of BATNEEC results in the BPEO. Government documents explain this terminology as follows.

- Best—means the selection of the most effective technology.

- Available—means any technology which has been tested, even if not in general use.

- Techniques—include both plant and process, from design, staff training, working methods and maintenance.

- Not Entailing Excessive Costs—serves to moderate BAT in view of economic reality. HMIPs have a duty to follow technological developments, and to review a company's introduction of new processes in the light of such developments. Existing processes may be required to be updated in due course.

(DoE 1993a)

While BATNEEC produces the Best Practicable Environmental Option (BPEO), resulting in cleaner processes according to state-of-the-art technologies, it does little to foster research into new, less polluting and more sustainable technologies. As a bolt-on approach to environmentalism, it fails to address the need for a fundamental reassessment of the relationship between industry, society and the environment. Research and development work in multinational corporations such as the Swiss firm Ciba-Geigy has led to the development and introduction of novel methods and technologies. R&D at Ciba-Geigy has followed two basic principles:

1. Questions of safety, health and the environment are pursued with the same scientific approach used for development of new products.
2. Wastes are handled, treated and disposed of with the same care as is devoted to sales products.

This approach has enabled Ciba-Geigy to improve or refine the following environmental technologies:

■ Chemical and biological effluent treatment.

■ Biodegradation of special wastes.

■ Wet air oxidation of non-biodegradable wastes.

■ Incineration of wastes.

■ Biofiltration for waste air purification/deodorization.

■ Off-gas purification by absorption, catalytic oxidation, incineration.

■ Flue-gas purification.

■ Immobilization and stabilization of slags and ashes.

■ Site remediation.

■ Groundwater decontamination.

■ Ecotoxicology.

■ Environmental trace analysis.

■ Biospheric monitoring.

■ Noise abatement.

(Rothweiler 1994)

The list indicates the range of potential for new and old technologies to be reassessed for their contribution to sustainability.

Sustainable technologies

Sustainable technologies respect the limits imposed by the need to remain within the carrying capacity of the earth in terms of its biological and environmental capital. Living off the interest is sustainable. Living off the capital is not. Living off the capital means exceeding the rate of sustainable use of renewable and non-renewable resources, and of the use of the environment as a sink for pollution and waste. As Herman Daly (1990) has explained:

■ The sustainable rate of use of a renewable resource should not exceed the rate of generation of that resource (its carrying capacity or sustainable yield).

■ The sustainable rate of use of a non-renewable resource should not exceed the rate at which a renewable resource could be substituted for it.

■ The sustainable rate of emission should not exceed the rate at which that pollutant could be recycled or absorbed by the environment (its critical load).

Alternatives to the old polluting technologies need to be found as a first step towards the achievement of sustainability, and on a global scale there has been no shortage of research projects into the feasibility of cleaner and more sustainable technologies. One of the fastest growing areas of technological research is biotechnology.

Biotechnology

Biotechnology is the harnessing of biological processes and techniques for human ends. It is one of the oldest of human technologies, dating back to the origins of farming, when humans used favoured strains of plants and animals for selective breeding. The cultivation of bacteria for the purposes of making beer, wine or bread is an equally ancient example of biotechnology. These age-old techniques evolved over generations, providing well-tried and tested results. By the late twentieth century scientific advances have come to offer quick-fix solutions to human problems through a new form of biotechnology. Genetic engineering, the ability to take genes for a particular characteristic and insert them in a different plant and animal species, raises new possibilities, and unknown dangers. Most of the world's major chemical companies have invested hundreds of millions of dollars researching the modification of plants and animals. By 1988 research into the agricultural potential for the new biotechnologies in the top 25 companies totalled US$330 million. On plant biotechnology alone, Shell was spending US$25 million and Monsanto US$55 million per year.

Areas of research for agricultural purposes include the development of:

- Strains of staple foods which are resistant to herbicides, insects, viruses or drought.

- Strains of fruit and vegetables with improved keeping qualities.

- Animals with improved productivity, such as increasing milk yield in cows.

Biotechnology and genetic engineering also have actual or potential applications in:

- Waste disposal technology involving treatment of industrial or sewage effluents through bacteria.

- Degradation of biological materials to produce fuels such as ethanol.

- Cultivation of fungi or algae to produce food for animals and humans.
  (For details of any of the above processes, see Mannion and Bowlby 1994)

The harnessing of natural processes to serve human needs has infinite and intriguing potential for practical applications. For example, domestic waste dumped in landfill sites degrades through natural microbial processes, resulting in an explosive and potentially hazardous discharge of methane. In a similar way, organic material from domestic waste, sewage or agricultural wastes can be biosynthesized by bacteria, to create methane, sometimes called 'biogas'. On a small and local scale, digesters have been widely used in China to provide fuel for domestic use (Mannion and Bowlby 1994: 152–3).

Energy-use technologies

Research, on both large and small scales, across countries and across industries has produced an infinite variety of means and mechanisms for reducing the human impact upon the natural environment. Flavin and Lenssen cite the work of small-scale inventors in Switzerland who have developed a series of two-passenger, battery-powered city cars made from lightweight fibreglass. The cars have a range of 50–80 kilometres and a top speed of 50–100 kilometres (30–60 miles) per hour. Research has shown that even in the USA 70 per cent of drivers average fewer than 80 kilometres (50 miles) a day. For most drivers most of the time, a 2000 kilogram car with a range of 600 kilometres is not necessary.

> From the outside, the small Swiss electric cars appear tiny, but inside they have ample room to seat two passengers and a full load of groceries. They weigh less than half as much as a normal car, accelerate rapidly, and are so short that the driver can skip parallel parking and just turn directly into the curb.
>
> **(Flavin and Lenssen 1994: 207)**

Flavin and Lenssen identify a range of similar inventions indicative of the coming shift from polluting and wasteful energy sources towards cleaner systems. They predict a 'rapid move to more efficient, decentralised and cleaner systems, echoing the shift from mainframe to personal computers during the 1980s'. However, they also forecast conflict, as the giant oil, auto and utility companies seek to preserve the status quo. Newer firms and their 'environmental allies' will inevitably face stiff opposition to pressure for change in government policies in favour of the new energy markets. Indeed, the continued growth in road-building and motor car use is predicated upon the now dated assumption that business travel is economically indispensable. As Brennan has explained (Berry 1993):

> If telephones, computers and fax machines have turned the world into a global village, why is it necessary to spend so much time shuttling around it, especially when such shuttling is a major ingredient in the production of greenhouse gases and ground level ozone pollution?
>
> **(Berry 1993: 11)**

The major business interests involved in the production of conventional fuels of oil, coal, natural gas and nuclear power and the technologies dependent upon their use have little to gain, and a great deal to lose, by the widespread utilization of alternative energy sources. Although the technologies exist for the production of energy from biomass, wind, water and solar sources, the introduction of those technologies is dependent upon removal of non-technical socio-economic barriers.

Hill *et al.* (1995) provide a comprehensive analysis of the history and use of different forms of energy. They provide a clear account of the technical and economic issues involved in energy policy. The implications for environment and society of the adoption of the various options available are explored. This includes alternative renewable energy sources such as biomass, wind, water and photovoltaics. The research also considers ways in which social and environmental costs could be introduced into energy planning and accounting, and emphasizes the need for global energy efficiency to limit overconsumption.

Hill *et al.* (1995) challenge the global energy industries to create a society we want rather than to allow an unsustainable society to be predicted and realized. They call for flexible sustainable energy policies that reflect the true impact they have on the environment, society, economic systems and political environment featuring the following aspects:

- Satisfaction of and right to basic human needs in both the developed and developing world.

- Creation of fair economic comparisons between conventional and renewable resources (the principal demand is for externalities to be internalized).

- Correct implementation of taxes on energies to assist in reducing environmental pollution, in particular, that the range of taxes is ascribed at real prices and to all pollutants.

- Promotion of energy-efficiency improvements and improved access to environmentally benign technology.

- Increased research and development in renewables technology.

- Generation of additional financial resources and equal access to these resources.

- Promotion of national and regional self-reliance.

- Incorporation of energy strategies that reflect the nature of all socio-environmental problems at a global level.

Energy source

Although it may seem at first glance that the source of energy used by a company is limited there are in fact alternative options available to the industrial decision-maker. Alternative sources of supply than fossil fuels exist, of which locally supplied renewable energy is one such alternative. As technology develops the option of locally supplied energy from renewable sources has become a more viable option.

Combined heat and power (CHP)

CHP is one such option. CHP is a system that produces heat and electricity simultaneously. Combustible materials used in production can be incinerated on site and used to fuel the energy supply. Freemans Mail Order Company (UK) installed an incinerator to use the combustible waste produced in their production processes (plastics and cardboard). The incinerator not only dealt with the problem of waste disposal, but also generated heat and hot water for the warehouse where it was installed. The system saves over £32 000 a year and paid for itself within four years (BiE 1992: 24). Heat losses can be reduced by as much as 15 per cent and CO_2 emissions reduced by 20–25 per cent. Electrabel (SGB) installed a methane-driven cogeneration system for Fiat that meets 50 per cent of its energy requirements. CO_2 emissions were reduced by 30 per cent.

Wind energy

In July 1994 the Welsh Affairs Committee on Wind Energy said, 'Wind energy has the potential to make a significant contribution to national electricity needs' (Welsh Office 1994). Wind energy itself is far from a new source of energy supply. Water and wind powered the beginning of industrial innovation over 2000 years ago. It is an ancient form of energy generation that has been superseded until recently by more technologically capable forms of energy generation. Today there is a resurgence of wind energy with more modern technological developments that are facilitating the generation of electricity on a larger more economic scale. New technologies include the charging of batteries and the driving of pumps to produce heat. There are currently over 20 000 wind turbines generating electricity world-wide (British Wind Energy Association (*BWEA*) 1995).

Commercial wind energy began in the UK in 1990; in the mid-1990s the turbines are producing enough electricity for the needs of 230 000 people and it is estimated that by the year 2010 as much as 10 per cent of the UK's electricity supplies could be generated by wind. It is estimated that two-fifths of Europe's usable wind potential is within the boundaries of the UK.

There are essentially two types of wind turbines, the vertical and the horizontal axis machines. In the early days the majority were horizontal axis types; however, there has been a move towards the vertical in recent years. Most machines have three blades; however, there are two-blade machines and even some one-blade turbines. Although the trend has been to build large machines, there is certainly a market for small-scale, private-use machines. Most machines operate at a constant rotational speed, typically 30–50 rev/min with the low-speed high-torque shaft connected via gears to an electrical generator rotating at 1000 or 1500 rev/min.

Just as all forms of commercial activities have an effect on the ecological surroundings, all energy generation incurs some form of environmental impact. The environmental impact, however, is relatively very low compared with other more traditional sources.

Wind energy produces:

- No carbon dioxide (the primary greenhouse gas).

- No sulphur dioxide or nitrous oxides (which contribute to acid rain).

- No hazardous or radioactive wastes.

Calculations have shown that the scrap value of the wind turbines pays for the installation, making them commercially and ecologically effective. The only major reservation has been their intrusive nature and attached visual amenity loss through aesthetic damage. It has been proposed that wind turbines are a blot on the landscape and ruin the beauty of the countryside. Although surveys undertaken by the DTI (at Delabole in Cornwall) and the Countryside Council for Wales have shown that the majority of people find their existence positive to their quality of life rather than negative as they show progression towards a more caring and sensitive society, there is in fact an even more powerful counter-argument in favour of progressive usage of wind energy.

The question that has to be posed is, which is more aesthetically intrusive and offensive: a hill with wind turbines generating electricity safely or a hill devastated by the effects of acid rain generated from fossil fuel consumption or the landscape surrounding Chernobyl? The precautionary principle would seem to favour further research and investment into the renewable source of wind energy.

Wind energy produces a significantly lower level of environmental impact than fossil fuel electricity. If the true price of energy generation were to be accounted for today, the price of electricity would be significantly higher after taking into account the environmental costs of acid rain and the greenhouse effect. Indeed measurement of their true costs of production would be difficult to collate, as we are not actually sure of the long-term damage to society of our present means of energy generation.

Other arguments in favour of wind energy include the fact that the electricity supplied is locally available, labour for construction is generally taken from local pools of labour and maintenance of the turbines provides long-term employment opportunities. With current reserves of UK oil due to be depleted by the year 2010 and gas by the year 2020 there is clearly a need to plan for alternative energy sources unless the UK intends to become energy dependent.

Wind energy not only has a significantly lower environmental cost than fossil fuel energy generation but also has a lower financial cost as well. Electricity from wind costs 6p a unit in the UK (which is estimated to be about 80 per cent of the price paid by UK customers for their electricity at present). The BWEA predict that this price will fall to 4.5p by the year 2000.

Other renewable sources
Project Arbre in the UK is a biomass renewable energy joint venture between Yorkshire Environmental Ltd, Yorkshire Water plc, Associated Energy Projects plc and TPS Termiska Processor AB (Case Study 10.1). The project (funded by the EU's Thermie programme) aims to develop renewable energy sources to fuel an 8 megawatt (MW) power generating plant near Eggborough, Selby, UK. Project Arbre is looking to encourage local landowners to turn their set-aside fields over to the cultivation of energy crops like short rotation willow coppice. The willow coppice is then to be used to fuel the new power station and generate renewable electricity.

In the UK the third *NFFO* (non-fossil-fuel obligation) Renewables Order for England and Wales was announced in December 1994. NFFO-3 aims to create an initial market for renewable-based electricity generation technologies which have the potential to compete against the more traditional forms of conventional generation sources. The UK government has committed itself to generating 1500MW of new renewable-based generation capacity by the year 2000 as a part of the process to restore carbon dioxide emissions in the year 2000 to 1990 levels. Technologies encouraged for development included in the NFFO-3 are wind, hydro, landfill gas, solar, municipal and industrial waste, energy crops, agricultural waste and forestry waste.

Current international practice in renewables

The Netherlands
With the current subsidy levels placed on conventional European energy sources, renewable energy sources or 'green power' is 50–57 per cent more expensive. However, in the

Netherlands customers of PNEM the (southern Dutch energy company) are considering offering their customers the option of buying green power at the full price to allow money to be pumped back into the research and development of renewable energy. This would be an extra Dfl 20 (US$3 a month) on the average energy bill. Nevertheless at present renewable sources of energy account for only approximately 1.5 per cent of energy consumption in the Netherlands.

Austria
Austria is proposing the development of an energy tax with or without EU backing, even if it means competitive disadvantage with neighbouring countries.

Denmark
Renewable energy resources provide 8 per cent of total energy consumption. Household waste and straw are currently the main suppliers of renewable energy in Denmark. Alternative renewable supplies also include wood, wood chips and bark, pelleted wood, straw, biogas, solar energy, wind and water power, heat pumps, fish oil.

Germany
In 1994 the German government launched a DM10 million (US$6.5 million) renewables support programme which has been extended into 1995, supporting solar, minihydro and windpower schemes.

Other countries
Wind energy projects have also been established in the Canary Islands (Fuerteventura), Spain and by Maharashtra State Electricity Board in India.

Waste minimization technologies
The introduction of cleaner industrial processes may face various economic and cultural barriers.

Economic barriers include:

■ Possible overall production cost increases, through raw material costs increase, production rate decreases or costs of new equipment.

■ Increased capital investment may be required beyond that necessary for pollution control or waste treatment.

■ Costs may render the project unprofitable, despite benefits.

■ Capital investment may appear attractive, but capital be unavailable.

Cultural barriers include:

■ Lack of commitment and responsibility in senior management.

■ Resistance to change, individual or corporate inadequate internal communication (bureaucratic opposition, especially on the generation of cost data).

Economic and cultural resistance to change can best be overcome through imaginative technological innovation involving lateral thinking and a combination of cost-saving outcomes. The DTI's (1989) first business guide to *Cutting Your Losses* provides an illustration of the potential for obtaining an impressive payback by combining:

■ Waste reduction at source.

■ Recycling.

■ Lower cost disposal routes.

The guide described an early project whereby Allied Colloids dealt with the waste from a liquid dispersion polymer (*LDP*) process. The resultant waste from the process mixed with water formed a viscous sludge, causing problems of treatment and disposal. A settlement tank introduced to the system in 1984 allowed the extraction of waste LDPs and solvent before the substances came into contact with large quantities of water. The waste was skimmed off and distilled. Waste solvent, in the form of 5 tonnes of white spirit per week, could be reused. Although there was no use for the LDPs, with the extraction of the white spirit it could be landfilled, at a cost of £100 per tonne. This compared favourably with the previous costs of incineration at £500 per tonne. Similar lateral thinking has given rise to the introduction of new technological processes such as PROJECT ARBRE (Case Study 10.1).

CASE STUDY 10.1
PROJECT ARBRE

In December 1994 the NNFO (non-fossil fuel obligation) contract was awarded to Project Arbre with funding from the EU's Thermie programme to encourage the development of renewable energy technologies. The project is run by Yorkshire Environmental Ltd, the waste management and environmental services business of Yorkshire Water plc.

The plan is to site a BMW power-generating plant near Selby, to supply sufficient power for a town of 18 000 people. The principal fuel source will come from 2000 hectares of short rotation willow coppice. Partners to the project, in addition to Yorkshire Environmental, are Associated Energy Products plc, a subsidiary of the French Compagnie Générale des Eaux (CGE) and the Swedish technology development company TPS Termiska Processor AB. The project will explore the potential of a new technology to generate a number of positive outcomes:

■ Studies have shown that the use of coppiced wood for energy production releases far more energy than is used in its growth and harvesting.

■ Treated domestic sewage sludge will be used to fertilize the willow organically.

■ Biomass could provide up to 40 per cent of the UK's current electricity needs. Presently, biomass meets about 14 per cent of the world's energy demand, being an important source of energy in many countries.

■ The project itself will create about 40 full-time jobs in operating the wood fuel generating plant and coppice management and transport.

■ Agricultural land that has been set aside will be brought back into beneficial use.

■ Local people will be provided with electricity generated by an environmentally acceptable and sustainable method. Biomass energy production does not add to global warming. The amount of carbon dioxide released by gasifying the wood is equivalent to the amount needed by the trees for photosynthesis.

Research has shown that the most cost-effective wood fuel sources in Britain come from fast growing deciduous trees such as willow and poplar. Traditionally, coppicing was carried out by hand. The process involves cutting back the stems after the first year of growth. Three years later, the stems are harvested in winter, with subsequent harvesting on a three-year cycle. Wood produced in this way was useful for fencing and basket-making. New technology has enabled this method of wood farming to be used to fuel an electricity generating plant.

Broad support for renewable energy schemes based on short rotation coppicing and using wood fuel generation technology has been forthcoming from a list of organizations, including the Department of the Environment (DoE), the Energy Technology Support Unit (ETSU), the DTI, the Forestry Authority, Ministry of Agriculture, Fisheries, and Food (MAFF), the Royal Society of Nature Conservation, CPRE, Greenpeace, RSPB, the Farming and Wildlife Advisory Group, the Countryside Council for Wales, the Countryside Commission, the Game Conservancy Trust and English Nature.

Source: Yorkshire Environmental (1994) and Project Arbre
Address: ARBRE, 2 The Embankment, Sovereign Street, Leeds, LS1 4BG

In their guide to waste minimization (Crittenden and Kolaczkowski 1995) the Institute of Chemical Engineers (IChemE) recognize that recycling may be an effective alternative to treatment and disposal. However, the elimination and minimization of waste at source are the preferred options in the hierarchy of waste management practices. Hazardous materials, including solvents and catalyst supports used in the production process, may be replaced by less hazardous or even non-hazardous materials. They list the following examples:

■ Replacement of chlorinated solvents in cleaning and degreasing operations by non-chlorinated solvents, water or alkaline solutions.

■ Substitution of chemical biocides by alternatives, such as ozone.

■ Replacement of solvent-based paints, inks and adhesive formulations with water-based materials.

■ Substitution of a more durable coating to increase coating life.

■ Increase in the purity of purchased raw materials to eliminate the use of trace quantities of hazardous impurities.

- Reduction of phosphorus in waste water by reduction in use of phosphate-containing chemicals.

- Replacement of hexavalent chromium salts by trivalent chromium salts in plating operations.

- Replacement of solvent-based developing system by a water-based system in the manufacture of printed circuit board.

- Replacement of cyanide plating baths with less toxic alternatives.

They cite a number of case studies of practical implementation of waste minimization. In one of these the Swedish firm Thorn Järnkonst minimized its use of organic solvents in degreasing and painting in the production of light fittings from aluminium and steel sheets. In the process, the alkaline degrease cost was reduced by $25 200 per year while avoiding the need for the installation of recovery equipment. Further changes in powder painting techniques brought annual costs savings over solvent-based painting including $206 000 for paint, $62 000 for cleaning and $47 000 for disposal.

These examples demonstrate the vast potential for industry to use cleaner technologies. Until the environmental crisis, 'dirty' technologies could be employed with impunity as policy-makers considered pollution as an inevitable by-product of profitable industrial development. Examples of the type cited above continue to mask the true costs to the environment resulting from industrial operations, since the 'cost savings' from waste minimization are calculated from known costs incurred by the firm. Environmental 'externalities' which do not feature on company balance sheets remain outside these calculations.

Clean technologies

Clean technologies have been defined by the UK government as: 'supplying goods which are cleaner or do not produce waste by processes that inherently prevent or reduce the production of dangerous or unpleasant by-products (hazardous or offensive filth, stench or noise)' (Department of the Environment 1995). The introduction of clean technology is an attempt to produce the same end result as conventional technology, with reduced environmental impacts. New 'low or non-waste' technologies are designed to reduce pollution at source. Introducing the UK Environmental Protection Technology (*EPT*) Scheme in 1989, Chris Patten, then Secretary of State for the Environment, observed that in the past industry had 'often been seen as a source of pollution. [Now] it is industrial innovation and new technology that offer the means by which we can clean up our environment.' The EPT Scheme was designed to promote research into and use of low- or non-waste technologies. Three types of process changes were featured in the project:

- A basic design change to the process itself which results in less pollution or waste being generated.

- Recycling materials, either within a process or between related plants.

- The conversion of previously dumped waste material into useful products.

The EPT Scheme focused initially on 'ingenious process changes' fitting into the three above categories. Admitting that 'the operations shown are not environmentally perfect', it was noted in the scheme that 'the manufacture of a "cleaner" alternative product' as one additional option to be explored at a later date. Case Study 10.2 gives examples of 'Cleaner Technologies'.

CASE STUDY 10.2
Cleaner Technologies

Recovery of copper from printed circuit board etchant

In the manufacture of printed circuit boards unwanted copper foil was etched away using an acid solution, resulting in surplus copper oxide being disposed of to landfill. The introduction of new technology in the form of a new material, PVC, and a process change resulted in improvement to the quality of the boards, virtual elimination of disposal costs, recovery of the copper in high value form and elimination of hazardous chemicals to be handled. The improved technology gave a payback period of two years on the capital investment of £55 000.

Reduction of pollution from diphenyl oxide plant

The Billingham ICI plant is a chemical processing plant with 6000 employees, producing alcohols and detergents as derivatives of oil. The processes gave rise to an effluent stream containing 10 per cent impure phenol which could not be discharged to estuary because of its high chemical oxygen demand (COD). The nearby Higher Alcohols plant manufactures products such as iso-decanol for use as plasticizers. The process results in a 'heavy-ends' stream which is used as fuel. Advances in the technology of process scale solvent extraction equipment, together with liquid–liquid mass transfer data, made it possible for ICI to use the 'heavy ends' to remove at least 95 per cent of the phenol from the effluent. Capital investment of £250 000 was paid back in 11 months. This provided an example of the effluent stream from one process being cleaned by a waste product from another process. At the same time the thermal value from the phenol was recovered.

Water-based screen printing ink

Sericol, employing 500 staff, supplies a wide range of screen printing inks for use in graphic displays and on fabrics. Traditional solvent-based inks give off fumes when in use, contributing to unpleasant working conditions and smog in urban areas. Heat generated in the drying processes represents wasted energy. The technological development of water-based inks through advances in organic and polymer chemistry, combined with development of radio-frequency dryers, made it possible to develop water-based inks. The result is avoidance of pollution and reduction in waste and energy use.

Cement kiln pollution and waste reduction by improved process control

Blue Circle Industries has 12 manufacturing plants and is the largest producer of cement in the UK. The firm co-operated with Image Automation, which trades in laser scanning systems and expert-system industrial control (LINKman system), to obtain the enabling technology. The manufacture of cement requires the burning of fuel together with limestone and clay. The resultant clinker is then ground with gypsum to produce cement. The process requires to be operated within a certain band of optimum temperature, which is difficult to achieve manually due to unpredictable disturbances to the process. Improvements in the science of expert systems control and measurement technology resulted in avoidance of wastage of coal at high temperatures, improved clinker quality, life extension of kiln liner, and reduction of NO_x and SO_x emissions. Capital investment of £203 000 was paid back in 3 months.

Source: Department of Environment (1993b)

The introduction of 'clean' technologies offers ample scope to the ingenuity of university research and R&D departments in the vast bulk of highly polluting industries. Recent examples of 'progress' include:

- Recycling vehicle wash: a company running 300 vehicles introduced a £70 000 'technically advanced' machine to keep the vehicles in pristine appearance, using 'recycled water and the latest biodegradable detergents'.

- Introduction of a No Clean Flux technology in the manufacture and installation of circuit boards.

- Introduction of laser and toner cartridge recycling schemes.

- Promotion of energy efficient computer equipment to reduce emissions of the primary greenhouse gas, carbon dioxide and the acid rain causing sulphur dioxide and nitrogen oxides.

- Anaerobic digestion stage added to sugarbeet processing, producing useful fuel and reducing load on aerobic treatment plant.

The availability of 'green technologies' across the entire range of production processes and industrial sectors indicated by these examples is no guarantee that ecologically sound technologies will be adopted. This is despite the work of organizations like Vesa (Video Electronics Standards Association) setting up helpful standards including DPMS (Display Power Management State). Research into the greening of IT, for example, noted that in practice:

the physical impact of green technology on the office environment is very low ... many IT managers had 'never heard of' the various manufacturer environmental initiatives. For example, 91% of IT managers had 'never heard of' Energy Star compliance, one of the main ways in which green computers and printer manufactures are promoting their product. Similarly, 41% had 'never heard of' cradle-to-grave manufacture; 82% were similarly unaware of Vesa DPMS; 41% of BS 7750; and 95% of ICER (Industry Council for Electronic Equipment Recycling).

(Coates, et al. 1994)

Nevertheless, in Germany the 'environmental technology' sector has been recognized as a major growth area. 'According to the most recent statistics of 1993, 6,000 companies in Germany are involved in environmental protection technology. In 1992 turnover in this area came to DM 55.6 billion.' A growth rate of 4.9 per cent was predicted, representing 'huge new market opportunities for those banks prepared to do business with those industries' (Bruns 1994: 191).

TECHNOLOGY AS A SOCIAL PHENOMENON

In the course of his review of the greening of risk assessment, Fischer (1993) demonstrates that technology is rooted within the society in which it is used, and does not have a separate, independent 'scientific' existence. Large-scale technological systems 'are integrated sets of techno-institutional relationships embedded in both historical and contemporary social processes. They are complicated technical processes functionally woven together by networks of socio-organizational controls' (Fischer 1993: 103). Fischer illustrates this point by reviewing the institutional failures which were the true source of technological hazards and catastrophes in the 1980s and 1990s:

- The tragedy at Bhopal chemical plant was the result of workers ignoring the misalignment of valves.

- The Chernobyl catastrophe occurred when plant operators overlooked established procedures.

- Three Mile Island occurred when workers misapplied established procedures.

- The Prince William Sound oil spill in Alaska resulted from neglect of standard practices by the *Exxon Valdez* tanker captain.

- The failure of the US space shuttle *Challenger* occurred as a result of management's unwillingness to heed the warnings of company engineers.

- A serious crash at Los Angeles International Airport was caused by air traffic controllers who cleared two planes to use a runway at the same time.

Advocating a participatory approach to institutional change, Fischer (1993) dismisses the technocratic approach institutionalized in current business practice, in which technical answers are sought to bring political discussions to an end. He cites a Californian experiment with 'siting contracts' in which a set of power- and risk-sharing procedures enable a host community to review new plant equipment and operations before installation. Management procedures of this type will be increasingly important in the adoption of greener technologies and their efficient operation.

Appropriate versus inappropriate technologies

Blind acceptance of the ability of technology to provide a solution to every problem created by industry can no longer be accepted as a rational approach to the solution of environmental questions. Problems and their solutions are rooted in the society which created them. The technofix solution can appear deceptively attractive, but if introduced without regard to the broader socio-economic and institutional context its results may be the reverse of those intended. A prime example of this phenomenon is offered by the 'Green Revolution' (the term 'green' in this case is not synonymous with 'environmental').

The Green Revolution

The development of high-yielding varieties of wheat and rice appeared to be a case of a new technology providing the answer to food shortages. The introduction of the high-yielding varieties to Third World countries in the 1960s without regard to the socio-economic implications of the introduction of a new technology offers a classic illustration of the symbiotic relationship between technology and society.

The technological advance was achieved through research in global research centres including the International Rice Research Institute in the Philippines and the International Maize and Wheat Improvement Centre in Mexico. The new wheat strains were first introduced to Mexico in the 1940s, and to India and Pakistan in the 1960s, followed by new rice strains. Following their introduction to India and Pakistan, yields doubled in less than a decade. The 'Green Revolution' appeared to offer the solution to the problem of providing enough food for the expanding populations of the Third World. In reality, the impact of the new types of wheat and rice was, for the majority of people, a disaster.

The problem was that in order to produce the high yields, the new types of wheat and rice required large inputs of fertilizer. Also, because they are totally devoid of natural immunity to pests, they require large quantities of pesticides. The use of chemical fertilizers and pesticides in Asia rose steeply, bringing new financial costs to growers of the new varieties. High yields were available only to farmers who could afford high inputs. The small peasant farmers who formed the majority did not have enough land or capital to enable them to use the new techniques. Large landowners who did have the resources became richer, expanded their holdings by buying up peasant land, and turned the subsistence farmers into landless labourers. Farmers adopting the new seed became totally dependent on imported fertilizers, pesticides and farm machinery and exported their produce on the world markets. The landless peasants had less food available and swelled the ranks of the unemployed, while their countries became net exporters of food.

Those who benefited were the agrochemical firms in the developed world and the small elite of landowners and exporters of food to the First World. The outcome was entirely foreseeable at the time the hybrid seeds were first introduced, and was predicted both by academics and small farmers. This did not prevent institutionalized interests from introducing a socially, ecologically and economically unsustainable system of food production. 'Westernized' agriculture is not more efficient than that of the Third World. Indeed, it is less efficient. It 'succeeds' because of its ability to purchase higher inputs, which ensure higher outputs, but at a cost of much higher energy throughput per unit of production. The increased grain production was not only used for human consumption. A quarter of the world's total grain production is fed to animals in the industrialized world, a method of food production which is highly wasteful in terms of energy throughputs. It also has environmentally disastrous side-effects, in terms, for example, of disposal of manures at locations remote from the grain-producing areas.

The net result was to erode forty centuries of agricultural knowledge. According to Vandana Shiva:

> The very meaning of agriculture was transformed with the introduction of the western green revolution paradigm. It was no longer an activity that worked towards a careful maintenance of nature's capital in fertile soils and provided society with food and nutrition. It became an activity aimed primarily at the production of agricultural commodities for profit.
>
> **(Shiva 1988: 23)**

Shiva demonstrates that the gains in yield from monoculture are illusory, since they fail to take account of the loss of by-products and the complex interrelationships involved in cultivation through traditional mixed farming methods. She cites Sir Alfred Howard, who observed in 1940 that the agricultural practices of the Orient were as sustainable as the primeval forest through creation of a perfect balance between manurial requirements of crops harvested and natural processes which replace fertility. The conservation of soil fertility is achieved by a combination of:

■ Mixed and rotational cropping with leguminous crops.

■ A balance between livestock and crops.

■ Shallow and light ploughing.

■ Organic manuring.

This type of mixed cropping follows nature in providing a balanced diet, giving better results than monocultures. As Howard noted: 'Here we have another instance where the peasants of the East have anticipated and acted upon the solution of one of the problems which western science is only now beginning to recognise' (Shiva 1988: 107). Howard was ahead of his time. Western science continues to view 'productivity' in narrow terms of output for markets and profit. By failing to contribute to the soil's organic fertility, western 'scientific' agriculture renders land unproductive and is fast turning the croplands of the world into deserts. By failing to take account of the socio-economic implications of the introduction of new technologies, policy-makers continue to create problems faster than solutions. Nevertheless, western policy-makers continue to view innovation in a positive light, while dismissing opposition to novel technology as indicative of backwardness and irrationality.

NIMBYism and the Flavr Savr Tomato

Invariably, novel technology is regarded with suspicion by users and consumers. Originating in the research laboratories of large commercial interests, novel products and processes have not been tried and tested over time, as was the case with pre-industrial changes in agricultural processes and practices. The introduction of new biotechnologies raises questions relating to the degree of unexplored risk attendant upon their long-term impacts on the physical and social environment. Although policy-makers and green pressure groups are united in dismissing *NIMBY*(Not In My Back Yard)ism as illogical, the phenomenon is as old as human society, and more rational than the immediate acceptance of change for the sake of change. It is more natural to hesitate than to embrace a philosophy that would throw caution to the four winds in pursuit of short-term gain. The use of genetic engineering in food production and for medical purposes is a journey into the unknown which can at best be described as 'brave' but more realistically appears intemperate. Medicine *may* benefit from the development of the 'oncomouse' patent, which breeds mice guaranteed to develop cancer. Agriculture *may* benefit from the invention of 'ice-minus', which breeds strawberries capable of resisting frost. But, as contributors to Wheale and McNally (1990) demonstrate, the introduction of any new technology of this type will have side-effects in terms of human health and environmental and climatic stability which have yet to be quantified.

The 'Flavr Savr' tomato provides an example of the types of issues raised by the introduction of technologies which are not rooted in society and community, and have not been tried and tested over time (see Case Study 10.3). Although the early trials of Calgene's Flavr Savr tomato were not a success, and the first crop had to be ploughed into the ground in Mexico, agricultural biotechnology continues to explore the potential for manipulation of a host of food crop varieties. The DNAP tomato, for example, 'ripens' only when immersed in ethylene gas. It is already common commercial practice when marketing fresh tomatoes to pick them green, keep them cool, and turn them red immediately prior to sale through the application of ethylene gas. The resultant tomato appears attractively red to the eye of the customer, but it is not really ripe and is hard, tasteless and acidic. Market research indicates that customers buy food with their eyes; agri-business and the supermarkets cash in on this knowledge. Technology itself may be neutral, but its application has wide socio-economic implications.

CASE STUDY 10.3
The Flavr Savr Tomato

In November 1994 the US corporation Calgene sought to conquer the European market with its patented tomato. However, its application to the European Patent Office for a 'European' patent was opposed by more than thirty NGOs on the following grounds:

The patenting of life forms by vast monopoly interests is contradictory to 'morality and public order' (Article 53a). Vast monopoly claims of this type enable a company like Calgene to own not only the tomatoes produced in their laboratories, but also all plants manipulated in the same way and the succeeding generations for twenty years. This particular patent includes manipulated 'long-living' apples, potatoes, squash and melons. The firm has developed a technology the use of which depends upon a change in legislation, since Article 53b of the European Community states that plant varieties cannot be patented. The Flavr Savr is clearly a plant variety.

Consumer deception

In the genetically manipulated tomato the decomposition of the cell wall is slowed down. Although the tomato rots less quickly, all the other ageing processes occur as in a normally ageing tomato, as vitamins A, C and other nutrients decompose. The Flavr Savr appears young and fresh when in reality it may be so old that its nutritive value approaches zero. As Swiss gastro-journalist Wolfram Siebeck noted: 'With this product the first and most important requirement of the good cuisine, its freshness, will become a complete farce.' The consumer is deceived at the point of purchase and consumption.

Risk of bacteria resistant to antibiotics

The Flavr Savr tomato has been genetically engineered to include two novel genes in each of its cells: an 'anti-sense' gene designed to retard rotting, and a kanamycin resistance gene used as a 'marker'. Scientists predict that the widespread use of kanamycin could create bacteria resistant to antibiotics. It is possible this would compromise the efficacy of the therapeutic use of kanamycin and the related antibiotic neomycin. If this occurs, a critical group of antibiotics could be rendered useless, putting public health at risk.

Risk of new allergies

The kanamycin gene codes for a special protein (the enzyme APH(3')II) responsible for kanamycin resistance. This protein could induce new allergies, since new proteins always have the potential to cause new allergic reactions with unknown risks. It may take as long as 10 years for the first allergic reaction to occur.

Increased transportation and centralization

The Flavr Savr has been specifically adapted to withstand long storage and transport times. It is the perfect high-tech tomato for industrial production systems. Its effect will be to undermine local and regional producers, while increasing transportation with all its attendant adverse ecological impacts. The diversity of tomato varieties will be endangered, as high-tech agriculture is expanded.

Third World cash cropping

The long-living Flavr Savr is an ideal cash crop for growing in Third World countries, where wages and other costs are low. But the social and environmental costs of cash cropping in Third World countries, including the use of agrochemicals, contamination of soils, loss of soil fertility and enforced economic dependence on multinationals, have been more detrimental than positive in their effects.

Although the US Pure Food Campaign has announced a boycott of the Flavr Savr, press reports have publicized the tomato as a successful technological feat, and products from genetically engineered tomatoes are on sale in major food stores across the world.

Source: Koechlin (1995)

Biosphere 2

The problems associated with perceiving sustainability as a purely technical matter, bereft of wider environmental, social or ethical implications are encapsulated in a grandiose experiment seeking to recreate the earth's ecosystems artificially (Case Study 10.4). The experiment arose out of commercial interests including:

- The generation of marketable pollution control and environmental management technologies.

- The potential sale of a small-space life-support system to the US space programme.

From a purely scientific point of view, the attempt to reproduce Planet Earth as a biological entity appears attractive, signalling 'a new stage in evolution, with biospheres likened to new biological organisms'. The commercial potential for living in the oceans or space, or creating 'oases for survival' on the earth itself in the highly populated, highly polluted world of the future, can appear attractive. Scepticism about the project from within the scientific community has tended to focus on the scientific feasibility, noting the project's lack of scientific rigour. The aim of seeking to reproduce Planet Earth has attracted little critical comment.

In the Biosphere 2 experiment, science and commerce have co-operated to create a vast artificial supermarket of life itself. Plants and animals selected for the experiment were limited to those deemed essential to the reproduction and maintenance of human life and its support systems. 'Thus all the biomes mechanically reproduced in Biosphere 2 are in effect "bionic engines" designed to produce particular outputs at some level of "sustainable yield" so as to fulfil the biodynamic requirements of artificial ecological models' (Luke 1995:

CASE STUDY 10.4
Historical Account of Biosphere 2

Space Biosphere Ventures (*SBV*), the private company which built and manages the project, brought together soils, plants and animals from a variety of naturally occurring ecosystems. The project originated in 1983 and arose from the work of the Institute of Ecotechnics, founded in 1974. Funded by Texas billionaire Ed P. Bass, the project was steered into existence by the eight-strong Decisions Team.

The 3-acre site in the Arizona desert is completely enclosed in a tightly sealed glass superstructure. It houses 3800 species of plants and animals, arranged according to the seven basic 'biomes' of Biosphere 1 (the earth). The biomes are:

1. Marsh.

2. Savannah.

3. Tropical rainforest.

4. Desert.

5. A 25-foot deep 'ocean and coral reef'.

6. Intensive agriculture.

7. Human habitat.

To design Biosphere 2, SBV employed the services of a range of ecological, engineering and environmental experts from the University of Arizona, the Marine Systems Laboratory at the Smithsonian Institution (Washington, DC), Kew Gardens in Britain and the University of Hawaii. The designer collage of plants, soils and waters is housed in a series of pyramids. The mechanical infrastructure of pumps, motors, fans and piping necessary to operate the enclosed system is hidden from sight. The complex of components keeps air and water moving, plants and animals alive, and temperature and humidity constant.

> In the north pyramid the rain forest flows into the ocean and savannah biomes and the fresh and salt water marshes. These zones blend into the thorn scrub and desert areas in the south pyramid. The two pyramids are connected via a smaller, pyramid-arrayed hall linked to another hall which is topped by three arched vaults: these in turn blend into three squat domed turrets and a short dome-capped tower. The arched vaults contain the intensive agriculture biome while the human habitat occupies the turrets and tower—a simulated micro-city.'

Biosphere 2 was designed for human habitation, and in September 1991 four men and four women entered the superstructure intending to spend 24 months sealed in and living off the top of the designer food chain. Problems occurred to thwart the plan to keep the eight people sealed up without interruption. These included:

■ The need for emergency surgery and immediate food supplies necessitated opening up the superstructure almost immediately.

■ The productivity of Biosphere's food systems was limited by an unusually cool and cloudy Arizonian winter.

■ The 'Biospherians' were too preoccupied with obtaining food supplies and keeping their environment in order to collect scientific data on the interactions of plants and animals.

■ Some animal species died off completely because of the build up of carbon dioxide, and extra equipment had to be installed to introduce oxygen and clean the air. This was despite the confidence of designers in the system's ability to balance itself.

On their emergence from the structure in September 1993 the Biospherians declared the experiment 'a success'. However, a second experiment in 1994 to test out modifications to the system in the light of experience was aborted after six months. It was concluded that little further was to be gained from the permanent presence of researchers within the structure, and the domestic animals were removed. Since then, people make only day trips inside.

Source: Luke (1995)

157–62). Even the intensive agricultural biome, intended to mimic a subtropical region, was unlike any actually operational system. Instead, the food mix mimicked the flow of products made available by the global food trade: 'this biome emulates, through intensive on-site production, what the average suburban consumer can feed on after extensive car trips to the supermarket in a US or European city' (Luke 1995: 157–62). Furthermore, there were no tiger sharks, grizzly bears, or even house flies. Pests and weeds were decreed dispensable by the designers of Biosphere 2, and were simply omitted.

The scale, grandeur and supreme chaotic excesses of the earth's deep oceans and vast land masses are reduced to a version of ecology designed to rationalize the commodification of the environment itself. 'Biosphere's version of ecology seems intent upon selling people a product that they once had for free. Fresh air, clean water and green grass, Biosphere 2 suggests, will soon be either a memory or a corporately produced analogue' (Luke 1995: 157–62).

This commercially based scientific experiment has been described as:

> a monument to scientific hubris. Far from replicating nature, it has engineered a denatured space where fragments of nature are shackled as slave mechanisms for the benefit of humans. As a totally managed environment it offers a glimpse of where 'sustainable development' might lead if sustainability continues to be viewed as a purely technical and managerial matter.
>
> (Luke 1995: 157–62)

The intricate and delicate balance of the earth's ecosystems are still way beyond our replicative ability, strengthening the case for increased conservation and earth care awareness. When the earth was made the instructions and the expertise to replicate it were not provided.

Appropriate technologies and material sufficiency

Pollution and waste in Europe has reached unmanageable proportions. The average European household creates 0.5 tonne of refuse annually, with food, drink and other consumables constituting a sizeable proportion of the pollution caused by agriculture and industry. Consciousness of public opinion coupled with legislative pressure has driven companies in the developed world to explore and introduce new technologies to reduce the environmental impact of their productive activities. On the whole, however, as in the individual examples cited above, approaches to cleaning up the environment have been adopted in a piecemeal fashion, with the final responsibility for initiating change resting on the management of individual firms as they respond to external pressures.

In some instances, such as the work undertaken by INFORM (see Case Study 10.5) research has examined the availability of new technologies and processes in a broader context. But the primary pressures on companies have been to produce and market first, and to consider cleaner methods as a secondary consideration. Cleaner technology can be good for business and better for the environment. But while technologies are available to minimize human impact on the environment, their use is dependent upon decisions at the investment stage. This places a duty on producers, consumers and legislators to examine the technical options available to them as economic actors and to take responsibility for the impact of their choices from cradle to grave.

A 'whole system' approach will go beyond the refining of techniques and move towards the selection of technologies based upon a concept of sufficiency, efficiency and security. A commonly used example is that of the tumble dryer. While it is possible to design more efficient steam turbine blades for the generation of electricity, it is also possible to place this single technological advance in a wider context. Tumble dryers can be replaced by a clothes line and a few clothes pegs, simple to produce, simple to use and simple to dispose of. A good case can then be argued, in terms of costs and benefits, for adoption of a policy of drying the washing in the fresh air:

■ It eliminates demand for the output of electricity from entire power stations.

■ Fewer power stations require building or decommissioning.

■ Fewer 'white goods' are produced and disposed of, again reducing energy consumption.

■ The washing smells fresher.

■ It represents an example of ecologically sound technology.

The primary aim of technology is to lighten work, but a technology which places an intolerable strain on the environment is, in the end, self-defeating. Such technology is ultimately unviable, as it consumes the very capital resource base upon which society exists. As Schumacher explained:

> The illusion of unlimited powers, nourished by astonishing scientific and technological achievements, has produced the current illusion of having solved the problem of production. The latter illusion is based on the failure to distinguish between income and capital where this distinction matters most ... namely, the irreplaceable capital that man has not made, but simply found, and without which he can do nothing.
>
> (Schumacher 1973: 136)

Appropriate technology meets the criteria of efficiency supplying a sufficiency which leads to resource security. According to Hill *et al.* (1995: 69), efficiency may be encouraged because:

■ The use of less fuel costs less.

■ If fossil fuels are used less, they will last longer.

■ Reduction of greenhouse gas emissions makes climate change less likely.

■ Smaller power requirements in total will enable all requirements to be met from renewable resources.

■ Reduced pressure on resources will leave greater stocks for future generations.

Efficiency in terms of energy use in buildings, whether domestic or commercial and public, can be achieved through improved design in basically two ways. First, improvements in the ways heat is put into a building. Second, in terms of heat retention. Efficient design of

CASE STUDY 10.5

Reassessing Refillable Bottles—INFORM

INFORM is a US research and educational organization. It is a non-profit-making organization which researches business practices that harm the environment and pinpoints ways to improve those practices. Since 1976 it has published more than 60 reports.

Until the Second World War, the normal practice in the USA, as in the rest of the developed world, was to return and refill beer and soft drink bottles. By the 1990s a mere 5–7 per cent of the volume of US beer and soft drinks was sold in refillable bottles. Instead, US residents used 120 billion beer and soft drinks containers annually. Disposal adds to the solid waste pile, and production of single-use packaging of this type adds to the consumption of materials and energy. At first glance, a return to the use of returnable bottles appears to offer the most environmentally sustainable option. But what are the facts? Does reuse generate additional costs in terms of transportation, cleaning and relabelling, rendering the option less attractive?

INFORM's detailed report covers all these questions. INFORM brought together data from government, business and pressure group sources to review the environmental and technical implications of transportation, washing and ultimately recycling refillable bottles (refillables do not have infinite durability). The results were compared with a thorough evaluation of the environmental effects of the manufacture, recycling or disposal of many types of single-use bottles and cans. INFORM reviewed materials used, energy consumption, waste generation and costs.

INFORM concluded that:

> refilling can offer one of the many routes to a more sustainable society. For example, INFORM calculates that under a scenario in which the 1990 market share of aluminium cans remained constant and all glass and polyethylene terephthalate (PET) bottles were refillable and were used 25–30 times, the weight of beer and soft drink container waste would be reduced by 73.6% from 1990 levels.

Additionally, INFORM documented the extent to which the reuse of bottles reduces energy consumption, as fewer bottles need to be manufactured or melted down in the recycling process. Reduction of production also leads to a decrease in air and water pollution.

INFORM further explored the length of time a bottle can stay in circulation before being recycled, according to its material composition. Fillings were:

- For a refillable glass beer or soft drink bottle.

- For a refillable plastic soft drink bottle.

- For a plastic milk bottle.

INFORM's findings established the technical case for protection of the environment through the use of reusable bottles. They further established that technical feasibility alone does not establish environmentally sound practice. While US use of reusables was at 5–7 per cent, the role of refillable bottles as a percentage of beer retail sales in other countries was: Austria 95 per cent, Canada 82 per cent, Denmark 100 per cent, Finland 86 per cent, Germany 84 per cent, Guatemala 90 per cent, Mexico 80 per cent, Netherlands 95 per cent and Norway 98 per cent. Comparable figures for soft drinks were similar. These figures illustrate the efficacy of economic and legislative pressures on industry to secure environmentally sound policies.

Mechanisms to promote refilling include deposits (most commonly used in refilling systems), and government policies such as taxes on one-way containers, quotas for refillable bottles, bans on one-way containers and separate retail systems for beverages. Combinations of these measures have resulted in widespread adoption of environmentally sound technology on a rapidly increasing scale.

Source: Saphire (1994)

end-use appliances for space heating, water heating, lighting, cooking and the running of other appliances can substantially increase efficiency of energy use. Efficient design of buildings and appliances can further minimize heat and energy loss, adding to overall efficiency. Similar savings can be made in respect of energy use in transport.

Sufficiency, the reduction of demand upon energy and material resources, can further reduce demand upon resources. This can be achieved by design of products and the siting of facilities so as to reduce the need to consume resources. Public transport systems, increased product durability and reusable packaging fit into this category. The trail blazers in this respect have been the Germans, with their 'Ordinance on the Avoidance of Packaging Waste' (*Verpackungsverordnung*). The effect of this legislation, passed in 1991, is to make industry pay for managing the waste generated by packaging. Industry must take back, reuse and/or recycle packaging materials independently of the public waste management system. The legislation is based upon the 'make the polluter pay' principle, and has the effect of motivating industry to adopt more resource-efficient technologies in order to cut down unnecessary packaging.

An INFORM study (Fishbein 1994) explores the German experiment in manufacturer responsibility as it extends to a requirement on manufacturers to take back products, for example automobiles and electronic equipment, at the end of the lifespan. Volkswagen and BMW have conducted pilot schemes in auto recycling, and it anticipated that cars and other consumer durables will increasingly be designed to be recyclable. As technology is encouraged to move in this direction through a combination of economic and legislative pressures, the extension of the product life itself will become increasingly attractive. Durability will require a shift from the manufacturing of goods for use and disposal to manufacture for repair, including spare parts, and servicing.

The technological achievement of efficiency and sufficiency is a means not only to environmental security but also to political security. Intemperate demands upon scarce resources can, as Hill *et al.* (1995: 33) observe, lead to expensive defensive action. The US Department of Defense safeguarded oil supplies in 1989 at a cost of $15 billion, with a further $30 billion spent on the war in the Gulf. 'Resource wars' are an expensive form of subsidy to support inefficient, wasteful and environmentally unsustainable technologies. Case Study 10.6 describes some appropriate technologies.

CASE STUDY 10.6
Some Appropriate Technologies

Reed Beds

Reed bed treatment (RBT) of sewage water, whereby plants are used as natural water filters, is an ideal application of the principle of BATNEEC. For example, specially developed reed beds have been planted to act as natural water filters to help prevent contamination of nearby streams from a disused waste tip. The £1 million clean-up of the 12-acre dumping ground at Burley-in-Wharfedale near Bradford, UK, was necessary because of the poor siting of a council waste tip in a wet area in the 1920s. Research using new soundwave techniques from the USA discovered additional problems with groundwater seeping into the site. The water is cleaned by flowing through a series of seven reed beds before going into a willow copse. Once constructed, the beds need very little maintenance, one bed needing to be dug out once every 10 years. The site can be planted with trees, providing a useful habitat for animals and wildlife.

In addition to the cleaning of contaminated land, reed beds can be, and indeed are, used for treatment of sewage. Severn Trent Water has over 80 working reed beds, and the system can be shown to be highly cost-effective.

> Nature is the finest water engineer. In terms of cost-benefit analysis this can be proven now through the development of reed-bed treatment, or constructed wetlands, a form of super-efficient grass plot whose construction costs are typically 50% of conventional sewage treatment costs, with running costs of only 10%.
>
> (Jones 1995: 42–5)

Restoration of wetlands for the purpose of sewage treatment in this way has additional advantages, since the areas provide:

- Flood relief.
- Water resource storage.
- Release of secondary resources for fertilization.
- Reeds, rushes and willow for biomass and other purposes.
- Conservation and leisure activities.

Reed beds are the ultimate in 'cradle-to-cradle' technology. The process allows *in situ* treatment in a decentralized system, such that water and wastes can be recycled at minimal costs. By contrast, centralized systems, involving expensive piping and pumps, results in a cocktail of contaminated effluents being released, deliberately or accidentally, to inland waterways and the sea. Jones argues, however, that widespread introduction of reed bed technology in the UK is inhibited by the sewage infrastructure. This needs to be expensive because water industry profits are calculated as a percentage of costs. Therefore, the higher the costs the better. Furthermore, by a neat trick,

> we pay massive subsidies for farmers to apply artificial fertilisers to their fields and then have to pay again to remove the resulting harmful levels of nitrates from our drinking water, whilst also paying over the odds to have our own natural fertiliser disposed of.
>
> (Jones 1995: 42–5)

Reed beds offer an excellent example of a technology ideally suited to ecological sustainability, being tried and tested and found efficient and effective. They also illustrate the institutional barriers to the wholesale introduction of environmentally sustainable technologies.

Source: Bradford Environment Action Unit and Jones (1995)

British Hemp Stores

Hemp is an ecologically sustainable crop which has been displaced by the introduction of fossil fuels and nylon and wood paper-making technologies. There are strong environmental arguments for the revival of production of hemp for the following purposes:

- **Textiles** The long-lasting fabrics created from hemp, which can be used in clothing and industry, are naturally biodegradable.

- **Paper** Paper made from hemp is excellent and durable.

- **Oil** Hempseed oil has a wide range of uses, as salad oil, in cosmetics, and for paints and inks in industry.

- **Fuel** Hemp creates large quantities of biomass, and can be used for fuel in cars and electricity generation.

- **Environmental** The crop helps to reverse the greenhouse effect by converting CO_2 to oxygen as it grows. It contains no sulphur, a major contributor to acid rain.

- **Economic** Hemp can be grown almost anywhere, and processed regionally, serving to strengthen local economies. 'On a global level, local communities would be able to provide up to 80% of their material needs themselves.' (British Hemp Stores pamphlet, available from 76 Colston Street, Bristol BS1.)

British Hemp Stores stocks hemp products from across the globe, including clothes, textiles, paper, oils, seed, cosmetics, rope, twine, wallets, hats and accessories. It provides a further example of the imaginative use of technology to introduce ecological sustainability in practice.

Source: British Hemp Stores, 76 Colston Street, Bristol, BS1.

SUMMARY

As this chapter has indicated, research has given rise to an abundance of new possibilities, especially in the field of the new biotechnologies and genetic engineering. However, as the experience of the 'Green Revolution' demonstrates, the introduction of a commercially attractive new technology may have unforeseen socio-economic effects. Equally, the effects of new biotechnologies on the environment are giving pause for thought. The release of plants genetically engineered to resist herbicides could have effects on the wild plant population, resulting in weeds which are virtually impossible to control. The effects of the use of pesticides, which has given rise to more virulent strains of pests, requiring use of more powerful poisons on foodstuffs, indicates the extent to which cause for concern is rooted in rationality. Growing public awareness of these issues suggests that in the future, companies with a cavalier attitude towards environmental and social questions will find it increasingly difficult to survive.

Just as a weed is simply a plant growing in the wrong place, technology is 'good' or 'bad' according to the context in which it is used and the end results of its use. Environmentally damaging technologies can be made 'cleaner' by individual companies on a piecemeal, *ad hoc* basis, as illustrated within this and other chapters. Nevertheless, in the long term, sustainability requires the adoption of green technologies developed within the holistic context of co-operation between the different sectors of the community. The Best Practicable Environmental Option has minimal negative externalities from cradle to grave. This cannot be achieved by business standing apart from the social institutions and environmental realities from which it draws its resources. As business co-operates with governmental organizations, pressure groups, community groups, and educational and financial institutions, sustainable technologies will emerge to satisfy the criteria of efficiency, sufficiency and security.

QUESTIONS

10.1 Case Study 10.3 on the Flavr Savr tomato presents the negative arguments associated with Calgene's patent application. Calgene developed the product at great expense. Present the case in favour of the application.

10.2 The Biosphere 2 experiment could potentially give rise to the development of marketable technology in the field of pollution control, hazardous waste mitigation and rationalized waste management. To what extent are these outcomes practicable?

10.3 Select one product of the new technologies currently in the news and explain the arguments for and against its use.

BIBLIOGRAPHY

Key texts

Fishbein, B. K., (1994) *Germany, Garbage and the Green Dot: Challenging the Throwaway Society*, INFORM, New York

At a time when US policy-makers and citizens were outfaced by the problems of mounting municipal and commercial waste, Germany was introducing sweeping new legislation designed to lead industry into reducing packaging and product waste. *Germany, Garbage and the Green Dot: Challenging the Throwaway Society* describes the German requirement that businesses be responsible for taking back used materials from packaging and products they have produced, and recycling, reusing or disposing of them. This intriguing adaptation of 'making the polluter pay' encourages and rewards innovation. As with all INFORM texts, this book is thoroughly researched and presents the inevitable problems and pitfalls which accompany the search for practical solutions to the problems of industrial waste management.

Wheale, P. and McNally, R. (1990) *The Bio-Revolution: Cornucopia or Pandora's Box?*, Pluto, London

At a time when the technofix of genetic engineering and the new biotechnologies appeared to offer solutions to the mounting problems of resource depletion and toxic waste production, an international conference brought together leading experts in the field to assess the potential of the new technologies. This book is the result of the deliberations of laboratory scientists, veterinarians, ecologists, government regulators and industrialists. They observed that for the first time in the history of the earth, it was possible to create new plants, animals, bacteria and viruses containing genes from different species, including human genes which have been inserted into farm animals. Although the promise appeared tantalizing, the potential risks to the stability and welfare of farming techniques, the environment and public health were profound. The ethical and moral questions raised by the contributors to this book will achieve a high profile in the early twenty-first century. This text provides a valuable introduction to this vast subject area.

Crittenden, B. and Kolaczkowski, S. (1995) *Waste Minimization*, Institution of Chemical Engineers, Rugby

This text is based on the US Environmental Protection Agency's *Waste Minimization Opportunity Assessment Manual*, and its draft *Guide for an Effective Pollution Program* and the UK Department of Trade and Industry's aptly named pamphlet *Cutting Your Losses*. It documents the benefits of waste minimization together with the methodology and practical techniques to minimize waste, illustrated with case studies. It is complementary to the IChemE's *Waste Minimization Training Package*, setting out principles which managers will need to adapt to their own national legislative requirements.

Warmer Bulletin, Journal of the World Resource Foundation

This free bulletin is published four times a year in English, German and French. It provides a world-wide information service on the potential recovery of resources from post-consumer waste. The World Resource Foundation is independent of commercial interests and is assisted by an advisory council of internationally eminent academics, waste management professionals and environmental specialists. Topics covered include company profiles, composting and anaerobic digestion, country/city features, eco-labels, economics, electrical and electronic wastes, legislation and policy, landfill, LCA, materials reuse and recycling, packaging, waste minimization, and waste to energy.

Warmer Bulletin is available from **The World Resource Foundation, Bridge House, High Street, Tunbridge, Kent, TN9 1DP, UK**. It is also available from World Resource Foundation Spanish and German Offices.

Tansey, G. and Worsley, T. (1995) *The Food System: A Guide*, Earthscan, London
In this comprehensive text the scientific, political and economic aspects of the production and distribution of food are drawn together, stressing their interrelated nature. Amounting to $1.5 trillion annually, the production and processing of food and beverages is one of the largest industries in the world. This book places the food manufacturing industry in context, exploring the place of food in human affairs, the role of agriculturists, food processors, distributors, caterers and customers, and the role of science, technology and management of food policy. Expertly researched, *The Food System* succeeds where many a text has failed in achieving an appeal to the serious student and to the general reader. It provides an invaluable guide to the operation of the food system on a global scale, at once well balanced and informed as a source of reference and a good read.

References and further reading
Berry, R. J. (ed.) (1993) *Environmental Dilemmas: Ethics and Decisions*, Chapman & Hall, London.
Bie (1992) *A Measure of Commitment—Guidelines for Measuring Environmental Performance*, Business in the Environment, 8 Stratton Street, London W1X 5FD.
Brennan, A. (1992) 'Environmental Decision-making', in Berry 1993 (details above).
British Wind Energy Association (1995) *BWEA: Wind Energy 'The Facts'*.
Bruns, V. (1994) 'Environmental Management in a Leading Bank', in R. Taylor, C. Hutchinson, P. Pollack and B. Tapper (eds) *Environmental Management Handbook*, Pitman, London.
Coates, N. F., Atkinson, S. and Staplehurst, J. (1994) 'The Greening of IT', *Greener Management International* 8 (October): 48–57.
Crittenden, B. and Kolaczkowski, S. (1995) *Waste Minimization: A Practical Guide*, Institution of Chemical Engineers, Rugby.
Daly, H. (1990) 'Towards some Operational Principles of Sustainable Development', *Ecological Economics* 2: 1–6.
DoE (1993a) *Integrated Pollution Control: A Practical Guide*, DoE, London.
———(1993b) *Clean Technology*, pamphlet, DoE, London.
DoE (1995) *The UK Environment*, Alan Brown (ed), Department of the Environment/GB Government Statistical Service, HMSO, London.
DTI (1989) *Cutting Your Losses: A Business Guide to Waste Minimization*, DTI, London.

Fischer, F. (1993) 'The Greening of Risk Assessment', in D. Smith (ed.) *Business and the Environment*, Paul Chapman, London.

Fishbein, B. K. (1994) *Germany, Garbage and the Green Dot: Challenging the Throwaway Society*, INFORM, New York.

Flavin, C. and Lenssen, N. (1994) *Power Surge: Guide to the Coming Energy Revolution*, Worldwatch Environmental Alert Series and W. W. Norton, New York and London.

Hill, R., O'Keefe, P. and Snape, C. (1995) *The Future of Energy Use*, Earthscan, London.

Jones, J. (1995) 'Back to the Sewage Farm', *Resurgence* 169: 42–5.

Koechlin, F. (1995) 'No Patents on Life', available from European Coordination, Blanenstrasse 15, CH/4142 Münchenstein.

Luke, T. W. (1995) 'Reproducing Planet Earth?', *Ecologist* 25 (4): 157–62.

Mannion, A. M. and Bowlby, S. R. (1994) *Environmental Issues in the 1990s*, John Wiley, Chichester.

Rothweiler, W. B. (1994) 'Reviewing and Monitoring Environmental Performance', in R. Taylor, C. Hutchinson, P. Pollack and B. Tapper (eds) *Environmental Management Handbook*, Pitman, London.

Saemann, R. (1992) 'The Environment and the Need for New Technology, Empowerment and Ethical Values', *Columbia Journal of World Business* 92, 27 (3–4): 186–93.

Saphire, D. (1994) *Case Reopened*, INFORM, New York.

Schumacher, E. F. (1973) *Small is Beautiful*, Blond & Briggs, London.

Shiva, V. (1988) *Staying Alive*, Zed, London.

Welsh Office (1994) *Wind Energy*, House of Commons Welsh Affairs Committee, July.

Wheale, P. and McNally, R. (eds) (1990) *The Bio-Revolution: Cornucopia or Pandora's Box?*, Pluto, London.

The New Millennium: Support Structures for a Post-Modern Sustainable Society

The truly crucial limits confronting mankind are not outer but inner. It is not the finitude of the planet, but the bounds of human will and understanding that obstruct our evolution towards a better future. ... We human beings are the cause of the problem, and only by redesigning our thinking and acting ... can we solve them.

(Ervin Laszlow George 1995: 141)

INTRODUCTION

Decades of environmental concern have produced a bewildering array of consultancies and scientific experts capable of monitoring in minute mathematical detail the environmental impact of every production process and product on earth. As the human species monitors its own predicament in accurate and elegant detail, environmental degradation has continued apace. Generations of public and private sector managers, trained to find technical solutions to technical problems through the application of science, engineering, law, economics and accounting, have been slow to recognize that the determinants of long-term environmental problems are social, not technical. Their training presents an almost insuperable barrier to rational thought, an essential precondition of progress towards sustainability.

This section explores some of the implications of the fundamental paradigm shift essential to the attainment of long-term ecological sustainability, premised upon inter- and intra-generational equity. The paradigm shift entails the rejection of the cosmetic technofix in all its guises. The following chapters document the growing recognition of the need for holistic solutions, taking account of the needs of the economy, the environment and the community based upon local needs and local knowledge. They are underpinned by an emerging theory of sufficiency.

THROUGH EFFICIENCY TO SUFFICIENCY

Wolfgang Sachs of the Wuppertal Institute for Climate, Energy and the Environment has neatly summarized the post-industrial paradigm that has emerged from critiques of the early, outdated business-as-usual approaches to the ecological crisis. Noting the obsession with perpetual expansion of output at escalating speeds of growth, Sachs (1995) questions the efficacy of reducing ecological concerns to efficiency in resource and waste management. The 'efficiency solution' embraces attempts to reduce the use of natural resources per unit of output by producing technically superior motor vehicles, goods from recycled materials and greener technology. Ecological sustainability would, however, require efficient resource management of an order well beyond scientific credulity.

> According to the current rule of thumb, only a cut-back of between 70% and 90% in the throughput of energy and materials in the decades ahead would do justice to the seriousness of the situation. Only a daring optimist would believe that such a target could be achieved merely by improvements in efficiency.
>
> (Sachs 1995: 6)

The speed at which cars are driven, and kilometres which they cover, so increased during the 1970s and 1980s as to eliminate all savings in energy efficiency. Speed is the watchword of the dying industrial era. Yet that speed is unfocused, lacking in rational goals and outcomes. 'Nothing is as irrational as rushing with maximum efficiency in the wrong direction,' observes Sachs. Speeding towards an integrated planetary economy is neither practicable nor an unavoidable necessity.

> Integration entails transportation and even more transportation. The distances between producer and consumer (and also between consumer and refuse dump) are increasing. Flowers from Kenya and shoes from Taiwan are well-known examples. In addition the

distances between suppliers and manufacturers are multiplying too. Through 'global sourcing' car manufacturers get parts from all over the world.

(Sachs 1995: 7)

Sachs quotes the famous example of the yoghurt carton and its contents, travelling a total of 9000 kilometres from source to consumer, and notes that 'lean production' leads to 'fat transportation'. Since the true social and ecological costs of transportation are thrown on to the environment and into society at large, transport costs are not truly reflected on the company balance sheet. The number of long-distance journeys by heavy goods vehicles multiplies so long as transporters can assume 'that the area between the destination is worth nothing, and can be crossed, concreted over, subjected to noise and poisoned at will.' As an alternative, Sachs recommends realistic prices based on long-distance taxes or local customs charges to 'increase the resistance of space against easy transit'. This type of approach to sustainability is echoed by progressive thinkers throughout the 'developed' and 'developing' world.

The theory of locally intensified economic development flows from recognition of the shortcomings of a concept of efficiency in use of resources and waste minimization not backed by recognition of the concept of 'sufficiency'. Sustainability requires the colourful diversity of economies and cultures which is evolving from the post-modernist regeneration of the sense of place (see bioregionalism, pp. 261–2).

THINK GLOBALLY, ACT LOCALLY

The pressures to 'Think Globally, Act Locally' come from many quarters, bringing with them the observation that the ecologically aware company is incapable of operating in a 'business-as-usual' vacuum, yet is unable to effect change without information and support structures which are based in the local community. Each enterprise exists in a dialectic relationship with its physical and social surroundings, subject to a multitude of social, economic, environmental and legal pressures and dependent upon co-operation and networking. Recognition of these complex inter-relationships has given rise to a shift in values and created a demand for the integration of land use and transport planning in order to reduce the physical separation of activities. Roberts (1995) has identified three themes dominating sustainable regional planning:

1. The search for forms of economic organisation that respect the environment and minimise the negative environmental consequences of development.
2. The desirability of moving towards spatial forms and modes of social organisation that minimise the excessive use of resources and maximise environmental benefits.
3. The desirability of meshing together sectoral and spatial elements to ensure the environmentally responsible and balanced planning and development of regions.

(Roberts 1995: 781).

The 'spatial elements' of planning include the design of urban and rural communities, the layout of industrial, commercial and residential areas and the interconnecting transport systems. Regional planning, as proposed by Roberts, may be based upon a river basin or a city and its immediate hinterland, taking account of geographic and cultural diversity. The city or local geographical region may exist as a political entity within the nation or state, and this may in turn fall within a larger federation. Within this multilayered system decision-making is ideally devolved to the lowest practicable level. In most countries, including the UK, the lowest political region is the local government area.

LOCAL AGENDA 21

The Local Government Management Board (*LGMB*) has co-ordinated Local Agenda 21 work in the UK. In its series of informative pamphlets, the LGMB argues that local authorities need find no conflict in their duties to provide for economic development and environmental activities.

> Nevertheless, there is sometimes believed to be a conflict between them, because economic well-being depends on consumption, which requires resource use, which causes environmental damage. If this were always true, 'sustainable development' would be a contradiction in terms. However, it isn't. A rising material standard of living does not necessarily mean more consumption. Things that are built to last (houses, furniture, etc.) are of high quality and require minimal maintenance.
>
> **(LGMB 1995: 147)**

The preconditions for the regeneration of local economic development are laid down in Chapter 28 of Agenda 21 (UN 1993) and have given rise to a wide diversity of local initiatives across the globe. As local needs are identified and met through local resources, skills and traditions, top-down management techniques are replaced by co-operative structures. Local authorities implementing development action plans based upon Chapter 28 are less inclined to tolerate resource degradation, pollution and local unemployment as a necessary price to pay for global economic growth.

> As the level of government closest to the people, local authorities play a vital role in educating, mobilising and responding to the public to promote sustainable development. By 1996, most local authorities in each country should have undertaken a consultative process with their populations and achieved a consensus on a 'Local Agenda 21' for the community.
>
> **(Chapter 28, Agenda 21, UN 1993)**

In the following chapters the theoretical and practical developments arising from Agenda 21 are placed in context, and the implications for business and commerce are reviewed. Chapter 11 covers the evolution of co-operation and networking within a region or locality. Chapter 12 looks at localized trading patterns and explores the core sectors, in this context, of agriculture and transport. Chapter 13, the concluding chapter, reviews the development of the concept of sustainable twenty-first century cities, drawing together the core themes of the book.

REFERENCES AND FURTHER READING

Laszlow, E. (1995) in J. George (ed.) *Asking for the Earth: Waking Up to the Spiritual/ Ecological Crisis*, Element, Mass., USA.

Local Government Management Board (LGMB) (1995) *Sustainability Indicators Research Project: Consultants' Report of the Pilot Phase*, LGMB, London.

Roberts, P. (1995) 'Sustainable Regional Planning', *Regional Studies* 28 (8): 781–7.

Sachs, W. (1995) 'From Efficiency to Sufficiency', *Resurgence* 171: 6–8.

UN (1993) Earth Summit Agenda 21: United Nations Programme of Action from Rio, UN, New York.

CHAPTER 1

CO-OPERATIVE STRATEGIES

Government and cooperation are in all things the laws of life; anarchy and competition, the laws of death.

(John Ruskin 1819–1900)

INTRODUCTION

This chapter explores a range of strategies open to the firm seeking to identify and implement ecologically sustainable strategies. First, the pressures placed on a firm in parallel with the profit motive are explored, with particular reference to the threats and opportunities faced by SMEs. A range of co-operative strategies are examined, illustrated with examples from environmental cities and local government initiatives throughout the UK. Second, opportunities for co-operation with educational institutions are explored through examples of progressive initiatives.

LOCAL COMMUNITY PRESSURES

The successful manager is one who reads the business environment, and reads it correctly. While national and international economic pressures will remain a predominant source of external pressure, strategic management is coming under increasing pressure from less traditional sources. The generic green consumer movement of the 1980s has given way in the 1990s to a more focused appraisal of the potential for sustainability, giving rise to sustainability indicators at global, national and local levels. Inspired by the Seattle Project (see Case Study 11.1), the Local Agenda 21 Steering Group of the UK Local Government Management Board commissioned Touche Ross Management Consultants, New Economics Foundation and the United Nations Association (the UNA Sustainable Development Unit) to undertake a pilot project on sustainability indicators. The indicators seek to provide evaluation of the progress towards sustainability within a particular local authority. In this study 10 local authorities worked with their local communities to develop indicators relevant to their particular locality. The objective was to develop techniques capable of adaptation to use in a particular locality. The evolution of an 'objective' set of indicators capable of global application was considered impractical, not least because an essential element of the project was to raise local awareness and generate local involvement. Although the business community was perceived as having a 'different agenda' in this pilot project, one of its final recommendations was to draw in business associations and local chambers of commerce to participate in future projects. As schemes of this type proliferate, stakeholder pressures will increase for firms of all sizes and in each industrial sector to provide evidence of having adopted an ecologically sustainable policy and strategy.

CASE STUDY 11.1
Sustainable Seattle

A set of local sustainability indicators was pioneered as a long-term voluntary initiative in Seattle in Washington State, USA. Set in spectacular countryside, surrounded by mountains and water, Seattle has been subject to growth in population and economic development which threatens the long-term sustainability of the city and its hinterland. The voluntary initiative sought to bring all sectors of the community together to provide 'a perspective based on visions of a more desirable future'. The initiative aims 'to enable and inspire people in the many different communities of greater Seattle to transform the values of sustainability into actions that will move Seattle, the region and the planet towards long-term cultural, economic and environmental health and vitality.' It is 'a concrete attempt to de-mystify the concept of sustainability and to involve the local community in future planning and decision-making.'

From the outset, the project was 'owned' by the community. Through a series of discussions and technical working groups, a list of 100 possible issues was refined to an initial 20 indicators which could 'provide a snapshot of the concept of sustainability [and] stimulate vision, . . . provoke discussion, draw criticism, challenge assumptions, and inspire actions.' Three types of indicators were developed:

1. **Primary indicators** The key measurements of progress to sustainability.

2. **Secondary indicators** These include the building blocks from which the primary indicators were created.

3. **Provocative indicators** These are measurements which stimulate thought about patterns or trends in particular issues and reflect a complex range of complex interlinkages, such as wild salmon returning to spawn in local streams.

Overall, the indicators showed that Seattle was still moving away from the goal of long-term sustainability. 'Eleven of the twenty (including wild salmon runs through local streams and percentage of children living in poverty) are moving away, while only four are moving towards sustainability, with five neither towards nor away.' The four trends towards sustainability were:

1. Number of good air quality days per year—up.

2. Gallons of water consumed per capita in King County—down.

3. Percentage of employment concentrated in the top ten employers—down.

4. Library and community centre usage rates—up.

To set against these positive trends, the project noted substantial increases in total population, generation of solid wastes, use of renewable and non-renewable energy and in juvenile crime rates. The project proved a useful exercise to:

1. Inform the public policy-making process.

2. Assist decision-makers to analyse trends.

3. Encourage the media to broadcast the indicators and inform the public.

4. Challenge individuals to assess the implications of their lifestyles.

The initiative gave rise to educational and cultural projects, publications and activities, and the findings are being incorporated in city and neighbourhood planning processes. This is not a one-off process, but it inspired further work on indicators as part of an evolutionary process. As demonstrated in the main text, this pilot project is being used as the basis for development of sustainability indicators through the UN Sustainable Development Unit.

Source: LGMB (1995: Appendix V)

SMEs AND SUSTAINABILITY

Despite the proliferation of industry initiatives on the environment and environmental laws and regulations, accompanied by a wealth of research projects and publications during the 1980s and 1990s, research indicates that management in general, and SMEs in particular, have been slow to progress from a reactive to a proactive response to environmental pressures. Despite targeting advice through publications by the Advisory Committee on Business and the Environment (ACBE), Business in the Environment (BiE) and other agencies, SMEs, which account for over 90 per cent of the industrial sector, are apparently not aware of, nor responsive to, changing environmental considerations. Being more preoccupied with survival, particularly in view of the recession, SMEs have viewed the environment in a negative light, seen as necessitating significant expenditure. Attempts to 'sell' environmental awareness through energy-saving programmes (which result in cost cutting) have failed to overcome the widespread preference for the status quo in UK SMEs. Several studies indicate that unless and until senior management in a company is fully committed to an environ-mental policy, environmental issues will fail to be positively cultivated. Delegation of responsibility for 'the environment' as an extra responsibility alongside other 'more important' duties is a common strategy, leading to conflicts of interest in which environ-mental issues remain merely a paper commitment (Hutchinson and Chaston 1994; Hutch-inson and Hutchinson 1995).

In many cases companies responding to the environmental challenge find it to be a minefield, with pressures from stakeholders, insurers and legislation. In the absence of resources to enable them to assimilate what is relevant to their business and how to respond, their response is usually to ignore it. There are also further problems in the relationship between large companies attempting to exert supply chain pressure for environmental improvement and the SMEs which supplied them. Although the object of the exercise is to extend awareness of environmental issues, lack of time and resources coupled with minimal guidance from the purchasing company converts the exercise into a 'paper chase', lacking substance and commitment.

COMPETITION AND CO-OPERATIVE ADVANTAGE

Traditional management literature has been modelled on competitive theories of the 'survival of the fittest' as derived from popular biology and game theory. This approach is reinforced by economic theory which accepts competition as a force apparently deriving from biological or natural law. As Nielsen (1988) has demonstrated, however, co-operative strategies can benefit competing organizations. Quoting from Astley and Fombrun (1983) he notes:

> Business policy's 'battlefield analogy' . . . must be de-emphasised. Exaggerating somewhat, the field seems obsessed with the idea of competitive survival. Organisations are seen as vying for optimal locations within their respective industrial areas, capturing a greater share of the market at the expense of others, engaging in 'price wars' and 'predatory' practices, measuring their financial success *vis-à-vis* the fortunes of their neighbours. All of this is conceived of as a game: organisations must strategically counteract each other's manoeuvres. Even apparent instances of collaboration with others are analysed from a game theoretic viewpoint. . . . Although such interaction appears to be co-operative, it is seen, more or less, as antagonistic, tongue-in-cheek, short term co-operation designed to allow each organisation to improve its own long term competitive position. However, many of today's organisational interactions cannot be explained adequately in terms of competitive warfare. . . . Business policy must pay attention to the institutionalization of these collective allegiances, for they play an increasingly important role in today's corporate society.
>
> **(Astley and Fombrun 1983, quoted in Nielsen 1988: 476)**

Competition may produce positive results in some circumstances. But it is possible, as Nielsen points out, for players in any game to adopt competitive strategies in which all players lose. Two competitors may bankrupt each other. Within a family a competitive dynamic may result in spouses and children hurting each other more than they help each other. Negative-sum strategies of this type derive from prevailing reasoning at the micro-interorganizational level which assumes a zero-sum (fixed pie) competitive system.

On the other hand, in a positive-sum game all players can win. This occurs as two or more players adopt a strategy which enables all players to increase the size of the pie pieces (benefits) they receive from playing the game. To summarize the three types of games:

- **Zero-sum games** The size of the pie remains the same over time. For one player to win an increased reward, another must lose rewards.

- **Negative-sum game** The size of the pie decreases over time. In this event, all can lose. For one player to maintain the same amount, another player must lose.

- **Positive-sum game** The size of the pie increases over time, offering benefits to all.

Where adopted in strategic management, game theory has most frequently been used in the light of competitive strategies. Normally, it is assumed that organizations live in zero-sum or negative-sum scenarios. Hence it has been rare for game theory to explore strategies which could transform zero-sum games into positive-sum games. However, as the evolutionary biologist Herbert Simon points out in respect of human activity in general (Simon 1983):

> Success depends on our ability to broaden human horizons so that people will take into account, in deciding what is to their interest, a wider range of consequences. It depends on whether all of us come to recognise that our fate is bound up with the fate of the whole world, that there is no enlightened or even viable self-interest that does not look to our living in a harmonious way with our total environment.
>
> **(Simon 1983, quoted in Nielsen 1988: 478)**

Simon's observation is borne out by an earlier experiment by Axelrod (Axelrod 1984), which explored types of strategies capable of being adopted to win a positive-sum game. A range of competitive and co-operative strategies was submitted by 14 game theorists drawn from psychology, economics, political science, mathematics and sociology. The strategies were tested in a computer-simulated prisoners' dilemma tournament. Surprisingly, the highly co-operative 'Tit for Tat' (TFT) strategy submitted by psychologist Rapaport proved the most successful over the long term.

> TFT starts with a co-operative choice and thereafter responds positively to a co-operative move by the other player and negatively to a competitive move by the other player. . . . Despite short-run situations in which its co-operative offerings are met with competition and attack, and result in losses to some other strategies, in the longer term the TFT strategy was able to build high co-operative interactions and scores with other co-operative strategies.
>
> **(Axelrod 1984)**

It therefore easily out-performed competitive strategies. These both destroyed each other, and were retaliated against for attacks on other strategies. According to Axelrod:

> What accounts for Tit for Tat's robust success is its combination of being nice, retaliatory, forgiving and clear. Its niceness prevents it from getting into unnecessary trouble. Its retaliation discourages the other side from persisting whenever defection is tried. Its forgiveness helps restore mutual co-operation. And its clarity makes it intelligible to the other player, thereby eliciting long-term co-operation.
>
> **(Axelrod 1984, quoted in Nielsen 1988: 479)**

Nielsen uses thirty-two cases to demonstrate the use of four inter-organizational co-operative strategies within four different market situations. The four co-operative strategies are:

■ *The pool strategy*, in which scarce resources are pooled in order to reduce duplication and redundancy.

■ *The exchange strategy*, where operations or facilities are exchanged, enabling organisations to specialise, increasing speed and reducing duplication.

■ *The de-escalation strategy*, where players reduce or eliminate attacks on each other. While this may have negative monopolistic-type effects, it may also be beneficial. For example, in 1983 the Council of European Federations of Industrial Chemicals in conjunction with the EEC reviewed the European and world petrochemical markets and agreed to 'de-escalate competition by mutually reducing production and production capacity.' The alternative was to over-produce, necessitating dumping if prices were to be maintained.

■ *The contingency strategy* enables organisations to agree to co-operate in specific ways depending upon future circumstances. This strategy enables organisations to increase the efficiency of the other three strategies according to circumstances.

(Nielsen 1988: 480–1)

The market situations with which these co-operative strategies are combined in the case studies are:

■ A negative-sum game/declining market.

■ A zero-sum game/mature market.

■ A positive-sum game/ growth market.

■ A changing game/market to positive-sum/growth.

More often than not, co-operative strategies are additive: used in combination, they become even more effective, freeing resources for further joint development, while in competitive strategies the reverse occurs. Nielsen (1988) demonstrates that even in the most market-orientated political economies, such as the USA, governments may co-operate with organizations to interfere in market processes 'for some purpose considered by the players to be socially desirable' such as agricultural support or trigger pricing. This type of 'internal co-ordination' is practised systematically by the Japanese to enhance their world share of the market within the 'triadic' trading system. Over the long term, inter-organizational co-operation makes more strategic sense than 'tooth and claw' competition. The individual company is, however, constrained by a number of factors in its ability to participate in co-operative strategies.

Networking and localities

The next stage is to examine those aspects of co-operative strategy which may be of particular interest to the environmental manager. As noted above, long-term co-operative strategies can be efficient, both within and between organizations, offering long-term growth overall. Such strategies may be adopted at national and global levels, as organizations and national governments combine to secure their long-term mutual interests. In so far as environmental factors are taken into account, these tend to benefit the market share of the large organization. Meanwhile the impacts of these strategies, whether positive or negative, is felt in particular localities.

National governments and large firms operating at national and international levels have a presence within a geographic locality in a physical sense. They cannot, however, be described as being *of* the locality, either in economic or non-economic terms. By contrast, the SME has a stake in a particular city or local government area. This offers considerable potential for participation in co-operative strategies to protect the environment. Theory suggests that local economic networks, composed mainly of small businesses in co-operation with a few large firms, should provide the opportunity for co-operation on environmental issues at local level. Networks would comprise:

- **Business-to-business links** as goods and services are exchanged between known players at local level.

- **Cross-sectoral links** through intermediary institutions, including chambers of commerce, enterprise agencies, rotary clubs, charitable trusts, banks and accountants.

In practice the strengths or weakness of local networks are highly dependent upon national circumstances. Where local government is strong relative to national government, for example in Germany, resource allocation can be determined at local level and co-operative strategies can flourish. In this climate, local banking facilities stimulate inter-organizational co-operation, offering long-term positive-sum benefits which extend beyond the purely economic and into the social and ecological fields. By contrast, in the UK in the 1990s weak local government structures fostered a climate of short-termism, offering little support for inter-organizational contacts and co-operation.

Studies by Curran and Blackburn (1994) paint a dismal picture of the potential for local co-operation in the UK. In theory, 'vertical co-operation' through supply chain pressure could serve to disseminate environmentally sound practice. As Curran and Blackburn demonstrate, however, 'subcontracting' or 'contracting out' in the UK provides minimal security for the small supplying firm, since each contract won tends to be on a 'one-off' basis. In this event, supply chain pressure to conform to environmental standards results in little more than minimalist adoption of environmental policies or strategies. Where an SME does have a long-term subcontract, it will most likely be with a large firm outside the local area. In these circumstances, supply chain pressure to conform to patterns of environmental excellence may have some effect. However, in a recession, a local firm remains in a precarious position if its fortunes are dependent upon a contract with a single company. Where the large company fails, or is forced to cut back on its activities, the small local firm's survival may be threatened. The same is true for a small firm dependent upon a single large supplier for its essential materials. In this light, 'networking', the generation of information flows through vertical contacts and contracts within an industry may be a limited vehicle for environmental change.

The pool strategy at local level
Despite the above limitations, 'vertical co-operation' is one of many strategies available for the dissemination of information on environmental issues. The problem of raising awareness

and generating a responsible attitude to pollution control, waste management and energy conservation can also be approached through the establishment of local 'clubs' and business forums. These may be formed in the course of a 'one-off' pilot study, or may constitute a longer-term association of business and community groups within a local area. The main feature of this type of association is its ability to offer information, support and guidance to a group of locally based SMEs which may individually lack the resources, in terms of personnel, finance, expertise and awareness, to explore the implications of new and impending legislation. The process of meeting with other firms in the area can raise awareness of new technologies and of waste and energy-saving techniques. In the process, heightened awareness can provide motivation to explore the potential for change through product adaptation or alternative transport systems. Examples of this type of co-operative strategy can provide incentives and act as a motivating force for new ventures. To be effective, individual ventures are grounded in a spatial or territorial concern, an urban area or a watershed region. In the UK projects of this type have taken a number of different forms.

Groundwork trusts

An early scheme to encourage commercial concerns to respect the environment has been developed in run-down industrial areas in the North of England, sponsored initially by the Countryside Commission and run through Groundwork Trusts. From the two initial schemes at St Helens and Knowsley, the Groundwork Foundation has expanded to fifty locally based trusts throughout the UK, with further projects in France and the Netherlands. The Groundwork Foundation has adopted the principle of securing public funding, from the Department of the Environment and the European Commission, to generate support for local projects from business and local authorities. Staff secondments from large private and public sector bodies have supplied management expertise, and funding has been augmented by the Trust's landscape design and project management.

Although projects are locally based, the policy is to blend national and local sponsorship from private and public sources with the physical and human resources of the area. Volunteer support is sought from local residents and employees of sponsoring organizations, thus offering a means of two-way communication on local knowledge and environmental expertise.

Waste minimization projects

A series of projects designed by CEST (Centre for Exploitation of Science and Technology) in the early 1990s sought to provide a comprehensive view of the extent of uptake of waste minimization in British industry and to assess the scale of the challenge which still remained. Funded by industry and the UK government, CEST works with industry, academia and government policy-makers to identify new technical and commercial opportunities and enable companies to exploit them. All its projects are participatory, designed to enable companies to identify new opportunities. As the projects evolved, it became apparent that the 'club' approach, bringing companies together on a local or regional basis, was particularly beneficial for smaller firms. As a result of the projects, several key issues were identified:

- It was essential to raise awareness among SMEs through local business support organizations, environmental clubs and networks.

- Successful involvement of any individual firm was highly dependent upon targeting the board and senior management levels.

- Targets and performance measures had to be integrated into management information systems.

By August 1994 participants in the Aire and Calder Project had identified a total of 900 measures to reduce waste, improve efficiency and save money. 'More surprising . . . in excess of two thirds of the savings achieved arose from reductions in the usage of inputs, *i.e.* raw materials, energy and water' (CEST 1994). This was achieved through the use of the 'club' approach, in which participants exchanged ideas and generated the motivation to continue, with the local media providing good coverage and favourable publicity for participants. Furthermore:

> The project also showed that the regulated and the regulators can work together without conflict of interest. In addition, both the regulators and Yorkshire Water have made considerable use of the results of the project to encourage others both nationally and more especially at local and regional level.
>
> (CEST 1994: 9)

A project manager was identified as a key element in the success of the project. The final report concluded:

> A strong steering group, meeting regularly and to whom the project manager reported was another significant factor in the success of the project. The knowledge and experience that the group contributed was of enormous benefit and the sponsors consider that the project benefited greatly from the leadership of CEST and the experience of the March Consulting Group. In particular, there is an amount of work that still needs to be done even if the project manager takes on the burden of recruiting and training the participants. Although one or more of the sponsors could, theoretically, absorb this effort, there is an efficiency gain in leaving this to another body, in this case, CEST.
>
> (CEST 1994: 10)

The waste minimization project demonstrated the benefits of establishing working relationships between the public sector and manufacturing and service businesses. In addition, it provided the basis for establishing a pool of expertise for identifying pollution hazards resulting from leakages, spills, accidents and other escapes which could result in one-off, and highly polluting, incidents.

The Aire and Calder Waste Minimization Project

The Aire and Calder Project demonstrated the value of regulators, businesses and business support organizations working together to produce evidence that 'pollution prevention pays'. According to Steve Humphrey, speaking for HMIP, the project has provided a body of evidence and expertise which demonstrates that companies can:

- Save money.

- Reduce the environmental impact of their activities.

- Begin to change the basic culture of their organizations.

Even before its completion, the pilot project had inspired a further 16 projects, involving 80 companies. Although the practical and financial aspects of this pilot project were highly significant, it is Humphrey's final point, the introduction of the possibility of change in the basic culture of organizations, which was considered the most important aspect of the project for British industry. Without a change in attitude towards the environment, industry will continue to adopt a reactive approach to the environment. The Aire and Calder Project illuminated the importance of co-operation if individual firms were to be motivated to change (see Case Studies 4.4 and 4.6).

In summary, the Aire and Calder Project had three broad achievements. First, practical techniques for reducing environmental impact were identified. These included

- Reduction in demand for water.

- Reduction in effluent production.

- Identification of the means to reduce the risk of accidental pollution.

The second achievement was that a methodology for recognizing key success factors for a project was identified. These included

- The need for commitment and support from senior management.

- The necessity for effective project managers.

- The need to provide training and involvement across the whole company.

- The importance of monitoring and targeting for continuous improvement.

Third, the key role of communication as a factor in the progression towards environmental sustainability was identified. A commitment to good practice is dependent upon the dissemination of information and methodology. This may be done through:

- Legislation.

- Printed communications, e.g. 'best practice guides'.

- Industry support organizations.

North West Business Leadership Team (NWBLT)
The North West Business Leadership Team (*NWBLT*) is based in Manchester and was founded in 1991 to co-ordinate the influence, expertise and resources of senior industrialists in North West England. The NWBLT was established to enhance 'the long term well-being of the whole region, economically and environmentally', and has worked closely with Business in the Environment, local authorities, Groundwork Foundation, the Civic Trust in

the North West, the CBI North West, the DTI North West and Department of the Environment, the Mersey Basin Campaign and the North West Chamber of Commerce. In May 1993 it identified the following issues regarding implementation of corporate environmental policies:

- Communication within the organization (middle management often a block).

- Lack of understanding of legislation.

- A failure to realize that the environment is a business opportunity not a threat.

- The need to identify issues that are particular to your company and its business.

- Getting the top management to appreciate the importance of the environment.

- The potential of reaching employees' families.

- The need to accept that the payback is long term.

- The need to see the cost of environmental management in the context of the competition.

- The limitations of what one company can do in isolation.

From the outset, NWBLT established its initial objectives as to:

1. **Ensure all team members' companies have an active environmental policy in action** This setting of standards is a core element of the team's work, and has resulted in the achievement of very high standards within the majority of member companies.
2. **Establish a core of companies to share their practice and develop collective recommendations for the team as a whole** This core Environment Action Group includes 'nine senior executives with direct responsibility for environmental affairs in their own companies.' The Group produced a list of environmental expertise available to all in the area.
3. **Identify development sites, in conjunction with local authorities, inward and other key agencies within the region** After more than two centuries of industrialization there are a large number of derelict sites in urgent need of improvement. NWBLT is one of the sponsors of a regional strategy to improve the region's image and environment.
4. **Advise smaller companies in the region on what they can do in the environmental area** NWBLT has organized seminars and environmental award schemes to encourage involvement of smaller businesses. It has used devices like competitions in conjunction with the Association of Small-Medium Sized Businesses, Groundwork Trust and Global Forum '94, offering free environmental reviews as prizes.

NWBLT lists the following achievements of its associated companies in the North West:

- **Grosvenor Estates** Conservation plan demonstrates the benefits of conservation for smaller landowners and farms. Grosvenor Farms Limited, a large farming enterprise, has been commended for its staff motivation, capital use, conservation of habitats and landscape and pollution control.

- **AMEC plc** A major construction and engineering company that uses specialist technologies to solve clients' waste problems.

■ **BICC Cables** Seeks to reflect its environmental commitment in its commercial and manufacturing operations. It is represented on both UK and European Cable Industry environmental committees.

■ **British Nuclear Fuels plc** *BNFL* has a long history of publishing annual reports on health and safety matters to the general public (since 1977). Its Environment Council includes leading academics among its independent external members, and its policy of monitoring discharges has been extended since 1992 to include non-radioactive wastes. BNFL is a founder member of the CBI Environmental Forum.

■ **Boddington Group plc** Has worked with the Blackburn Groundwork Trust to identify and implement sound environmental practices in its public houses, hotels, nursing homes and distribution depots.

■ **British Aerospace plc** Seeks to minimize environmental impacts within its facilities and within the communities in which they are located. It has increased its use of renewable resources and instituted a staff training programme.

■ **British Airways plc** BA's operation at Manchester Airport is its third largest in the world. Drawing on the expertise of its Environmental Department in London, BA commissioned a technical review of its environmental performance in Manchester. BA sponsored the Tourism for Tomorrow Award, which was won by the Castlefield Urban Regeneration Project, a Manchester project, in 1993.

■ **The Co-operative Bank plc** Carried out an environmental audit in 1992. Already it was using lead-free petrol in its company cars and recycled 'environmentally friendly' paper, and had introduced energy conservation measures. It has since introduced an environmental plan and appointed an executive director to head an Environmental Management Team. As a result of its ethical policy it refuses to do business with companies which 'continue to needlessly damage the environment.'

■ **Granada Television Ltd** Has used its educational role to the full. It has produced a series of Green Life Guides to back up its on-screen output of information. These 'free, easy to understand fact sheets' enable viewers to make contact with the companies featured on the show. Granada has worked with the Countryside Commission to sponsor the Granada Landscape Awards to local projects. Granada has also helped to finance the Mersey Basin Waterwatch Scheme which aims, among other things, to clean up all the 1725 km of rivers and streams in the Basin. Further, it has introduced an in-house policy of environmental vetting of suppliers.

■ **James Cropper plc** Manufactures paper and board in Cumbria. It has introduced an environmental policy which, among other measures, seeks to co-operate with customers, suppliers, the workforce and the public in implementing its objectives.

■ **Johnson Group Cleaners plc** Has formally accepted responsibility from the highest levels for improvement and monitoring of its environmental performance in its dry-cleaning shops. The Group is a member of national and international trade associations, and is a party to a Charter of Co-operation with its solvent suppliers seeking to reduce solvent consumption and emissions to the environment.

■ **Kellogg Company of Great Britain Ltd** Has introduced a variety of initiatives relating to the environment. These have included raising employee awareness, monitoring and control of air and water emissions, waste management, waste minimization and recycling.

■ **Lancashire Enterprises plc** Are involved in a series of environmental initiatives, including work on the Leeds–Liverpool Canal Corridor Project, with funding from the European Commission.

■ **Littlewoods Organization plc** Favours legislation as the major instrument for environmental reform, seeing its first commitment as being to satisfy the commercial requirements of its customers.

■ **Manchester Airport plc** Published its first environmental policy document in 1989, and has long had a strategy for monitoring environmental performance. It established an Environment Department in 1992.

■ **Manweb plc** The first regional electricity company to publish an environmental report. It has a programme to minimize environmental impacts and to maximize staff awareness. Where possible it is replacing overhead powerlines with underground cables. Its tree management policy ensures minimum trimming of trees, and replacement where felling is necessary. Its Queensbury Depot recovers CFCs from old refrigerators and freezers.

■ **North West Water Group plc** Fish and other wildlife are returning to rivers in the Mersey Basin following a £5 billion investment programme by North West Water. Training programmes foster environmental awareness among staff, and where practicable public access to reservoirs and other sites for recreational purposes is being improved. Conservation bodies are represented on the company's advisory committee on environmental matters. The company also provides nature reserves, sponsors research projects and four county Wildlife Trusts. It is the largest funder of the British Trust for Conservation Volunteers, many of whose projects are conducted on company land.

■ **NORWEB plc** Has a programme of promoting staff awareness of conservation issues when working in rural areas and on farmland.

■ **Paterson Zochonis plc** Cussons (UK) Ltd, the Group's principal UK subsidiary, has concentrated its environmental policy on the area of packaging, raw materials, energy saving and waste disposal product design. Its Nottingham soap factory has reduced waste consumption by 20 per cent, and its programme for the reduction of the polymer content in its plastic bottles has resulted in a 15 per cent reduction in plastic use.

■ **Pilkington plc** Is committed to the introduction of best practices in the recycling of glass and related materials and has undertaken maximum research and educational processes on environmental issues. For example, a dust and spillage reduction exercise at Pilkington Glass reduced waste by over 1000 tonnes per year, saving £50 000 per year in dumping and replacement costs. Programmes to reduce energy consumption and atmospheric pollution have reduced the amount of heat required to produce a tonne of glass by half since the mid-1960s.

■ **Refuge Group plc** This assurance company has two main approaches to the environment. Internally, it ensures that its head office building is energy efficient, having won awards, and that its waste-paper management is carefully controlled. Externally, it promotes environmental issues through leaflets and posters on environmental matters circulated through its large customer base for use in homes and groups.

- **Royal Insurance (UK) Ltd** Through its underwriting practices, risk management and control advice the company contributes to loss prevention, safer working methods and the environment. Through an environmental audit it was able to demonstrate good environmental practice in respect of its own buildings, waste management, paper usage and vehicle fuels.

- **Shell Chemicals Ltd** According to the Chairman and Chief Executive of Shell UK Limited, the company's environmental policy 'is not about words, but deeds: our performance should speak for itself!' Best practice throughout the company is co-ordinated through an integrated environmental management system. In 1992 it budgeted £35 million for the first phase of its Environmental Quality Improvement Project at Stanlow, a purely environmental investment 'with no payback other than a reduction of emissions and a continued license to operate'. At Carrington it reduced emissions to air and water and achieved an 80 per cent energy saving per tonne over the existing plant.

- **Unilever** The Environment Division and Environmental Engineering Section provide scientific support for the company's Research Laboratory at Port Sunlight, with an annual budget of £4 million. This research benefits Uniliver's products and operations world-wide. Ten Unilever companies in the North West are investing roughly £1.5 million annually in environmental control activities.

- **VSEL Consortium plc** Plays a leading role in the Furness Waste Consortium, pooling expertise and resources to minimize waste and reduce energy consumption.

- **ZENECA Specialities** Forms part of the ZENECA Group plc formed by the demerger of ICI Group bioscience and fine chemical interests. All new processes are systematically examined at the development stage, and action is taken to reduce potential environmental impacts. An inventory has been taken of waste streams, with a view to reducing all hazardous wastes over time. Staff environmental awareness training has been introduced, and each major site has a community liaison arrangement.

The process of working together to pool environmental awareness and expertise has enabled the NWBLT to identify environmental pressures on company decision-makers. These include:

- Regulators/government.
- Pressure groups.
- Shareholders.
- Bankers.
- Insurers.
- Customers.
- Suppliers.
- Unions.
- Employees.
- Community.
- Trade associations.
- Media.

(NWBLT 1993)

The major companies participating in the NWBLT have recognized and used these sources of pressure as a means to a two-way flow of information. As the experience of individual NWBLT companies shows, concerns expressed by customers, the media and pressure groups and so on were translated into specific environmental policies. A vital part of the success of those policies is their communication back down the line to and through the pressure sources. Compliance with regulations, employee training and media presentations enable the company to communicate its environmental policies to the wider community. In this type of example a large part of the expertise is inspired and developed through co-operation with the other companies in the local group.

Many of the companies in NWBLT form part of a large national or international consortium. As such they are in a position to influence the development of environmental legislation in so far as it affects their own industrial sector. Furthermore, there are ample resources at their disposal for research and development of their environmental strategies. These resources can be put to good use in developing the company's green marketing strategy. From the outset, however, like many public authorities and environmental organizations, the NWBLT noted the need to make environmental advice available to small companies in the area. In general, SMEs have little awareness or expertise in environmental issues, and fewer resources at their disposal with which to develop an environmental strategy.

Co-operation on a local scale

The need for local support structures offering advice and assistance on environmental issues to local firms, particularly to SMEs, has been recognized on a global scale. The types of structures which have evolved depend very much on local cultures and local circumstances. Even within one country such as the UK there is no uniform blueprint of the form such structures might take. Neighbouring towns and local authorities have moulded local knowledge and expertise to meet local needs in the light of national and international legislative requirements. Inevitably, key individuals and sponsoring organizations have stamped their characteristic concerns and enthusiasms upon the local environmental scene. Here, two examples of local schemes in practice in the UK are examined.

Business and Environment Support Team (BEST)

In 1994 Bradford Council's Economic Development Unit recognized the need for practical assistance and environmental information to be made available to small and medium-sized companies. Over 90 per cent of firms in the area of Bradford employ fewer than 50 people, but account for 42 per cent of local employment. Most of these firms have limited resources, and lack time to research and implement environmental policies. Meanwhile they have come under increasing pressure on environmental issues, not least in view of national and EU regulations and legislation. Bradford Council's Economic Development Unit therefore launched the Business and Environment Support Team (*BEST*).

BEST offers the following facilities:

- Practical and financial assistance to local firms, subsidizing audits, reviews and consultancies. An Environment and Business Support Officer is available to provide practical and financial support, including baseline environmental reviews, assistance with BS 7750 and other environmental management systems, full environmental audits, energy efficiency audits, interpretation of audits, development of environmental policies, environmental training, contaminated land studies and best practice feedback.

■ A free information service to companies in Bradford and in the neighbouring local authority areas of Kirklees and Calderdale. The Environment Information Officer supplies details of environmental legislation and standards, funding opportunities, potential new environmental markets and other environmental opportunities. The officer is based at the West Yorkshire European Business Information Centre, and is therefore ideally placed to monitor new legislation and market opportunities.

■ Close co-operation with Bradford's Business and Environment Forum. The forum was set up by Bradford University Management Centre in conjunction with Bradford Council's Economic Development Unit. It provides an opportunity for companies to co-operate and pool ideas to gain expertise on the implications of environmental issues and legislation so that best practice can be spread throughout the area. The forum provides an opportunity for local businesses to make their views known to local councillors, local MPs and government ministers. Over 200 firms attended events in the first 18 months of its existence, including seminars on eco-audits, environmental legislation, waste minimization and the phasing out of ozone depleting chemicals.

■ *Business and Environment News* is a newsletter which is made available to local businesses and policy-makers describing the services offered by BEST, free and priced publications on facilities, regulations and consultancies, and examples of good practice within the local business community (see Case Study 11.2).

■ Two-way communication with the EU and European firms for West Yorkshire companies. BEST works with West Yorkshire European Business Information Centre (WYEBIC), which assists West Yorkshire firms in finding new environmental markets through a computerized 'dating agency'. Relevant European firms are listed on a database and in WYEBIC's quarterly publication *Euro-Notes*. BEST and WYEBIC have represented the interests of Bradford and the UK at international conferences, such as Enterprise Ecobusiness '94 held in Italy.

Bradford's Business and Environment Forum has demonstrated the value of bringing together different interest groups on a local basis in anticipation of new legislation and environmental measures. Meetings explore the implications for local firms of, for example, the new European Packaging Directive, legislation facing the printing sector and the implications of Integrated Pollution Control (IPC) for the textile industry. In the same way, the different interests of Yorkshire Water, the Confederation of British Wool Textiles and the Transport and General Workers' Union (TGWU) were aired at a meeting called to discuss the proposed Yorkshire Water Reception Charge.

Business and the local community
During the 1990s, largely inspired by Local Agenda 21 of the Rio Earth Summit, cities and local authorities in 178 countries have brought together different interest groups within their

CASE STUDY 11.2
Three Companies Assisted by BEST

Contaminated Land Study

Company A sought to expand on to the site of a former dye works which had also been used for dumping topsoil, tyres, building and other materials. Finance for the expansion was dependent upon completion of a contaminated land survey. The company qualified for assistance on geographical criteria and BEST was able to provide a 50 per cent grant towards the cost of the environmental survey. As a result of the contaminated land study the land was deemed suitable for industrial development.

An Environmental Package

Company B sought to make several environmental improvements. These included:

- Finding a new recyclable packaging material in order to target European markets.

- Reduction of oil and fat in their effluent.

- Recovery of waste heat from a cooling process.

BEST provided 50 per cent of the financial costs of employing consultants. They were able to suggest an alternative packaging material and ways to reduce the firm's effluents which would enable the company to cut its water charges. A further government scheme available to SMEs provided 50 per cent funding for an energy efficiency audit. This audit also examined the possibility of a heat transfer scheme.

Environmental Management Review

Company C sought to cut costs and ensure full compliance with relevant legislation in order to minimize its environmental impact. BEST recommended a baseline environmental review and secured an Environmental Audit Grant from Bradford's City Challenge Ltd to meet 60 per cent of the cost of consultancy. As a result the total cost to the company was £600. The review offered the company the ability to satisfy supply chain demands and to reduce the cost of energy consumption and effluent treatment. The review also provided a basis for the initial stages of an environmental management scheme such as BS 7750 or EMAS.

Source: *Bradford Business and Environment News* (winter 1994)

boundaries in order to co-operate in establishing environmentally sound policies and strategies. In the process local companies have faced threats and opportunities. Highly polluting processes, in terms of noise and discharges to air, water and land and large containerized transport systems have become the focus of adverse publicity through the bringing together of local communities and pressure groups with local councils and educational bodies. Companies introducing less polluting products or production measures have benefited from being able to work with and through the local community in promoting their products and services. This type of initiative is relatively novel, and presents a host of opportunities for highly cost-effective 'green' sponsorship of local environmental projects and pressure groups. Examples of good practice can be found throughout the UK, including *Environment City Schemes*.

Environ

Based in Leicester in the Midlands of England, Environ is the largest local environmental charity in Europe. It was formed in 1993 through the merger of Leicester Ecology Trust and Leicester Environment City Trust, and works through professionals and volunteers to improve the quality of life in Leicester through practical environmental projects. Its headquarters are situated next to its 'Eco House', a greener living show home, and it is supported by the European Commission, the Department of the Environment, Leicester City Council, Leicestershire County Council, Leicestershire Training and Enterprise Council, WWF, local businesses and many other organizations. Its activities and projects include:

> Advice and Comment, Awards, Business Support, Car Sharing, Cash for Trash, Community Development, Composting, Conferences, Conservation, Consultancy, Cycling, Development, Eco Drama, Eco House, Eco Roadshow, Economic Development, Energy Efficiency, Environmental Auditing, Environment City, Events, Exhibitions, Festivals, Friends of Vrindavan, Grants, Green Accounts, Green Housing, Green Shopping, Greener Driving, Guided Walks, Habitat Creation, Interpretation, Kerbside Recycling, Landscape Design, Local Agenda 21, Nature Reserves, Office Recycling, Organic Growing, Partnership, Publications, Recycling, Renewable Energy, Research, School Activities, School Nature Areas, Surveys, Sustainable Development, Talks, Telephone Helpline, Third World Links, Training, Transport, Tree Planting, Vision for Society, Viva Podcarpus, Volunteering, Waste Reduction, Wildlife.
>
> **(Environ publicity)**

The above list indicates the range of lateral thinking available to generate interest and expertise in sustainability within a locality. Waste minimization and energy conservation, which form the basis of the initial steps of business and commerce towards sustainability, are promoted alongside cultural, educational and farming activities and the promotion of sustainable planning and transport facilities.

Leeds Environment Business Forum

Leeds Environment Business Forum (*LEBF*) was established in 1992 to facilitate the sharing of environmental expertise within the city. It has made energy efficiency and waste disposal advice available to businesses in the city, and has organized meetings, seminars and a regular newsletter. LEBF has found that the production of a good practice guide is the most effective method of communicating with local SMEs. The *Good Environmental Business Practice Handbook* (available from **LEBF, Room 5, Stansfield Chambers, 6 Great George Street, Leeds LS1 3DW**) offers a series of case studies demonstrating that environmental good practice can be good for business. The case studies publicize the environmental achievements of local businesses and offer a local network of contacts to facilitate the exchange of

TABLE 11.1 *LEBF case study profiles*

Company	Size	Type	Problem	Savings
Holdene plc	100 staff	Computer resellers	Waste management	£31 111
M&E Network	40–50 staff	Insurance brokers	Waste management	£4750
Royal Mail North East	17 903 staff	HQ North East	Waste management	
Waterloo Metals	15 staff	Non-ferrous scrap metal merchants	Monitoring after product left premises	
Warwick International	70 staff	Speciality chemicals	Acid waste treatment/min	£66 000 pa
Rhône-Poulenc	70 staff	Speciality chemicals	Pollution control and waste minimization	£52 139
Orcol Fuels Ltd	100 staff	Oil recycling	Oil sludge treatment	£45 840 pa
Pickersgill-Kaye Group Ltd	150 staff	Lock/valve/ handle manufacturers	Energy efficiency	£8800
Royal Mail North East	17 903 staff	Postal services	Energy efficiency	£43 000 pa
Joshua Tetley & Son Ltd	600 staff	Brewers	Energy efficiency	£18 400 in nine months
DuPont Howson	750 staff	Producers of lithographic printing plates	Process design	£477 000
Leeds Metropolitan University	20 000 students	Education	Green purchasing	£9941
National Power plc	100 staff	Power station	Social responsibility	£200

information and expertise. Case study profiles are listed in Table 11.1. Each case study covers some aspect of the following:

Waste and pollution

■ Waste management.

■ Pollution control.

■ Noise.

Energy efficiency and transport

- Electricity and gas.

- Company transport.

Product and process design

- Product durability.

- Process design.

Purchasing and materials

- All material inflows.

- Water consumption.

Environmental policy and management

- Environmental management systems.

- Marketing and promotion.

- Personnel training.

- Social responsibility.

- Premises and built environment.

Examples of good practice
The case studies highlight specific instances of good practice. For example, BSD Lye Spencer Steel Service Centre, with 62 staff, saved £5000 a year by reusing wooden pallets when transporting goods. The M&E Network, a small insurance company, saved £4750 by employing a small firm to refill toner cartridges. In the process, 139 cartridge cases were saved from going to landfill in a year.

The reuse of existing packaging saves Holdene plc over £31 111 pa on purchase of new packaging. Furthermore, the exercise identified suggestions for practical co-operation between firms. An employee of Holdene noted that often the quantities of waste generated by individual companies are too small to make collection a paying proposition for recycling industries. This problem could be overcome with the provision of a central storage facility. Savings generated from reuse of materials could be used to pay the salary of an employee to facilitate the collection and transfer of waste products for reuse and recycling, both within and out of the company premises.

Royal Mail North East has had a long-standing relationship with local organizations, including Meanwood Valley Urban Farm and the West Yorkshire Playhouse. Both have received waste stock in the form of baskets and containers. The reuse of this equipment has reduced the need to incinerate or add to landfill problems. This type of co-operation can lead to a range of contacts and outcomes.

Environment cities and local co-operation

Cities throughout the UK, mainland Europe and the other signatory countries of the Rio Earth Summit Local Agenda 21 have recognized the value of co-operation at local level to achieve sustainability. In the UK, the Local Government Declaration on Sustainable Development, signed in 1994, recognized that local communities have a powerful part to play in solving environmental problems like the greenhouse effect and holes in the ozone layer. Local action is particularly effective, for example, in protecting natural habitats and reducing air pollution as a cause of ill health, and in recognition of this local initiatives have proliferated throughout the UK.

LEBF is one of three sectoral bodies organized by Leeds City Council as part of its Leeds Environment City Initiative (*LECI*). Leeds, like Leicester, is part of the BT Environment City Scheme and has therefore been required to develop specialist working groups in areas of environmental concern. The groups which comprise members from public, private and voluntary sectors are co-ordinated by the Environment City Unit and share their findings with the three other environment cities, Middlesbrough, Peterborough and Leicester. The specialist working groups are:

■ Economy and Work.

■ Energy.

■ Transport.

■ Natural Environment.

■ Built Environment.

■ Environmental Quality.

■ Waste and Recycling.

■ Food and Agriculture.

Leeds Environmental Action Forum (*LEAF*), a part of the Leeds Environment City Initiative (*LECI*), works in conjunction with the Leeds Environment Business Forum, (*LEBF*). Launched in 1992, LEAF is an umbrella organization linking charities, voluntary groups, residents' associations, conservation groups, civic societies and individuals working to conserve the environment in and around Leeds. These three bodies comprise the Leeds Environment City Initiative, providing the means for communication between different sectors in the local community.

SUMMARY

Environmental degradation proliferates where decision-making is not locally accountable, whether under capitalism or communism. As was the experience in eastern Europe, the root causes of environmental degradation were organizational factors rather than technical factors. Under communism, where property was government owned, the environment was regarded as a free resource, and pollution was rife. As a result, 95 per cent of water in Poland was unfit for human consumption, while in former East Germany 80 per cent of the surface water was classified as being unsuitable for drinking or leisure purposes. Under capitalism, distant decision-making is also just as unlikely to tolerate unsustainable and polluting practices. On the other hand, locally based forms of co-operation between different industrial sectors, and between industry and commerce in general along with other sectors of the community, offer the route forward to sound sustainable practice.

Ecological sustainability is wholly dependent upon the construction of social 'software', the building of organizational structures and institutional capacity based upon co-operation. Economic and technological solutions are tools available for use in appropriate circumstances which emerge within social systems. The social factors which determine the uses to which the technical tools are directed are themselves determined by relationships among people and the value systems they create. Local forms of co-operative interaction offer the most promising guarantees for protection of natural resources.

This chapter has introduced some of the fundamental organizational shifts that need to occur if sustainable development is to be achieved within post-modern twenty-first-century trade. One central element to these paradigm shifts is the need to recognize that co-operative advantage (where all win, including the environment) is not purely an abstract concept, but just requires a realignment of our traditional business thinking.

The chapter also covers the need for local support structures to be established to enable (particularly smaller) firms and organizations to deal with the environmental challenge. There is no perfect structure for support organizations as the local culture is often the primary determining variable; however, merits of various case study examples are considered.

QUESTIONS

11.1 NIMBY (Not In My Back Yard) has been used in a derogatory sense, to describe protests against road and industrial developments by people who nevertheless accept the products of industrialization when they arrive on their doorsteps. Compare and contrast NIMBY protests with the evolution of a post-modernist regeneration of a sense of place.

11.2 To a large extent the environmental policy of a large company will be a product of the nature of its operations. The most highly polluting firms will be the first to organize and implement environmental strategies, alongside firms which have been set up to supply clean technologies. Using examples from this chapter and general reading, produce evidence for and against this assumption.

11.3 What evidence can you find in your locality of co-operation between local companies and the local community on environmental issues?

BIBLIOGRAPHY

Key text

Andruss, V., Plant, C., Plant, J. and Wright, E. (eds) (1990) *Home! A Bioregional Reader*, New Society Publishers, Philadelphia, PA, Gabriola Island, BC, and Santa Cruz, CA

This collection of writings by over 40 writers introduces the political philosophy of 'living in place'. Bioregionalism is founded on the perspective that by living within the limits and resources of a particular place it becomes possible to create a sustainable way of life based upon the realities of the earth's limited resources. Inevitably, with so large a collection of contributors, the quality and resonance of this book is variable. Nevertheless, it contains pieces from leading thinkers in this field whose work has been widely read since the original publication of this work.

References and further reading

Astley, W. G. and Fombrun, C. F. (1983) 'Collective Strategy: The Social Ecology of Organisational Environments', *Academy of Management Review*, vol 8, no. 3, pp. 578/586.

Axelrod, R. (1984) *The Evolution of Cooperation*, Basic Books, New York.

CEST (1994) *Waste Minimization: A Route to Profit and Cleaner Production: An Interim Report on the Aire and Calder Project*, CEST (Centre for Exploitation of Science and Technology) 5 Berners Road, Islington, London N1 0PW.

Curran J. and Blackburn, R. (1994) *Small Firms and Local Economic Development: The Death of the Local Economy*, Paul Chapman, London.

Hutchinson, A. and Chaston, I. (1994) 'Environmental Management in Devon and Cornwall's Small and Medium Sized Enterprise Sector', *Business Strategy and the Environment* 3 (1): 15–22.

Hutchinson, A. and Hutchinson, F. (1995) 'Sustainable Regeneration of the UK's SME Sector: Some Implications of SME Response to BS 7750', *Greener Management International* 9 (January) 73–84.

Johnson, N. and Stokes, A. (1995) *Waste Minimization and Cleaner Technology*, CEST (Centre for Exploitation of Science and Technology) 5 Berners Road, Islington, London, N1 0PW.

Nielsen, R. P. (1988) 'Co-operative Strategy', *Strategic Management Journal* 9: 475–92.

NWBLT (North West Business Leadership Team) (1993) *Setting the Standard: A Synopsis of Combined Corporate Action*, NWBLT, Manchester.

Simon, Herbert A. (1983) *Reason in Human Affairs*, Stamford University Press, Stamford, CA.

12 LOCALIZED TRADING

Trade's unfeeling train; usurp the land and dispossess the swain.

(Oliver Goldsmith 1728–74)

INTRODUCTION

The co-operative structures outlined in Chapter 11 form an initial stage in raising environmental awareness within the business community and fostering a proactive approach to sustainable development. The multibillion pound market for environmental goods and services in the UK alone is further indicative of the high value being placed on the environment. Individual examples of good practice will not, however, lead to environmental sustainability. In the long run, sustainability requires the production of goods and services within an integrated infrastructure which recognizes the spatial element in the relationship between the economy and the environment.

In this chapter we examine the implications of the evidence that environmental quality now features at the top of the list of considerations in planning and investment strategies. We further explore the type of local infrastructure which encourages ecologically sound inward investment. Working together at the local level, business and the wider community can provide the physical infrastructure and support services necessary to secure sustainable development within a particular region. In pursuit of ecologically sound and sustainable economies, planners are confronting the general requirement for territorial integration and the allied issues of transport, finance and regional planning. These topics and the more general overriding themes of bioregionalism, permacultural design, local agriculture and food distribution are outlined in this chapter.

TERRITORIAL INTEGRATION

Ecology and economy interact in particular localities. However, the implications of this physical reality can be ignored in a global market-place where capital is mobile and economic growth measurable in purely monetary terms. As Daly and Cobb have explained:

> A world of cosmopolitan money managers and transnational corporations which, in addition to having limited liability and immortality conferred on them by national governments, have now transcended those very governments and no longer see the national community as their residence. They may speak grandly of the 'world community' as their residence, but in fact, since no world community exists, they have escaped from community into the gap between communities where individualism has free reign.
>
> **(Daly and Cobb 1989: 215)**

This ability for production policy decisions to be shaped by the whims of individuals in the global market has profound implications for ecological sustainability. It has occurred through the detachment of 'the economy' from social and physical reality and is dependent upon a concept of 'freedom' uprooted from the realities of social and ecological responsibility. It is a product of the Fordist paradigm and is incapable of producing solutions to the serious environmental and economic problems which it has created. Recognition of this dilemma has come from a number of different sources.

Friedmann and Weaver (1979) have distinguished between 'territorial integration' and 'functional integration':

■ Territorial integration emphasizes the interaction between natural and socio-economic systems within a particular territory.

■ Functional integration considers the role of places and their resources within a wider economic order.

Functional integration prioritizes economic growth over all other considerations, and its continued ascendancy threatens the viability of a sustainable development paradigm. Territorial integration, on the other hand, recognizes that the protection of natural resources and the minimization of waste are dependent upon the substitution of physical movement by other forms of interaction.

The development of a spatial strategy goes beyond mere energy saving. It implies, as Roberts (1995) has recognized, the integration of land use and transport planning in order to reduce the physical separation of activities. Roberts advocates a system of comprehensive regional planning for sustainability to replace the '"slash and burn" regional philosophy that has dominated much of the past 40 years.' The common elements of such a system are as follows:

1. The 'standard' elements of sustainable development related to environment, futurity and equity.
2. Elements related to the diversification of the regional economy intended to make it better able to deal with adversity.
3. The question of self-sufficiency—intended to minimize environmentally and economically wasteful resource inputs or transfers.

4. The question of territorial integration both within the individual region and between regions.

The 'slash and burn' economy is dependent upon freedom of access to raw materials and human resources, on the continued availability of capital and consumer markets divorced from culture and locality, and on the continued ability to dump wastes, packaging and products in somebody else's 'back yard'. As national and international legislation restricts the options to produce and pollute, and as consumer pressures reject polluting products, a proactive approach to sustainability is emerging. Working in partnership with the broader regulatory framework, territorially integrated planning comprises the two key elements of local self-reliance and diversity. It results in:

- Minimization of transportation.
- Reduction in resource utilization.
- Minimization of waste production.
- Maximization of motivation for recycling and reuse.
- Local economic regeneration.

As Roberts (1995) has explained, territorial integration cannot be achieved by individual firms working in isolation, however environmentally enlightened those firms might be. What is required is ecologically sound 'hard' and 'soft' infrastructures, individually tailored to particular localities.

'Hard' infrastructures include

- Planned location of residential areas, industry and distribution to minimize the need for travel and transportation.
- Provision of facilities to maximize production of basic necessities from the local physical resource base.

'Soft' infrastructures include:

- Local finance and investment.
- Local training and employment.
- Local education and skills and cultural awareness.

The twin themes of transport minimization and maximization of local self-reliance in terms of basic necessities have emerged with increasing frequency. In the following pages we examine these issues.

A QUESTION OF TRANSPORT

The role of transport in the context of the economic, social and environmental debates in Europe has been explored in detail by Whitelegg (1994). His considered view is that 'transport is at the heart of current environmental concerns'. He dismisses early government actions aimed at reducing environmental impacts as:

> nothing more than rhetoric . . . based on playing with technology in the hope that fundamental changes in behaviour can be avoided. Catalytic converters and electric vehicles fall into this category. There is, in consequence, a dark side to the sustainability issue which can be summarised in the commitment to existing patterns of resource consumption whilst installing end-of-pipe technologies to solve any problems that might result from consumption.
>
> **(Whitelegg 1994: 154)**

In 1994 there were over 25 million motor vehicles (those with up-to-date licences) in the UK. The projected number for the year 2025 is 42.8 million (Department of Transport) (*DoT* 1994). If we accept that there are significant environmental and health risks today then clearly the implications of this massive increase in motor vehicle transport over the next quarter of a century demands serious analysis and action. In the mid-1990s the UK government came to believe that there is no link between the economic well-being of our societies and the number of motor vehicles on the road (a view which it previously held). They intend, therefore, to address this problem by looking at the possibilities of integrated transport strategies. The implications for industry are apparent and the current trend to make road transport more costly in proportion to other modes of transport, will continue.

In the short term, a firm may consider taking anti-polluting and energy-saving measures to reduce the environmental impact of its transportation. Such measures may include:

■ Improving maintenance of company vehicles.

■ Recycling engine oil.

■ Retrieving CFCs from replaced or reconditioned refrigeration equipment.

■ Using unleaded petrol or other fuels.

■ Disposing safely of used antifreeze.

■ Purchasing energy-efficient vehicles.

■ Retraining employees in driver-efficiency to reduce fuel-use.

Palliatives like these are predicated upon the assumption that transportation of goods and people from place to place can and should continue at present levels. Whitelegg presents the case for a deceleration in vehicle use on the following grounds: 'If we accept the accelerating upwards trend in vehicle use in the developed societies then we must accept it for the remainder of the planet' (Whitelegg 1994: 3). He argues that if it is not acceptable to convert all Third World countries to European levels of transport consumption and use, global inequality and exploitation must increase. This is incompatible with the Rio Earth Summit or any other declaration of sustainability. It logically follows that vehicle use in the developed world must be reduced. Pioneering work on transport policy for sustainability suggests that:

■ Transport is a vital element in economic and social activities but must serve those activities rather than be an end in itself.

■ The consumption of distance by freight and passengers should be minimized as far as possible whilst maximising the potential for locally based intersection and locally based economic activity.

(Whitelegg 1994: 157)

Whitelegg argues that sustainability is basically a scale problem. Sustainability is practicable 'at the right spatial scale where social and environmental objectives are genuinely high on the agenda . . . A small community knows that it wants safe streets, clean air and a vibrant, friendly neighbourhood.' A small community is unlikely to get what it wants from a planning system dominated by EU and national policies based on an unsustainable agenda. The single market is based on the philosophy of removing barriers to the movement of goods and capital, and discriminates fiscally in favour of road transport. Hence the 'grandiose military style transport planning that routes international highways through local communities with no thought for the consequences and a set of vague notions about linking the periphery or binding the community together' (Whitelegg 1994: 158–9).

As experience in California, Amsterdam and Zurich demonstrate, local autonomy is essential to the delivery of environmentally sound solutions to traffic problems. In this respect, Britain has been less favourably placed. Although 96 per cent of the UK road network is under local authority control, the funding of major transport schemes and the planning process itself are centralized. In England and Wales the annual process of Transport Policies and Programmes has the potential to direct local transport and land use to meet local objectives rather than the national requirements as set out by the Department of the Environment. However, the Local Government Management Board, in its Local Agenda 21 Roundtable Guidance on Planning, Transport and Sustainability, can merely point out that local authorities '*should* resist proposals for transport investment and road construction likely to conflict with agreed land use and environmental objectives' (LGMB 1993: 5). In the UK local authorities have very little power to prevent such developments in practice.

The location of development has an impact upon the need for travel and the choice of transport mode. On a local scale, out-of-town business parks and shopping areas increase the need for transport. A mix of development in urban areas of residential and employment, retail and leisure uses in one locality can reduce the volume and frequency of transport. On an international scale, the growing interdependence of economies across Europe has inevitably led to the building of tunnels, bridges and routes through Alpine passes, bringing swathes of environmental destruction in their wake. Whitelegg explores the inconsistency of this 'pursuit of an elusive economic utopia':

> The EC intends to add 1200 km of motorway to the present 3700 km in the next ten years. Of the new routes, 40% will be established in Greece, Ireland, Portugal and Spain so that these countries can be incorporated more successfully into the system of large producers and log distance travel to the detriment of more local production and

consumption. This plan is costed at 120 billion ECUs and comes from the same stable as the car free city concept and the green book on the urban environment. Clearly there is some inconsistency in EC policy.

(Whitelegg 1994: 161)

Given the determination to reject illogical and unsustainable development, the EU could in theory, through the principle of subsidiarity, encourage local autonomy and environmental sustainability at a local level. The development of sustainable transport systems is necessarily dependent upon overall planning structures being evolved to create sustainable communities. As Whitelegg indicates, a great deal of the problem of unsustainable development lies in the determined opposition by centralists to the devolution of powers to the lowest practicable levels.

The *SAFE* (Sustainable Agriculture, Food and Environment) Alliance has provided further statistical evidence to support the view that local production of food for local markets would reduce much unnecessary waste of energy and resources. *The Food Miles Report* (Paxton 1994) documents global statistics on food transportation, advocating decentralized structures of distribution to reduce long-distance food transportation and its attendant environmental and health costs. 'Food Miles' come in two varieties. First, mileage is built up within countries, as food is processed, packaged, stored, taken to distribution centres and retail outlets and on its final journey to the point of consumption. Second, food travels between the country where the produce is grown and the country where it is eaten. Most food in the UK has travelled vast distances to reach the consumer:

> Granny Smith apples 14,000 miles from New Zealand, prawns 8,000 miles from Bangladesh and green beans 5,000 miles from Kenya are just some of the everyday items available in supermarkets.

(Food Miles Campaign in Paxton 1994: 6)

Even within a country, many 'surplus' transport miles may be covered. Paxton (1994) cites the example of a vegetable grower in Wales who sells through two outlets in the local town:

■ **The greengrocer** Produce travels from the farm to the shop, where it is bought by the consumer. Transport distance—5 miles.

■ **The supermarket** Produce goes 5 miles to the packhouse, then almost 100 miles to the distribution centre, and 100 miles back to the consumer. Total almost 200 miles.

Food is being transported over longer and longer distances. Although the *amount* of food being transported remained the same between 1979 and 1994, the *distance* it was transported increased by over 50 per cent. This has two environmentally detrimental results:

1. Increased transport distances covered by lorries and planes increases pollution and contributes to global warming and health problems.
2. Food transported over long distances must be over-processed, sprayed with pesticides and over-packaged, contributing to further pollution.

The increase in distance travelled is an inevitable result of ecologically unsound management practice. This takes two forms:

1. **Central distribution** Retailers achieve economies of scale by reducing the number of warehouses required. Since retailers normally pay the same for the product regardless of the distance it has come, the costs fall on the farmers, and the environment. Cheap bulk imports from countries where environmental standards and wages and conditions are low can undercut local food producers.

2. **Just in time (JIT) deliveries** Sales-based ordering, whereby growers deliver at short notice, perhaps only two hours, is possible through computerized systems linked to the supermarket till. Lorries used in a system of this type will make a journey when goods are needed, regardless of whether it is full or not. Large vehicles may be less than half full, increasing the distances travelled and adding to congestion, road damage, noise and air pollution.

Food Miles, and the distances travelled by the vast range of consumer goods, increase for two reasons. First, road transport is heavily subsidized. Second, the financial system is weighted in favour of unsustainable development and against local production for local consumption within local economies. Before turning to the question of finance, we look briefly at the 'invisible' costs, or externalities, which fall upon the community as a whole from motorized transport. It is estimated that air pollution from road transport accounts for some £2.8 billion of damage annually. This cost is not met by the individual firms which benefit from increased mobility. Vehicle emissions account for:

- About one-fifth of the UK's carbon dioxide emissions.

- Half the emissions of nitrogen oxides (NO_x).

- Volatile Organic Compounds (VOCs).

- Black Smoke.

- Almost all emissions of lead and carbon monoxide.

In addition to pollution, road transport causes environmental and financial costs in terms of noise, road traffic accidents, land taken up by roads and parking. Respiratory and other illnesses increase with the increase in urban air pollution, children's freedom is restricted in traffic-congested towns and cities, and wildlife sites are lost. The burden of these costs are met by the community and by the environment. In so far as commerce and industry were to incorporate these in terms of economic costs, mass transportation would cease to be an economic proposition. This leads to a consideration of the financing of environmentally sustainable and socially equitable production and distribution systems.

A QUESTION OF FINANCE

Money is the tool by which urban civilisations were built. It is as fundamental to city life as the vote is to politics and the wheel is to transport. Historically it has been used by individuals for personal profit and empire building, but there is no reason why it cannot be used by individuals, groups and communities in a socially conscious way to build a better world.

(Conaty 1993: 118)

Conaty (1993) links the poverty resulting from unemployment and over-indebtedness with environmental degradation. A leading figure in the UK Social Investment Forum (UKSIF: see Chapter 9), Conaty supports calls for a new economic order focused upon meeting finite needs through community development and neighbourhood economics. Of the trillion pounds a day which is traded on the London money markets, less than 5 per cent is connected with world trade. And yet

> this dominant form of pure speculation has come to have . . . a powerful effect on both national and individual welfare. It is obscenely ironic that this gambling activity is plied both in the Square Mile in London and on Wall Street in New York within short walking distance of growing armies of homeless people sleeping rough, either off the Strand in London, or in the Bowery in Lower Manhattan.
>
> **(Conaty 1993: 118)**

New financial institutions offer the potential for 'socializing' conventional banking and credit practices, and are being adopted across the globe. In addition to Socially Responsible Investment (SRI), Socially Directed Investment (SDI) aims to 'create social wealth by developing the capacities of people as a resource.' SDI comes somewhere between conventional loans (as finance expecting financial reward) and conventional grants (as gifts to encourage development). As a form of both investment and aid, SDI is a particularly effective means to promote sustainable development at the local level (see Case Study 12.1). Conaty cites the results of twenty years of research by the Center for Neighbourhood Technology in Chicago into the vitality of local economies. According to this research, neighbourhood economies fall into three broad categories:

- Workless.

- Import-export.

- Working.

Since the 1960s 'working neighbourhoods' in North America have been undermined through the impact of urban planning, corporate policies and economic development. Conaty draws attention to the fact that 'banking funds everything else'. Over-indebtedness may seem a less obvious pollutant than toxic waste or acid rain, but it leads as surely to social inequity and environmental degradation. The financial system's performance in managing resources is vitally important. In the USA and the UK, wild speculative lending by large banks and financial institutions in the 1980s led to collapse and compensation from government funds. This did not, however, ameliorate the plight of consumers caught in debt or negative equity, or small businesses subject to bank foreclosure. The main result was to stimulate development of alternative, community-based banking and finance institutions.

In the UK, the social and environmental record of banks has been researched with a view to promoting local economic regeneration based on good banking, accountability and community obligation. Less than competent banking has social and financial costs and is a sign of lack of accountability. Accountability, on the other hand, allows valuable feedback from

CASE STUDY 12.1
South Shore Bank, Chicago

Regional or community banks still exist in the United States, which has a more decentralized banking system than the UK. Acquired in 1973 by 11 socially committed investors, the South Shore Bank in Chicago has used banking techniques to assist the local Afro-American community to pull local neighbourhoods out of economic decline. When the bank was taken over, its books revealed that the total savings of local residents on deposit was $33 million, but of this only $120 000 (0.3 per cent) was either invested in the area or on loan to those living in South Shore neighbourhoods. The new owners resolved to reverse this capital flight.

The new owners were determined to recycle local money to meet local needs, while attracting new money to the area from outsiders to finance redevelopment. As a result, by 1992 the South Shore Bank had achieved the reputation of being the only bank in the USA to lend to its local community more than it takes from the same community by way of deposits. Its development deposits stood at $106 million, and development loans were in excess of $200 million. Default rates on loans were 1.5 per cent, well below the US average.

Companies capitalized by its holding company, Shorebank, included:

■ City Lands Corporation, a property development company.

■ Neighbourhood Institute, a not-for-profit venture.

■ Access, a self-employment and business development initiative for women.

■ South Shore Enterprise Centre, a small business incubator facility.

■ Neighbourhood Fund, an equity finance fund for black businesses.

■ South Shore Advisory Services, banking consultancy services.

The South Shore model has been copied by communities in Arkansas and New York, and the concept has been translated to accommodate British banking practice in pilot schemes in Birmingham (England: the Aston Investment Trust), in Glasgow (Scotland) and Derry (Northern Ireland).

Source: Conaty (1993: 124–6)

stakeholders, enabling the bank to set and change its course. More information should not, however, be mistaken for better information.

'Relationship banking' has lost out to communication technology and computer models which create a 'virtual reality' of finance. If the assumptions are wrong (having a telephone, for example, made you creditworthy in the credit explosion of the mid-1980s) the first law of computing holds. Garbage in, garbage out.

(Mayo *c.* 1994: 4)

Locally based banking and financial institutions offer a sounder means to promote social, environmental and business good practice than global financial institutions capable of moving capital on a whim.

REGIONAL PLANNING FOR ECOLOGICAL SUSTAINABILITY

In the ninteenth century, at the height of the industrial revolution, Sir Titus Salt (an entrepreneur from the North of England) was able to provide his workforce with healthy housing close to the place of work, with good wages, clean air and sanitation, shops supplying wholesome food and chapels ministering to their spiritual needs. He took a holistic line to the total environmental picture. However laudable the ethical line that Sir Titus Salt and many since have taken, the ecological problems faced by industry at the turn of the millennium are unlikely to be solved by individual paternalists, no matter how impeccable their ecological credentials.

Although co-operation between companies and other organizations on a spatial basis is emerging as the most feasible alternative, structured co-operation between disparate interest groups requires planning and co-ordination. Theoretical and practical expertise in local economic regeneration was not initially motivated by environmental considerations. Nevertheless, the series of studies on industrial districts collated by the International Institute for Labour Studies at the International Labour Office (*ILO*) in Geneva in 1990 provides evidence of the potential for local co-operative development.

The research programme explored the phenomenon of small-firm industrial agglomerations or 'industrial districts' in a number of regions, drawing upon case studies from Italy, where this type of model was first identified. Other studies provided evidence from Spain, Denmark, Germany, Canada, Cyprus and the USA. In addition to economic development, studies focused on specific policy issues of relevance to local authorities, trade unions and employers' organizations. They concluded that co-operative mechanisms improve the competitive capacities of small-firm communities and networks by overcoming the 'resource gap' problem and improving economics of scale and scope. Joint procurement, development, utilization and financing of resources offer benefits even when firms in the region are competing to produce similar products or are at the same stage of a productive process. According to Pyke and Sengenberger (1992), co-operation at local level may take the form of:

■ Collaboration on design and technical specifications between individual firms at different phases of the production cycle.

■ Acceptance of orders beyond the normal manufacturing capacities of individual manufacturers.

■ Collective provision of skills through collaboration in training labour for the district as a whole.

■ 'Good neighbourliness', including the lending of tools and spare parts, sharing of advice and lending of assistance in emergencies.

(Pyke and Sengenberger 1992: 4–39)

This contrasts with the practice of providing incentives for impetus, know-how and financial inputs to come from exogenous sources. Financial incentives to attract business from outside the area rarely generate stable and permanent development. The incentives may be used by firms to set up plants in boom periods, but these may be nothing more than 'extended workbenches', to be closed down in times of recession. On the other hand, endogenous regional development commits local enterprises to continuous development within a specific region which has its own identity, economically, politically and culturally. This offers the potential for integration of key actors on a regional basis for regional development. Key actors include firms, business organizations, trade unions, local and regional government, employment exchanges and banks.

The organization of economic relations in industrial districts offers scope for a 'new localism' with the potential to reshape the relationship between business and the community and business and the environment. Refocusing development at the local level has the effect of blurring the boundary between the spheres of business and community. The result is that community norms and expectations impact upon economic behaviour and standards. The local community becomes supportive of businesses which do not prioritize short-term economic gains at the expense of general welfare. An essential element is the potential for the cultivation of trust as a guiding principle in business relationships. The evidence suggests that the ability to act on trust brings a new dynamism to the economy by increasing the security of trading relationships.

> Firms do not, contrary to textbook descriptions of the ideal competitive market, seek every opportunity to destroy their rivals. In the ideal industrial district model, the individual firm does not see survival and success in terms of a fight to the death with rivals; rather, the accent is on collective growth, where each individual unit benefits from the success of the whole.

(Pyke and Sengenberger 1992: 9)

In the world of practicalities and realities, trust and co-operation are highly valued, while stress and uncertainty are viewed as counterproductive, both locally and globally. The ILO study provides compelling evidence of the disadvantages of the global division of labour, whereby firms from the advanced industrial economies migrate to low-paying developing countries. Economic development of this type is destabilizing economically, socially and environmentally, both for developed and developing countries. Furthermore, endogenous economic development from local resources under local control provides both motivation and resources for preservation and protection of the physical environment. In other words, 'districts as they develop, with all their political, manufacturing and tertiary resources, need to behave as multinational companies both in terms of technological and commercial monitoring and of the renewal of internal resources (Pyke and Sengenberger 1992: 9).

Business networks cannot, however, undertake such long-term change on their own. They require the support of local institutions and the territorial state (Pyke and Sengenberger 1992). The evidence indicates that ecological sustainability is based upon the principles of permaculture and bioregionalism and practised within geographically and culturally defined spatial areas. Before exploring these concepts in more detail we examine the general case for subsidiarity of decision-making in developed countries.

Beatley and Brower (1993) have argued that developed countries, as major consumers of the world's resources and major sources of waste and pollution, are most in need of sustainable development. They urge planning professionals to create sustainable communities which:

1. Recognize environmental constraints and work to live within biological limits.
2. Reduce exposure of people and property to natural hazards.
3. Reduce air and water pollution.
4. Promote a sense of place.

As Kinnersley (1988) has shown in the matter of water, sharing resources is a social, not a technological, process:

> viewing it [sharing] as a problem of social organisation leaves less scope for hoping that, somehow, the next step or two in technological progress will make it all easier or better. . . . The evidence of the last 200 years or so is that ... the advances in technology taken together have been two-edged. The development of sewage treatment, for example, has helped us to moderate the pollution loads we thrust into the river at certain points: but the discovery and wider application of fertilisers, pesticides and other features of intensive agriculture expose rivers and even groundwater to new hazards which, by their diffuse nature are far more insidious.

> (Kinnersley 1988: 195–6)

Technological advances have contributed to the growing need to understand the relationship of individuals and communities with their water environments. Pressures on water resources increase as rivers are used for the conflicting purposes of drinking, irrigation, waste disposal, recreation and transport. Similar pressures on other natural resources lend support to the case for local planning based upon local knowledge and co-operation.

The concept of locality

Traditionally, the political economy of the developed world has been based upon the concept of the nation-state. Legislative and economic measures are framed within the context of a geographically defined sovereign state with designated borders. People and places within the borders are subject to the laws and dictates of the nation. People and places outside the borders are not. You are either in, or out. Nevertheless, particular areas within a nation-state may be the subject of differential policies designed to alleviate economic or social deprivation which has been identified at a 'regional' or local level.

Much intellectual effort can be wasted in seeking a definition of a subnational 'region' for planning purposes on the lines of physical boundaries such as define a nation-state. A lot depends upon the purposes to be served by such definition. Whether for physical planning, economic development or environmental protection, the selection of a local authority, city area or river basin will vary according to the nature of the problem for which a solution is being sought. No particular purpose is to be served in delineating one definition for all purposes, particularly in an environmental context. Human and natural systems form a complex series of overlapping and interconnecting networks: as a river flows across human boundaries to the sea, a transport system traverses different natural regions and human territories. While a national economic plan may be based within the territorial boundaries of a nation-state, regional planning with special reference to the environment is less easily confined within human-made borders.

The concepts of bioregionalism and permaculture have evolved to re-root human activity within a locality which is not defined by human-made boundaries. Both concepts place each and every activity within the context of a series of concentric circles which, much like the ripples caused by throwing a stone into a pool, impact upon the surrounding human and physical neighbourhood.

Bioregionalism
Bioregionalism has become increasingly influential throughout North America and the developed world. Its social and economic visions flow from the landfalls, water flows, climate and natural communities within neighbouring localities. Unsustainable development has thrived upon three mistaken assumptions:

1. The cumulative effects of incremental change on the physical and natural environment are irrelevant to the development project.
2. The welfare of the human community is a peripheral consideration for commercial enterprise.
3. The knowledge of where food comes from and how to produce it is dispensable.

Sustainable development based upon bioregionalism replaces the consciousness of place, community and food security. It fosters a sense of place, a respect for sentient beings within each locality, and it requires mastery of information about the state of the bioregion and its governance.

Permaculture
Bill Mollison, inventor of the term 'permaculture', dismisses the 'free market' as a cover for unethical monetary and monopoly supply systems (Mollison and Holmgren 1978). According to Mollison, uncontrolled materialism will continue to damage soils, forests, air quality, water and basic nutrition. Hence our 'only real freedom is to choose those areas where we can act responsibly in relation to conserving and regenerating the earth's resources' (Bell 1992: Foreword).

Permaculture is a way to make conscious decisions to redesign our lives, manage our resources well and reduce waste. In 1978 Bill Mollison and David Holmgren wrote *Permaculture 1* (Mollison and Holmgren 1978) an outline of a vision for rebuilding sustainable and ecologically benign human settlements.

Systems which pollute are wasteful, nor just financially, but in that they create unnecessary work. Nature does not waste, it is a complete system in which each element produced by one part of the process is indisputably needed somewhere else as a resource. Humans work far more than other creatures in nature, setting greater demands for their satisfaction, and creating yields for which they have no use. Each plant, animal, bird and micro-organism is placed within the natural system at a point where its needs can be met and its wastes supply someone else's needs. By conscious design we can improve the situation.

(Bell 1992: 22)

As Bell (1992) points out, human creativity has outstripped human ability to govern, or even to know, the results of human activity. As world governments notice that something is wrong in their relationship with the environment, they create commissions to study the matter, and claim never to have been worried about anything else. The results of their deliberations may be a crack down on litter louts, while the contribution of the companies who produce and use disposable packaging may be considered a natural and permanent feature of the economic order. Although permaculture provides a more holistic approach, it is not a religion. It is a practical system for designing based upon connectedness which can be adapted to any culture or any place.

Regional environmental management

Welford (1993) has proposed the creation of an interactive computerized database to monitor environmental quality in a region, as a planning aid. His model would be based on Geographical Information Systems (*GIS*) and would incorporate environmental and socio-economic data. This management tool would enable land use and climatic factors to be incorporated into decision-making alongside more traditional data, facilitating regional environmental management by companies, industries and local communities.

The GIS would have a number of uses. These include:

■ Monitoring of infrastructure developments.

■ Fostering of communication between industry and local communities.

■ Development of models and environmental targets.

■ Identification of opportunities for new investment and growth.

■ Development of strategies to promote 'green' companies within the region.

The Earth Centre described in Case Study 12.2 and similar projects focus not only upon education, training and industry for sustainable development, but also on farming, horticulture and food security. The environmental case for localizing food production is particularly powerful. While regions and localities may continue specialist production of clothing and textiles, furniture, steel or car production in terms of traditional industrial location practice, concentration of diversified systems of farming, food processing and distribution around urban and industrial areas has the advantage of reducing transportation, energy usage and pollution and waste generation. It also maximizes the potential for packaging reuse.

CASE STUDY 12.2

The Earth Centre Millennium Initiative, South Yorkshire

The Earth Centre is a project designed to demonstrate the potential for sustainable living in the third millennium. After five years of research and planning, at a cost of £1.3 million, the initial facilities at the Earth Centre were opened to the public. Coopers & Lybrand led the initial feasibility study, which concluded that the Earth Centre had the potential to become a financially self-sustaining popular visitor centre and a 'new national institution'. According to the business plan, the project will attract 2.5 million visits by the year 2000. An award of £50 million has been secured from the Millennium Fund, which is funded by the National Lottery, with the balance of capital being provided from private sector borrowing and equity, the EU, corporate and other partnerships, charitable trusts and public subscriptions.

The Earth Centre project is situated in 350 acres of land in Conisborough in the Dearne Valley of South Yorkshire. Originally an area of natural beauty, this former mining area suffers from economic stagnation and post-industrial blight. It is therefore an ideal place in which to develop the twin themes of environmental best practice and sustainable development. 'The Earth Centre has been designed to exemplify the highest environmental standards in the design of the buildings, in its energy, waste and transport infrastructure and in ecological land restoration and management.' It comprises a range of learning opportunities for a large and diverse audience. It has been designed to demonstrate best practice by working with local communities through a series of 'green corridor' projects and innovative Agenda 21 economic regeneration initiatives.

The first phase of building started in 1994, and involved site restoration and small-scale ecology demonstration projects. Three Millennium Pavilions will be opened in the year 2000.

The Sustainable Futures Centre

The slogan 'visit today, live it tomorrow' will be demonstrated through:

- 2000 Global Case Studies.
- Future Town.
- Community Planning for Real.
- The Forum.
- Sim Earth.
- Green Audit.
- Internet.
- Media Centre.

- Environmental Film Pavilions.

- Video, Films, Slides, Music, Drama.

The Ark

The slogan 'bringing the future to life' will be demonstrated through:

- Earthwatch and Wildsound, The Ride of Time.

- Children's Theatre.

- Global Village.

- Diversity of Life.

- Solar Age.

- Rainforest Adventure.

- Resource and Energy Centre.

- The Tree.

- Electronic Forum.

The Sustainable Science and Industry Gallery

Science and industry ideas to change the world will be demonstrated through:

- Earth, Air, Water, Fire.

- Communications Gallery.

- Business Centre and Corporate Hospitality.

- Industrial Ecology.

- Niche Trade Fairs.

- The Green Office.

- Library.

- Intermediate Technology Gallery.

The three Millennium Pavilions support the residential, educational, artistic and training programmes being developed at the centre. These programmes have been designed to offer facilities to local communities to develop practical 'Green Renaissance' initiatives for new business and industry based upon the example of the Earth Centre Project itself. The project will retain links with kindred projects and places of outstanding ecological interest throughout the world.

Source: Earth Centre publicity material.

Address: The Earth Centre Project, Kilner's Bridge, Doncaster Road, Denaby Main, Doncaster, South Yorkshire, DN12 4DY, UK.

LOCAL AGRICULTURE AND FOOD DISTRIBUTION

Localization of food production has great potential for reducing the environmental impact of commerce and industry, offering potential for business development in the field of customized supplies based on new forms of information flow and new patterns of trade. Local food sourcing implies a move away from monocultural agriculture, with its reliance on mechanization and agrochemicals, towards diversified agriculture which is light on chemical and energy inputs, correspondingly light on transport, processing and packaging, and low in non-recyclable waste generation. Local food production also serves to decrease ignorance among consumers, thereby reducing the necessity for promotional advertising and packaging, with all the attendant waste entailed. In the short term, however, it can increase the need for innovative firms to educate their customers by presenting the case for ecological sustainability and making the connection between theory and company practice. Established trading patterns which are heavily reliant upon concentration and centralization militate against the practice of local food sourcing and localized trading.

This was not always the case. In the early decades of the twentieth century New York, like most urban settlements throughout history and across the world, was supplied by agricultural enterprise in the immediate hinterland of the city. Local shops were supplied by local farms, and it was common practice for urban dwellers to view the fields and farms supplying the livestock and arable produce to local shops. Processing, packaging and transportation were at a minimum, with a correspondent minimization of energy usage and toxic waste generation. 'Progress' led to the increase in 'Food Miles', the distance travelled by food components and packaging from farm to table. While the economic desirability of increasing 'Food Miles' has appeared incontestable, the ecological implications have only recently become apparent. As Schumacher (1973: 246) summed it up: 'Modern man talks of the battle with nature, forgetting that if he ever won the battle he would find himself on the losing side.'

Growing consumer appreciation of the disadvantages of centralization and distribution of food has given rise to a variety of local trading initiatives, offering guidelines for new directions in trading patterns. Paxton (1994) explores some of the issues raised by research into 'Food Miles' and examines some of the countervailing tendencies.

Concentration of production and distribution

Two large bakeries dominated the baked bread market in the UK in 1992. Allied Bakeries and British Bakeries accounted for 60 per cent of all bread production. The two bakeries are owned by large national food corporations and are supplied by grain-milling operations within their groups. The remaining 40 per cent of plant-baked bread is supplied by around 4000 bakers, a reduction from 12 500 in 1950. Although bread has a short shelf life, rapid transport systems and the technological development of part-baking has led to an increase in the import and export of bread products. The concentration of supplies and the increase in imports and exports has increased transportation distances, adding to ecological costs with no proven value added to the food value of the product. In conventional management terms the logistics of centralized production and distribution signifies success. In terms of ecology, it signifies disaster. The *Food Miles Report* offers several examples of 'the insanity of central distribution'.

- **Bananas** Imported by Geest, a fruit and vegetable distributor, they arrive in Southampton, travel by road to Lancashire for ripening, then to a Somerset warehouse before being distributed all over Britain.

- **Dairy produce** For all Safeways stores in the UK this is supplied from one single distribution depot in Warwickshire.

(Paxton 1994)

Centralized distribution is nothing new. The practice was noted by Schumacher in the 1970s, as he observed lorries loaded with identical packs of biscuits passing each other on the newly built motorways between London and Edinburgh. It is, however, a practice difficult to recommend as ecologically sound and suitable for adoption on a global scale.

Paxton (1994) follows through the ecological implications of the long-distance trade in foodstuffs under four headings:

1. Agricultural production.
2. Processing, packaging and preservation.
3. Transport.
4. Energy use in the food chain.

Agricultural production

The production of farm produce for distant consumption has a number of implications:

- Resources are allocated to production for export (i.e. out of the locality, region or country) rather than for self-sufficiency and local food needs.

- Specialization of crop production implies the use of intensive agricultural methods, whereby a limited range of crops are grown. Such crops are heavily dependent upon agrochemicals, both to increase yields and decrease the pests and diseases which thrive on monoculture.

- The separation of food production from consumption leaves consumers uninformed about the conditions under which their food is produced, and the degree of its possible contamination by toxic substances.

- As machinery displaces farm workers, rural unemployment rises.

- Intensive agricultural methods are both high in energy consumption and destructive of the natural environment.

Processing, packaging and preservation

To ensure a long life in transit and on the supermarket shelf, food needs to be preserved and packaged. These processes may themselves generate further transportation, as food is moved to and from packaging and preserving plants. In addition, the processes consume resources and increase pollution as follows.

Processing
Industrial processing of foods from raw ingredients is highly energy intensive, using up to 10 times the energy necessary to grow the crop in the first place. Although food processing is an extremely profitable business, the loss of nutrients during storage and the addition of flavourings, preservatives and other additives reduces nutritional value of foods sold to the consumer.

Packaging
Long-distance transport of food and drink renders the reduction and reuse of packaging problematic, since packaging is necessary to enable food to be consumed far away from where it was produced. Roughly two-thirds of packaging is used to protect food and drink, adding considerably to the volume of household waste. Reuse, particularly of glass bottles, is highly energy efficient, but favours local distribution systems over long-distance transportation.

Pesticides
Long-term storage of fruit and vegetables in transit and on the supermarket shelves necessitates the use of pesticides. These are by their very nature poisonous. Some, like methyl bromide, are not only toxic, but also cause a significant amount of ozone loss. Many fruits and vegetables are sprayed with several toxic substances on the way from farm to table.

Transport
On its way from farmer to consumer, food may pass through a number of intermediaries, as it goes to processors, wholesalers, distributors and retailers. Each stage may involve transportation over considerable distances, even where foods are eventually sold within a few miles of their origins. All forms of transport consume energy and emit pollution to air, water or land in combination or severally.

Energy use in the food chain
A 1978 study found that the distribution and processing stages of the UK food system used roughly 11 per cent of total UK energy use, while growing the food used only 6.2 per cent. Findings of this type support the view that ecological sustainability may best be promoted by a highly localized system of food production.

Energy saving and waste minimization projects have their role to play in the initial consciousness-raising stages of heightened ecological awareness. Nevertheless, continued reliance upon extensive trading systems which depend upon intensive monocrop agriculture and high energy usage in production, transportation, processing, packaging and preserving with the attendant generation of waste appears an unpromising route to long-term ecological sustainability.

The case for green farming
Until the 1990s the Precautionary Principle was applied in reverse by chemistry, toxicology and fertility departments in universities and hospitals across the world. As cash for yet more research was handed out, different industrial and commercial interests battled to deflect

culpability for environmental degradation and potential causes of deteriorating health standards to 'natural' causes. Nevertheless, mounting evidence of cause for concern led to a growth in support for locally based agriculture and reduced agri-chemical use.

According to the British Medical Association (*BMA*)

> until we have a more complete understanding of pesticide toxicity, the benefit of the doubt should be awarded to the environment, the worker and the consumer. More particularly, where there are serious concerns relating to the safety of a particular pesticide, its use should be withdrawn or restricted until a new risk analysis can be made.
>
> **(BMA 1990: 11)**

The Institute for Environment and Health's (1995) report was not particularly reassuring. It listed as causes for concern:

- Phyto-oestrogens—plant chemical oestrogen mimics.

- Alkyl phenolpolythoxylates—used in detergents, paints and cosmetics.

- Polychlorinated biphenyls—PCBs used in electrical equipment.

- Dioxins—poisonous chemical by-product of the manufacture of herbicides such as Agent Orange and bactericides.

- Phthalates—added as plasticizers in food wrappings.

- Organochlorine pesticides—including DDT, dieldrin and lindane.

Organochlorine pesticides continue to be used in the growing and preservation of foodstuffs. Although DDT has been banned in the UK since 1984, it is persistent in the environment, having a half-life of about 100 years, and it is used on imported foods. Brazil and Mexico still use about 1000 tonnes annually. Lindane is used in the UK on a host of crops, including cereals, grassland, oilseed rape, cabbages, Brussels sprouts, apples, pears, tomatoes, cucumbers, strawberries and sugar beet. Lindane has been linked to reproductive and endocrine deterioration, and is suspected as contributing to the high incidence of breast cancer in the farming area of East Anglia.

Mounting evidence links use of this type of agrochemical with deterioration of health in both workers and consumers, and the use of environmentally benign strategies with benefits to human and environmental health. In 1994 Danish research found that a test group of organic farmers and growers had sperm counts higher than the national average.

> The study of reproductive effects of pesticides in male greenhouse workers . . . found an unexpectedly high sperm density in members of an association of organic farmers, who manufacture their products without the use of pesticides or chemical fertilisers. This is of interest in the light of evidence that indicates a world-wide decreasing trend of sperm density in the general population.
>
> **(quoted from *The Lancet* by Maynard 1995: 9)**

Findings of this type have added impetus to the growth of locally based organic farming schemes.

In March 1995 the Council for the Protection of Rural England (CPRE) published the report of a study undertaken by the London-based Institute for European Environmental Policy. The report explored the extent to which the design of 'agri-environment' schemes required by EC Regulation 2078/92 reflected local environmental goals and priorities. The study covered schemes in Denmark, France, Ireland, Germany, Spain and the UK. The report noted that conflicts arising from differences in policy approaches by agricultural, environmental and land use planning systems could be resolved if agri-environmental schemes were 'more focused on specific zones and landscape types . . . Thus several of the scenarios for the reform of the CAP which now appear plausible would involve payments to farmers which are more closely linked to their environmental role' (CPRE 1995: 13–15).

Local influence and participation was seen as a growing factor in the development of agri-environmental schemes by both statutory and non-governmental organizations (see Case Study 12.3). However, agricultural support policies developed in Europe and the USA continue to favour intensive farming methods. Under this system, environmentally expensive farming methods remain the least costly in purely monetary terms. The same remains true in respect of centralized distribution systems, just-in-time deliveries and out-of -town shopping centres, which maximize Food Miles and minimize environmental protection. The possibility of reducing intra-European Food Miles by improving the competitiveness of the UK food industry has, however, received some attention.

The Strathclyde University Food Project has worked with companies which process food, buyers from the major supermarkets, representatives of the catering sector and other industrial bodies, including the National Farmers' Union and the Meat and Livestock Commission, to explore ways to decrease Britain's 'food trade gap'. Most of the food eaten in Britain is affected by these organizations, and their co-operation on the project is likely to result in a reduction in the transportation of foods like bacon, salad vegetables and fruit from the Netherlands, Denmark, Belgium, Ireland and Germany.

CASE STUDY 12.3
Examples of Community Involvement in Food Production

Seikatsu Club in Japan

Although originally formed in 1965 as a co-operative to supply cheaper food products, the Seikatsu Club's primary concern has become respect for the environment. No goods considered harmful to the environment or to health are supplied to its 153 000 members. Bulk orders of dried goods are delivered to groups of families on a monthly basis, with weekly deliveries of fresh produce. In common with similar schemes throughout the world, the club has fostered strong customer-supplier relationships.

Self-Sufficiency in Chinese Cities

Despite development pressures, 14 of China's 15 largest cities continue to obtain food from their own farm belts, and are largely self-sufficient. The cities, which include Beijing, Shanghai, Tianjin, Shenyang, Wuhan and Guangzhou, keep their agricultural suburbs fertile with treated human waste.

Community Supported Agriculture

The Community Supported Agriculture movement brings organizations of producers and consumers into an ongoing relationship to mutual benefit. While the producers agree to supply foodstuffs which are free of pesticides and preservatives, the consumers guarantee not only to buy the produce but also to support the producers in terms of finance and practical assistance. Other local produce marketing schemes strengthen links between grower and consumer, enabling a diversity of crops to be sold on a small scale within a limited local area.

Source: Adapted from Paxton (1994)

SUMMARY

The bulk of food should be grown near where people live, which would: reduce the need for transport, create useful home-based employment, enhance human health through contact with nature, and improve freshness and therefore quality of food, stimulate local area trading and co-operation, and increase decentralised political autonomy.

(Peter Bane, quoted in Paxton 1994: 51)

On a global scale, economic development and environmental protection are conflicting goals. At the local level, however, sustainable economic development and environmental sustainability are fully compatible. This fact has been widely recognized. In 1994, for example, Dr Richard Tapper of WWF drew the attention of the International Chamber of Commerce to the necessity for local economic development, and for local communities to retain the benefits from local economic regeneration. This may well entail the development of local or regional economies as autonomous enterprises, with industry and commerce working in partnership with statutory and voluntary organizations. However, recognition of the necessity for ecological sustainability does not necessarily lead to the development of the infrastructures necessary for sustainable development. For progress towards sustainability to occur a recognition of the complex interplay of social, economic and ecological factors is necessary at all levels of government, from local to national and international.

This chapter has considered the plausibility of localized trading and analysed elements of co-operative trading. Focusing primarily on agricultural production it has given the reader a basic understanding of regional trading and management and has put forward a case for ecologically sound inward investment in local sustainable infrastructures.

QUESTIONS

12.1 How much do you know about the sources of the food you eat? Take one main meal of the day and break it down into individual components. Where does each component come from? How far has it travelled? Under what conditions of agriculture and labour relations was it produced, preserved and packaged?

12.2 Name 10 food crops grown in your locality and identify the seasons when they are harvested. Are locally grown supplies of all 10 crops available in local shops?

12.3 Outline the implications for sustainability of the adoption of the policy of self-reliance in food production by regional communities on a global scale.

BIBLIOGRAPHY

Key texts

Whitelegg, J. (1994) *Transport for a Sustainable Future: The Case for Europe,* **John Wiley, Chichester**
Taking the view that transport is at the heart of environmental concerns, this review of European transport policy explores the philosophy which underlies the urban policies that cause pollution and congestion. The author forcefully presents evidence to reduce the need for a constant increase in the mobility of people and freight from the planners' perspective as well as the decision-makers' perspective. A valuable contribution of facts and information.

Paxton, A. (1994) *The Food Miles Report: The Dangers of Long Distance Food Transport,* **SAFE Alliance, London**

Since the early 1990s a growing number of organizations in the USA, Germany and the UK have produced studies to guide policy-makers and industrialists in making decisions which will affect the environment. INFORM in the USA, the Wuppertal Institute in Germany and the SAFE (Sustainable Agriculture, Food and Environment) Alliance in the UK have been pioneers in this field. In *The Food Miles Report*, Paxton and the SAFE Alliance document a wide range of highly significant but little known facts on the issues of food, transportation and trade. The pros and cons of transport and distribution techniques, including central distribution and just-in-time (JIT) deliveries, are explored from the point of view of producer, customer and wider society. Reports like these present evidence of the growing acceptance that the scope for the individual firm to focus exclusively on the bottom line, ignoring the broader holistic implications of its impact on society and the environment, has been severely reduced. The Wuppertal Institute (1995) has also produced a report on *Sustainable Germany* which documents the causes for concern and the steps necessary to create a sustainable industrial base in Germany.

References and further reading

Beatley, T. and Brower, D.J. (1993) 'Sustainability Comes to Main Street', *Planning* 59(5): 16–19.

Bell, G. (1992) *The Permaculture Way*, Thorsons, London.

British Medical Association (BMA) (1990) *Guide to Pesticides, Chemicals and Health*, BMA, London.

Conaty, P. (1993) 'Socially Directed Investment: An Appropriate Use of Excess Credit', in Birmingham Settlement, *Consumer Debt in Europe: The Birmingham Declaration*, Birmingham Settlement, UK.

Council for the Protection of Rural England (CPRE) (1995) *Local Influence: Increasing Local Involvement in the Development of Green Farming Schemes*, CPRE, London.

Daly, H. and Cobb, J. (1989) *For the Common Good*, Beacon Press, Boston, MA.

DoT (1994) in R. Smithers (1996) 'Minister Voices Doubts over Future Car Society', *Guardian*, 18 January: 7.

Friedmann, J. and Weaver, C. (1979) *Territory and Function*, Edward Arnold, London.

Institute for Environment and Health (1995) *Environmental Oestrogens: Consequences to Human Health and Wildlife*, Medical Research Council, London.

Kinnersley, D. (1988) *Troubled Water: Rivers, Politics and Pollution*, Hilary Shipman, London.

LGMB (1993) Local Government Management Review Board, LGMB, The Arndale Centre, Luton, Beds, W1 2TS.

Maynard, R. (1995) *'Sperm Alert'*, *Living Earth* 188 (October).

Mayo, E. (ed.) (c. 1994) *Bank Watch*, New Economics Foundation, London.

Mollison, B. and Holmgren, D. (1978) *Permaculture 1, A Perennial agriculture for human settlements*, Permanent Publications, Tyalgum, Australia.

Paxton, A. (1994) *The Food Miles Report: The Dangers of Long Distance Food Transport*, SAFE Alliance, London.

Pyke, F. and Sengenberger, W. (eds) (1992) *Industrial Districts and Local Economic Regeneration*, International Institute for Labour Studies, Geneva.

Roberts, P. (1995) 'Sustainable Regional Planning' *Regional Studies* 28(8): 781–7.

Schumacher, E. (1973) *Small is Beautiful*, Blond & Briggs, London.

Welford, R. (1993) 'Local Economic Development and Environmental Management: An Integrated Approach', *Local Economy* 8(2): 131–42.

Whitelegg, J. (1994) *Transport for a Sustainable Future: The Case for Europe*, John Wiley, Chichester.

Wuppertal Institute (1995) *Sustainable Germany: A Contribution to Sustainable Global Development* (Résumé) Doppersberg 19, Wuppertal, Germany.

CHAPTER 13

TOWARDS SUSTAINABLE REGENERATION

Sustainable Development means that we use our unlimited brain capacity instead of our limited natural resources.

(Juha Sipilä, Director of the Helsinki Metropolitan Council)

INTRODUCTION

Piecemeal, remedial, bolt-on green measures will do little to convert the triadic trading system (see Chapter 4) to long-term ecological sustainability Rising labour costs and environmental legislation in the developed world will shift manufacturing and agri-business to the developing world. This will result in a continued rise in the percentage of the earth's population living in overcrowded and unsustainable urban settlements where problems are created faster than they can be solved. Crime will continue to rise and health standards deteriorate, as cash crops force millions more small farmers in developing countries off the land. As the urban unemployed form a pool of cheap labour for the manufacturing and service industries of the multinational corporations, the landless and rootless unemployed from north and south will increasingly live in unsustainable social, economic and environmental conditions. Under these circumstances, the 'civilized' world will need to house itself in fortified economic and social ghettos in an attempt to maintain an illusory security.

In this chapter we review alternatives to this gloom-laden scenario. Sustainable development will require radical changes in industrial, agricultural, educational transport and trading policies and strategies. The ecological company's role will be to set its policy options within the wider cultural infrastructure of a new society emerging within a sustainable framework. Industrialization has given rise to the phenomenon of the city, a large urban conglomeration which is of itself unsustainable. To survive, it relies on inputs of raw materials and energy from outside its borders, and exports of pollution and wastes. The haphazard adoption of a global hinterland is neither scientific, rational, nor is it sustainable. The alternative is to develop the concept of a city within the context of a bioregion. In this scenario, the city and its suburbs, agricultural regions and wilderness form one, interacting and sustainable entity. Within this broad framework each city, set within its bioregion, will be idiosyncratic and diverse, reflecting its own individual setting. Nevertheless, sustainable cities based upon a renewable economy, will share common characteristics. Policies will:.

- Prioritize holistic and cyclical strategies formed within a bioregional framework.

- Be rooted in a sustainable agricultural base.

- Minimize the need for transportation.

- Educate for sustainability.

- Promote sustainable tourism.

- Be based on inter-generational and intra-generational equity.

- Require adaptations in management structures and work patterns.

THE PLANNED ENVIRONMENT

Haughton and Hunter (1994) explore urban living in the light of the environmental and social sciences. They note that towns and cities draw their resources in unsustainable ways. In the case of water, for example, urban areas drain regional freshwater supplies while wasting their own water supply. Water is taken from other users in the hinterland while urban fresh rainwater is run off from streets as rapidly as possible, often contributing to flooding downstream.

> Urban areas rely on salt and fresh waters for drinking water, industrial activities, food supply, amenity and recreation. Yet they pollute these resources to the detriment of aquatic ecosystems and organisms and, therefore, ultimately, of themselves. It is almost beyond belief that urban activities are allowed to pollute groundwater, for example, when this source is so often of crucial importance in maintaining urban life.
>
> **(Haughton and Hunter 1994: 196–7)**

The water pollution costs of urban living extend far beyond urban boundaries, and these costs are rapidly rising. Cities are major contributors to oxygen depletion in fresh waters and in the marine environment. Dense human populations give rise to sewage, a mixture of wastes from human faeces and urine, laundry, bathing and cooking. Added to this, wastes from some industries, in particular pulp and paper waste and waste from food-processing plants, increase the biological oxygen demand. While the dangers of water-borne diseases have led to major efforts to provide clean domestic water supplies in cities, less attention has been paid to the disposal of sewage from urban areas. Haughton and Hunter note that a survey of OECD countries found that in 1989 only 60 per cent of the population was served by waste treatment plants. 'Between 1981 and 1991 the number of people in cities globally without access to sanitation facilities grew by 81 million' (Haughton and Hunter 1994: 180). Often, in developing countries, little or no domestic waste is treated, and industrial and domestic wastes are discharged together into the sewage system and directly from there to streams, rivers, estuaries and inshore waters. In terms of sustainability, this is disastrous on three counts:

1. Waters are contaminated from the overload of biological materials.
2. Waters are contaminated from toxic waste materials.
3. Biological wastes are removed from the land without being replaced.

Vast cities operating in this way are unsustainable. They make unrealistic demands upon the environment, sucking in materials and spewing out wastes in an uncontrolled and uncontrollable fashion. They arise from the linear industrial mentality of exploitation and the profit motive based upon rights without responsibilities, deriving from a philosophy which views nature as a productivity machine, stripped of enchantment, sacredness, truth and, in the end, of productivity as well.

The unsustainable 'ecological footprint' of cities arises from their dependence upon what Herman Daly has termed the linear 'economics of the digestive tract'. Simple inputs and outputs are viewed in isolation from the broader contexts in which they occur. Cities developed in this way fail to reflect the reality that all human development has impacts—a footprint—far beyond the site in question. The impact of a housing estate can be traced to the quarries supplying the building materials, the reservoirs providing the water for the household taps and the landfill sites accepting the solid wastes. New residents make journeys to work and to shops, adding to the numbers of journeys in the locality and making demands on transport routes. In the past, the added pressures on the environment could be disregarded. With 80 per cent of the population of a country like the UK now living in towns and cities, this is no longer the case. According to the CPRE, the urbanization of rural England is expanding at the rate of 11 000 hectares a year. In England, 15 per cent of the land area is under urban use; this is set to rise to 20 per cent (one-fifth of the land area) by 2075. This irreversible loss of land to development may be unsustainable.

The failure to account the long-term implications for human health and environmental sustainability of industrial activity is now recognized as irrational and unscientific. Sustainability is dependent upon the development of an 'economics of the circulatory system', which respects the scientific realities of the natural environment and works within that framework. A sustainable city has an economy in which degraded resources are renewed and reused. Such an economy demands the application of increased scientific sophistication. By contrast, the blanket application of agrochemicals on the land, and the widespread use and disposal of laboratory-developed preservatives, paints, cleaning agents and solvents have been introduced with a total lack of scientific rigour and total disregard for sustainability.

Unsustainable cities draw on food produced by unsustainable methods on unsuitable lands. Massive soil erosion has followed the cultivation of the Great Plains of Khazakhstan and over-grazing of the clear-felled tropical forests of South America. One-third of the topsoil of the USA has already been lost as a direct result of unsustainable farming methods, and the southern boundary of the Sahara desert has moved south by over 120 miles in the 17 years before 1975. Soil erosion and other forms of environmental degradation occur where the relationship between urban and rural economies is fragmented. As regional planners realized as long ago as the 1920s:

> Cultural man needs land and developed natural resources as the tangible source of bodily existence; he needs the flow of commodities to make that source effective; but first of all he needs a harmonious and related environment as the source of his true living. These three needs of cultured man make three corresponding problems:
>
> (a) the conservation of natural resources
> (b) the control of commodity flow
> (c) the development of environment.
>
> **(Benton MacKaye 1928, quoted in Haughton and Hunter 1994: 76)**

The CPRE advocates that land-use and planning policies for town and country should be developed together in order to make best use of land and other resources in both. This necessitates enhancing all the features that make cities attractive places to live.

A high quality urban environment:

■ Makes the best use of scarce land resources.

■ Increases the cost-effectiveness of public transport.

■ Reduces the loss of countryside.

■ Provides a positive alternative to building which damages landscapes and habitats.

■ Supports urban facilities and services.

■ Reduces the need for car travel and reduces journey times.

■ Tackles the problem of urban dereliction and provides homes.

■ Revitalizes vacant buildings.

■ Supports existing business investment.

■ Makes positive use of empty offices and vacant industrial land.

■ Improves town centres and supports existing infrastructures.

(Adapted from CPRE 1994)

National initiatives seeking to implement sustainable planning strategies are supported by a number of international programmes offering examples of best practice.

SUSTAINABLE CITIES

In summary, therefore, there is a need to rethink the urban–rural relationship in order to refine policies in the direction of sustainability (Elkin *et al.* 1991). In place of unplanned urban-sprawl, policies are required which encourage:

- The countryside to revive its role as urban hinterland.

- The city to govern planning functions, especially of location of food processing, distribution and retailing companies.

- Growth of more food within cities.

- Raised consciousness of city dwellers of their interdependence with the countryside.

- Sustainable agriculture and healthy food production.

- Sustainable leisure opportunities in urban and rural areas.

A number of initiatives are moving in this general direction. 'Sustainable Cities' is one of the programmes being developed by the International Council for Local Environmental Initiatives (ICLEI), which is responsible for co-ordinating a world-wide Local Agenda 21 programme. Its policy is guided by the following principles:

- The creation of sustainable societies will require that local governments have the *capacity* to maintain, improve and transform the basic human systems that they manage.

- Local governments need new *solutions* to unprecedented environmental problems.

- Global environmental problems result from human activities in the place where people live their daily lives. For this reason no global environmental agenda will succeed without a co-ordinated *strategy* for local action.

(ICLEI 1995)

ICLEI co-ordinates research, conferences, conventions and publications, drawing on the expertise of public managers, statutory and voluntary agencies, locally elected officials, management professionals and academics to establish the communication, information and training services necessary to meet the global environmental challenge. They observe that traditional institutional structures are unable to handle the rapid change necessary to solve the growing tensions. Founded at the World Congress of Local Governments for a Sustainable Future at the United Nations in New York in 1990, the ICLEI opened its World Secretariat in Toronto, Canada in 1991, its European Secretariat in Freiburg, Germany in 1992, and an office for the Asia and Pacific Region in Tokyo, Japan in 1993. It constitutes the environmental organization of the International Union of Local Authorities (*IULA*), and its European Secretariat serves the Council of European Municipalities and Regions (*CEMR*). In March 1995 municipalities who were signatories to its Cities for Climate Protection numbered 56 in Europe, 37 in North America, 2 in the Middle East, 1 in Asia and 1 in Africa.

According to ICLEI: 'The ecological development of our cities and towns requires the establishment of systems that maximise the efficient use of resources and minimise the export of wastes into the environment.' Their projects seek to bring together experts who are pioneering new policy frameworks, management instruments and financing mechanisms. In addition to projects concerned with individual aspects of the need for climate protection, the ICLEI European Local Agenda 21 campaign has given rise to the European Sustainable

Cities and Towns Campaign, and 80 European local authorities signed the Aalborg Charter with the objective of promoting good environmental practice. The Charter of European Cities and Towns: Towards Sustainability (the Aalborg Charter), signed in Denmark on 27 May 1994, contained the following statements:

- We understand that our present urban lifestyle, in particular our patterns of division of labour and functions, land use, transport, industrial production, agriculture, consumption, and leisure activities, and hence our standard of living, make us essentially responsible for many environmental problems humankind is facing.

- We, cities and towns, understand that the limiting factor for economic development of our cities and towns has become natural capital, such as atmosphere, soil, water and forests. We must therefore invest in this capital.

The Charter goes on to recommend investment in natural capital in the following categories:

- Conservation of groundwater stocks, soil and habitats for rare species.

- Stimulating growth of natural capital stocks and reducing consumption of non-renewable energy.

- Relieving pressure on natural capital stocks, e.g. by creating inner city parks to relieve recreation pressure on natural forests.

- Encouraging efficiency through energy efficient buildings and transport.

The first report of the European Sustainable Cities and Towns Campaign (1994) recognizes that cities themselves have the potential to solve:

- The problems within cities.

- The problems caused by cities.

  City managers must seek to meet the social and economic needs of urban residents while respecting local, regional and global natural systems, solving problems locally where possible, rather than shifting them to other special locations or passing them on to future generations.

                          (European Sustainable Cities and Towns Campaign: 1994: 5)

The report notes the weaknesses of 'conventional good management practice'. Although some professional and technical expertise can be useful, the general reductionist approach seeks to make 'complex problems manageable by forcing them into narrow frames of reference. ... Rather, there is a need to ground management practices more firmly in ecosystems realities.' To do this, composite policy instruments which have multiple objectives will need to be devised. Thus the solution to each problem will require a combination of tools, while each tool can assist in solving more than one problem.

Urban management for sustainability will operate within a city-wide policy framework, using a range of tools to formulate and integrate local environmental policies. These tools include:

- Specific environmental management systems and environmental impact assessment.

- Collaboration and training across disciplines, including professional education and training and values, formal and informal partnerships between private organizations and public authorities.

- Local environmental taxes, charges and levies, investment appraisal, utility regulation, environmental considerations in budgeting, tendering and purchasing, and other tools designed to bring the market mechanisms in line with sustainability.

(Ibid. 1994: 8)

As yet, as the European Union's Fifth Action Programme notes: 'Few cities possess an institutional framework which permits genuine co-ordination of investment, development and environmental decision-making' (Commission of the European Communities 1992). However, as towns and cities across the globe seek to pursue the objectives of Agenda 21 with the support of organizations like the ICLEI, managers of companies in both the private and public sectors can expect to require a familiarity with these complex tools. The ability to focus upon the complexity of local ecological, fiscal and economic, educational, and social realities in addition to the company's bottom line will make considerable demands upon the capabilities of management in the future. Radical action at city level is proposed within the EU Fifth Action Programme, in which industry is one of the five target sectors. Cities will increasingly focus on such measures as:

- Promotion of green consumerism.

- Targeted inward investment strategies.

- Promotion of the environmental business sector.

Supported by national legislative measures, this must necessarily occur with an integrated local planning framework.

Integration of the urban environment and land-use planning

The greening of economic development is dependent on the social stability necessary to provide secure living conditions for the local labour market. European cities are experiencing inner city decay and the deterioration of post-1960s urban fringe settlements which now house the most disadvantaged residents and the lowest quality environments. To these residents global environmental issues appear less pressing than current personal survival, and historically the pressures have been to address the pressing problems of present urban residents. Belatedly, recognition has grown at European level that economic growth could not be indefinitely divorced from questions of resource allocation and welfare. A new approach to economic development is emerging from what started as separate environmental and social equity standpoints.

In the case of all urban settings, whether historic city centres, suburbs or new settlements, the EC document *Europe 2000+: Co-operation for European Territorial Development* (1994) is indicative of the shift among land-use planning professionals towards more ecological analyses. The necessity for this emerges from recognition of the unsustainability of policies which continue to foster the decentralization of population and employment from central cities. The resultant suburbanization, with the increasing separation of home from work, leads to:

- Increasing demands for personal transport.

- Consumption of rural land on the edge of cities.

- Dereliction of town and city centres.

- Reduced quality of urban environment.

- Threatened historic town centres.

- Reduced quality of life.

Reversal of these trends occurs as new planning policies are developed alongside research into the ecological and economic 'footprints' of urban settlements. Planned provision of amenities and infrastructure, of private and public space within cities and towns, sustainability will depend upon the planned development of the relationship between urban and rural. Environmental considerations re-emerged in regional planning in the UK during the 1990s. As Haughton and Hunter (1994) explained:

> Regional planning can be redefined to place at its very heart the need to support business to make a positive contribution to improved sustainability, including policies to reduce pollution and excessive resource demands, and policies to reduce transport needs for raw materials, goods and services. Here it is not so much the size and location of settlements that take centre place, but the relationships between individual activities and, the implications of this for energy and transport demand.
>
> **(Haughton and Hunter 1994: 12)**

Sustainable planning on a regional basis takes account of the relationship between the survival requirements of city, suburb, countryside and wilderness and their spatial interconnections. A rapidly growing area of concern centres on the need to evaluate and recognize the impact of industrialized cities upon the global and local countryside. Urban centres remain totally dependent upon a sustainable agricultural base.

PLANNING FOR SUSTAINABLE AGRICULTURE

One of the least sustainable legacies of the late industrial revolution is belief in the 'global village', with its ability to blur the distinction between town and country. In the quest for an urban lifestyle lived within a rural idyll, commuters or 'telecommuters' sprawl across the countryside, creating super-highways to supply their physical and cultural needs from across the globe while degrading the sustainability of the land where they actually live. To counter this type of unsound development, sustainable planning is increasingly evolving mechanisms whereby urban settlements may be supplied with foods grown in the rural hinterland of cities. Local supply of foodstuffs reduces the need for long-distance transportation with its attendant requirement for the excessive use of preservatives and packaging. When cities take their rural hinterlands into account, regional planning builds up mutual understanding between town and country. As a result, urban dependence on the countryside for essential supplies comes into focus, offering scope for close monitoring of methods of food production and preservation, and solution of common problems.

In the UK, as in other developed countries, over-intensive farming methods have resulted in a featureless landscape, with hedgerows, trees, dry stone walls and small barns and buildings removed. Farming methods requiring excessive inputs of fertilizers and pesticides have reduced soil and water quality and accelerated soil erosion. The use of intensive farming methods in preference to more sustainable traditional mixed farming is encouraged by the EU Common Agricultural Policy (CAP). Total UK expenditure on the CAP in 1994–5 was in the region of £2.6 billion. In an attempt to reduce food 'surpluses', generated by such methods, farmers are paid to take their land out of production. This 'set aside' policy is unsustainable. It encourages farmers to farm even more intensively on the remaining land, while encouraging the 'development' of 'surplus' land through extending the built environment. Instead, the CPRE and others recommend direct payments to farmers to enhance and maintain the countryside. Protection of the countryside is best achieved through the introduction of mixed farming methods, and with the co-operation and leadership of farmers.

The need to revise the reductionist, single-issue approach to farming subsidies in respect of the EU CAP has been recognized in a report commissioned from the Institute for European Environmental Policy (IEEP London) by the CPRE (Baldock and Mitchell 1995). Accounting for around 80 per cent of rural land use, agriculture has an immense impact on the environment. However, although significant public finance is devoted to agriculture, there are few connections between public policy decisions on the allocation of those resources and other land use policies. The report examined the arrangements made in six EU member states to implement Regulation 2078/92. This regulation requires member states to implement an 'agri-environment' programme to pursue environmental objectives. The programmes, although small initially, represent a move away from subsidies based purely upon agricultural production, towards funds designed to protect the environment. As the agri-environment budget grows, continued public support for farming subsidies will depend increasingly on high-profile benefits at local level.

The CPRE study focused on the institutional arrangements and the respective roles of national, regional and local authorities in Denmark, France, Ireland, Germany, Spain and the UK (Baldock and Mitchell 1995). It concluded that a more environmentally sustainable agricultural industry will require policies which reflect:

■ Growing public consultation and participation in planning, particularly at local level.

■ The diverse natural and agricultural circumstances in the countryside.

■ Stronger links between agricultural policy, environmental policy and the land-use planning system.

Many local authorities are launching countryside initiatives of various types, encouraged in the UK by such organizations as the County Planning Officers' Society, the London and South East Regional Planning Conference and the SAFE Alliance. On a global scale there are many examples of sound practice, including some cities which have retained a strong agricultural sector and remain self-sufficient in food. In China, 14 of the 15 largest cities fall into this category, the bulk of supplies coming from the suburbs being kept fertile by treated human waste. Agriculture remains the dominant land use within a number of legally defined metropolitan areas in Canada, Japan, Spain and Costa Rica (see Haughton and Hunter 1994: 121).

Sustainable agriculture

The IIED study of sustainable agriculture in Britain (Pretty and Howes 1994) is one of a number of initiatives lending support to the view that sustainable agriculture is economically and environmentally viable (see Case Study 13.1). Narrow policy goals as pursued by the EU CAP, following 'high-input/high-output' agricultural policies, have brought hidden costs to farmers and the wider society. Rural poverty and environmental resource damage motivated a reappraisal of the performance of integrated farms. The report suggests that mixed farming methods have the overall advantage in comparison with conventional farming methods. Integrated farming has, after all, been sustainable over long periods of human history across the globe. As Vaclav Havel explained:

CASE STUDY 13.1
Community Supported Agriculture

The rapid growth of Community Supported Agriculture (CSA) across the USA has given rise to a wealth of literature on the subject, and to the spread of the basic concepts across Europe and into Russia and the former Soviet Union. The practice originated in a growing awareness that people no longer retained any appreciation of the origins of their food. Food had become a substance to be found, packaged and labelled, on the supermarket shelves. Generations were growing up who have never seen a cow in a field, an apple on a tree, or a beanstalk full of beans. A latent realization that farms have something to offer beyond food gave rise to appreciation that farms have educational and cultural significance.

Based upon sound mixed farming practices, CSA is focused on the social and economic conditions which make sustainable farming possible. It reconnects farmer with consumer in such a way as to reinforce mutual responsibilities. The mass market requires mass production of uniform products, achievable only through mass, monocultural farming methods. The farmer prepared to use traditional farming methods is by definition, limited to a smaller and local scale and becomes dependent upon the specialist local consumer. Through CSA, consumers become directly involved in the finance and marketing of the farm produce. The process has social, economic, educational and health benefits for farmers and consumers in their particular localities.

Source: Groh and McFadden (1990)

it was rooted in the nature of its place, appropriate, harmonious, personally tested by generations of farmers and certified by the results of their husbandry. It also displayed a kind of optimal proportionality in extent and kind of all that belonged to it; fields, meadows, boundaries, woods, cattle, domestic animals, water, toads and so on. For centuries no farmer made it the topic of a scientific study. Nevertheless, it constituted a generally satisfactory economic and ecological system within which everything was bound together by a thousand threads of mutual and meaningful connection, guaranteeing its stability as well as the stability of the farmer's husbandry. Unlike present-day 'agri-business' the traditional family farm was energetically self-sufficient.

(quoted in Conford 1992: 106–7)

Reductionist science had no role in the traditional farming system. It is, however, simplistic to dismiss traditional farming as 'unscientific', based as it is upon close monitoring of cause and effect within a holistic setting. In comparison, agri-business, which monitors only a narrow selection of causes and effects, appears crude and unscientific. The growing recognition that ecologically sustainable agriculture is both economically and ecologically viable presages vast changes in the production and marketing of agricultural produce, with repercussions throughout the global economy. These changes will rely upon vast changes in the planning system, in particular with regard to transportation systems.

TRANSPORTATION

Throughout the developed world urban and rural areas suffer from problems generated by increasing mobility of goods, services and people associated with traffic growth and urban mobility. The introduction of cleaner technologies which reduce energy use and emissions of pollutants offer limited means to provide solutions over the long term. Road transport takes land from other uses, not only in the actual road space (a total of 2848.3 sq. km in UK), but also for the connected activities such as the construction of cars and lorries, quarrying for building materials and parking of cars. Land blighted by car-parking includes:

- Car-parking on and off streets in city centres and business districts.

- Street parking in residential areas.

- Front gardens put down to tarmac.

In 1992 the CPRE provided the following statistics:

- Of the rock aggregates quarried in England and Wales, 43 per cent is used for road construction and maintenance.

- A significant proportion of the UK's CO_2 emissions comes from road transport, which is growing faster than any other industrial sector.

- The majority of Department of Transport's staff are involved in car and lorry-based transport. The remaining 10 per cent cover rail, bus, air and sea transport combined.

- Each kilometre of motorway takes about 7.5 hectares of land and uses 120 000 tonnes of quarried aggregates.

- In 1988, transport was the largest single consuming sector of energy in the UK. In 1990 transport used 33 per cent of all energy consumed, of which road transport was responsible for 80 pcr cent.

(CPRE 1992)

There is a growing appreciation that in order to meet environmental and transport objectives an integrated approach to transport, environmental and spatial planning is essential. The shift from private cars to public transport, cycling and walking may have some effect for personal and leisure activities. Schemes to reduce the environmental impact of company vehicle fleets and employee travel may have some short-term impact. But such measures will not of themselves lead to long-term sustainability. Over the long-term, planners will be required to reconcile accessibility with economic development and environmental objectives. Measures which bring about a reduction in the need to travel will, over the long term, prove sounder than continued attempts to reduce the speed of travel.

The reduction of human mobility may be achieved by a combination of a variety of measures, each of which has considerable potential to reduce undesirable environmental impacts without detracting from the quality of life. Such measures include:

- The revitalization of urban spaces, as e.g. in Freiburg.

- Renovation and subsidy for public transport, as e.g. in Freiburg.

- Retention of high street shops, as e.g. in Leicester.

- Comprehensive planning for cycling and pedestrians, as e.g. in Copenhagen.

- Telecommuting.

- Energy taxation and removal of hidden automobile subsidies.

The wholesale movement of employees from homes in the suburbs to offices and industrial premises in city centres is environmentally costly. It creates noise, production of vehicles, vehicle emissions and growth of road networks, requiring revised planning and employment patterns. As future planning is redirected to minimizing travel and transportation, firms will need to shift their transportation policies to adapt to the new measures.

As part of the UK response to Local Agenda 21 the Local Government Management Board is working with local authorities in the UK to 'encourage the use of the right mode of transport for the right journey'. Local authorities are encouraged to:

- Set objectives to reduce the proportion of car-based movement.

- Plan development in locations where there are alternatives to car travel.

- Through management of the existing transport structure, optimize its use.

- Reduce the overall areas of land devoted to roads through area-based management initiatives.

- Reduce the amount of space allowed to non-residential parking.

SUSTAINABLE TOURISM

Tourism is one of the fastest growing industries and has, since the early 1960s, developed into the world's largest industry. In Europe alone tourism now directly accounts for more than 4 per cent of both UK and EC GDP; with the secondary and tertiary effects of spending taken into account the figure is probably closer to 10 per cent and increasing (Ravenscroft 1992).

The costs of tourism are, however, also increasing. Tourism costs can be divided into three main categories; in Britain the Countryside Working Group (Ravenscroft 1992) define these as:

- **Economic costs** these are not borne by the tourist industry or consumers, e.g. road congestion.

- **Social and cultural costs** e.g. resentment of undesirable tourism development.

- **Environmental costs** e.g. erosion, pollution, and impairment of visual amenity.

The environmental impact of mass transit tourism is immense, having adverse effects upon the natural, social and human-made environment. Green or eco-tourism providing for smaller, less price-sensitive markets are only superficially more sustainable, giving rise to the suspicion that the only good tourism is no tourism (see Case Study 13.2).

The strategic planning of the tourist industry, like any other forward-looking industry, needs to reflect the current paradigm shift of public opinion towards sustainability. It requires a strategic vision that will harmonize its activities with the environment while concurrently allowing space for commercial expansion.

The long-term success and health of the environment is of course a central external variable for the tourist industry. If there is any industry that requires a healthy sustained environment it is the tourist industry. It is in their interests, therefore, to actively promote truly ecological values. The responsibility lies in the main with individual businesses who are on the leading edge of or interface between policy and the environment. They must seek to allow the ethical values of the strategic plans to filter through to action implementation in the field. This can be through:

- Implementation of environmental management systems.

- Promotion of ecological activities and sustainable initiatives.

- Protection and conservation of ecologically sensitive areas.

CASE STUDY 13.2
Spot the Difference—Green Tourism

With green tourism expanding so rapidly, Ted Trainer offers this checklist for the environmentally concerned traveller (see Figure 13.1).

Tourism: ecologically unacceptable (e.g. a holiday in Bali or Thailand)

- Travel a long distance by air or car using a huge quantity of scarce energy and polluting the atmosphere.
- Stay in hotels built from scarce local resources, at a daily cost equal to the annual income averaged by half the world's people.
- Spend a lot of money on duty-free goods you don't need.
- By your affluent lifestyle, video camera, etc., help to teach the natives the superiority of western culture.
- Eat food airfreighted in, or produced by local people at starvation wages.
- Spend your time not looking at trees, animals or landscape.

John McConnell

FIGURE 13.1 *Green tourism (Artist: John McConnell) (Source: Real World, 1995)*

Green Tourism: ecologically acceptable (e.g. a Kenya safari trip)

- Travel a long distance by air or car using a huge quantity of scarce energy and polluting the atmosphere.
- Stay in hotels built from scarce local resources, at a daily cost equal to the annual income averaged by half the world's people.

- Spend a lot of money on duty-free goods you don't need.

- By your affluent lifestyle, video camera, etc., help to teach the natives the superiority of western culture.

- Eat food airfreighted in, or produced by local people at starvation wages.

- Spend your time looking at trees, animals or landscape.

Source: Ted Trainer, with permission

- Environmentally deleterious activity diversification.

- Values diffusion to stakeholders and customers.

- Political lobbying for ecologically sustainable infrastructural developments.

In the creation of sustainable development, sustainable tourism has a vital role to play. It completes the logic of creating sustainable cities through a system of regional planning which integrates urban and rural land use and incorporates sustainable agriculture and transport.

Mass tourism has evolved as the package tour industry has refined and reinforced the need to 'get away from it all' once a year among the urban working class. The annual flight from unpleasing living and working conditions in industrial areas has moved from national seaside resorts to southern European and Third World resorts. The negative effects of mass holidaymaking in this way are outlined in Case Study 13.2 on 'Green Tourism'. Low-priced high-volume tourism is not compatible with sustainability. Sustainable tourism, on the other hand, can regenerate urban and rural areas in sustainable ways. It follows the following principles:

- Run by small companies with specialist knowledge of markets.

- Locally owned and managed.

- Culturally connected to the host culture.

- Minimal environmental costs.

- Managed on a long-term basis.

The first principle of sustainability in tourism is the development of a holistic approach in the living environments of travellers and hosts. More sustainable cities in industrialized countries, with more sustainable living and working conditions, reduce the motivation to 'get away from it all' on any terms. The revival of the city as an attractive place to be, whether as resident, worker or tourist, has many advantages, as the experience of Copenhagen, Freiburg and a number of other European cities have shown. The reversal of the flight from city centres through transport and planning measures promotes civic pride and culture and improves the quality of life within the built environment. The 'rediscovery' of city life leads to:

- Conservation of the natural and built environment.

- Reduction in travel.

- Preservation and development of open spaces.

- Reduction in pollution.

- Increased educational awareness of environmental issues.

A locally managed tourist industry, drawing upon locally produced food and based upon the local cultural inheritance of buildings, arts and hinterland, brings economic prosperity to a city and its region at the price of minimal environmental impact.

EDUCATION FOR SUSTAINABILITY

The final requirement is for local, long-term sustainable development for change to be pioneered through education for sustainability. This has been recognized along the spectrum from the more cautious conventional approaches to greening, as in Case Study 13.3 on the Skelton Grange Project, to the more radical holistic approaches. Environmental initiatives escalated in numbers as Local Agenda 21 programmes were introduced in local authority areas across the globe, reaching virtually every town and city. Many ecological and environmental projects have been designed to incorporate an educational aspect.

Furthermore, the process of statutory and voluntary bodies coming together with local businesses to establish individual schemes has generated a more focused consciousness of the need for firms to accept responsibility for environmental impacts which were once regarded as incidental externalities. In these circumstances, managements have become increasingly conscious of the value of being involved in, and being seen to be involved in, co-operative environmental schemes which have an educational dimension. This may involve working with schools, colleges and universities on many different levels, including:

- Product design.

- Waste management.

- Pollution control.

- Protection or clean-up of specific sites.

- Staff training.

- Media presentation and publicity.

Environmental education is a multidirectional process. Firms with environmentally sound employment, purchasing and waste disposal policies may have much to offer towards the 'greening' of educational establishments which continue to act as 'silent destroyers'. Favourable publicity for local firms through educational establishments can attract local custom, benefiting the local community and local authority through the generation of jobs within a

CASE STUDY 13.3
Skelton Grange Project, Leeds

As part of its environmental management policy the Skelton Grange Power Station runs an environmental education centre. Skelton Grange is a coal-fired power station owned and operated by National Power plc, the leading electricity generator in the UK. The Chief Executive of National Power is active in the Advisory Committee on Business and the Environment (ACEB) and a key member of the Leeds Environmental Business Forum (see Chapter 11). Through its environmental programme Skelton Grange has reduced the risk of major environmental accidents and has improved the landscaping and general environment on the site. As part of the process, an area of the Skelton Grange site has been dedicated to an environmental education centre.

The centre is fully accessible to local schools and community groups, providing opportunity for the learning of indoor and outdoor skills. It is jointly funded by National Power and the Countryside Commission, and is administered by the British Trust for Conservation Volunteers. The centre is sited in a wildlife area of over 1 hectare in size. On the site are located a large meadow, a cornfield, with a riverside path, bird hide, mature and young hedgerows and two ponds. The area is managed by regular volunteer workdays to maintain the wildlife areas on the site. Educational sessions for schools provided on the site include such subjects as:

■ Minibeasts.

■ Ponds.

■ Hedgerows.

■ Seasons.

■ Electricity.

■ Electricity generation.

Educational ventures of this type are becoming an increasingly vital aspect of company policies, bringing enhanced communication between management, local community and conservationists.

Source: Leeds Environmental Business Forum

cleaner environment. The partnership between educational providers and the local community is particularly important in fostering environmental awareness. It can provide motivation for the establishment of community projects to strengthen social stability and environmental standards within the region. It is also vital to inform local consumers on choices of goods, transportation and leisure patterns for environmental sustainability. The role of education is crucial in establishing a sustainable quality of life in any specific region. It sets the scene for the adoption of the vital tools of sustainability. These include:

- Valuing the locality formally through local indicators.

- Regional planning for sustainability.

- Public works for environmental protection.

- Landscaping.

- Green architecture.

Education for sustainability implies a significant shift away from cultural values which perpetuate the dualisms between industry and community and between industry and the environment. It is grounded in multidimensional tools offering the capacity to respond with accuracy to the aesthetic, cultural, natural, social and psychological implications of policy decision and strategy formation. Failure by businesses and educational establishments to make responsive provision for these developments would render them increasingly marginalized and redundant. Case Study 13.4 on conservation in the Bradford and Leeds conurbation is an illustration of the revolutionary changes occurring from the 'bottom up'. The

CASE STUDY 13.4
Education to Conservation in the Bradford–Leeds Conurbation

During the 1990s UK towns, cities and local authority areas have witnessed an upsurge in local environmental awareness, giving rise to a wealth of locally focused conservation projects. The establishment of schemes has acted as an educational process, extending knowledge of both problems and solutions, giving rise to lifestyle changes and reducing tolerance of polluting and environmentally degrading activities.

The Bradford–Leeds conurbation provides a typical example of the growth of environmental consciousness leading to planning for sustainability through concerted actions in business, transport, education, wildlife conservation and the home environment. Following extensive research in the adjoining metropolitan districts of Leeds and Bradford, Education to Conservation (1994) produced the first *Leeds and Bradford Green Directory*, sponsored by local business and statutory organizations. The research revealed a wide range of plans and projects already in place in the field of sustainable development, environmental education and nature conservation. They found:

- A good communication network between local authorities, charities, volunteer and other environmental organizations.

- New environmental education and learning centres.

- The Schools Environment Improvements Programme.

- Local community/nature conservation projects.

- Large-scale tree planting schemes.

■ Business and industry participation in waste reduction and environmental management systems.

The research resulted in publication of a 100-page booklet providing precise and concise information on environmental problems and solutions within the locality. The booklet contains three parts:

1. Save Time, Save Money, Save the Environment.

2. Doing a Little More.

3. A–Z of Local Environmental Organizations.

Save Time, Save Money, Save the Environment

This section explains why the environment needs to be protected, and how to set about reducing environmental impacts. Information, practical guidance and local contacts are offered on the following subjects:

■ A home environmental review.

■ Transport and fuel efficiency.

■ Energy.

■ Insulation and energy-saving tips.

■ Central heating.

■ The natural garden.

■ Water clean-up and preservation.

■ Global warming (the greenhouse effect).

■ Protecting the ozone layer.

■ The world's forests.

■ Britain's woodlands in world context.

■ The business environment.

■ Waste not want not.

■ The A–Z of recycling.

Doing a Little More

This section offers 10 methods to enhance environmental sustainability locally and globally. Nine are listed here, including:

■ Getting an environmental education.

■ Use the power of the pound in your pocket.

■ Use the power of expression.

- Recognize environmental improvements.

- Support environmental organizations and projects.

- Support or organize a conservation initiative.

- Implement a company environmental review policy.

- Raise funds.

- Keep up to date.

A-Z of Local Environmental Organizations

The booklet lists over 150 local environmental organizations and projects within Bradford and Leeds, with details of work done, services and advice offered and opportunities for voluntary and educational work. This section provides a wealth of information on the extensive networks already in place to promote and develop environmental issues. In this context, the wider initiatives of Leeds Environment City and Bradford Environmental Action Trust (with its *BEATroot* Newsletter) provide supportive frameworks. In addition to information on council services on waste management and energy conservation, details are included on:

- Schools Environmental Improvements Programme.

- Groundwork Trust.

- Shell Better Britain Campaign.

- Wildlife Garden and Grounds Consultancy.

- National Rivers Authority.

- Local finance and Local Employment and Trade System (*LETS*).

In addition, the area supports a range of individual projects, from urban farms, permaculture and wildlife reservations to firms offering energy conservation and recycling facilities and a number of college and university departments offer environmental education initiatives.

The holistic approach to environmental issues is encapsulated in this area in the promotion of local awareness of food and the importance of the cyclical nature of sustainability. Bradford is a pilot project in the Growing Food in Cities project, aimed at identifying existing and potential local sources of food production. The project is linked to the more general Agenda 21 initiatives, and aims to heighten awareness of food sourcing and methods of production. An early venture was the supply of modestly priced compost bins to householders (reduced from £45 to £25, and £10 for pensioners and unemployed people). The project is designed to reduce by up to one-third the amount of household waste going to landfill. This has the potential to further reduce transport and energy use while converting the waste into organic, and therefore sustainable, fertilizer. The project is an example of using 'unlimited brain power' to save limited natural resources.

Adapted from Education to Conservation (1994)

incorporation of the culture of ecological awareness within the planning process is the key to success both in industry and education if both are not to be increasingly alienated from contemporary reality.

As David Orr (1994) has demonstrated, it is vital to reform education in order to halt the rapid decline in the habitability of the earth. 'Discipline-centric' education which merely seeks to prepare the young to compete effectively in the global economy is not a useful preparation for healing the damage caused by industrialization. It is *possible* to continue to dismiss calls for a saner relationship with the planet as 'sensationalism' (see Case Study 13.5) to be swept aside as an irrelevant stumbling block on the path to 'development'. However, it seems more rational to accept that the disruption of ecological systems and the disordering of the vast biochemical cycles of the earth reflect an underlying disorder in the industrial mind, a failure of perception, imagination, intellectual priorities and loyalties. Orr calls for 'ecological design intelligence':

> *ecological design intelligence* is the capacity to understand the ecological context in which humans live, to recognise limits and to get the scale of things right. It is the ability to calibrate human purposes and natural constraints and do so with grace and economy. Ecological design intelligence is not just about things like technologies; . . . At its heart ecological design intelligence is motivated by an ethical view of the world order and our obligations to it. On occasion it requires the good sense and moral energy to say no to things otherwise possible and, for some, profitable.

(Orr 1994: 2)

CASE STUDY 13.5
Ecological Dodos: The Ecology of Extinction

In a special issue on 'Environmental Risk' in winter 1995, the Journal of the Institute of Economic Affairs advanced the view that although the environment is 'inherently risky', the wealthier we become the 'more flexible and robust' will be our attempts to reduce risks and improve the quality of our lives.

Assessing the Political Approach to Risk Management

Dismissing as 'alarmist' concerns about water and air quality, food contamination and holes in the ozone layer, Fred Smith, President of the Competitive Enterprise Institute, Washington, DC, in the above-named article in *Economic Affairs*, likens such fears to superstitious beliefs in evil forces.

> Today, these same fears exist, but the villains are American business and modern technology, the substances are 'toxic' chemicals, electro-magnetic fields (EMFs) and anything associated with radiation, and the charges are brought by the environmental establishment.

In fact, Smith assures us, 'The world is made safer by dangerous products and processes—that are less dangerous than the products and processes they replace.' It is all a question of how you look at it. Smoking is a statistical risk factor, 'causing 500 000 lung cancer deaths per year in the USA'. Driving is also risky. About '50 000 people die in highway related incidents per year'. On the other hand, the risk of shark attacks in the United States is 'small—perhaps one or two per year in the US.' 'Yet,' scoffs Smith, 'if one were to stand on a dune on a beach in America and cry "Shark! Shark!", almost everyone would rush from the water, and some would light up a cigarette and most would soon drive home!'

Smith's point is that through the political system, environmentalists are 'shamelessly' exploiting people's irrational fears.

Lessons from the Brent Spar

In the same vein, Roger Bate, Director of the IEA Environment Unit, attributed concern about marine pollution to the 'selective use of science' which 'stirred up the emotions of European middle-class Greens'. Unfortunately, Bate does not produce any alternative 'science', save to argue that the 'stone-throwers ignored the fact that more pollutants than are contained on the Brent Spar flow from the mouth of the Rhine every 20 minutes.' Ignoring this excellent reason for *reducing* the industrial impact on the environment, Smith proceeds to quote Professor Frits Böttcher of the European Science and Environment Forum, a group of scientists 'sceptical about the consensus on global warming'. Böttcher warns of the potential dangers of 'precautionary principle folly'.

Fred Smith describes the response to the recent

> near miss by asteroid scare, [when] the US Congress commissioned NASA to assess the risk of a direct hit. Ladbrokes would have given enormous odds and gleefully taken bets; NASA, on the other hand, convened two expert panels, on detection and interception, proposed a 25 year investigation and the building of at least six new ground-based telescopes. On the agenda of the interception panel was discussion of 'deploying a nuclear armada of missiles to deflect a doomsday asteroid from its path'. This, in the name of precaution.

Smith concludes his article rhetorically, accusing the environmental movement of 'anti-science rhetoric'.

Sincerely held though these views may be, they are at best misleading to the young. In the winter of 1995–6 this particular issue was circulated free of charge to secondary schools throughout the UK, making these half-digested ideas more readily available than the slowly emerging information and skills required to develop 'ecological design intelligence'.

Source: *Economic Affairs* (Journal of the Institute of Economic Affairs: winter 1995)

Orr (1994: 3) calls for the redesign of education itself, starting with the educators who must become students of the 'ecologically proficient mind and of the things that must be done to foster such minds'.

EQUITY AND SUSTAINABILITY

The separation of industry from the land, and the conversion of the land itself into agro-industrial estates, has led to unsustainable development. Not only in the developed world, but also in the developing world, peasants have been driven from the land and turned into landless labourers. Their villages razed to the ground, they have joined the growing army of the urban unemployed. The divorce of people from the land, of town from country, is counterproductive. As Robert Waller has explained:

> The only way to create a sustainable society and economy is to create a proportionate balance between urban and rural. In a balanced world in which the rural have access to the urban and urban access to the rural, so that the best qualities of both can converge, the truths of religion revealed in the rural past can still mould the way people live, but they cannot in a wholly urban world.
>
> **(Waller 1992: 213)**

The prerequisite for sustainability is to study the natural properties of the soils on the land in order to understand the secrets of nature and secure optimum productivity over the long-term. Waller raises the question of the wisdom of attempting to teach nature how to perform its own operations. Scientifically, ethically and economically, the end result of industrialization divorced from the land is unsustainable, as demonstrated in Case Study 13.6 on beef imports.

The added ethics of pursuing economic development through science, technology and finance which disregard the needs of the land and its people results in the destruction of the land and its people. The vast inputs required for even diminishing outputs indicate the unviability of the continuation of a development model bereft of sound ethical values. The need to consider inter-generational and intra-generational equity in terms of access to the land as the basis of all material resources takes environmental management beyond the principles and applications of traditional management theory.

CASE STUDY 13.6
Beef Imports and Export Dumping

Intensive livestock production in Europe is largely dependent upon imported feeds, with additives and supplements. Non-cereal animal feeds, such as soya, are allowed into the EU without application of tariffs. As a result, EU wheat which would otherwise have been used as animal feed becomes surplus, and is exported with a further subsidy. The result is:

■ Soils in countries exporting animal feeds are depleted.

■ Importing countries have an excess of nutrients, for example a 40 million tonne mountain of manure in the Netherlands.

■ Export of animal feeds from Third World countries casts an 'ecological shadow over the land'.

In a country like Brazil, for example, large, mechanized soya monoculture has been a major factor in the devastation of the Cerrados plateau. About 12 million acres produce soya, 80 per cent of which is exported. Soya production has resulted in:

■ Loss of tropical forest.

■ Soil erosion.

■ Loss of biodiversity.

■ Contamination of water by fertilizers, pesticides and lime.

■ Growth of pests and disease as natural predators are eliminated.

■ Loss of food security for local people.

In Europe, the surpluses of beef resulting from intensive livestock production leads to storage at taxpayer's expense and/or export dumping at prices lower than meat produced by locally reared animals. The EU exported 70 000 tonnes of mainly low-grade beef to West Africa in 1992, with the help of huge export subsidies. The dumping is disastrous, ecologically and economically. It ruins local graziers in the developing country, and ruins the environment as the graziers encroach further onto marginal lands in a desperate attempt to stay in production.

Meanwhile, the UK imports beef, a total of 140 000 tonnes in 1993, mostly from the EU but also from Australia, Central America and sub-Sahara Africa. This was of course before the UK BSE crisis and has drastically increased since. Since the CAP keeps beef prices in the EU artificially high, exporters receive a better price for their product. Hence countries suffering or on the brink of famine are at the same time exporting to the EU, over distances of 7100 km (Zimbabwe), or 5200 km (Botswana and Namibia).

Source: Paxton (1994)

BEYOND THE WINTER MODEL

The Winter Model (see Chapter 4) encapsulates the best use of traditional management tools for the purpose of developing more ecologically sound management. With its starting-point of the firm, it prioritizes:

- **Prevention** Through the employment of cleaner technologies to reduce ecological damage at the outset.

- **Reduction** Through the use of technologies designed to minimize 'unavoidable' damage.

- **Recycling** Through the re-use of waste materials within the firm or within the industrial system.

- **Disposal** Through safe disposal of inevitable resultant waste.

Although Winter goes further than traditional management theory in many respects by stressing management and employee creativity and responsibility for the ecological realities both within and outside the workplace, the model takes the requirements of the productive system as the starting-point. From these tentative beginnings, ecological management will evolve a diversity of structures capable of delivering sustainable regeneration based upon social and ecological reality. Progress can be negative, and it is necessary to be selective, drawing the best from the past and rejecting the unworkable, be it in technology, economics or strategic management itself.

Ecological management evolves as businesses rooted in locality co-operate with statutory and voluntary organizations as a matter of course, working with particular initiatives such as Local Agenda 21 or the European Sustainable Cities where such ventures occur. Sustainability is dependent upon industry's ability to supply cities and the surrounding countrysides with goods and services while making a light 'ecological footprint'.

The alternative is to await definitive proof that the earth's fragile ecosystem has been irreparably damaged. The 'sobering' consensus statement from the second Municipal Leaders' Summit on Climate Change stated in Berlin in 1995:

> Humanity is conducting an unintended, uncontrolled, globally pervasive experiment whose ultimate consequences could be second only to a global nuclear war. The earth's atmosphere is being changed at an unprecedented rate by pollutants resulting from human activities, inefficient and wasteful fossil fuel use and the effects of rapid population growth in many regions. These changes represent a major threat to international security and are already having harmful consequences over many parts of the globe.
>
> (quoted in ICLEI 1995)

This text has attempted to draw together experience from all over the globe to prove that ecologically sustainable management is a desirable and a feasible possibility. Examples of best practice provide ample scope for the development of ecologically sound management practice. A theme that has been apparent throughout the book is that ecological sustainability will be moved forwards only if management accept that present practices not only are unsustainable and damaging to the environment but also are poor management practices. An unsustainable trading system is not in the interest of the environment or business.

Some of the possibilities for movement towards an ecologically sustainable trading system and society have been delineated within the pages of this book. This work is not intended to be exhaustive in nature, a task quite impossible for an academic area as eclectic as the environment. It attempts simply to point the reader towards sources of inspiration to move towards a more co-operative win-win society. A society where humankind pays a greater regard to our earthly playground keeping it in such a well-oiled condition as to allow our children to derive as much utility out of it as we have been allowed.

SUMMARY

In this chapter we have seen how changes in our global and local thinking towards industry, agriculture, education, transport and trade can provide a route towards ecologically sustainable development. The concept of the sustainable city is developed and it is argued that ecologically sustainable development will not be achieved without an integrated holistic strategy for the city. There is a need to rethink and reprioritize our sense of place. Where do cities fit into the larger environmental picture and what effect do they have on the long-term prospects for sustainability? Details of urban management are considered, as are blueprints for sustainable transport, agriculture and tourism.

The chapter also covers the importance of education in the sustainability vision, and how a society can not be sustainable if it is not aware of the implications of its commercial and individual actions. The final section draws together themes from the book and argues for the need to move beyond management systems and traditional approaches to sustainable development towards a more integrated, accessible, and radically achievable blueprint for ecologically sustainable development.

QUESTIONS

13.1 Assess the extent to which the company-specific Winter Model approach to environmentalism is capable of delivering long-term sustainability.

13.2 Discuss the view that: 'It is ridiculous to pretend that business can operate in an ethical vacuum.' The statement was made by a journalist in reference to Shell's failure to take a moral stand on the 'judicial murder' of Ken Saro-Wiwa by the Nigerian military regime in November 1995.

13.3 It is essential for the environmental manager to be aware of major environmental projects and initiatives within the firm's local authority area. Using your local government offices as a starting-point, draw up an outline report on local environmental schemes involving co-operation between two or more types of organization, for example business, statutory body, school, college or university, voluntary or community group.

BIBLIOGRAPHY

Key texts

Elkin, T., McLaren, D. and Hillman, M (1991) *Reviving the City*, FoE and Policy Studies Institute, London
This book documents the changes in urban land use and transport developments in cities in the UK and across the world, documenting the arguments for change to move towards more sustainable planning systems. The book is illustrated with examples of best practice across a range of issues, including energy and transport, waste and pollution and food production and supply. The issues are placed within the broader context of a holistic approach to sustainability.

Haughton, G. and Hunter, C. (1994) *Sustainable Cities*, Regional Studies Association, London
Haughton and Hunter have linked environmental sustainability with urban development, taking the lead from the World Commission on Environment and Development's 1987 observation that the 'future will be predominantly urban, and the most immediate environmental concerns of most people will be urban ones'. This well-researched global review of the relationship between cities and the environment arose from work undertaken by the authors in producing the book *Environmental Policies for Cities in the 1990s* for the OECD (OECD 1990). This holistic approach to regional urban planning is a valuable, carefully structured resource for policy-makers from economic, ecological and managerial perspectives.

References and further reading
Baldock, D. and Mitchell, K. (1995) *Local Influence: Increasing Local Involvement in the Development of Green Farming Schemes*, CPRE, London.
Conford, P. (ed.) (1992) *A Future for the Land*, Green Books, Bideford.
Commission of the European Communities (1992) *Towards Sustainability: A European Community Programme of Policy and Action in relation to the Environment and Sustainable Development*, Commission of the European Communities, Brussels, Belgium.
Council for the Protection of Rural England (CPRE) (1992) *Wheeling Out of Control*, CPRE, London.
———(1994) *Urban Footprints* (pamphlet), CPRE, London.
Education to Conservation (1994) *Leeds and Bradford Green Directory*, available from Education to Conservation, 3 Cromack View, Pudsey, LS28 7PX.
Elkin, T., McLaren, D. and Hillman, M. (1991) *Reviving the City*, FoE and Policy Studies Institute, London.
European Sustainable Cities and Towns Campaign (1994) Rue du Cornet 22, B-1040 Brussels.

Groh, T.M. and McFadden, S.H. (1990) *Farms of Tomorrow*, Bio-Dynamic Farming and Gardening Association Inc., Kimberton, USA.

Haughton, G. and Hunter, C. (1994) Sustainable Cities, Regional Studies Association.

ICLEI (1995) *Cities for Climate Protection Change Newsletter* 1 (March), in London. Introductory Pack, 8th Floor, East Tower, City Hall, 100 Queen St. West, Toronto, ONM5H 2N2, Canada.

OECD (1990) *Environmental Policies for Cities in the 1990s*, Organization for Economic Co-operation and Development, Paris.

Orr, D. (1994) *Earth in Mind: On Education, the Environment and the Human Prospect*, Island Press, Washington, DC.

Paxton, A. (1994) *Food Miles Report*, SAFE Alliance, London.

Pretty, J. and Howes, R. (1994) *Sustainable Agriculture in Britain: Recent Achievements and New Policy Challenges*, IIED, London.

Ravenscroft, N. (1992) 'The Environmental Impact of Recreation and Tourism Development: A Review', *European Environment* 2(2): 8–13.

Trainer, T. (1995) Unpublished material, Professional Studies, University of New South Wales, Sydney 2052, Australia.

Waller, R. (1992) 'Earth and Spirit: A Tradition Renewed', in P. Conford (ed.) *A Future for the Land*, Resurgence Books, published by Green Books, Ford House, Hartland, Devon, EX3 96EE.

GLOSSARY

ACBE Advisory Committee on Business and the Environment, UK, jointly established by the Department of Trade and Industry and the Department of the Environment in 1991.

Acidification The result of changes in chemistry in any area which results in a more acid environment. Acid rain can result in the unnatural acidification of habitats that have limited capacity to neutralize such changes in chemistry.

Acid rain The burning of fossil fuel results in the emission of sulphur dioxide, nitrogen oxide and other gases into the atmosphere. These travel long distances in the atmosphere before being washed out of the air as acid rain.

Agenda 21 Rio Earth Summit document pertaining to sustainable development (UNCED).

BANANA *see* NIMBY.

BATNEEC Best Available Technology Not Entailing Excessive Cost.

BAUM Bundesdeutscher Arbeitskreis für Umweltbewusstes Management (German environmentalist society).

BCSD Business Council for Sustainable Development. Similar aims to WICE. *See also* WBCSD,

BEST Business and Environment Support Team (Bradford, UK).

BIC Business in the Community. A not-for-profit campaigning organization which supports the economic and social regeneration of communities by raising the quality and extent of business involvement, and making community involvement a natural part of business practice.

BiE Business in the Environment. A business-to-business organization which campaigns to raise awareness of environmental issues in corporate Britain. It encourages good environmental management by devising and promoting practical tools to implement the principles of sustainable development, through action and partnership.

Biodiversity (biological diversity) The total range of the variety of species and life forms.

Biodiversity Convention Convention on Biological Diversity signed by 150 Heads of State or Governments at the Earth Summit (UNCED) in Rio de Janeiro in June 1992. Under Article 6A of the Convention, signatories must develop national strategies, plans or programmes for the conservation and sustainable use of biological diversity.

Biomass The total weight of living organisms in any area.

Bioregionalism Local sustainable development within specific ecologically delineated areas.

Biosphere The thin layer of covering of life-support systems surrounding the earth.

BNFL British Nuclear Fuels plc.

BPEO Best Practicable Environmental Option.

BREEAM Building Research Establishment Environmental Assessment Method.

BS 7750 British Standard 7750, the UK specification for Environmental Management Systems.

BSI British Standards Institution.

BUND Bund für Umwelt und Naturschutz Deutschland (Germany). An environmental pressure group.

CAP Common Agricultural Policy (EU).

Carbon tax A tax on fossil fuels. It is designed to encourage industry to use less fuel and to seek alternatives.

CBI Confederation of British Industry.

CEC Commission of the European Communities.

CEMR Council of European Municipalities and Regions.

CEN Comité européen de normalisation (European Standardization Committee) (EU).

CER Corporate Environmental Report.

CERES Coalition for Environmentally Responsible Economics (USA).

CEST Centre for Exploitation of Science and Technology is an independent not-for-profit organization, funded by industry and the UK government, which exists to identify emerging global issues and to relate these to commercial and technological opportunities.

CFCs Chlorofluorocarbons.

CHP Combined heat and power (energy use). Power stations and generating plants provide both heat and electricity. The heat in the form of hot water and/or steam is used locally rather than being discharged into the atmosphere.

CIMAH Control of Industrial Major Accident Hazards Regulations 1984 (UK).

Clean Air Acts The first environmental legislation to combat the hazards caused by industrialization.

Climate Change Convention Convention on Climate Change signed by 150 Heads of State or Governments at the Earth Summit (UNCED) in Rio de Janeiro in June 1992. The Convention established a framework for action to reduce the risks of global warming by limiting the emission of so-called 'greenhouse gasses'.

COD Chemical oxygen demand.

Command and Control An approach to environmental standards regulation with shortcomings such as expense, bureaucracy, detection can be evaded, there is little incentive to improve process and technology.

COPA Control of Pollution Act 1974 (UK).

COSHH Control of Substances Hazardous to Health (UK).

CPRE Council for the Protection of Rural England. It campaigns for more sustainable use of land and other resources in town and country.

Cradle-to-grave Manufacturers are expected to take responsibility for all aspects of product design and use, from the procurement of energy and raw materials, through production to the use and disposal of the product.

Cryosphere Ice caps, glaciers, seasonal snow cover, permafrost.

CSA Community Supported Agriculture.

DDT Dichloro-diphenyl-trichloro-ethane. An insecticide.

Deep ecologist Argue that the rights of the non-human world should be prioritized over human welfare.

Dioxins These are poisonous by-products of the manufacture of herbicides (such as Agent Orange) and bactericides, produced when PVC and other chlorinated materials are burned at low temperatures. They cause cancer in animals and humans.

DoE Department of the Environment (UK).

DoT Department of Transport (UK).

DTI Department of Trade and Industry (UK).

EA Environmental Assessment.

Earth Summit United Nations Conference on Environment and Development (UNCED).

EBS Ecology Building Society.

EC European Commission; *also* European Community (*see also* EU).

EC Directive A legal instruction from the European Commission which is binding on all member states of the EU but which leaves the method of implementation to member governments.

ECJ European Court of Justice.

Eco-economics An environmentally-friendly, cost-saving measure.

Eco-efficiency Competitively priced goods and services designed to satisfy human need and enhance quality of life, while reducing environmental impacts and resource intensity.

Eco-labelling An EU labelling scheme designed to give the customer reliable environmental information about the purchase.

Ecological footprint The international environmental impact of a company's goods and services may be described as its 'ecological imprint'. The overall impact on the environments of human activity in a particular area or country can be described in the same terms.

Ecology The science of the relationship of living things, including human beings, to their living and inanimate surroundings. The study covers the environments created by human beings, and explores the interactions between plants, animals and other living organisms.

Eco-sponsoring The sponsoring by industry of an environmental pressure group or a specific conservation project.

Ecosystem A community of interdependent living organisms, plants and animals, set in the non-living components of their surroundings.

EC Regulation European Commission legislation that has legal force in all member states of the EU.

ECU A European currency.

EDP Environmentally adjusted net domestic product.

EEB European Environment Bureau. It is a federation of 160 environmental NGOs from all 15 EU member states and is committed to seeking sustainability within the EU in partnership with governments and industry.

EIA Environmental impact assessment. This presents information to decision-makers in national authorities of the environmental impact of a proposed major industrial or infrastructure development.

EIRIS Ethical Investment Research Service.

EMAS Eco-Management and Audit Scheme. A regulatory scheme introduced by the EU.

EMS Environmental Management System.

Environmental auditing Auditing the application of a company's policies. Environmental auditing is a management tool evaluating the performance of a firm's environmental organization, management and equipment in safeguarding the environment. It is used to assess compliance with company policy, including the need to meet regulatory standards.

Environmentalist One who is informed by the ideologies and practices which flow from a concern about preservation of the environment.

Environment City Scheme A scheme operated by the Royal Society for the Conservation of Nature (UK) in co-operation with local authorities.

EPA Environmental Protection Agency (USA).

EPA 1990 Environmental Protection Act 1990 (UK).

EPE European Partners for the Environment.

EPT Environmental Protection Technology.

ERT European Round Table of Industrialists.

ESD Ecologically sustainable development.

Ethical egoism The belief that to act contrary to one's own self-interest is immoral.

Ethics Moral principles, philosophy.

ETSU Energy Technology Support Unit (UK).

EU European Union. With the passing of the Single European Act 1986 the European Community (EC) was subsumed within the broader body now known as the European Union (EU). Hence the continued use of the initials EC in respect of legislation.

European Fifth Environmental Action Program A program of policy and action for the European Community in relation to the environment and sustainable development.

Eutrophication over-rich in nutrients, either naturally or as a result of artificial pollutants.

FIMBRA Financial Intermediaries, Managers, and Brokers Regulatory Association.

FMCG Fast-moving consumer goods.

FoE Friends of the Earth.

Food chain All organisms are dependent upon others in a community. Each member of a food chain feeds on one below and may be eaten by one above.

Food miles Cumulative miles food has travelled from source to consumption.

Fordism Acceptance of the Taylorist scientific management paradigm.

Fossil fuels A natural fuel such as coal or gas formed in the geological past from organisms.

Free rider In an environmental context, a 'free rider' is a profit-maximizing firm seeking short-term rewards and assuming that everyone else's environmental care will minimize the effects of their own pollution.

GATT General Agreement on Tariffs and Trade. Formed in 1948 with 23 signatories, GATT, as a system of regulations on world trade, comprised 108 member countries by 1993. About 90 per cent of world trade is governed by GATT, which is one of the most influential world institutions.

GDP Gross domestic product.

GEMI Global Environmental Management Initiative, 1828 L Street NW, Suite 711, Washington DC, 20036, USA.

Genetic diversity The range and frequency of different genes and genetic stocks.

Geosphere The solid portion of the earth.

GHGs Greenhouse gases.

GIS Geographical Information Systems.

Global warming The increase in average temperatures on the earth caused by the greenhouse effect.

GMO Genetically modified organism.

GNP Gross national product.

Green consumers People who declare that they have selectively purchased a product because of its environmentally friendly packaging, formulation or advertising.

Greenpeace The largest international pressure group to campaign non-violently in defence of the natural world.

Greenwashing Superficial greening of corporate image.

GST General Systems Theory.

HCFCs Hydrochlorofluorocarbons.

Heavy metals Lead, cadmium and mercury are toxic, while zinc, copper and manganese can be. They can be spread to humans through the air and through animal and vegetable foods.

HGV Heavy goods vehicle.

HMIP Her Majesty's Inspectorate of Pollution, the UK government's main environmental watchdog.

IBCC International Bureau of Chambers of Commerce.

IBE Institute of Business Ethics.

ICC International Chamber of Commerce.

ICLEI International Council for Local Environmental Initiatives. It is the associated environmental organization of the International Union of Local Authorities (IULA) and was established at the World Congress of Local Governments for a Sustainable Future held at the UN in New York in 1990.

IEA Independent ethical adviser.

IEEP Institute for European Environmental Policy (London).

IFA Independent financial adviser.

IIED International Institute for Environment and Development. An independent organization promoting sustainable patterns of development through research, policy studies, consensus building and public information. It has headquarters in London, a sister organization in Latin America and an associated institution in North America.

ILO International Labour Office (Geneva).

INEM International Network for Environmental Management.

IPC Integrated Pollution Control. Land, water and air are policed by HMIPs on a holistic basis (UK).

IPCC Intergovernmental Panel on Climatic Change (UN).

ISEW Index of Sustainable Economic Welfare.

ISO International Standards Organization.

IT Information Technology.

IUCN International Union for Conservation of Nature and Natural Resources.

IULA International Union of Local Authorities.

JIT Just-in-time (deliveries).

Landfill Disposal of solid wastes to the ground.

LA21 Local Agenda 21.

LCA Life Cycle Assessment (or Analysis). The evaluation of the environmental impact of a particular material or process from inception to disposal. This 'cradle-to-grave' form of analysis facilitates the design of industrial processes to minimize environmental impact.

LDC Less developed country.

LDP Liquid dispersion polymer.

LEAF Leeds Environmental Action Forum.

LEBF Leeds Environment Business Forum.

LECI Leeds Environment City Initiative.

LETS Local Employment and Trade System *or* Local Exchange Trading System. A scheme which enables individuals to exchange goods and services without the use of money.

LGMB Local Government Management Board.

Libertarianism An extreme *laissez-faire* political philosophy which advocates minimal state intervention in the lives of citizens and the predominance of private morality over state codes of ethics.

LWMI Leicestershire Waste Minimization Initiative.

MAFF Ministry of Agriculture, Fisheries, and Food.

MEP Member of the European Parliament.

Meta-theory A higher order theory.

Monoculture Cultivation of a single crop or variety over a large area. The system generates increased attacks from pests, disease and weeds, necessitating the use of agrochemical pesticides and herbicides. In the absence of manure from stock animals, soil fertility has to be maintained by application of agrochemical fertilizers. The single input–output system takes no account of the loss of secondary outputs from more diverse systems.

NAFTA North American Free Trade Agreement.

Natural capital The stock of renewable and non-renewable resources which make up the planet's life-support system.

NDP Net domestic product. Gross domestic product less depreciation.

NEF New Economics Foundation (UK). Research on sustainable economics, including indicators and product durability.

NFFO Non-fossil-fuel obligation.

NGOs Non-governmental organizations. These are not government agencies, but may be voluntary organizations, community groups, trade unions, educational establishments or corporations.

NIMBY Not In My Back Yard. Applied to people who approve of controversial developments as long as the developments are not close to where they live. They can be distinguished from the *BANANA* species of the human race. BANANA people are those who say we should 'Build Absolutely Nothing Anywhere Near Anyone'.

NNP Net national product. Gross national product less depreciation.

Non-renewable resources Resources which, once used, can never be renewed. They include minerals and fossil fuels such as coal or oil.

NRA National Rivers Authority (UK).

NSCA National Society for Clean Air and Environmental Protection (UK).

NWBLT North West Business Leadership Team.

OECD Organization for Economic Co-operation and Development. Founded in 1961 to promote economic growth and expansion of multilateral world trade in order to raise the living standards of member countries, originally Austria, Belgium, Canada, Denmark, France, Germany, Greece, Iceland, Luxembourg, the Netherlands, Norway, Portugal, Spain, Switzerland, Turkey, the United Kingdom and the United States. Subsequently joined by Japan, Finland, Australia, New Zealand and Mexico.

Ozone As a layer 25 km above the earth's surface, ozone helps to keep out ultraviolet rays from the sun. When it occurs at ground level it can prove an irritant and cause breathing problems.

PCB Polychlorinated biphenyl (toxic constituent of plastics, etc.). Old electrical equipment contained PCBs, which are toxic substances and not biodegradable, requiring incineration at 1200°C.

Permaculture Permanent sustainable agricultural technique.

PEST Political, Economic, Social and Technological (framework for analysing these aspects of a business environment).

PESTE Political, Economic, Social, Technological and Ecological. *See also* STEEP.

Polluter pays principle Those who cause pollution should bear the costs of damage and clean-up.

ppm Parts per million.

PRAIRE Pollution Risk from Accidental Influxes into Rivers and Estuaries.

Precautionary Principle Cost-effective measures to prevent environmental degradation may be introduced before irreversible damage occurs, even in the absence of full scientific evidence of the damage impact. The environment is given the benefit of the doubt on the grounds that risk prevention is likely to be more effective than cure over the long term.

Prescribed processes are industrial processes which may not breach the regulations of the Water Resources Act (1991) or the Environmental Protection Act (1990) without incurring penalties.

PRISMA Project Industrial Successes with Waste Production (Netherlands).

Protocol Formal agreement that defines means of working together, usually by different organizations.

PVC Polyvinyl chloride (synthetic resin).

Quango Quasi-autonomous non-governmental organization.

R&D Research and Development.

RBT Reed bed treatment.

RSNC Royal Society for Nature Conservation.

RSPB Royal Society for the Protection of Birds.

SAFE Alliance Sustainable Agriculture, Food and Environment Alliance. An association of pressure groups and organizations concerned to promote environmentally sustainable and healthy food.

SBV Space Biosphere Ventures.

SCEEMAS Small Company Environmental and Energy Management Assistance Scheme (EU).

SDI Socially Directed Investment.

SEA Supplier environmental audit.

SEA 1986 Single European Act 1986.

SEEC Scottish Environment Education Council.

SME Small and medium sized enterprise.

Seveso Directive Issued by the EC in an attempt to minimize the effects of chemical industrial accidents on people and the environment.

Social ecologist Believes that only a society free from social exploitation can operate in a harmonious relationship with the planet.

SPOLD Society for the Promotion of LCA Development.

SRI Socially Responsible Investment. It includes non-financial criteria as part of the investment assessment and may include social or environmental criteria.

SSSI Site of Special Scientific Interest. An area of land notified under the Wildlife and Countryside Act 1981 as being of special nature conservation interest (UK).

Stakeholder capitalism Companies accept obligations to employees, suppliers and the local community as well as to shareholders.

STEEP Social, Technological, Economic, Environmental and Political. *See also* PESTE.

Subsidiarity The principle that a central authority should have a subsidiary function and perform only those tasks that cannot be performed effectively at local level.

Sustainable development Improvement in the quality of life which does not impair the ability of the ecosystem to sustain life.

SWOT Strengths, Weaknesses, Opportunities, Threats. A strategic management model for assessing the business environment.

TNC Transnational corporation.

Tradable permits Companies are allowed to pollute to a certain level. If a company does not pollute to this level it can trade the permit with another company. This serves to control the overall level of pollution.

Triadic Trading System Three globally competing trading blocs.

TUC Trades Union Congress.

UKAS United Kingdom Accreditation Service.

UKSIF UK Social Investment Forum.

UNCED United Nations Conference on Environment and Development.

UNDP United Nations Development Programme.

UNEP United Nations Environment Programme.

Utilitarianism Philosophical theory that an action is right in so far as it promotes happiness and that the guiding principle of conduct should be to achieve the greatest happiness or benefit for the greatest number.

UV-B Ultraviolet radiation (wavelength 280–320 m).

VOC Volatile organic compound. A by-product of industrial solvents, paint and degreasing agents.

WBCSD World Business Council for Sustainable Development. Evolved from the BCSD and WICE.

WICE World Industry Council for the Environment. Established by the ICC after the Earth Summit to provide business input into the international environmental policy debate and to promote sound environmental management at the international level. *See also* BCSD and WBCSD.

WRA Waste Regulatory Authority.

WRI World Resources Institute.

WTA Willingness to accept. An integral part of the economic concept of contingent valuation.

WTP Willingness to pay. An integral part of the economic concept of contingent valuation.

WWF Worldwide Fund for Nature (formerly World Wildlife Fund).

INDEX